American Labor and
the Cold War

American Labor and the Cold War

GRASSROOTS POLITICS AND POSTWAR
POLITICAL CULTURE

☼

EDITED BY

ROBERT W. CHERNY

WILLIAM ISSEL

KIERAN WALSH TAYLOR

Rutgers University Press
New Brunswick, New Jersey, and London

Library of Congress Cataloging-in-Publication Data

American labor and the Cold War : grassroots politics and postwar political culture / edited by Robert W. Cherny, William Issel, Kieran Walsh Taylor.
  p. cm.
  Includes bibliographical references and index.
  ISBN 0-8135-3402-X (hardcover : alk. paper) — ISBN 0-8135-3403-8 (pbk. : alk. paper)
  1. Labor unions—United States—Political activity—History—20th century.
2. Anti-communist movements—United States—History. 3. Cold War. 4. Political culture—United States—History—20th century. 5. United States—Politics and government—1945–1953. 6. United States—Politics and government—1953–1961.
I. Cherny, Robert W. II. Issel, William. III. Taylor, Kieran Walsh.
HD6510.A45   2004
331.88′0973′09045—dc22
                                                                         2003020095

British Cataloging-in-Publication data for this book is available from the British Library

This collection copyright © 2004 by Rutgers, The State University
Individual chapters copyright © 2004 in the names of their authors
All rights reserved
No part of this book may be reproduced or utilized in any form or by any means, electronic or mechanical, or by any information storage and retrieval system, without written permission from the publisher. Please contact Rutgers University Press, 100 Joyce Kilmer Avenue, Piscataway, NJ 08854–8099. The only exception to this prohibition is "fair use" as defined by U.S. copyright law.

The publication program of Rutgers University Press is supported by the Board of Governors of Rutgers, The State University of New Jersey.

Manufactured in the United States of America

Contents

List of Abbreviations *vii*
List of Illustrations *ix*
Acknowledgments *xi*

Introduction 1
Robert W. Cherny, William Issel, and Kieran Walsh Taylor

Labor and the Cold War: The Legacy of McCarthyism 7
Ellen Schrecker

Uncivil War: An Oral History of Labor, Communism, and Community in Schenectady, New York, 1944–1954 25
Gerald Zahavi

Mixed Melody: Anticommunism and the United Packinghouse Workers in California Agriculture, 1954–1961 58
Don Watson

The United Packinghouse Workers of America, Civil Rights, and the Communist Party in Chicago 72
Randi Storch

"An Anarchist with a Program": East Coast Shipyard Workers, the Labor Left, and the Origins of Cold War Unionism 85
David Palmer

The Battle for Standard Coil: The United Electrical Workers, the Community Service Organization, and the Catholic Church in Latino East Los Angeles 118
Kenneth C. Burt

Popular Anticommunism and the UE in Evansville, Indiana   141
SAMUEL W. WHITE

"A Stern Struggle": Catholic Activism and San Francisco Labor, 1934–1958   154
WILLIAM ISSEL

Memories of the Red Decade: HUAC Investigations in Maryland   177
VERNON L. PEDERSEN

Negotiating Cold War Politics: The Washington Pension Union and the Labor Left in the 1940s and 1950s   190
MARGARET MILLER

The Lost World of United States Labor Education: Curricula at East and West Coast Communist Schools, 1944–1957   205
MARVIN GETTLEMAN

Operation Dixie, the Red Scare, and the Defeat of Southern Labor Organizing   216
MICHAEL K. HONEY

"A Dangerous Demagogue": Containing the Influence of the Mexican Labor-Left and Its United States Allies   245
GIGI PETERSON

Contributors   277
Index   279

List of Abbreviations

ACTU	Association of Catholic Trade Unionists
ACWA	Amalgamated Clothing Workers of America
AEC	Atomic Energy Commission
AFL	American Federation of Labor
AFSCME	American Federation of State and County Municipal Employees
ALCO	American Locomotive Company
AMC	Amalgamated Meat Cutters and Butcher Workmen of America
CDA	Committee for Democratic Action
CIO	Congress of Industrial Organizations
CLS	California Labor School
CNDP	Comité Nacional de Defensa Proletaria (National Committee in Defense of the Proletariat)
CP	Communist Party
CPAC	Citizens Public Assistance Committee
CPUSA	Communist Party of the United States of America
CRC	Civil Rights Congress
CROM	Confederación Regional Obrera Mexicana (Regional Mexican Workers Confederation)
CTAL	Confederación de Trabajadores de America (Confederation of Latin American Workers)
CTM	Confederación de Trabajadores de México (Confederation of Mexican Workers)
FEC	Federal Employees Committee
FTA	Food, Tobacco, Agricultural and Allied Workers
GE	General Electric Company
HLEC	House Labor and Education Committee
HUAC	House Un-American Activities Committee
IAF	Industrial Areas Foundation
IAM	International Association of Machinists
IATSE	International Association of Theatrical and Stage Employees
IBEW	International Brotherhood of Electrical Workers

ILA	International Longshoremen's Association
ILGWU	International Ladies Garment Worker's Union
ILWU	International Longshoremen's and Warehousemen's Union
IUE	International Union of Electrical, Radio and Machine Employees
IUMSWA	Industrial Union of Marine and Shipbuilding Workers of America
IWA	International Woodworkers of America
IWW	Industrial Workers of the World
LAPD	Los Angeles Police Department
Mine-Mill	International Union of Mine, Mill and Smelters Workers of America
NAACP	National Association for the Advancement of Colored People
NACFL	National Advisory Committee on Farm Labor
NAM	National Association of Manufacturers
NAWU	National Agricultural Workers Union
NDMB	National Defense Mediation Board
NLRB	National Labor Relations Board
NMCSA	National Marine Cooks and Steward's Association
NMU	National Maritime Union
NWRO	National Welfare Rights Organization
RCMS	Reference Center for Marxist Studies
RGASPI	Russian State Archives of Social and Political History
SACB	Subversive Activities Control Board
SCEF	Southern Conference Education Fund
SCHW	Southern Conference for Human Welfare
SISS	Senate Internal Security Subcommittee
SOC	Southern Organizing Committee
SOS	Sweethearts of Servicemen
SP	Socialist Party of America
STFU	Southern Tenant Farmers Union
TWEC	Total War Employment Committee
TWU	Transport Workers Union
UAW	United Auto Workers of America
UCAPAWA	United Cannery, Agricultural, Packing and Allied Workers of America
UE	United Electrical, Radio, and Machine Workers of America
UFWA	United Farm Workers of America
UMW	United Mine Workers of America
UOM	Universidad Obrera de México (Workers University of Mexico)
UPWA	United Packinghouse Workers of America
USF	University of San Francisco
USWA	United Steelworkers of America
WPU	Washington Pension Union

List of Illustrations

1.1	United Electrical Workers pamphlet number 156, *Red Baiting* (1950)	*17*
2.1	Schenectady GE workers celebrating the IUE victory at GE (1954)	*31*
3.1	Field workers during the Imperial Valley lettuce strike (1961)	*67*
4.1	Herbert March speaking at "Unite and Fight" rally (1952)	*73*
6.1	Tony Rios preparing to speak for the IUE at Standard Coil (1952)	*127*
7.1	Indiana State Police and UE strikers at the Bucyrus-Erie plant (1948)	*146*
8.1	*The Monitor* cartoon, "The May Day Celebration We Want" (1935)	*159*
10.1	Washington Pension Union delivering signatures for Ballot Initiative 172 (1948)	*199*
11.1	David Jenkins, Paul Robeson, John Howard Lawson, and Revels Cayton at the California Labor School (probably 1948)	*209*
12.1	Nickey Brothers strike, Memphis Tennessee (1946)	*229*

Acknowledgements

The idea for this volume originated at a meeting of the program committee of the Southwest Labor Studies Association, when it met to choose a theme for the 1999 annual meeting of the organization in San Francisco. The editors would like to thank David Brundage, Susan Englander, and Don Watson, who also attended that meeting, for their contributions to the discussion that led to the decision to organize the conference on the theme of Labor and the Cold War. Most of the papers assembled in this anthology began as presentations to the 1999 conference, and we acknowledge with pleasure the participants at the sessions for their thoughtful and stimulating questions and comments.

The editors would also like to thank the contributors to this volume for their cooperation—and their patience—during the lengthy process that led to their work appearing in print. Our editor at Rutgers University Press, Melanie Halkias, who inspired us with her enthusiasm and efficiency, has made the final process of assembling the book a real pleasure. We also thank Paul Buhle for his evaluation of the manuscript for Rutgers University Press, as well as a second anonymous reader for the Press.

Robert Cherny and William Issel thank our colleagues in the history department and the labor archives at San Francisco State University for helping to create a scholarly, collegial and friendly working environment. Kerry Taylor thanks his parents, friends at the Cesar Chavez House in East Chicago, and colleagues at the Martin Luther King, Jr. Papers Project and the Southern Oral History Program for their support and encouragement over the years.

We dedicate this volume to our teachers, past and present.

American Labor and the Cold War

Introduction

☼

ROBERT W. CHERNY, WILLIAM ISSEL, AND KIERAN WALSH TAYLOR

The American labor movement seemed poised on the threshold of unparalleled success at the beginning of the post-World War II era. Fourteen million strong in 1946, unions represented 35 percent of non-agricultural workers, and federal power insured collective bargaining rights. The contrast with the pre-war years was strongest for those workers who retained vivid memories of the 1920s and early 1930s. Then, the labor movement lacked government legitimacy, and, at the worst point of the Great Depression, the union movement barely enrolled 5 percent of the non-farm workforce; one out of every four workers lacked a job. Now, the future seemed to hold unlimited possibilities.

Like the aspirations for world peace that were shattered by the sudden onset of the Cold War, the hopes unionists held for solidarity and continued growth of prestige and power collided with unhappy realities: the persistent disunity caused by dissension among workers and renewed attacks by employers. The American Federation of Labor (AFL) competed with the Congress of Industrial Organizations (CIO) for members, and "raids" by one or the other proliferated. White workers disagreed among themselves about the importance of racial equality, and efforts by nonwhite workers to achieve dignity and justice met with continuing resistance. Catholic unionists, historically suspicious of Socialist and Communist programs and activists, joined forces with employers, anticommunist politicians, and disaffected radicals critical of Soviet policies in Eastern Europe to challenge the legitimacy of left-wing officers and organizers. In 1949–1950 the CIO expelled eleven national unions, approximately one-fifth of its membership, for alleged Communist control.

When the war ended in 1945, so did the shaky wartime truce between business and labor, and a business offensive against unions brought external pressure to bear on the internally divided labor movement. *New York Times* columnist James Reston wrote in September "both sides seem to take the view that they have taken a lot of guff from the other side during the war and are now free to fight it out." Influential economists and business leaders ridiculed unions' professions of civic responsibility, characterizing them instead as "militant labor monopolies"—their officials inherently untrustworthy, their organizations hostile to the market system. Even a sympathetic analyst such as labor economist John T. Dunlop, who later served as secretary of labor under President Gerald Ford, likened labor unions to diseases, "points of infection" among employees who occupied strategic market or technological positions in their industries.[1]

Unions demonstrated their disapproval of President Truman's policies for reconversion from war to peace by authorizing a wave of strikes during the latter part of 1945, and 1946. Rank-and-file workers vented their frustration over inflation by walking out in unauthorized "wildcat" strikes. The disputes rocked the maritime, trucking, railway, coal, oil, auto, electrical equipment, telephone, meatpacking, and steel industries. More members participated in more strikes during these months than in any similar period before or since. In 1946 alone, 4.5 million workers walked the picket lines. Critics denounced their actions as fresh evidence of labor irresponsibility.

The National Association of Manufacturers (NAM) took advantage of widespread outrage against the strikes to weld together a coalition of trade associations and corporations, determined to enforce industrial peace by means of federal legislation to amend the 1935 National Labor Relations Act (Wagner Act). Frankly pro-union, the Wagner Act protected the worker's right to join a union, and placed the federal government in the position of "encouraging the practice and procedure of collective bargaining." The act also provided for secret ballot elections as the means by which workers would decide whether to be represented by a union, and it established a federal National Labor Relations Board to enforce the law. Frustrated in their attempts to invalidate the Wagner Act when the Supreme Court declared it constitutional in 1937, business activists eagerly rejoined the battle during the 1946 strike wave.

The NAM led off with a "Declaration of Principles" that appealed to the bias in American political tradition against federal government power and in favor of local control by insisting upon the need for decentralizing the collective bargaining process. The group also reiterated the theme that business owners functioned as the stewards of civic well being, while union officials were merely parochial defenders of the selfish interests of their members. This official NAM position, in addition to the more hard-line proposals of dissidents within the organization who wanted the Wagner Act abolished altogether, became the basis for the Taft-Hartley Act passed in June 1947. In forging a majority that favored the act, the NAM appealed to anti-labor Republicans and conservative southern Democrats, along with moderates from both major parties who believed that the public demanded a check on union power. Congress passed the law over President Truman's veto, and the NAM promptly took credit for the new measure and assumed the role of its defender.

Although the Taft-Hartley Act did not repeal the Wagner Act, it fundamentally changed the character of federal government regulation of labor relations. For the first time, controls were placed upon the actual substance of the collective bargaining agreement, as well as on procedural matters. The closed shop, prohibiting the hiring of non-union employees, was made illegal. Other measures likewise limited union activities. Management could sue unions for breaking contracts or damaging company property during strikes. The law established a new federal agency, the Federal Mediation and Conciliation Service, to seek resolution of conflicts without resort to strikes, and the government could obtain injunctions requiring a "cooling-off" period of 80 days during a strike considered dangerous to health or safety. Several provisions placed the government in the position of supervising the internal operations of unions. Officers had to swear that they did not belong to the Communist Party. Unions had to make their financial statements public and could not make financial contributions to political campaigns. In 1951 Congress amended the act to allow contracts establishing a union shop, providing that employees must join the union within thirty days of being hired, without a majority vote of the employees.

The Taft-Hartley Act also included a clause that allowed states to prohibit union shops. No one was surprised when anti-labor coalitions in eleven states immediately succeeded in lobbying for such "Right to Work" (anti-union shop) state-level legislation. All these states were in the Sunbelt or Midwest regions, where unionism had made little headway by 1945, usually in the face of widespread hostility and determined resistance. Six more states in the same regions passed similar laws during the 1950s, but the vigorous opposition by unions stopped the campaign in 1958, when all but one of six right-to-work proposals on state ballots were quashed by the electorate. Voters in Indiana repealed that state's law in 1965, but Louisiana voters established one as late as 1976.

The Taft-Hartley Act likely contributed to restricting unionism to those areas of the country and sectors of the economy in which the labor movement had made its greatest successes by the end of World War II. The act hurt labor by slowing down the expansion of union membership and bargaining rights. It also established government monitoring of internal union decision-making and financial accounting practices that provided safeguards against potential abuses, but at the cost of onerous and burdensome reporting requirements.[2]

The setbacks to the labor movement stimulated by Taft-Hartley coincided with the election of President Dwight D. Eisenhower, a Republican, in 1952. In 1955 George Meany and Walter Reuther, new presidents of the AFL and the CIO, decided to merge their organizations. The goal was to strengthen unionism against the certainty of continued efforts to stop the expansion of union membership, limit collective bargaining gains, and pass additional anti-union legislation.

The merger curtailed the expensive and fruitless practice of "raiding," but even the combined efforts of the AFL-CIO and its allies in Congress could not stop the passage by Congress in 1959 of the Labor-Management Reporting and Disclosure Act (Landrum-Griffin Act). The background to Landrum-Griffin was a series of investigations, including those by New York State in 1952–1953 and the United States Senate's McClellan Committee in 1957, into corruption and racketeering in the unions. In 1954 George Meany's AFL expelled the International Longshoremen's Association and followed suit in 1957 with the Teamster's and two other unions, for harboring criminal elements. Teamster president Dave Beck was convicted of embezzlement in 1957, and his successor Jimmy Hoffa was convicted of jury tampering, fraud, and conspiracy in 1964.

The AFL-CIO tried to limit the damage to the reputation of organized labor by expelling the offending unions and by adopting a code of ethics, but the abuses uncovered by investigators were genuine and could not be explained away. The officers of several unions, including the nation's largest—the Teamsters—enriched themselves by racketeering, used union funds for personal aggrandizement, abused the democratic process by intimidating members who dissented from their policies, and severely violated the civil rights of members. Congress intended the Landrum-Griffin Act to remedy such abuses by union officials, as well as to increase federal government regulation of internal union activity.[3]

The new legislation imposed four major responsibilities on unions. They had to comply with a "Bill of Rights" that protected individual union members. They needed to make financial disclosures and demonstrate their freedom from transactions where a conflict of interest existed between the parties. They were prohibited from improper trusteeships, and they were subject to federal safeguards against the manipulation of union elections in favor of incumbents.

Like the Taft-Hartley Act of 1947, the Landrum Griffin Act was imposed upon organized labor, rather than resulting from union desire for government regulation. By 1960, the 1945 expectations of leaders and the rank and file of American unions of maintaining and even expanding upon the gains made between 1933 and the end of the war had come to little. The National Labor Relations Act stood, and collective bargaining still enjoyed federal government protection, but unions faced the future in a defensive mode. They were still divided internally by race, limited by region, heavily concentrated in aging industrial cities, and faced widespread public suspicion. Union membership was on the decline, never to recover; by 1980, only 20 percent of the workforce belonged to unions. Today, union members make up only about 13 percent of the workforce.

This anthology addresses the history of labor in the postwar years by exploring the impact of the global superpower contest between the United States and the Soviet Union on American workers and labor unions during the decades after World War II. Most of the following chapters began as contributions to the annual meeting of the Southwest Labor Studies Association in May 1999, a meeting that focused particularly on the tensions, conflicts, and contests that the labor movement faced during the early Cold War years. The authors of this collection are not the first to ask what happened within the labor movement and between unions and their opponents in the years from the end of World War II and the 1960s.[4] Nor are they the first to try to explain the failure of labor to build on the gains made between 1933 and 1945 and the reasons for the success of business in reestablishing public confidence and dominance in labor relations. A substantial body of work exists on various topics related to these questions. This literature includes numerous biographies that illuminate the life and work of particular national leaders, monographs on specific national unions, and particularly rich writings on the labor left, including the Communist Party. This book seeks to build on the existing literature by asking: what do we learn about the period from 1945 to about 1960 when we look in detail at the grassroots? What kinds of relationships existed among labor unions of the AFL and CIO, the radical left and the conservative right, business and other interest groups in American communities? How did these groups, voluntary associations, relate themselves to local, state, and national governments during these years?

The book begins with Ellen Schrecker's elegant synthesis of the research assessing the nature of the damage done to the labor movement by the red scare and McCarthyism in the postwar period. Gerald Zahavi uses extensive oral history sources to present a richly textured account of Communism and unionism in the UE in Schenectady, New York during the first postwar decade. Two essays explore how members of the United Packinghouse Workers members coped with the Cold War during the 1950s. Don Watson draws on newly available archival sources to analyze the case of California, and Randi Storch describes the Chicago story. David Palmer provides an incisive account of how, in the East Coast shipyards of World War II, the clash between the labor left and anticommunists in the Industrial Union of Marine and Shipbuilding Workers of America foreshadowed Cold War unionism. Kenneth C. Burt contributes a perceptive account of the efforts by UE to displace the IBEW at a manufacturing plant in Los Angeles, an episode that underscores the ways that ethnicity, religion, and gender shaped inter-union rivalry.

Samuel W. White's essay identifies the emergence of consensus in Evansville, Indiana, for a popular anticommunism that undermined the wartime gains of the local labor movement—most particularly the United Electrical Union, which had organized the city's largest employer. William Issel describes how the Cold War influenced the campaign begun by the Catholic Church and militant Catholic unionists in the early 1930s to shape the San Francisco labor movement. Vernon Pederson details the mixed results of the investigations conducted in Maryland by the House Committee on Un-American Activities. Margaret Miller analyzes the impact of the red scare on the Washington Pension Union, a labor-sponsored project during the 1940s and 1950s that united old age pensioners in an effort to secure better welfare benefits from the state of Washington. Marvin Gettleman presents an original account of how the Communist Party's labor schools in New York City and San Francisco adapted to the challenges posed by the red scare and McCarthyism. Michael Honey details the impact of the red scare on the efforts of the CIO to recruit southern workers in its Operation Dixie program. In the concluding essay, Gigi Peterson, using recently declassified English and Spanish materials, offers fresh insights into how the Department of State worked to contain the influence of the Mexican labor-left and its allies in the labor movement in the United States.

Each essay in this volume stands on its own as a contribution to historical knowledge on the topic of labor and the Cold War, but two themes characterize the collection as a whole. First, the authors in this anthology ask: to what extent did union members and labor leadership actually experience state repression? To what extent did the red scare and McCarthyism harm working-class communities and labor unions? To what extent did the red scare and McCarthyism draw upon a genuine and principled anticommunism in the working-class communities of the nation? The second theme that links together the essays in this book is the importance of regional variation and local tradition and culture, in the context of American political life, to the history of workers and their unions. Previous scholarship on labor and the Cold War, for all of its strengths, has overemphasized the importance of the Communist Party, the automobile industry, and Hollywood. Scholars have paid insufficient attention to politically moderate and conservative workers and union leaders, the medium-sized cities that housed the majority of the population, and the Roman Catholic Church.

Each of the essays in the collection makes a contribution to the literature on unions, politics, and postwar political culture. Some are original forays into topics that have so far not attracted the attention of professional historians; and others use archival research and oral history to shed revealing new light on existing historical knowledge. Together, the chapters in this volume provide the most comprehensive study thus far of how workers in specific unions and communities across the nation lived through, experienced, and indeed shaped the character of the Cold War at the grassroots.

Notes

1. James Reston quoted in John Barnard, *Walter Reuther and the Rise of the Auto Workers* (Boston: Little, Brown, 1983), 102. John T. Dunlop, "The Development of Labor Organizations: A Theoretical Framework," in *Insights into Labor Issues*, ed. Richard A. Lester and Joseph Shister (New York: Macmillan, 1948), 180. See also Elizabeth A. Fones-Wolf, *Selling Free Enterprise: The Business Assault on Labor and Liberalism, 1945–1960* (Urbana: University of Illinois Press, 1994).
2. Howell John Harris, *The Right to Manage: Industrial Relations Policies of American Business in the 1940s* (Madison: University of Wisconsin Press, 1982), 118–125.
3. Doris McLaughlin and Anita L.W. Schoomaker, *The Landrum-Griffin Act and Union Democracy* (Ann Arbor: University of Michigan Press, 1979), 180–181.
4. Ann Fagan Ginger and David Christiano, eds., *The Cold War Against Labor*, 2 vols. (Berkeley: Meiklejohn Civil Liberties Institute, 1987); Steve Rosswurm, ed., *The CIO's Left-Led Unions* (New Brunswick: Rutgers University Press, 1992); George Lipsitz, *Rainbow at Midnight: Labor and Culture in the 1940s* (Urbana: University of Illinois Press, 1994); Ronald L. Filippelli and Mark D. McColloch, *Cold War in the Working Class: The Rise and Decline of the United Electrical Workers* (Albany: State University of New York Press, 1995).

Labor and the Cold War
The Legacy of McCarthyism

☼

ELLEN SCHRECKER

The political repression of the McCarthy period had a deleterious impact on American labor. Only the Communist Party was as deeply affected. Not only was the entire left wing of the labor movement destroyed, but many of the people who came under fire had union ties, such as the Hollywood Ten, or the thousands of maritime workers thrown out of their jobs because of the federal government's Korean War Port Security program. We cannot ignore the damage that McCarthyism did to the lives and careers of these men and women; but if we are to understand its broader impact on American labor, we need to focus on its institutional fallout. We should not exaggerate that impact nor blame it for negative developments that stemmed from structural economic change. Nonetheless, the anticommunist crusade of the late 1940s and 1950s did make a difference to the labor movement, even if that difference manifested itself mainly in shifted priorities and lost opportunities. If nothing else, McCarthyism tamed American labor and brought it into the Cold War political consensus. Moreover, by preventing the nation's unions, if so inclined, from building a broad-based social movement that challenged corporate values and championed social justice, McCarthyism narrowed political options for all Americans.

I use the term "McCarthyism" advisedly here. The phenomenon that we are looking at encompasses much more than the political career of the aberrant senator from Wisconsin who gave it a name. It began years before he burst into the headlines, waving his ever-changing lists of Communists in the State Department; and it continued for several years after he self-destructed in the eyes of the nation's television viewers at the Army-McCarthy hearings in the spring of 1954. Nonetheless, the word has historical specificity. It is a convenient and concise way to refer to the anticommunist political repression of the early Cold War, to the multi-stranded domestic campaign to destroy the influence of every idea, institution, and individual connected to American Communism.

There were many reasons why McCarthyism targeted the labor movement. Ever since the late nineteenth century, red-baiting has traditionally been associated with attempts on the part of hostile employers to suppress unions and weaken community support for organized labor. The McCarthy era's focus on labor was thus, in part, an updated version of all those earlier campaigns. Certainly, in those industries where antagonistic employers faced militant left-wing unions, anticommunism was a useful way to roll back the gains those unions had made since the late 1930s.[1] Similarly, red-baiting had long been a useful weapon for conservative labor leaders and their allies to wield against their left-wing rivals.[2] But perhaps the most important reason why McCarthyism focused on American labor was because Communism focused on American labor.

If we are to understand how McCarthyism operated and how it affected the labor movement and the rest of American society, we must relieve ourselves of the myth that most of its victims were "innocent liberals," apolitical folks who somehow turned up on the wrong mailing lists, or whose parents had once subscribed to the *Daily Worker*. True, such unfortunate individuals did exist, and they often got a lot of attention.[3] But most of the men and women who were called before congressional investigating committees, hauled before grand juries, or blacklisted by the entertainment industry were or had been in or near the Communist Party (CP). And many of them were union activists.

This should not surprise us. After all, whatever else it stood for, the Communist Party claimed to speak for the working class. Naturally, it sought a niche within those organizations that most directly represented the interests of American workers: their unions. And, at least for a few years during the 1930s and 1940s before McCarthyism drove them out, Communists did have some influence within American labor. Never as extensive as its supporters hoped or its enemies feared, that influence was nonetheless of some significance within a number of unions. Eliminating it affected the labor movement in ways we are just coming to understand.

Although the Cold War is over, American Communism has been such a demonized and contradictory movement that it still provokes impassioned debate.[4] On the one hand, the Communist Party was an authoritarian political sect whose adherents tried to conform to an inappropriate Soviet model and closed their eyes to the crimes of Stalin. On the other hand, it was the most dynamic sector of the left in the 1930s and 40s. An entire generation of idealists embraced the Communist Party as the most effective vehicle for their political aspirations, whether it was organizing labor unions, opposing racial discrimination, or fighting fascism, imperialism, and war. At the same time, party members were also concealing their membership, repressing all internal opposition, and even, we must now admit, spying for the Soviet Union.[5] The CP's record, in short, is mixed.

Within the labor movement the party threw some of its best cadres into the early organizing campaigns of the CIO. They were effective, experienced organizers who played important roles in building unions in the maritime, automobile, steel, and electrical industries, as well as among white-collar and professional workers. These people recruited few ordinary workers into the party, but they did rise to leadership positions in quite a number of unions. They were honest, hardworking union leaders, and recognized as such. By the 1940s, Communists and their allies led unions that contained about 20 percent of the membership of all CIO unions. They had a sizable, though dwindling, position of influence within the UAW and dominated the leadership of United Electrical, Radio and Machine

Workers of America (UE), International Longshoremen's and Warehousemen's Union (ILWU), Mine, Mill, and Smelter Workers, and about a dozen smaller unions that represented workers everywhere, from the salmon canneries of Alaska to Alcatraz Penitentiary.[6]

It is hard to assess the extent to which the party shaped the unions it controlled. Many of the Communists who rose to positions of leadership were trade unionists first and party members second. It was not unusual for these people to ignore party directives that clashed with union priorities, and in fact some of these labor leaders actually left the CP when they felt that its demands were contrary to the interests of their unions.[7] They had, after all, joined the party in large part because they felt it would help them build a strong labor movement. None of them even tried to transform their unions into revolutionary organizations. Nor was there any specifically Communist component to the normal trade union functions of the organizations these people led. The most explicit support these unions gave to the party's non-labor policies was what one former Communist called "the resolution bit"—endorsing CP causes in conventions and newspaper editorials.[8]

Still, the Communist unions *were* different. Their leaders were usually better educated, more militant, more class-conscious, and, in most cases, more democratic. And they rejected bread-and-butter unionism, committing their organizations to a wide range of social reforms.[9]

That commitment was particularly striking in the area of race relations. During the 1930s and 1940s, the Communist Party was the only political organization not specifically part of the civil rights movement that was dedicated to racial equality. At a time when workplace segregation was common, the party pressed its labor cadres to fight discrimination. Such an agenda was not always popular with the rank-and-file. The leaders of New York City's Transport Workers Union were reluctant to confront the racism of their mostly Irish members. But racial equality had become such a central issue within the Communist movement that the TWU's leaders eventually began to seek the hiring of black bus drivers and motormen. During World War II, when African Americans finally began to break the color line, some Communist-led unions pioneered an early form of affirmative action called "Super Seniority," as a way to ensure that the newly-hired black workers would be able to keep their jobs after the war ended.[10]

Though these measures did not increase the left-led unions' popularity with the large majority of white workers, they did appeal to minority ones. They enabled unions like the ILWU, Mine-Mill, and Food, Tobacco, Agricultural and Allied Workers Union (FTA) to get a foothold in the South and in such racially diverse areas as the Southwest and Hawaii. In keeping with the party's emphasis on racial equality, these unions often sought ways to promote minority-group members to leadership positions. In some places, these unions actually functioned like civil rights organizations.[11]

A good example of this kind of rights-based unionism was FTA Local 22 in Winston-Salem, North Carolina. The union imbued the African American women who were working for the R.J. Reynolds Company with a sense of self-worth, and enabled them to challenge the demeaning way the company treated them. Local 22 also encouraged its members to vote and to join the NAACP. These efforts were rewarded with the election of an African American to the Winston-Salem Board of Aldermen in 1947 and with improved public services to the city's black community.[12]

The left-led unions also paid attention to women's issues. From the cigarette factories of North Carolina to New York City's public welfare agencies, these unions sought out the subjugated, poorly-paid, and often non-white female workers overlooked by the rest of the labor movement. Not only did these unions address women's issues, but some of them also encouraged the development of strong women leaders. The UE, which had more female members than the other big industrial unions, was a pioneer. During and after World War II, it fought for such women's issues as equal pay for equal work and opposed the inequities involved with shunting women off into "women's jobs."[13] As the historian Daniel Horowitz has discovered, none other than Betty Friedan wrote many of the UE's most important policy statements about women's issues during the late 1940s and early 1950s.[14]

McCarthyism brought most of these efforts to a halt. Friedan was an indirect victim. She lost her job when the debilitated UE had to downsize and dropped her from her job on its newspaper. Though the UE was one of the few party-led unions to survive the McCarthy era, it emerged weakened and no longer able to push for women's rights or any of the other social reforms that it had previously championed. Most of the other left-wing unions simply went under, unable to withstand the unrelenting assault directed against them.[15]

The anticommunist crusade against the labor left was effective because it came from so many different sources and employed so many different weapons. Employers, federal officials, rival union leaders, Catholic priests, former Communists, right-wing journalists, and politicians all combined to drive the Communist Party out of the labor movement. As part of an informal network of professional anticommunists, many of these people had been fighting the party for years. The Cold War not only conferred legitimacy on their campaign, but also brought new forces onto the field, in particular the federal government.

As a result, from the late 1940s on, the Communist-led unions were under constant attack. Their leaders were hauled before congressional investigating committees and grand juries, subjected to criminal prosecutions, kept under constant surveillance by the FBI, audited by the IRS, and, if they were foreign born, threatened with deportation. The unions were equally harassed. Not only did they have to contend with internal schisms, external raids, and intransigent employers, but they also were denied the protection of the NLRB, called before the Subversive Activities Control Board, and expelled from the CIO. They were soon so beleaguered and preoccupied with defending themselves and their leaders that they could barely perform their regular economic functions, let alone carry out any kind of program of ambitious social reform.[16]

The most serious damage was caused by the 1947 Taft-Hartley Act. Designed to roll back many of the gains that the labor movement had made since the late 1930s, the measure also included an anticommunist provision. Inserted as an afterthought, this provision revealed how pervasive the anticommunist consensus had become. The only debate it occasioned concerned the best way to remove Communist influence from the labor movement, not the advisability of doing so. The measure that was finally incorporated into the law was Section 9(h), which required all union officials to sign an affidavit affirming that they neither were in the party—identified as a movement that sought the overthrow of the government by force and violence—nor had any sympathy for its doctrines. Unions that did not comply with the law were to be denied the services of the NLRB.[17]

It was not immediately apparent that Section 9(h) would have any impact. Many mainstream labor leaders opposed the measure not only because it infringed on civil liberties, but also because it seemed to be placing a burden on the labor movement that other sectors of society did not have to bear. In addition, because of the act's unclear language about "belief in" and "support for" for the Communist Party, it was obvious that a constitutional challenge was in the making. After Harry Truman's upset victory in the 1948 presidential election, there was also the possibility that the law itself might be repealed. Instead, much of the opposition to Taft-Hartley petered out. Most labor leaders learned to live with the law, especially when the anticommunists among them realized how damaging it was to the left-led unions.[18]

Hostile employers took advantage of those unions' inability to rely on NLRB assistance to process unfair labor complaints. Claiming that the unions' failure to sign the affidavits revealed their lack of patriotism, these employers refused to bargain. Unable to obtain federal support, the left-wing unions were all too often forced to engage in unpopular and debilitating strikes. At the same time, rival unions stepped up their raids on the non-signing unions and, for the first time, were able to attract large numbers of workers. Unable to participate in NLRB elections, the left-led unions found themselves in no-win situations where they had to appeal to their supporters to vote for a "no union" option. These unions' vulnerabilities emboldened their internal opponents as well. Anticommunist factions challenged the leadership of the UE and the other left-wing unions and, with the help of such allies as the House Un-American Activities Committee and the Catholic Church, began to win some significant battles.[19]

By the middle of 1949, it was clear that the left-led unions' failure to comply with Taft-Hartley was inflicting serious damage and was, in fact, threatening their very survival. There was little hope that the law would be repealed and an equally dim prospect that the Supreme Court might overthrow it, especially after the Steelworkers—the most important union involved in the litigation—dropped the case and two of the Court's most liberal justices died.[20] Accordingly, the left-wing unions abandoned their opposition to the law and authorized their leaders to sign the affidavits. Compliance, however, created problems in itself, for many of these unions' leaders *were* Communists. In order to bring their unions into compliance, they either had to quit their positions or else quit the party. Most of them left the CP, often accompanying their resignations with public statements defending their political commitment and explaining why they supported Communism.[21]

Complying with the Taft-Hartley Act did not, however, bring relief to the embattled unions. Their opponents immediately questioned the authenticity of such resignations from the party, insisting that, despite their formal protestations, they were still Communists at heart. Employers continued to stonewall, refusing to bargain with the left-led unions and pressing the NLRB to stop processing their complaints. And the NLRB, equally skeptical about those unions' compliance but unsure about its jurisdiction in the matter, urged the Justice Department to prosecute the unions' leaders for perjury.[22]

Nor did signing the affidavits prevent the CIO from expelling the left-led unions. Though the organization's president, Philip Murray, had been under pressure for years to purge the Communist-led unions, he had resisted out of a reluctance to split the labor movement. But as the CIO became increasingly tied to the Truman administration in the aftermath of Taft-Hartley, Murray's resistance began to fade. The party's insistence that its labor cadres support the third-party presidential campaign of Henry Wallace in 1948 provoked the break. After the left-led unions refused to go along with the CIO's requirement that they refrain from backing Wallace, Murray came around. Truman's electoral victory, in the words of one historian, "sealed the doom of the Communists within the CIO." At its 1949 convention the CIO formally expelled the UE (which had already walked out) and launched charges against ten other unions.[23]

The proceedings before the three-man panels that considered the charges against each of the left-wing unions were almost identical to the operations of all other anticommunist investigations in the McCarthy era. There were two types of evidence: testimony from former Communists identifying specific union leaders as party members and texts of resolutions and newspaper editorials that seemed to parallel the party line. Significantly, the literary materials that the CIO's prosecutors produced dealt almost entirely with matters of foreign policy, not trade union issues. But the substance of the evidence was largely irrelevant, since the unfavorable verdict had been reached even before the tribunals began.[24]

By the summer of 1950, when the Supreme Court finally rejected the left-led unions' case against the Taft-Hartley affidavits, the pathetic condition of these marginalized and ostracized unions had become obvious. The Court's majority echoed the prevailing wisdom that considerations of national security justified the imposition of restrictions on Communist influence within the labor movement. If the United States went to war against the Soviet Union, so the standard reasoning went, the left-wing unions might encourage individual members to engage in physical sabotage or call political strikes to shut down defense plants. Troubled by early 1930s party directives to sabotage shipping and defense industries, J. Edgar Hoover and his allies had been hyping the Communist threat for years. The advent of the Korean War intensified these concerns.[25]

Even before the Korean War, businessmen and federal officials invoked national security to rationalize the measures taken against the left-wing unions. In 1948 the Atomic Energy Commission (AEC), citing the standard litany about potential sabotage, ordered the General Electric Company to refuse to let the UE represent the workers at its new nuclear facility near Schenectady, New York. A similar order barred the left-led United Office and Professional Workers of America from operating at the AEC's own laboratories in Illinois.[26] The government's various security programs also hampered the activities of the left-led unions in defense industries. It was common, for example, for federal officials to deny security clearances to shop stewards and other union activists, thus making it impossible for them to circulate throughout their factories and fulfill their normal obligations.[27]

Official harassment came from the legislative as well as the executive branch of the U.S. government. From the start, the main congressional investigating committees targeted the labor left. Only a very few of the left-wing union leaders were not subpoenaed by HUAC or one of its siblings and grilled about their connections to the Communist Party. Unlike many of the committees' other witnesses, these labor leaders did not lose their jobs for refusing to cooperate with the committees. However, the unfavorable publicity that their hearings generated could be quite damaging, especially if the investigation coincided with a strike or union election; that so many hearings did pointed to intention, rather than coincidence.[28]

One of the most damaging congressional investigations occurred during a 1947 strike by the FTA Local 22 against the R.J. Reynolds Tobacco Company. The union was already under attack when HUAC arrived in North Carolina to investigate the Communist affiliations of the local's leaders. By holding its hearings in Winston-Salem, the committee ensured that the allegations against the union would get extensive publicity and weaken the local's support within the broader community. Since the FTA had not signed the Taft-Hartley affidavits, Local 22 was also vulnerable to raids from outside unions. Reynolds further weakened the union by redesigning its manufacturing process to eliminate the jobs of the unskilled black women who formed the union's most loyal members. By the time the CIO expelled the FTA in the spring of 1950, Local 22 was no longer functioning.[29]

A similar process broke a strike and destroyed another militant union, the United Auto Workers Local 248 at the Allis-Chalmers Company outside Milwaukee, Wisconsin. Even if there had been no Communist influence within the local, the company's hostility to organized labor ensured that its dealings with the union would be stormy. Work stoppages and red-baiting were endemic throughout the 1930s and into the '40s. In 1941 a major seventy-six-day strike got nationwide attention for the company's allegations that the walkout had been inspired by Moscow. These charges resurfaced when Local 248 went out on strike in the spring of 1946. Allis-Chalmers mounted a massive publicity campaign, planting a series of fifty-nine articles in a local paper, detailing the Communist connections of the local's leaders. It gave similar information to several congressional committees, outside journalists, and the FBI.[30]

The company's campaign came to a climax in March 1947 when the House Labor and Education Committee, which was drawing up the Taft-Hartley Act, questioned Local 248's president and past president about their party ties. After both men denied that they were Communists, the committee heard from Louis Budenz, the former managing editor of the CP's *Daily Worker* and one of the nation's leading professional witnesses. Budenz testified that he had been present at a meeting in December 1940 when top party officials told the local's president, Harold Christoffel, to call a strike in order to damage the nation's defense efforts. Though there is evidence that Budenz's story may have been a fabrication, it got wide circulation and became the main justification for all the measures designed to eliminate Communists from the labor movement. HUAC reinforced the message with a second set of hearings, and a subcommittee of the House Labor and Education Committee topped it off with a final session in Milwaukee. A week later the strike was over. Within six months Local 248 had fallen from eight thousand members to 184.[31]

The committee hearings had another after-effect. Christoffel was soon indicted for perjury and after several years of appeals and retrials had to serve a term in prison. He was not alone. Several other left-wing labor leaders faced criminal prosecutions during the McCarthy era. The usual charges were contempt of Congress or perjury for falsifying their Taft-Hartley affidavits. Unlike Christoffel, most of these people did win their cases on appeal, especially if they could keep them in the courts until the political climate changed in the mid-1950s. Nonetheless, the defense effort was costly—not only in money but also in the time and energy of the left-wing unions' top leaders and staff members.[32]

Deportation proceedings could be equally draining. The repeated attempts to expel the Longshoremen's leader Harry Bridges are notorious. The campaign against him began in the late 1930s and, by the time it finally waned twenty years later, Bridges had faced two Immigration and Naturalization Service deportation hearings and two federal conspiracy cases. Twice, when the initial decision was against him, he had to appeal to the U.S. Supreme Court. Again, as in so many of the McCarthy era cases, Bridges was ultimately exonerated. But the battle took a serious toll on him and on his union.[33]

Besides having their leaders subpoenaed and indicted, the left-led unions encountered official harassment in many other forms. The IRS audited them. The Justice Department brought UE and Mine-Mill before the Subversive Activities Control Board. The federal government's loyalty-security program cut a swath through the ranks of the United Public Workers union, while the Port Security program, instituted soon after the outbreak of the Korean War, hit the left-wing maritime unions, wiping out the small Marine Cooks and Stewards union. Though the unions resisted, fighting the official onslaught in the courts where they sometimes won, the struggle was extremely draining. Labor lawyer Victor Rabinowitz, who handled many of these cases, recalls that he felt fortunate if his embattled union clients could manage to cover his train fare.[34]

The anticommunist crusade was so debilitating for the left-led unions that by the time it came to an end in the mid-1960s, few of them were still around. In some cases, a larger union absorbed a smaller one. In others, the left-led union merged with a rival organization, as Mine-Mill did in 1967 when it joined the United Steelworkers. Only the ILWU remained intact. The UE, though maintaining its institutional independence, lost many of its members and most of its clout. It would, however, be incorrect to assign to McCarthyism all of the blame for the demise of the left-wing unions. Some of them, like the maritime unions and the fur workers, operated in declining industries. Nonetheless, it is clear that the hardships imposed by the anticommunist crusade increased the difficulties these unions faced and often made it impossible for them to fulfill their normal trade union functions.[35]

Obviously, the men and women who were most directly affected by the disappearance of the left-led unions were the members of those unions. After all, the UE and the other Communist-influenced unions had been effective labor organizations, negotiating work rules and economic packages that were as favorable as those any other union had obtained.[36] However, once those unions came under attack, it became increasingly difficult for them to service their members as effectively as they once had done. Weakened by having to fend off so many internal and external enemies, the leaders of these unions could not always stand up to the demands of management. They were too vulnerable to outside raiders and internal dissidents to risk pulling a strike and so were sometimes forced to accept unfavorable contract provisions that, had they been stronger, they would certainly have rejected.[37]

The rest of the labor movement suffered as well from the demise of the left-led unions. Participation in the anticommunist crusade diverted AFL and CIO leaders from dealing with issues that were more central to their mission. Thus, for example, labor's campaign against its own left wing kept the mainstream from following up on its early opposition to the Taft-Hartley Act. This was a serious mistake, for the 1947 law was designed to weaken all labor unions, not just the Communist-led ones. Its provisions against secondary boycotts and the organization of supervisory workers were particularly damaging, rolling back some of the gains organized labor had made since the late 1930s and making it much harder to recruit new members. Whether or not an all-out mobilization to repeal the measure would have been effective is unclear. What is clear, however, is that after an initial burst of activity, mainstream unions like the UAW accommodated themselves to Taft-Hartley and took advantage of the non-Communist affidavits to eliminate their Communist rivals.[38]

Such a shortsighted approach proved debilitating; Taft-Hartley created an unfavorable legal environment for the entire labor movement. Prevented from using the aggressive organizing tactics that had served them so well in the late 1930s, the nation's unions found it hard to expand. As a result, when the industrial sector's postwar economic boom faltered and the traditional well-paid blue-collar jobs that the labor movement's core members relied upon began to disappear, organized labor was unable to mobilize the economic and political clout needed to protect its earlier gains. Its numbers dropped, and its percentage of the overall workforce declined even more dramatically. In 1945, 35 percent of all the nation's non-agricultural workers were unionized. Today the figure is below 16 percent, and only 10 to 11 percent in the private sector.[39]

Though Taft-Hartley certainly increased the obstacles to labor's expansion, the movement's own internal purges contributed as well, diverting it from any serious efforts to increase its membership. Instead of trying to organize the unorganized, mainstream unions raided their Communist rivals. The elimination of its left wing also kept the labor movement from reaching beyond its traditional white male constituency to bring in new types of workers. The left-led unions had, after all, been particularly active in those areas of the economy where organized labor most needed to grow. The destruction of these unions disrupted their organizing campaigns in the service sector and among white collar and professional workers, as well as their efforts to bring in the women and people of color whom the traditional unions had largely ignored.

It would be wrong to assign all the blame for the attenuation of organized labor to the anticommunist crusade. The business community was strong, well organized, and determined to reassert its dominance within the economy. Its successful drive to transform the nation's labor laws after World War II was, as Elizabeth Fones-Wolf has so clearly demonstrated, only one facet of the corporate sector's broader campaign to undermine the power and legitimacy of organized labor.[40]

Nonetheless, its own internal purges weakened the ability of organized labor to confront this corporate campaign. Not only did McCarthyism divide the labor movement, but it also destroyed its ability to confront the corporations by depriving it of those activists who could have most effectively mounted a strong defense of collective action and challenged the business community's promotion of privatization and individual gain. After all, the Communists and their allies were labor's most militant voices. Their ideology encouraged them to champion workers against bosses. They understood capitalism and were willing to challenge management at every level. They were the first to raise the issue of deindustrialization and the first to oppose runaway plants—as the UAW's huge left-wing Local 600 tried to do in the early 1950s, when it sued the Ford Motor Company to stop it from moving its production facilities away from the River Rouge plant outside Detroit. That effort also fell victim to the anticommunist furor, for the UAW's leadership refused to back the suit and purged Local 600 instead.[41]

Its collaboration with the anticommunist crusade may also have made the labor movement less democratic, increasing the distance between labor's leaders and its rank-and-file members. Here it is important to recognize that because of the rapid expansion of the labor movement during World War II, many unions, including many left-wing ones, were already experiencing a marked diminution in the union consciousness and commitment of their members. Still, the Communist-led unions, while not always democratically administered, did try to promote an enlarged sense of community. Aware that their political affiliations ensured that they would come under attack, the leaders of these unions recognized the importance of retaining the loyalty of their rank and file. A typical left-wing local like the one Harold Christoffel led in Milwaukee often held dances and offered classes, while also aggressively pursuing grievances. Moreover, as long as Communists were a presence within the labor movement, their opponents also had to work the grassroots.[42]

But once the left-wingers were ousted, labor lost much of its dynamism. The radical organizers who had done so much to build the CIO were replaced with less imaginative officials who lacked their predecessors' vision and drive. Much of the labor movement became more centralized and bureaucratic. Perhaps such a transformation was inevitable and might have occurred with or without the Communist presence. American workers had never been particularly class conscious and might never have supported a militant union movement; they barely supported a

FIGURE 1.1 The cover illustration of this 1950 pamphlet, Publication 156 of the United Electrical Radio and Machine Workers of America, provides an explicit argument linking red-baiting and the anti-union campaigns by organized business after World War II. *Credit: Labor Archives and Research Center, San Francisco State University.*

nonmilitant one. When they no longer viewed their union membership as central to their identity, they stopped participating in union activities.[43] In response, the apathy of their rank-and-file members forced the unions to rely ever more heavily on the federal government instead of their own members to fight their battles. As a result, when the Reagan administration turned against organized labor in the 1980s, the nation's unions were blindsided and unable to recoup.

The retrenchment of the labor movement and its failure to organize the unorganized also affected the rest of American society. Here, of course, we must speculate, for much of what we are looking at are things that did not happen. We must also guard against exaggerating the impact of the destruction of the labor left. It is by no means clear how much influence even a strong left-wing labor movement could have exerted within a polity that had been moving toward the right ever since the late 1930s. Still, some possibilities are suggestive.

Had there been a strong labor movement in the South in the 1940s and 1950s, it might have been possible to challenge the conservative politicians who held so much power in Congress. While we cannot assign full responsibility to the anticommunist crusade for labor's failure to organize Southern workers, it did play a part. When the CIO organized Operation Dixie, its 1946 campaign to bring unions to the South, it decided not to challenge the region's power structure and dominant values. It also focused its efforts on white workers and consciously distanced itself from those left-led unions like FTA Local 22 in Winston-Salem, North Carolina, that had been so successful in recruiting African Americans. Whether Operation Dixie would have been more effective if it had welcomed blacks and reds is unclear. Certainly, there was so much opposition to unions within the South that, despite the CIO's moderation, Operation Dixie was heavily red- and race-baited; it folded within six months.[44] Without a strong labor movement behind it, Southern liberalism withered, strengthening the conservative forces within that region's political elite that were pushing the entire nation to the right.[45]

The civil rights movement also felt both directly and indirectly the impact of the destruction of the labor left. The decline of Southern liberalism deprived black Southerners of a base of support within the white middle class. The anticommunist crusade destroyed some of the unions that were the main institutional support of the civil rights movement within the black working class. The destruction of these unions transformed the nascent drive for racial equality into a more middle-class movement, one whose leaders fought for legal and political rights but ignored the economic problems that plagued most Southern blacks. Though the more liberal sectors of organized labor outside the South did support the civil rights movement once it got under way, they often did not put their mouth where their money was and confront the racial discrimination that prevailed within their own ranks. As recent work on racial issues by a number of labor historians reveals, it is by no means the case that, even if the left-led unions had survived, they would have been able to overcome the racism of their white members. Still, it is clear that the disappearance of the labor left silenced the main voices calling for both economic and racial equality. And, as the contemporary political scene reveals, the severing of race from class has not been good for the United States.[46]

Besides transforming labor's relationship with the African American community, McCarthyism also cost the labor movement its political independence. The purge of the left-led unions deepened organized labor's dependence on the Democratic Party. With labor's dissenting voices stilled, there was no longer any question about its support for American foreign policy. Both the CIO and the AFL enlisted in the Cold War and, by the time they merged in the mid-fifties, most of the labor movement had been so thoroughly co-opted that its leaders provided cover for the CIA, and its conventions endorsed the war in Vietnam.[47]

On the domestic front, the destruction of its left wing transformed organized labor from a social movement to a special interest group. Though it constituted the left of the Democratic party, it was a timid left that advocated a rather mild program of reforms. In the 1940s, labor had been more forceful. The CIO—and not just its left-wing unions—had called for an expansion of the welfare state, pushing for a wide range of measures that included universal health insurance, public housing, and guaranteed economic security. The Communist-influenced unions were active here, pushing the rest of the labor movement to champion what was essentially a social democratic agenda. But in the aftermath of the McCarthy era purges, labor's political center of gravity shifted to the right. And, as in the rest of society, the fear of being tainted by supporting causes that Communists also backed weakened labor's commitment to social and economic change.[48]

Organized labor turned inward. It no longer gave more than lip service to reforms that would benefit the rest of society. Instead it focused on its own constituents, seeking and winning higher wages and benefits for its own members. But, by developing what was in effect its own private welfare system, the labor movement not only abandoned its previous role as the main institutional proponent of social reform, but it also contributed—albeit indirectly—to the delegitimization of state activism that has so seriously eroded the public sector today.[49]

We can't turn the clock back to the mid-1940s to recoup the opportunities for social change that were lost when the anticommunist crusade overwhelmed the labor movement. Still, we can look more closely at what happened during those years and perhaps gain a new hearing for some of the voices that McCarthyism forced out of the national conversation.

Notes

1. The most thorough historical treatment of the use of anticommunism in combating labor unions is in M. J. Heale, *American AntiCommunism: Combating the Enemy Within, 1830–1970* (Baltimore: The Johns Hopkins University Press, 1990). See also Robert J. Goldstein, *Political Repression in Modern America From 1870 to the Present* (Cambridge, Mass.: Schenkman, 1978).

2. For a good example of the red-baiting indulged in by conservative labor leaders, see the testimony of Matthew Woll, 17 June 1930, in "Investigation of Communist Propaganda," *Hearings Before a Special Committee to Investigate Communist Activities in the United States*, House of Representatives, 71st Cong., 2d sess. See also Bruce Nelson, *Workers on the Waterfront: Seamen, Longshoremen, and Unionism in the 1930s* (Urbana and Chicago: University of Illinois Press, 1988), 118–26, 143; Roger Keeran,

The Communist Party and the Auto Workers Unions (Bloomington: Indiana University Press, 1980), 97–117; and Harvey A. Levenstein, *Communism, AntiCommunism, and the CIO* (Westport, Conn.: Greenwood Press, 1981), 23–31, 104–109.
3. For a contemporary compilation of such cases, see Adam Yarmolinsky, ed., *Case Studies in Personnel Security* (Washington, D.C.: The Bureau of National Affairs, 1955).
4. For a recent example of the contentiousness of the issue, see Jacob Weisberg, "Cold War Without End," *New York Times Magazine*, 28 November 1999.
5. The history of American Communism remains controversial. As a result, charting its vicissitudes is a subject in itself. Works such as those published during the '50s and '60s at the height of the Cold War by Irving Howe and Lewis Coser, *The American Communist Party: A Critical History, 1919–1957* (Boston: Beacon Press, 1957) and Theodore Draper, *The Roots of American Communism* (New York: Viking, 1957) tended to be hostile to the CP. Later publications by Maurice Isserman, *Which Side Were You On? The American Communist Party During the Second World War* (Middletown, Conn.: Wesleyan University Press, 1982), Robin D. G. Kelley, *Hammer and Hoe: Alabama Communists during the Great Depression* (Chapel Hill: University of North Carolina Press, 1990), and Fraser M. Ottanelli, *The Communist Party of the United States: From the Depression to World War II* (New Brunswick: Rutgers University Press, 1991) take a more nuanced and sympathetic perspective. The work of Harvey Klehr and his various collaborators, however, reverts to the earlier anticommunist stance: Harvey Klehr, *The Heyday of American Communism: The Depression Decade* (New York: Basic Books, 1984); Harvey Klehr, John Earl Haynes, and Fridrikh Igorevich Firsov, *The Secret World of American Communism* (New Haven: Yale University Press, 1995); and Harvey Klehr, John Earl Haynes, and Kyrill M. Anderson, *The Soviet World of American Communism* (New Haven: Yale University Press, 1998).

There is also a growing body of ex-Communist memoirs. Among the most useful are Peggy Dennis, *The Autobiography of an American Communist: A Personal View of a Political Life, 1925–1975* (Westport and Berkeley: Lawrence Hill & Co., Creative Arts Book Co., 1977); John Gates, *The Story of an American Communist* (New York: Thomas Nelson & Sons, 1958); Dorothy Healey and Maurice Isserman, *Dorothy Healey Remembers: A Life in the American Communist Party* (New York: Oxford University Press, 1990); Steve Nelson, James R. Barrett, and Rob Ruck, *Steve Nelson, American Radical* (Pittsburgh: University of Pittsburgh Press, 1981); and Junius Irving Scales and Richard Nickson, *Cause at Heart: A Former Communist Remembers* (Athens: University of Georgia Press, 1987).

The most useful treatment of the party's involvement with espionage is Allen Weinstein and Alexander Vassiliev, *The Haunted Wood: Soviet Espionage in America—The Stalin Era* (New York: Random House, 1999). See also John Earl Haynes and Harvey Klehr, *Venona: Soviet Espionage in America in the Stalin Era* (New Haven: Yale University Press, 1999).
6. There are dozens of works that touch in one way or another on the CP's work within the labor movement, including memoirs and monographs about individual unions. Among the most useful general sources are Bert Cochran, *Labor and Communism: The Conflict that Shaped American Unions* (Princeton: Princeton University Press, 1977); Harvey A. Levenstein, *Communism, AntiCommunism, and the CIO* (Westport, Conn.: Greenwood Press, 1981); and Steve Rosswurm, "Introduction: An Overview and Preliminary Assessment of the CIO's Expelled Unions," in *The CIO's Left-Led Unions*, ed. Steve Rosswurm (New Brunswick: Rutgers University Press, 1992), 1–16.
7. Probably the most famous union leader to abandon the party was the Transport Workers' Mike Quill. The best source on Quill and his union is Joshua B. Freeman, *In Tran-*

sit: *The Transport Workers Union in New York City, 1933–1960* (New York: Oxford University Press, 1989). See also Rick Halpern, *Down on the Killing Floor: Black and White Workers in Chicago's Packinghouses, 1904–54* (Urbana and Chicago: University of Illinois Press, 1997).

8. Paul Lyons, *Philadelphia Communists 1936–1956* (Philadelphia: Temple University Press, 1982), 126.
9. The positive assessment of the CIO's Communists comes from Robert H. Zieger, hardly a party sympathizer, in *The CIO, 1935–1955* (Chapel Hill: The University of North Carolina Press, 1995), 255.
10. For information about the role that the party played in encouraging racial equality within the labor movement, it is necessary to look at the literature on specific unions. See, for example, Freeman, *In Transit*, 151–56; Rick Halpern and Roger Horowitz, *Meatpackers: An Oral History of Black Packinghouse Workers and Their Struggle for Racial and Economic Equality* (New York: Monthly Review Press, 1999), 16, 46; Michael K. Honey, *Southern Labor and Black Civil Rights: Organizing Memphis Workers* (Urbana and Chicago: University of Illinois Press, 1993); Robert Korstad and Nelson Lichtenstein, "Opportunities Found and Lost: Labor Radicals, and the Early Civil Rights Movement," *Journal of American History* 75 (1988): 786–811. See also Michael Goldfield, "Race and the CIO: The Possibilities for Racial Egalitarianism During the 1930s and 1940s," *International Labor and Working-Class History* 44 (1993): 1–32.
11. Halpern and Horowitz, *Meatpackers*, 60; Horace Huntley, "The Red scare and Black Workers in Alabama: The International Union of Mine, Mill, and Smelter Workers, 1945–1953," in *Labor Divided: Race and Ethnicity in United States Labor Struggles, 1835–1960*, ed. Robert Asher and Charles Stephenson (Albany: State University of New York Press, 1990); Karl Korstad, "Black and White Together: Organizing in the South with the Food, Tobacco, Agricultural & Allied Workers Union (FTA-CIO), 1946–1952," in *The CIO's Left-Led Unions*, ed. Rosswurm, 69–94; Honey, *Southern Labor and Black Civil Rights*, passim; Korstad and Lichtenstein, "Opportunities Found and Lost"; Louis Goldblatt, interview by Estolv Ethan Ward, 1978–9, Regional Oral History Office, Bancroft Library, University of California, Berkeley.
12. For an overview of FTA Local 22, see Korstad and Lichtenstein, "Opportunities Found and Lost," 786–811.
13. On the UE, see Lisa Kannenberg, "The Impact of the Cold War on Women's Trade Union Activism: The UE Experience," *Labor History* 34 (1993): 309–323. On other unions, see Daniel J. Walkowitz, *Working with Class: Social Workers and the Politics of Middle-Class Identity* (Chapel Hill: University of North Carolina Press, 1999) and Sharon Hartman Strom, "'We're No Kitty Foyles': Organizing Office Workers for the Congress of Industrial Organizations, 1937–50," in Ruth Milkman, ed., *Women, Work, and Protest: A Century of U.S. Women's Labor History* (Boston: Routledge & Kegan Paul, 1985), 227–28; Mark McColloch, *White Collar Workers in Transition: The Boom Years, 1940–1970* (Westport, Conn.: Greenwood Press, 1983), 34.
14. Daniel Horowitz, *Betty Friedan and the Making of The Feminine Mystique: The American Left, the Cold War, and Modern Feminism* (Amherst: University of Massachusetts Press, 1998), 102–52.
15. For a survey of the fate of the left-led unions, see F. S. O'Brien, "The 'Communist-dominated' Unions in the United States Since 1950," *Labor History* 9 (1968): 184–205.
16. For an overview of McCarthyism's assault on the left-led unions, see Ellen W. Schrecker, "McCarthyism and the Labor Movement: The Role of the State," in *The CIO's Left-Led Unions*, ed. Rosswurm, 139–157.
17. The most thorough treatment of the early history of the Taft-Hartley Act can be found in

Harry A. Millis and Emily Clark Brown, *From the Wagner Act to Taft-Hartley* (Chicago: University of Chicago Press, 1950); see also Gerard D. Reilly, "The Legislative History of the Taft-Hartley Act," *George Washington Law Review* 29 (1960): 298–299.

18. On the initial response to Taft-Hartley, see James A. Gross, *The Reshaping of the National Labor Relations Board* (Albany: State University of New York Press, 1981); R. Alton Lee, *Truman and Taft-Hartley* (Lexington: University of Kentucky Press, 1966); and Melvyn Dubofsky, *The State and Labor in Modern America* (Chapel Hill: University of North Carolina Press, 1994), 199–208.

19. Millis and Brown, *From the Wagner Act to Taft-Hartley*, 546–54; Vernon H. Jensen, *Nonferrous Metals Industry Unionism, 1932–1954* (Ithaca: Cornell University Press, 1954), 233–42; Levenstein, *Communism, AntiCommunism, and the CIO*, 254–78, 289–90; Goldblatt, interview, 457; Howard Kimeldorf, *Reds or Rackets? The Making of Radical and Conservative Unions on the Waterfront* (Berkeley and Los Angeles: University of California Press, 1988), 148; George Lipsitz, *Class and Culture in Cold War America* (South Hadley, Mass.: J. F. Bergin, 1981), 155–68.

20. On the litigation over Section 9(h), see Victor Rabinowitz, *Unrepentant Leftist: A Lawyer's Memoir* (Urbana and Chicago: University of Illinois Press, 1996), 47–56.

21. "NLRB Summary of Section 9(h) Problems," undated memorandum, NLRB records, 60-A-387–694, Record Group 25, National Archives; Jensen, *Nonferrous Metals Industry Unionism*, 248–49.

22. For a discussion of the various attempts to decertify the left-led unions after their officers signed the non-Communist affidavits, see Schrecker, "McCarthyism and the Labor Movement," 151–52.

23. Levenstein, *Communism, AntiCommunism, and the CIO*, 273–83; Cochran, *Labor and Communism*, 297–315; Zieger, *The CIO*, 269–93.

24. For an example of the kinds of arguments used in the expulsions, see "Resolution and Report Expelling the International Union of Mine, Mill, and Smelter Workers from the Congress of Industrial Organizations," 15 February 1950. There are copies of these resolutions in all the major labor archives; the one I used was printed by the United Steelworkers of America and came from Box 1 in the Archives, Western Federation of Miners and Mine-Mill, Historical Collections, University of Colorado, Boulder.

25. For the Supreme Court's language, see *American Communications Association v. Douds* 339 U.S. 94 (1950). On Hoover's assessment of the dangers of sabotage, see J. Edgar Hoover, memoranda to Edwin "Pa" Watson, 15 November 1939, 13 July 1940, in Franklin Delano Roosevelt Papers, OF 10-B, Franklin Delano Roosevelt Library, Hyde Park, New York.

26. The most useful discussion of the AEC's actions is *in Hearings Before a Subcommittee on Labor of the Committee on Labor and Public Welfare on Communist Domination of Unions and National Security*, 82nd Cong., 2nd sess., 1952; for a survey of the way in which politicians and others viewed the threat to security from the Communist-led unions, see Schrecker, *Many Are the Crimes*, 187–90.

27. McColloch, *White Collar Workers in Transition*, 72; Lipsitz, *Class and Culture in Cold War America*, 169; Carl Bernstein, *Loyalties: A Son's Memoir* (New York: Simon and Schuster, 1989), 173–258; James J. Matles and James Higgins, *Them and Us* (Englewood Cliffs, N.J.: Prentice-Hall, 1974), 174–80; Albert J. Fitzgerald to President Truman, and enclosure, 24 August 1948, in Hymen Schlesinger Papers, Series I, folder UE Dist. 6, Union Miscellany, Archives of Industrial Society, UE/Labor Archives, Hillman Library, University of Pittsburgh, Pittsburgh, Pa.

28. Levenstein, *Communism, AntiCommunism, and the CIO*, 247; Lipsitz, *Class and Culture in Cold War America*, 159–61; Rosswurm, "Introduction," 17–18; William D. An-

drew, "Factionalism and Anti-Communism: Ford Local 600," *Labor History* 20 (1979): 227–55.
29. Korstad and Lichtenstein, "Opportunities Found and Lost," 801–3; Barbara S. Griffith, *The Crisis of American Labor: Operation Dixie and the Defeat of the CIO* (Philadelphia: Temple University Press, 1988), 150–52; Larry J. Griffin and Robert R. Korstad, "Race as Class and Gender: Making and Breaking a Labor Union in the Jim Crow South," *Social Science History* 19 (1995): 425–54.
30. For an extended look at the Allis-Chalmers situation, see Stephen Meyer, *"Stalin Over Wisconsin" The Making and Unmaking of Militant Unionism, 1900–1950* (New Brunswick: Rutgers University Press, 1992). See also Schrecker, *Many Are the Crimes*, 185–7.
31. Keeran, *The Communist Party and the Auto Workers Unions*, 266–78; Martin Halpern, *UAW Politics in the Cold War Era* (Albany: State University of New York Press, 1988), 173–83; House Committee on Education and Labor, *Hearings, Amendments to the National Labor Relations Act*, 80th Cong., 1st sess., 1, 13 March 1947.
32. For a more extensive discussion of the various prosecutions that left-wing labor leaders faced, see Schrecker, *Many Are the Crimes*, 340–58, and Schrecker, "McCarthyism and the Labor Movement," passim.
33. The best treatment of Bridges' various ordeals is in Stanley I. Kutler, *The American Inquisition: Justice and Injustice in the Cold War* (New York: Hill and Wang, 1982), 118–51. See also Charles Larrowe, *Harry Bridges* (New York and Westport: Lawrence Hill and Co., 1972), and Ann Fagan Ginger, *Carol Weiss King: Human Rights Lawyer, 1895–1952* (Niwot, Colorado: University Press of Colorado, 1993), 253–534.
34. On the IRS, see Goldblatt, interview, 737, and Julius Emspak, interview, 1960, Columbia Oral History Project (hereafter cited as COHP), 14. On the SACB, see Ellen Schrecker, "Introduction" to *Records of the Subversive Activities Control Board, 1950–1972*, (Frederick, Md.: University Publications of America, 1989). For the UPW see Bernstein, *Loyalties;* for the Port Security Program, see Ralph S. Brown and John D. Fassett, "Security Tests for Maritime Workers: Due Process Under the Port Security Program," *Yale Law Journal* 62 (1953): 1163–1208; David Caute, *The Great Fear: The Anti-Communist Purge under Truman and Eisenhower* (New York: Simon and Schuster, 1978), 349–401; and Schrecker, *Many Are the Crimes*, 266–70. Victor Rabinowitz, interview, COHP, 83.
35. Robert S. Keitel, "The Merger of the International Union of Mine, Mill and Smelter Workers into the United Steelworkers of America," *Labor History* 15 (1974): 36–43; O'Brien, "The `Communist-dominated' Unions," passim; David Brody, *The Butcher Workmen* (Cambridge: Harvard University Press, 1964), 259–61; Levenstein, *Communism, Anticommunism, and the CIO*, 325; McColloch, *White Collar Workers in Transition*, 77.
36. Judith Stepan-Norris and Maurice Zeitlin, " 'Red' Unions and 'Bourgeois' Contracts?" *American Journal of Sociology* 96 (1991): 1151–1200; Mark McColloch, "The Shop-Floor Dimension of Union Rivalry: The Case of Westinghouse in the 1950s," in *The CIO's Left-Led Unions*, ed. Rosswurm., 186.
37. Levenstein, *Communism, Anticommunism, and the CIO*, 313; Keitel, "Merger," 37–40.
38. Martin Halpern, "Taft-Hartley and the Defeat of the Progressive Alternative in the United Auto Workers," *Labor History* 27 (1986): 204–226. For an admittedly partisan assessment of the damage caused by Taft-Hartley, see Irving Richter, *Labor's Struggles, 1945–1949, A Participant's View* (New York: Cambridge University Press, 1994), 96–133.
39. For an intriguing recent discussion of deindustrialization, see Judith Stein, *Running Steel, Running America: Race, Economic Policy, and the Decline of Liberalism* (Chapel Hill: University of North Carolina Press, 1998). For another explanation of labor's

decline, see Michael Goldfield, *The Decline of Organized Labor in the United States* (Chicago: University of Chicago Press, 1987).
40. Elizabeth A. Fones-Wolf, *Selling Free Enterprise: The Business Assault on Labor and Liberalism, 1945–1960* (Urbana and Chicago: University of Illinois Press, 1994). See also Howell John Harris, *The Right to Manage: Industrial Relations Policies of American Business in the 1940s* (Madison: University of Wisconsin Press, 1982).
41. On Local 600, see Korstad and Lichtenstein, "Opportunities Found and Lost," and Thomas J. Sugrue, "'Forget about Your Inalienable Right to Work': Deindustrialization and Its Discontents at Ford, 1950–1953," *International Labor and Working-Class History* 48 (1995): 112–30.
42. Kimeldorf, *Reds or Rackets?*, 128–141; Judith Stepan-Norris and Maurice Zeitlin, "Insurgency, Radicalism, and Democracy in America's Industrial Unions," *Social Forces* 75 (1996): 1-32; Meyer, *"Stalin Over Wisconsin,"* 68–9; Freeman, *In Transit*, 120–27.
43. Lipsitz, *Class and Culture in the Cold War*, 170.
44. On Operation Dixie see Griffith, *The Crisis of American Labor: Operation Dixie and the Defeat of the CIO*, and Michael Goldfield, "The Failure of Operation Dixie: A Critical Turning Point in American Political Development?" in *Race, Class, and Community in Southern Labor History*, ed. Gary M. Fink and Merl E. Reed (Tuscaloosa: University of Alabama Press, 1994).
45. On Southern liberalism, see Sullivan, Patricia, *Days of Hope: Race and Democracy in the New Deal Era* (Chapel Hill: University of North Carolina Press, 1996); and Linda Reed, *Simple Decency and Common Sense: The Southern Conference Movement, 1938–1963* (Bloomington and Indianapolis: Indiana University Press, 1991).
46. Robert J. Norrell, "Caste in Steel: Jim Crow Careers in Birmingham, Alabama," *Journal of American History* 73 (1986): 669–94; Thomas J. Sugrue, *The Origins of the Urban Crisis: Race and Inequality in Postwar Detroit* (Princeton: Princeton University Press, 1996), chaps. 4 and 6; Nelson Lichtenstein, *The Most Dangerous Man in Detroit: Walter Reuther and the Fate of American Labor* (New York: Basic Books, 1995), 370–95; John Dittmer, *Local People: The Struggle for Civil Rights in Mississippi* (Urbana and Chicago: University of Illinois Press, 1994), 23–24; Bruce Nelson, "Organized Labor and the Struggle for Black Equality in Mobile During World War II," *Journal of American History* 80 (1993): 979–81.
47. For a detailed look at labor's involvement with American foreign policy during the Cold War, see Ronald L. Filippelli, *American Labor and Postwar Italy, 1943–1953: A Study of Cold War Politics* (Stanford: Stanford University Press, 1989); see also Ronald Radosh, *American Labor and United States Foreign Policy* (New York: Random House, 1969). There is a disappointing biography of labor's chief advocate of opposing Communism abroad, Ted Morgan, *A Covert Life: Jay Lovestone: Communist, Anticommunist, and Spy* (New York: Random House, 1999).
48. William C. Berman, *America's Right Turn: From Nixon to Bush* (Baltimore: The Johns Hopkins Press, 1994), 38; Ira Katznelson, "Was the Great Society a Lost Opportunity?" in *The Rise and Fall of the New Deal Order, 1930–1980*, ed. Steve Fraser and Gary Gerstle (Princeton: Princeton University Press, 1989); Nelson Lichtenstein, "From Corporatism to Collective Bargaining: Organized Labor and the Eclipse of Social Democracy in the Postwar Era," in *Rise and Fall of the New Deal Order, 1930–1980*, ed. Fraser and Gerstle.
49. For two thoughtful overviews of the political evolution of the postwar labor movement, see David Brody, *Workers in Industrial America: Essays on the Twentieth Century Struggle*, 2d ed. (New York: Oxford, 1993), 156–239 and Nelson Lichtenstein, *State of the Union: A Century of American Labor* (Princeton: Princeton University Press, 2002).

Uncivil War

An Oral History of Labor, Communism, and Community in Schenectady, New York, 1944–1954

☼

Gerald Zahavi

During the first half of the twentieth century, Schenectady—lying at the eastern boundary of New York's Mohawk Valley—was a small, bustling, and ethnically diverse industrial city that depended on two major industries for its economic survival and growth: the behemoth General Electric (GE) Works located at the center of the city, and the smaller adjacent American Locomotive Company (ALCO). Though both constituted the economic foundations of the city, the GE plant—by virtue of its size—clearly figured as the more significant force in the city's development. The GE Works drew skilled and unskilled workers to the city; first, Anglo-Saxon and German machinists and engineers, then Italian, Canadian, and Eastern European workers. Men and women labored in the dozens of shops that together comprised the "Schenectady Works" of the GE. They fabricated or assembled refrigerators, wires and cables, electrical switches and controls, porcelain insulators, large and small motors, turbines, and—in wartime—hundreds of military-related products, including, in later years, nuclear power generation components.

Along with industry and a diverse laboring population came socialism and Communism. Though Thomas Edison had sought to flee trade unions and worker militancy when he relocated the Edison Machine Works from New York City to Schenectady in 1886, the corporation he helped found failed to adequately insulate itself from union or radical assault. Throughout the first half of the twentieth century, anarchists, syndicalists, and Communists pounded at the gates of GE. In 1906, the Industrial Workers of the World staged the first sit-down strike at GE's Schenectady plant. In 1913, over 14,000 workers struck the firm, and five hundred women walked out of one GE plant, led by socialist labor organizer Ella Reeve Bloor (later a Communist Party leader). During this latter confrontation, the city was led by a pro-labor Socialist administration headed by Mayor George R. Lunn. Even some of the firm's white-collar workers and managers sometimes brought with them ideological traditions anathema to corporate capitalism. The firm's most famous research scientist, Alfred Proteus Steinmetz, was a German-born socialist who sometimes hosted local Socialist Party meetings at his home on Wendell Avenue, located in the prestigious "GE Realty Plot."

In the 1930s the city's radical tradition was passed to a new generation of activists, many of them Communists active in the GE Works. Eliminating the firm's company union, they and their non-Communist allies helped establish a strong left-wing CIO-based labor movement in the city and in the region, a movement that revolved around Local 301 of the United Electrical, Radio and Machine Workers of America (UE). Through the late 1930s and into the 1940s, the local grew to include between 20,000 to 30,000 GE workers. Throughout these years, Communist organizers were sent into the community, most arriving from New York City. Schenectady was a major concentration point for the party, mainly because of its heavy industrial base, and because the largest number of party members in the 1930s were employed in the GE plants, scattered among the thousands of unionized workers.

With time, particularly during the post-World War II years, the party's ties to the union that had led GE's workers since the Great Depression became a major liability for the union and for individual workers. As Truman, Eisenhower, McCarthy, and hundreds of politicians were warming up the Cold War in Washington, D.C., Schenectady—with its radical tradition, and with its core industry increasingly dependent on government contracts for military production—could hardly remain insulated from America's second "red scare." Between 1944 and 1954 a series of confrontations took place within and outside the massive General Electric complex, replicating similar conflicts in other industrial regions throughout the land. Local 301 and its very popular and able business agent, Leo Jandreau, came under increasing pressure from distant and local sources. In 1949 the Congress of Industrial Organizations (CIO) expelled the UE and Local 301. It formed an opposition "right wing" union, the International Union of Electrical, Radio and Machine Workers (IUE), which very quickly established a beachhead in Schenectady to battle against Jandreau and the UE. Local clergy preached against Local 301 leaders; local politicians and former community supporters encouraged them to sever their ties to the Communist party and the UE, and to affiliate with the more conservative union. The Schenectady NAACP even entered the fray against the UE, backing the local IUE group. A series of federal congressional and senatorial hearings conducted in Albany and Schenectady from 1948 through 1954 (including two headed by Senator Joseph McCarthy in 1953 and 1954) sought to expose the Communist "domination" of the local and placed its leadership under very close scrutiny. The hearings led GE, in early 1954, to fire seven party members for assertion of their Fifth Amendment rights.[1]

While a vast literature exists chronicling labor's Cold War during the McCarthy era, much of it focuses on struggles at the national and institutional levels.[2] Close and detailed studies of the local dimensions of the domestic Cold War and its impact on labor and communities are still somewhat rare. Even more rare are profiles of local protagonists and antagonists and their motives. What follows is precisely that: autobiographical sketches of Communists and anticommunists recalling their participation in Schenectady's own "uncivil" war, the conflict between Local 301 of the UE and their antagonists—particularly those in the IUE. Since the fields of battle of this war extended well outside the gates of the local GE Works, and often had quite complex and multifaceted personal and social implications, I have included accounts that touch on these dimensions of the struggle.[3]

☼

Pasquale Vottis' father had come to Schenectady to work at American Locomotive in 1900. In 1923, at the age of sixteen, Pasquale—like many other members of his family—went to work for General Electric. More than a decade later, he became involved in the successful movement to break GE's company union, the Works Council, and establish an independent union, Local 301 of the UE. He became an early board member of the new Local. Pasquale's more famous brother, Salvatore ("Sal") Vottis, was an early Communist Party (CP) activist in the Local, though he dropped out of the party in 1939. In 1944, for personal and ideological reasons, Sal and Pasquale both turned on the Local's left-wing leaders and on the CP. The union expelled Sal. In 1948 he testified at a local hearing conducted by the Labor Sub-Committee of the House of Representatives (chaired by Charles J. Kersten) against local party members, claiming that he himself had recruited the local's business agent, Leo Jandreau, into the party in 1936.[4] Here, Pasquale Vottis recalls the early relationship between Communist Party members and Local 301 and the emergence of tensions during World War II that would resurface in the early 1950s.

I had a brother, Sal, about two years older than I. Sal went to work for the GE and he worked there . . . I guess the whole family at one time or another worked for GE, every one of us did. Now Sal and [Leo] Jandreau came over to me, and they started talking about organizing the union and trying to break up the company union [the Works Council]. So then we discovered that the ones who were working on this thing and promoting it were the commies. They were skilled in organizing; this was their job. They were organizers and they worked with Jandreau and my brother Sal. So the first thing they had to do is talk to the people in the shops. It was a little difficult because you couldn't just go walking around talking to people because they [GE management] didn't like that. The Wagner Act hadn't been approved yet, and all this kind of stuff, and the company was fighting them. But they were managing to get ahold of people in different shops. The Labor Relations Board was going to have a referendum of some kind and they were going to have a vote . . . with the help of the commies. I don't know where the hell they came from; come up from New York. They used to introduce themselves [as] labor helpers. Sal used to go with Joe [Rotundo, a local left-wing professor at Schenectady's Union College interested in labor and labor relations issues]; they talked about what was going on in the shops. Joe was accumulating all sorts of data on us. So now, finally the vote came, and the company union was broken; we broke the company union.

[After Local 301 was established in 1936] I was a board member. In fact, I was one of the first board members. We used to have board meetings—I think we started in the morning, every Thursday morning, all day, with management on one side and the union on the other, with Jandreau as our leader. And we'd bring up different grievances.

This was not a Communist Party union, and that's where the trouble started—when guys started coming in with . . . the *Daily Worker,* and they were madder than hell, saying "What the hell is this, the Communist Party's taken over now?" In fact, Jandreau and the rest of them had to stop that kind of stuff. Leo Jandreau was a very nice guy. But Leo went along with the commies, up to a certain point. After the union had gotten to a point where it was pretty strong, the commies wanted to come out in the open. Hey, this is our union; we built it, and they start peddling *Daily Workers* out the gates! They came out with the *Daily Worker* and grievances from the shop were front page in the *Daily Worker:* foreman so and so does this . . . that . . . in building so and so; this was all in the *Daily Worker.* Sal was going along with them for the same reason that most of—some of us—were. We needed them at first. But when they decided they were going to take over the union, that's when things started to get bad. I mean that's when a war started between Sal and Jandreau, and some of the others.

During the war I went to a couple of the conventions, and one of the big issues was the second front . . . they were fighting to ease the front there against Leningrad. I don't think [the workers] knew what the hell the difference was. But the delegates at the convention did, because there was some pretty good speakers for and against it. In fact it was the biggest fight on the floor—the convention floor—the opening of the second front. Now here this definitely brings out the commie . . . I mean, what the hell does this got to do with wages, what's it got to do with grievances? Here's something going on the other side, we were in it, but why should this become a big union issue? It was strictly a Communist issue.

Well, he got into a little argument there with Leo about the commies see, and Sal has always been, always been a freethinker of his own. I don't think he was enthralled with what was going on in Russia. That was too far away. Sal was a pretty powerful guy. In fact, he had me under his thumb there for a little long while. I used to have to go along with whatever Sal did. . . . I don't think Sal ever was at heart a Communist. None of us really were. There was only a very few who were actually into the party. There were not many, and you could not say that the workers were being drawn into the party because they were not, no.

I don't think I can quite put the point across, but the worker was not a very smart guy. They could have done any damn thing. There was never an uprising or anything of that sort against anything. They had to force them to go and vote. They had to push them to do this and push 'em to do that, and all the worker wanted to know was when do I get my raise after I've been here three months? That's all he wanted to know. I tell you, the workers did not support the union a hell of a lot. There rarely was a meeting where there was a quorum. Seventy-five was a quorum, and many times they had to go down to the bar downstairs and bring the guys up to vote. The workers would next day find out something had been passed that they didn't know anything about. Yeah, that was an old trick.

I used to hold a meeting with my stewards, seventy-five stewards that I held a meeting with. Let me tell you, the commies had taught me so many tricks on how to run a meeting, the minute you have someone on the floor heckle you or refute what you're saying, bother you, either you called him up to the stage, you called him up [and] say "Look, don't tell me about it, tell everybody here about it, tell everybody about it." Never hold a small meeting while you're standing up on the stage. Go among the people and hold the meeting, hold the meeting right among the group. That was another thing, and you would be amazed at how well that worked. A guy had a grievance and you called a meeting at noontime, you say you want to settle a little grievance here this afternoon. "I want to get you all in here. I want to see what you all think about it," see. All you had to do is start off telling what the grievance was and keep quiet; don't say a word. These guys were talking back and forth, knocking each other the hell, "What the hell's he talking about, my God, that's not so at all," and the other guy says, "Well he's got a right to do this." You listen, listen, you take it all apart and say, "Now, look, I think this is your problem." These are all the tricks that the commies taught. Max Gordon[5] and the rest of those guys used to tell you how to work.

☼

A. C. Stevens worked in Schenectady for the General Electric Company from the mid–1920s, when he took his first job as a summer employee, until his retirement in 1965. Stevens worked his way up from engineering trainee (he came into the firm through the famous GE "Test Course") to works manager of the Schenectady Plant, a position he attained in the early 1950s. The following account is drawn from a series of interviews conducted with him back in the spring and summer of 1991. Stevens died in 1996.

The Communist influence began to manifest itself as the Depression began to take its toll. Of course, it made a lot better sense for the people to line up behind any elements that would act in their behalf against the company. I would say about 1942 I was made assistant general superintendent of the plant. Increasingly, I was involved in labor relations. In those days our meetings [were] with the UE. Now, there wasn't anything that we could do about it, here in Schenectady. We accepted the fact that the union picked certain of those fellows as their leaders. And up until about 1950, McCarthy suspected, and had reason to believe, that the American Communist Party was really controlling at least the UE union—the United Electrical Workers. There was not much question but what we had right in Schenectady quite a number of people that were very closely influenced, and in some cases identified with, the American Communist Party. So I think the thing that opened the situation up was McCarthy's effort to expose this. He came to Schenectady. He contacted us.

Not long after the formation of the UE there was an allegation on the part of quite a few employees and some of the union—of the old UE leadership—that it had been infiltrated by Communist sympathizers. Well, nobody ever really knew whether this was true or not. Because there was no proof one way or the other. Finally, this developed into quite a split within the union, with this man, Jim Carey, taking sides and sort of taking over the command of the anticommunist group. Now, of course there was an awful lot of people [who] didn't know whether this was true or not, whether he was—whether this was a front or what it was. But he was obviously looking to be—to become personally in control of the UE union. The original founders of the UE, and I knew 'em all, they of course stoutly resisted any contention that they were Communists or Communist sympathizers. Anyway, this thing, over a period of several years, got to a point where you had two camps in the union, one the anticommunists and one, the Communists, and Carey heading up the one that was supposed to be anticommunist. He finally got through the NLRB. They had a vote and IUE, that is, Carey's faction, won out. I can't remember now whether this was by plants or whether it was a vote for the whole company.[6] The people that the UE had represented, I guess they were given the choice as to whether they would go with Carey or whether they would stay with . . . [the UE].

Well, [Leo] Jandreau was one of the original fellows affiliated with the UE, but I don't think Jandreau ever, ever wanted to be affiliated with fellows that were subversive in any way. On the other hand, he was in on it early—so early that he was branded with a certain amount of these accusations. I think he was in a very ticklish position. He wanted to retain his leadership, and he didn't like Carey personally. But on the other hand, he saw that it wasn't going to be in his best interest, personally, to be affiliated or connected with a group that were increasingly being identified with the Communist activity. I don't recall how he got over there, but finally he got into Carey's camp.

Well, we built the Campbell Avenue plant during the war to produce aircraft radio transmitters and receivers. And this was a new venture; we never made those before. We went into that during the war and built up very high production. And the employees in that plant were mostly women. It was assembly. I don't recall anything that went on during the war, as far as sabotage—there might have been some suspected stuff. But we had quite a show of security, we had guards all over the place. But I don't think they were very well trained. In fact, when the war was over, that's when I came into the picture. My predecessor, Louis Male, and I concluded that we hadn't had very good security, even though we spent a lot of money on it. We had satisfied all the requirements of the armed forces, because they were our principal customers, and they dictated what we had to do for security. That's when we got this fellow Charlie LaForge [of the New York State Bureau of Criminal Investigation] in the picture.

Male and I both decided that we'd gotten that far without any major scandals, but we felt that even during the war we had been wide open for subversive activity. So we went looking for somebody that was professionally trained, and about that time, Kefauver was holding his hearings up there in Saratoga on racing.[7]

FIGURE 2.1 Schenectady GE workers marching on the UE hall on 30 June 1954, just after the NLRB election closed and the ballots had been counted. The IUE won. *Credit: IUE Local 301 Records, M. E. Grenander Department of Special Collections and Archives, University Libraries, University at Albany, State University of New York.*

And LaForge was quite prominent in that . . . and his name got in the paper quite a little so we got hold of LaForge. We got acquainted with him and we found that he would be amenable to an offer to come down and head up our security. So we hired him. And from then on he headed the security up until he retired from General Electric—I think it must have been about '67 or '8. And, of course when we brought LaForge on, he was no shrinking violet, and he let it be known that he was going to get into some of these things. And he made contacts that we never could have made before—with the FBI, and with the Un-American Activities Committee, and those people. And through his contacts, we got to be pretty well-versed in the activities of the security people in Washington, largely the FBI. When Charlie got there it began to mean more. We began to get closer to this thing. Because then Senator Joe McCarthy got in the act and we began to become sophisticated.

I had taken over as Works Manager in '53, and it was along about the latter part of '53 that I got a call from a guy, a lawyer, who turned out to be the senator's counsel. He called me up. I didn't know him from Adam. And he said that the Senator had in mind coming up into the Albany area to hold some hearings. There was some people that they would like to subpoena to appear at the hearing, and they worked for General Electric. And he said, "If we gave you the names, would you make it possible for them to appear?" "Well," I said, "I don't—I don't know what you mean, make it possible." I said, "If you'll tell us who they are, we'll confirm whether they are employees or not. And then if you want to talk with them, if you want to subpoena them, you can go ahead and do so. We won't stop you. But I don't think we want to become a party to hauling them over before your hearings." Well, that seemed to be satisfactory to them. So, when they came up they gave us the names, and we confirmed whether they were or weren't employees. It so-happened that most of 'em were fellows that we'd always had some suspicion ourselves [about]. But we didn't say that, because we didn't know. So they held the hearings over in Albany. And they were all, of course, coached by the UE lawyer.[8]

They called these fellows, and they all took the Fifth Amendment. They didn't deny or agree that they were members of the Communist Party; they refused to answer. So I got hold of our attorney, in New York, who handled this sort of thing for the company, and I said, "We're getting in a tight spot here, because it is going to appear, if we don't look out, as though we're trying to protect these fellows." "Now," I said, "we have no reason to accuse them or protect them, either one. But," I said, "it's being alleged that we're harboring subversive people in our plant. And the fact that they refuse to answer makes us look kind of bad." So I said, "I think we've got to develop a policy somehow." So this went to the president of the company, [Ralph] Cordiner. And I talked to Cordiner and told him the same thing. And he said, "Well I think maybe you're right." He said, "We'll have to do something on this right away." So I met with this lawyer and we developed a policy that would apply for the whole company, which simply said that any employee summoned before a properly-constituted Senate or legislative committee charged with the responsibility of holding a hearing, who refused to answer—and I don't remember whether we said based on the Fifth Amendment or otherwise, but refused to answer—we would no longer employ. We didn't believe we should employ them any longer. Now that went into effect, and the result was we fired several of these fellows.[9]

Well, the UE turned around and sued us for a million dollars. And I remember I was supposed to appear in Washington and I got down there and I came down with the flu! So I never did appear. They finally took a deposition from me. But that's the last I ever heard of it.

☼

In the early 1950s Frank MacIntosh assumed responsibility for Employee and Community relations when A. C. Stevens became Works Manager. Here he elaborates on the impact of McCarthyism on the firm's security policies (a theme introduced above by A. C. Stevens) and on his respect for Leo Jandreau, suggesting the complex relationships that existed between local union leaders and plant managers—relationships that were threatened by the involvement of government and top-level corporate hard-liners.

Leo Jandreau and I had an excellent relationship. Argue, fight, you know—but in a business way. I think he was one of the finest guys I ever had to work with. You really want to give credit for what he was trying to do—he had a very difficult job, trying to control those people that he had. Argue, fight like hell, but I've never once [heard him go] back on his word. We'd make a deal, and that was it. I respected him and he respected me. But we had a lot of battles. You would sit across the table from him for eight hours. You would know you'd done a day's work, believe me. But, in all, I held him in high regard. I didn't like his ideas, but I knew he had a job to do. Several times we'd be asked to come out and speak. He'd take one side of his telling of a story and I'd tell it the other one, be on same platform . . . diametrically opposed in our theories. But I knew him well, as I say, I enjoyed working with him, if you could call it enjoyment.

[McCarthy] . . . was trying to embarrass Schenectady, embarrass everybody involved, Jandreau and the whole crowd of 'em. And here we were trying to keep . . . out of troubled waters, and McCarthy came up here and just raised hell. Of course, as a result of it, why the company had to put in some new standards, about hiring of Communists and all that stuff. I've forgotten all the specific details, but I know we were concerned over what was going to happen, whether we were going to continue to get the business and everything else, you know, with the commies in there. But we got rid of a few of 'em.

Yeah, we got rid of some of 'em, the ones that were really the bad ones. It could have [cost] a lot of business to the company, you know. So then, we didn't know what—we [were going to do]. Well, the whole thing got exposed at all the McCarthy hearings. The damn drunken bum! Jeez, he was a dandy. We took good care of him! We got him drunk anyway. This was at the hotel after some of the hearings [in Albany]. We had one of the guys over that were our security men, made sure that he had enough to drink.

[Charles LaForge] was in charge of security, which was part of my job. Oh, he hated 'em. He hated 'em. Yeah, if we'd had followed Charlie's idea we'd have really gone a lot stronger than we did. He had a file on every—it was a government file—on all these guys. Charlie had a lot of information on [Jandreau]. Charlie gave us a lot of dope. And Charlie did a lot of good for us. He made us aware of a lot of things that were going on, that we didn't know about, you know. Well, he had built this file up. I presume he started with—as part of the state police, somewhere. But Charlie LaForge knew everybody in charge of any police all over the country. He'd call up somebody in Kansas City and say, "Hi, Bill. I need some information on so-and-so." Charlie used to drive me crazy. He used spend most of his time driving between here and New York City. And I finally told him, I said, "For God's sake, lay off, will you?" He was a very unusual guy. Of course, he had spent twenty-five years or more with the state police. We brought Charlie over when he retired from the New York State Police, and we brought him into the plant in charge of security. But he was a tough guy to handle, for me. Because he was—just a wild man, that's all. He'd go anywhere. He didn't stop for nothing. Going where angels fear to tread never bothered Charlie. But he was quite a guy. He did a lot of good for us. He ran a hell of a show. He certainly brought security to . . . raised the whole level of what we had, of our whole program.

[Lemuel R.] Boulware came up here one day.[10] He went up and down Steve's [A. C. Stevens] back and mine, insisting that we come out in the papers with what we knew about Jandreau. And we just as strongly insisted that we wouldn't. And we didn't. Now, we were hated by Boulware from then on, I guess. But anyway, we didn't do it. Now it wasn't too many months after that [actually in 1960], when Carey was trying to pull off a company-wide strike. And he got all the plants except Schenectady. He never got Schenectady. And we think our relationship with Jandreau had a lot to do with it. Jandreau was the one to stop that. Now how do you evaluate that? You know, we never got any credit for it, I don't think, but I think it was through our efforts. Had we gone ahead and showed Jandreau up, I'm sure just as well as anything he'd have said, "To hell with it." And the company would've had a company-wide strike. The strike was broken. I mean they couldn't, they couldn't get it without Schenectady, not for any length of time. And you know what that's worth to a company. There's no way you can put dollars on that one.

☼

Frank Fiorello—first generation Italian-American, second-generation GE worker, and a devout Catholic—was a major figure in the local opposition to the left-wing UE and its leaders. Fiorello left the shop floor in the midst of the battles of the late 1940s and early 1950s and went on to have a distinguished career in the national office of the IUE, as Secretary of the GE Conference Board and as Director of Organization in upstate New York. Here he provides details of his growing involvement in union politics and of the organization of the opposition forces to the UE and to Leo Jandreau.

I didn't really start participating [in the union] until after the [1946] strike. . . . I got a call one day from my cousin [Frankie Sibitello]. He was a shop steward. They were having a meeting; he called me up, and he says, "Frank, there's a bunch of guys here, they want to get rid of the Communist control of the union." So I says, "It's about time."

There was no difference between the *UE News* and the *Daily Worker* [on] everything . . . foreign policy and everything. As a matter of fact, during the '46 strike, there was a pledge amongst all the CIO unions, the Auto Workers, the Steel Workers, and so on, that no union would . . . settle before there was a joint settlement of all the companies together. The UE broke that pledge. That's how it started. That fight went on until 1949, when they finally were expelled from the CIO.

Well, I never missed a membership meeting and raised my voice every time—and many times I was there all by myself. You know, people didn't want to go to meetings in those days, except the real die-hards. The only time they showed up at meetings was when there was a big issue at hand. And so many times, Marty [Stanton], Carmen [DiGirolamo] and myself were the only three of our group at the meetings, and just a handful of others. But this went on for, you know, '46, '47, '48, well that's a few years to carry on that torch all by ourselves, just to let 'em know we were there and they weren't going to intimidate us, or push us out, by any means, and quiet us. It was just loose-knit. Frank Kriss was part of another group that was opposing the incumbent officers of the local. We finally merged, and that's how we formed one . . . group. We amalgamated our two forces together and split up the offices, and that's how Frank Kriss and myself got elected. As a matter of fact, I and Marty and Carmen were expelled from the union in 1947. They made a big mistake, doing that.[11]

At that time, we had a maintenance-of-membership clause in the contract, which meant that the company had to fire us. It was a way of firing us from the plant, to get rid of us! That's why we had to go to court and defend our rights. There was supposed to be a membership meeting scheduled in the latter part of November, where there was to be nomination of officers. And that was the urgency of going to court, so that we'd get our membership reinstated so we could participate in that meeting to elect and nominate the people that we wanted to run for office. . . .

By virtue of the injunction that the court gave us to reinstate our membership, we went to the meetings—not without much ado. They kind of harassed us. We didn't take it serious. I mean, there was no violence or anything like that. They'd follow us around, and half of the meetings that we had—well they had their spies there, and I knew who they were. Sidney Friedlander was one of them.[12] He would sit outside the door. One time we had a meeting over at the Mohawk Hotel here on Broadway, and he and several other guys were sitting in the lobby. [He pretended] like he was fast asleep, like he didn't want to see us, so I had to go over there and wake him up. I said, "Hey, Sid! Come on, wake up, you're slowing down on your job." That's how much they intimidated us. . . .

[Sid Friedlander and I] argued trade union issues. It was nothing personal. I didn't like him representing me, being that he was a member of the Communist Party. There was no way that I could trust him. [The left-wingers] were in the company's back pocket. And we put it that way. And there wasn't much redress for grievances and things like that from their representatives. . . . I had one specific example that I can recall. I was working in Building 37 at the time. And one of my guys that I work with was complaining about his rate. He wasn't getting paid enough for the job that he was doing. So I said, "Look, put in a grievance, call the shop steward; put in a grievance," and he did. So they tried to talk him out of it. . . . And I told him, I says, "Look, you deserve more than that, so you stick to your guns." So they told him after the thing, "No way." They says, "This is it." You know, and, it was the union that backed off on that case.

And there were other cases that I heard of too, especially down there in Building 69. It was a piecework place—milling machines—and Marty Stanton was their shop steward down there. He had to protect himself against the Local, because they were consistently trying to come in and find out why his rates were higher than any other milling machine operator in the whole plant. And what they did was they policed their work—the shop stewards did themselves—because they didn't want the guys to turn in too much, so that the company would come down and cut their prices. They did that very effectively. But in the other areas, the guys went hog wild and the first thing you know the company came and slashed their prices, and the union never did anything about it. They did try to get on Marty and his crew down there and different things like that.

I met Marty in 1946 or '7. But even before that, there was that kind of strange relationship going on between his group and Leo. He ran against Jandreau at one time, Marty did. [The other group that opposed the left wing] were from the shops, too. I knew a lot of the boys who were in that group, and we knew that we couldn't stand a chance if we had three groups running—two groups opposing the incumbent. We knew we didn't have a chance. I didn't hear too much talk about being anticommunists, so much from them, from that group as from *our* group. We had several meetings together, you know. We had to wrangle it out, and we finally did. Some of the people we had on our slate we had to take off, and intermingle who they had. We had socialists . . . Dave Fisher was chairman of the Liberal Party. He was the first president of the union when it was organized, back in 1936 or '37, and he was in our group. Charlie Campbell [was] another one. I don't know if he was a socialist or not, but he was certainly not a Catholic. It was a mixed group. We sorted out our slate of officers and [in 1948 we won], except for Leo Jandreau. [I was elected] Recording Secretary. . . .[13]

[Father Edward LaRoe ran the labor school]. Most of the things it covered, like, you know, what was going on in the unions, the Communist Party, and the history of the Communist Party, and what they were doing and what they were up to. That's about it; [he took] no other active role other than conducting the school, and once in a while he'd have a speaker talk. They were democratic unionists. They were told how to do that, but most of it was about the Communist Party. There was nothing formal. It was just open discussion. It was just a group of guys getting together, no materials, just listening to everybody talk. [Father Charles Owen Rice] came up here a couple of times. One time he came up here when we were electing delegates to the UE convention—in 1948, I think it was, or '49. He was a very effective speaker—fiery.

[In 1954 Leo Jandreau] had a choice to make. You know, the Machinists were in here after the local too; this was 1953, I think it was. I got ahold of my assistant pastor, Father Lamanna, and I asked him to go down and see Jandreau, to see if he could negotiate with him to join the IUE. And he did. I think he was the one that was instrumental in getting [him to switch]. . . . I made a mistake in going there and asking him to do what I did. But that was the only role—he didn't get involved in any other kind of politics. Jandreau knew the handwriting on the wall. Come on now, he was not that dumb. So he joined the IUE. And it was not for any love of Jim Carey, I'll tell you that right now.

[The Company] always claimed that they were neutral. They did get involved at one time when they put out that full-page ad by Boulware, you know, "a plague on both your houses." Yeah, they got involved. A guy came up one day, to one of those meetings we had, a caucus . . . and he claimed he worked for the Hearst newspapers, and he was a freelance writer now, and he saw the ad, and he wanted to write an answer to it. And we said, "Go ahead." And, he didn't know what the hell to write. And he really put down together a pretty good piece of paper. . . . It goes on to describe what I thought Jim Carey himself would say about what Boulware was trying to do, putting the Communists and the anticommunists all under the same bushel basket. We were all collectivists and no matter what they were, they were all the same, and all that bullshit . . .

That was the greatest experience of my life. I tell you. I never heard about unions, really, until I got involved, and especially in the GE negotiations. The fight we had with the commies was nothing, compared with the fight we had with the company. Jeez, it was fierce.

☼

> Helen Quirini was a major force in the Schenectady UE from 1946 until the 1954 switch to the IUE. During these years she served as a shop steward, recording secretary of Local 301, and as a board member of the union. She became particularly active in fighting for working-women's rights in the local and within the national union. Here she recalls her entry into General Electric, her growing activism in local union politics, and the changing atmosphere in the shops and community that accompanied the battles between left- and right-wing trade unionists. Today she remains an activist, fighting for pension rights for retired GE employees and other workers.

I started at GE on April Fools Day—April 1, 1941. . . . The war ended in '46 or '45. And then when I thought about going to school, I had five years service. Everybody else was losing their jobs. My father had died, and I said, who's going to support me. There's no scholarships or anything like that. Not even to live, not to say anything about having your way paid. So, you give up your dream. And then I thought, well, what the heck. I wanted to be a social worker, and being in a factory like this, in a sense you are a social worker and you are a part of a great movement. I didn't realize how great it was until after, and so I guess I always thought that maybe someday I would get a better job within the company. I didn't know what a better job might be. I loved my job because I could use my brain. On these piece works, some of them—not all of them, but some of them—took a lot of brains because you had to work on blueprints, against time. You either did it, or you didn't make out.

I was a member of the YWCA. And we went to a meeting, and we had a woman—she and I have since become very good friends—who was a wife of the chief engineer of the General Electric Company. She was head of public affairs. And she was talking, and what she said was, "If you believe in what you're doing, get involved." She said that there are rumors that there are Communists down in the plant. And if you don't like it, get involved. That's the reason I got involved in the union, believe it or not. I definitely became a steward after the '46 strike. I was recording secretary right after the '46 strike. I was dying to become—the union had set up a woman board member at large, and I thought, gee, I'd like to be that. They offered me the secretary job. And I said, "I'm not qualified to be recording secretary." But I had done so much during the strike, they were impressed apparently, and they said, "No, no, we want you to be recording secretary." So, I had the privilege of taking every note, every minutes of every grievance that happened in the company for several years. . . .

The women were very active during the '46 strike, and the union had filed a case with the War Labor Board about women's rights and because of the war's end it never got really enforced. So it was part of the negotiations. Every time they talked about raises and anything else, end of discrimination was there—women's rights—and we slowly made progress every year in some contract negotiation. Of course, during the '46 strike the men stayed out longer, a couple of weeks longer, because the company said they weren't going to give the raises to "bobby soxers," meaning we women. So many people stayed out to make sure that women got the raises, and most of the people were men. It's hard to say, but I think at any time there were never more than one-third of the people in the GE factory who were women. The UE has always had beautiful programs about women's rights, women's wages. They recognized what a powerful force women were and how important it was to keep them involved.

The reason I became a shop steward was because I didn't like the conditions I saw around me—even though my father told me it was no good and they were a bunch of Communists and all that stuff. I think I even did the stupid thing of going on second shift to become a shop steward because I was so upset about what was happening. I hated second shift. When they first asked me to be shop steward, I went up the union hall and I said to Sal [Vottis], "I want to see your books." He said, "What are you saying?" I said, "I want to see your books." I said, "They asked me to be a shop steward. I want to know what I'm getting involved in." I said, "I hear you're making a hell of a lot of money and you're not spending it right." He said, "Come on in."

Jandreau was the business agent and he was up in the office. He was not an officer. He was a staff person. So, I opened up all of the books and I see—I've forgotten—let's see, we got three dollars a month, and fifty cents went to national, and fifty cents went to the district. I don't think there's ever been any absconding of money in our union, regardless of all the internal fights they've had. Part of it was that the membership was always active and alert. (I'm not saying that we always caught everything). So, when I saw that I said, "It's not that bad." But I was still scared about becoming a shop steward. I never was sure of my job in GE. That's why I always had an income property; never was sure of my job. Instinctively I knew that someday I was going to take a principal position, and somebody was going to be on my tail. And it happened. Because when I was an officer, I would go to meetings—and I was the only woman officer for years—and I would go into a meeting with the officers. What the officers do, of course, it's like [any] other executive board, you debate what's coming up, and policy decisions and everything, and they would bring up some stuff that I couldn't agree with, and I would argue with them. And then they weren't going to do it. Then I would say, "OK, then I'm going to make up a minority report." "Well, wait, wait, wait. What do you mean you are going to make up a minority report?" Like they were going to get rid of one of the second-shift board members; I didn't like him, but he was doing a good job. "I'm going to fight this at the membership [meeting]." "You really are?" "Yes, I am." "Let's talk about it." I never had to give a minority report.

When I first started getting involved, you know, I started looking around to see who all the Communists were. I looked in the paper, and there was my name. I said, "What the hell!? If they are accusing me, who else are they accusing wrongly?" Because during some of the campaigns, some of my best friends said, "Helen, why don't you get up in front of everybody and announce that you're not a Communist." "Because our constitution says that we let everybody in." And I said, "Who's going to believe me? Who's going to believe me?" And I said, "I won't, I'll look like the great white heroine on the white horse because I'm supposed to be pure because everybody else is not pure." I said, "I'll resign first. . . ."

Any religion I had from the Catholic religion got kicked out of me from when they got involved in the split. One of the things that they did—you know, I was Polish, OK, I never went to church very religiously—I had friends who were at other churches, and I used to go visit with them and everything. And they passed, before a Sunday session, a list of the Communists, and they had *my* name on it . . . a leaflet, for people going to church, as you walked in.

What we did was went down to the shop, we got good Catholics, [and we asked them to] please sign this statement. And we put it out: "To the Catholic Church. Please keep your hands"—something to that effect—"off of our election." And everybody signed it. When I went to some of my women, oh did I get hell! "We don't like what you're doing. You are condemning the Catholic Church." And I said, "I'll tell you something. If this Sunday your church does not preach against us, I will apologize to you personally. But if they do, you come in and apologize to me." And the churches did it in our area. People got up in church, they tell me, they got up in church and walked out. . . . Back in those days, in the '50s, that was a mortal sin, to talk against your priest. They got up and walked out. Guys got up and said, "You got no right to say that!" What happened is, these guys went and talked to the bishop's henchmen, or whatever you call them, and he said, "Well, we don't know what's going to happen, but we'll see what we can do." And the priests told our guys, "We're forced to do this. Forced to do this." One woman told me, she said, "Helen, I felt worse in my church when my priest did this, than when my daughter was laid out in front of the altar."

One of the churches used their basement to put out propaganda against us. They were the backers of the IUE in Schenectady. They were the great Communist fighters. Billy Mastriani was a good Catholic; they did a job on him. A guy named Whitbeck, good Catholic, they did a job; they smeared everybody. . . .

You always had that cloud of fear within the company, because everything you did you knew was under scrutiny. You never knew when it was going to be used against you. And all they had to do was [use] insinuation. I remember, one day, I almost killed a guy. Frank Kriss came over to me before a meeting and he said, "Do you know that they had a Communist meeting at the. . . ." Frank was an anticommunist; he got elected by that. "Did you know they had a Communist meeting at the Red-something hall?" They used to have a hall there in Schenectady. I said, "No." I didn't. "That's interesting." We went to the meeting and this bastard says to the people, "There was a Communist meeting at this hall and Helen knows about it." I got up and I said, "You are a bastard." I said, "The only reason I know about it is because you told me." But, I mean, this is the kind of stuff that happened. I mean, you know, this is the kind of stuff you put up with—innuendo. "Helen knew all about it." I just found out about it!

[When the split finally came in 1954] I went up there and he [Jandreau] had . . . about five men in the office with him. And he said, "I want to tell you," he said, "that we're going to go IUE." I said, "What!?" And then I started to cry. I said, "How could you do this? How could you do this, when we fought so hard? We've been red-baited and everything else by this outfit." And what happened when we went IUE!? Jandreau was no longer a Communist. Billy [Mastriani] was no longer a Communist. The same leadership of the UE in Schenectady that was so dangerous, that was a "pipe line to Moscow," the same leadership is there and nobody talks about it.[14] All of a sudden, you know, they give him the blessing, including the Catholic Church. You're a one hundred percent pure American. So, if that doesn't tell you how phony the whole issue was, what does. What does? Don't forget, Jandreau was red-baited as a leader of the whole UE, not just Schenectady, not just Schenectady. [Now] he was one of the guys.

I was the only one that did not go, I was the only one in leadership who didn't go IUE. And don't you think that that didn't have some kind of effect on some of the people I worked with all my lives. If I had gone then, everything, you know, it's a one hundred percent; everything's fine. But in a sense, I was needling their conscience about all the things that we had fought for over the period of years. Jandreau controlled everything down in the shop. He controlled the shop stewards. And if you ever tried to do much action down in the shop, you know, you always had to worry. I didn't do much because as I say, I was numb. I was just completely—I just didn't do anything. These were people that I had worked with from '46 to '54, fighting every struggle with—you know, the leadership who went IUE. And then I—you know—what the heck, you are fighting against something that's bigger than a lot of people.

Whenever the vote was, then I was no longer anything [in the shops]. I [became] active in the community. I always was active in the community. I just spent a little more time. A little more time, that's all. Oh, people would talk to me about [joining the IUE]. . . . Nobody ever offered me a card or anything. And the people told me that they were out there arguing with Jandreau. No, he wasn't going to let me in, and I wasn't about to go up to him and tell him I made a mistake. Because after this, our union did not have the strength it used to have. The kind of stuff that happened to some of the people in the plant, in my estimation, never would have happened if the UE was there.

☼

> James C. Carey was a Schenectady leader in the "right-wing" faction of the UE and later an IUE member. Though he shares his political beliefs—and his name, less the middle initial—with the national IUE leader, James B. Carey, he is not related to him. In the late 1940s and early 1950s, Jim was very active in the conflict against the left-wing leadership of Local 301 and the movement to join the IUE. He came to this battle as a liberal—an "FDR Democrat," as he calls himself. Today, he is a close friend of Helen Quirini, his former UE adversary.

This city was a very conservative Republican city, and that included a lot of people in the shop. Even though it was strongly conservative Republican, you had left-wing people running the union. . . . No more than 4 percent of people in the shop had the slightest ideological idea of what was going on in the union. No more than 4 percent of any people at any time in the shop ever had any knowledge of the UE and their political position on Henry Wallace, but also on the Marshall Plan, or the Truman Doctrine, invasion of Greece, or any of the things that the UE was expounding on—international affairs or even national affairs. They had little or no knowledge of it, and certainly didn't even care.

They belonged to the UE for two reasons. Number one, because it had raised their conditions of employment very radically from the old days, even from the old days of the Works Council, which was fairly effective by company union standards. But it raised their standard of living, it created piecework, and some of them were living pretty well. That was the greatest allegiance that they had. The other allegiance they had to the UE was that the locomotive company here [was organized by the] CIO steelworkers union. [It] was either striking or out on the street with no work about every year, so these people would look at that and look completely flabbergasted, and it got to mean to them later that the CIO union was a thing that struck, like the steelworkers, the auto workers, or even the coal miners. And here they could sit with the UE union, let people call their union leaders Communists, but at least they were living a good standard of living and they weren't out on the street striking, or out on the street for lack of work. So that was the basis of peoples' thoughts. It was all bound together in a beautiful package by a man who was perhaps the greatest labor leader of them all, and that's Leo Jandreau—a man with a terrific mind and great moral character, in my opinion, but who was also capable of speaking, and leading people. And so they felt that not only the UE but particularly Leo Jandreau might have been the one who provided them with a high standard of living and a good working union, without ever having to strike.

Thus in the years 1950 and '51, when the IUE tried to raid here, there was never, never, never a chance they would go to the IUE-CIO union because they were told by Jandreau and the other UE leaders that they would have no opportunity to vote on a strike if . . . Jim Carey, who was leading the anti-UE movement and who was a secretary-treasurer of the CIO, had anything to do with it. He would write a constitution for his union in which the executive board would vote on strikes, when to take people out on strikes, and they would have no opportunity to vote on whether to strike or not. So being that that constitution [of the newly formed IUE-CIO] was passed around the shop before every election, it scared most people away from the CIO. That was the most priceless page that the UE people ever ran into, because all they did was to mimeograph that page and bring it in the shop, and it provided thousands and thousands of votes, right off the bat, because the people felt, my God, I'll be striking like those other CIO unions.

In those days I didn't belong to any political organization. I was a young man—had other interests outside of unions. I had been looking at the girls some, and the nightclubs or what have you, the football games. So I wasn't up to my ears in crusades at this point, but eventually I was forced into being up to my ears in crusades because I would stay over late, perhaps because I loved the meetings at the UE, and eventually I saw some things that rather intrigued me. In these meetings there always seemed to be a certain number of people who were not only verbose, but who were quite accomplished in controlling the meeting, usually through parliamentary procedure, points of order and that type of thing—very knowledgeable in parliamentary procedures which, of course, the rest of the people weren't. And these people who were knowledgeable happened to be dispersed throughout the room. Later we found out that it's called a "diamond," where you put one person in the back and one in the front, and one on each side, and if they have some friends with them and they're pretty noisy and have some other support in the room, you could control a meeting almost completely with parliamentary procedures. Well, of course, I saw some of that and I was intrigued. Later at night after the rest of the people had left, and the average person had gone out for a beer or something, we used to get off on social issues; usually the ones that stick out in my mind most were issues on race relations. There was always some black man being hung in the South for raping a white woman, or something of that nature, and there was quite a concentration on that issue.

In the early part of the meeting it would be on wages and working conditions, or grievances, or somebody's complaining about a particular grievance or something of that nature. It did not get off on politics or foreign affairs or social issues. It was all strictly union stuff, and if there was a group of people who thought they had a real problem in their shops they would descend upon the hall *en masse*. Maybe they'd bring fifty people, maybe as many as one hundred, and it was their intention to take over the meeting and get their resolution through to make the raise, let's say the wages of all the welders. And, of course, the union leaders had to be pretty nimble. Leo Jandreau—a terrific speaker and a terrific man with psychology as far as the workers are concerned, [was] very loved in his community and the essence of everything that happened between the UE and the IUE. But he would certainly have a lot of assistance in holding down these momentary uproars of a certain number of people, because he had a certain machine, so to speak—appeared to have certain friends who were distributed through the rooms who would yell the right things at the right time, and he would always come up with a soothing answer, perhaps a compromise if possible, and hold down the uproar.

These people's support might be on one side one day and one side on another. It wasn't an obvious thing, but it was something that I did notice. There were certain people who were always bright-eyed, bushy-tailed, good speakers, to-the-point, real versed in parliamentary procedure, real versed on the issues that were up, real high IQs for the most part, and could jump up and turn an issue, start an issue, call for a point of order, call for adjournment, used all of the tricks of the trade.... I could see that there were certain faces of people I didn't necessarily know, who were always supporting the administration here, there, and the other place against these masses of men who decided to take it over. And of course, if I was alert at all I probably would be somewhat sympathetic to that, because the union leaders had to have someone to keep [order], and remember, this union even in 1950 had 20,000 members. Now during the war it was 30,000, 35,000—a huge number.[15] Now I'm not talking about during the war, at this point. After the war, we're probably down, pretty close to 20,000 members. But if you only had 150 to 300 people attending a union meeting and you could bring 50 to 100 or 150 people up, you could change the entire agenda of anything, change everything but the constitution, as a little delay point, but you could change everything else in the union in one hour if you could bring up—and of course, the other 20,000 people aren't in the union hall, so I probably realized that a union administration has to have some protection from a group of people descending on them with fire in their eyes, and I'm talking about real noisy, robust individuals. There's a little muscle work and a little fighting ... there might be scuffles, that type of thing, you know, might get that way. So I realized I got to have some protection, but at that point I didn't realize just how deeply ingrained this, what I'll say is a machine. I didn't realize it was so deeply ingrained, but I knew it was rather interesting that the same people were doing all the controlling....

☼

Irving Horowitz was active in the Schenectady City unit of the Communist Party from 1946 and well into the 1950s. He served on the central committee of the local organization for a time and recalls the events and the repressive atmosphere that pervaded the Schenectady community and the local GE shops during this period. His account offers compelling testimony on the crisis faced by many community-based party organizations during the height of the domestic Cold War.[16]

The intensity of the McCarthy period here in a town like Schenectady [was incredible]. Schenectady was the center home of the GE, and as such it was a concentration point of both the UE's by-far-biggest local, and of the CP—*and* of the FBI.

I grew up in Troy until I was thirteen, came to Schenectady, and I lived in Schenectady until I was in my thirties and I had to leave because I couldn't possibly get a job doing anything. And when I say anything I mean *anything*. I was fired from parking lots, from a dog shelter. I was hired at International Harvester, a little place on Union Street. I was hired there at about 12:15, and by the time I drove home where I lived, off of State Street, I got a call from the person that hired me that I was fired. And I was a nobody; I was a young fellow, just recently out of college. I was not a leader of the party. I was on the central committee [of the City of Schenectady], but I wasn't known publicly as any particular important person.

I started my activity in Schenectady when I came out of the service, which was in '46. From '46 to '48 I was very active in Union College; we had a branch there. Then I was ill for two years, but I was still involved. In 1950, in '51 and '52, that's when the height of the McCarthyism hit Schenectady. The reason I mention about myself is because I was just one of many little people that was harassed by the FBI as if we were somebody really of tremendous importance. I'll give you one other little thing to try to set the tone. I, and a number of other people, were doing all kinds of crazy little jobs to make a living, and collecting unemployment very often. We had a demonstration in Washington, I believe it was on universal military training—against it. And a group of us went from Schenectady and Albany and we went and we visited Representative [Bernard William] Kearney. I think there were something like twenty or twenty-five of us. And we were with thousands of people, and we each went to our different representatives, and so forth. We went to his office, and we presented our petition and I started to talk—I wasn't the leader of the delegation; we actually didn't have any. But we met with a representative of Kearney; he wouldn't meet with us. And I did a lot of the talking, and he said, "Well the congressman will be very interested in your views, I'd like to take down your names." And we gave him our names. The demonstration was on a Saturday. This was before the [New York State] Thruway, before the New Jersey Turnpike—it took us a long time to get there [and] to get back home. We got home very, very late on Sunday, and tired. The next morning, the *Gazette*—the [*Schenectady*] *Gazette* is the morning paper—had a headline like this [gestures size]: "Communist Group Petitions Kearney." We had been collecting signatures in downtown Schenectady, and most people were signing it. That night we met, and we agreed we had to go out again and we went down . . . nobody would talk to us.

The next day I went to the unemployment office. And I went up to the window and the guy said to me, "Were you ready, willing, and able to work?" That's the question they asked us. And he pushed the paper to me and he said, "Read it carefully before you sign it." Well, a bell went off, but . . . what the hell, I had gone this far. I signed it. As soon as I signed it, he said, "Come with me." He took me to an examiner and the guy said to me, "You know, you just committed perjury." And I said, "What do you mean?" He said, "You were in Washington on Saturday, and you said you were ready and willing and able to work, and you couldn't have been if you were down there." So I said I was looking for a job down there. And he said, "Well no you weren't, you were there on a political . . ." And he said, "I'm going to offer you one of two choices." He said, "Either you take the punishment of not being able to collect unemployment for two years, or it'll go to court and you'll be tried for violating the Unemployment Act," which had a five year sentence, if I remember correctly, and a $10,000 fine. So, I said I wanted to think it over, and I went home and talked to people, and then I went to see Mike Perlin, who was the . . . [attorney for the UE].[17] And I went and he said to me, "Irv, if you go to court on this, you're going to go to jail. Take the punishment," which is what I did.

They hounded us. They followed us. They knew every meeting we had. We thought we were so smart. We went in cars, and we went around corners, and we went here; they knew everything that we were doing. They had stool pigeons all over the place. . . .

Senator McCarthy came to the Capital District about Schenectady; Albany was relatively unimportant. He came to Schenectady three times. He had two open public hearings on television. The Walters Committee had three public hearings, as I remember it. All of us were named, all of us. A Mr. Getz . . . was dead. He had been a supporter of left-wing activities. I don't think he was ever actually in the party. Mr. Getz was named as a member of the party, and he was dead when this guy said, I can't remember his name—the guy that gave all the names, it was like hundreds of names. He was dead.[18]

So the atmosphere in Schenectady was [completely different than] in New York City, where you could get lost amongst the millions of people there. Here in Schenectady, we'd go and march around the Capital in Albany like a bunch of, I don't know what . . . and there were ten of us, or twelve of us. So the pressure on the people was immense.

The members of the party that were working in the GE, I knew them all. I wasn't involved with them directly, except socially, because we kept what we called the community group separate from the shop group. But I met with their wives, because the wives of the guys in the shop—there were very few women in there. If you worked in the shop, you might have made $80–$100–$120 a week. If you worked in the community, you made $40 or $45 a week. The people that worked in the shop were the stars of the party, and they also had more money than we did.

In the community group there was Marshall Garcia, and there was me and Guy, and this other young black guy . . . Jerry; everybody else were women.[19] There were a lot of women. Just in Schenectady, I would say twenty women. So, when the community group met, it was all women, with a few exceptions . . . so when I would go to a meeting, I was always surrounded by women. . . . One of the jobs that I had—talk about male chauvinism—we used to give out leaflets, and we gave it out at the subway gate. So, the first time we went, I had a car and I picked up a few other women . . . and we went down to the gate, about five or six of us, myself included, and we started giving out the leaflets. At this time there was an awful lot of tension. A couple of guys made motions as if to hit me. And after we gave out the leaflets, the decision was, after that, that they wouldn't hit a woman. So I drove them, and I used to sit in the car and they would give out the leaflets. I used to feel very guilty. We decided as a group that it was too dangerous for me, but it wasn't too dangerous for them. We would go down there once a week—I think it was on a Monday . . . and we would give out the Schenectady Peace Council [literature]; we gave out stuff against universal military training, but we also gave out the *GE Worker*.

The party, when they came down with a line—and that line was given to us—nine hundred and ninety-nine times out of a hundred, we followed it in the community group. I was a bit of a rebel, but basically we all went along. The shop group was very different. Sid Friedlander . . . was the most important person in the shop by far. Sid was a chief shop steward, known as a Communist. In fact, Sid gave out his own paper . . . he called it the *GE Worker*. What he put in that paper, Sid believed it. They could have brought [Eugene] Dennis down from New York, and if Sid didn't agree with it, it didn't go in. And no matter who came from headquarters, they had to listen to Sid, and Sid was a very bright but a very, very stubborn guy. The one issue that the party forced on the shop members—where the shop members raised it through the UE at an open meeting of the UE—that got them in trouble, was the Korean War.

When Wallace ran for president, we canvassed mainly over in Mt. Pleasant because that's where an awful lot of the GE workers lived. We got a nice response for Wallace, but we got a nice response for Wallace because the UE was supporting Wallace. When it came to Communists actually running as Communists in Schenectady, we got—we all knew who voted and who forgot to vote.

When Jandreau—after all these hearings and all the Communist, traitor business, and so on—when Jandreau switched, he set up a meeting in the Erie Theater. He set up a meeting there and he called in the shop stewards one at a time and he told them, they were switching, and in effect he told them, you come with us you're OK, you don't come with us, swoosh (gestures) . . . and most of them went with him—not the party guys, but most of the other shop stewards. When the top UE sent some people in here to Schenectady to organize for the fight with the NLRB, the local leadership here was all gone; it was all IUE, except the party people. And the party people used to come home and say, the guys in the shop say, "We know you did the best for us, we know you worked in our interest, but we can't help it." But they did a job. UE brought in a good, strong force, and the guys in the shop worked like hell and we all, the rest of us, aided. And a campaign took place—I don't remember how long it was—but it was [great]. When we started out we thought if we got 10 percent of the vote it would have been a lot. We got 44 percent of the vote, as I remember it![20]

It was the most amazing election in my seventy-three years that I know of, and the whole reason that the UE did so well was because the guys in the shop had done such a marvelous job from 1936 until 195[4].

☼

David Meyers, an African American with deep roots in Schenectady, offers an ambivalent evaluation of the Communist Party's contributions to Schenectady's small black community.

I got the GE job. I was washing cars down at the Van Curler [Hotel]. When the war started, that's when they started hiring Negroes, 1940. But the best I could do was get a job sweeping. It came out, we learned, the GE—Roosevelt was the cause of the GE—started hiring Negroes. They were forced to hire Negroes, but they wouldn't give you nothing but a job as cleaning or something—nothing, no machine work or nothing.

I don't remember the questions, but you had to fill out an application. They give you a thorough examination, but no tests, because you weren't going to get nothing. In those days all you were going to get were the laborers' jobs—cleaning, scrubbing, or something . . . or waiter. I got in the GE. It didn't take long before I went to work.

I asked them for a job . . . well, 'round about the war you had a chance of getting probably a better job. They started giving them crane-follower jobs, but you couldn't even become a crane follower. [There] was no opportunity at all if you were [black and] skilled. They had people there who couldn't read or write working on machines, Italian, especially Italians working on machines, cutting steel, getting good salaries, [and they] couldn't read or write. And I could read or write, and all I got was a broom. And that was forced through [by] the army—that I had to go there, or I would have never been there at all.

The union got really started during the war years. The union was not much of anything then. Union, you could forget it. It wasn't going to do nothing for no black in those days! No, union wouldn't do nothing for a black in those days! UE was all white. The Communists did fight, they tried to put up a fight, I remember the Communist Party, they had their office down at the corner of Liberty and Walsh Street, because I know a couple of boys got tied in with them, but it was a good party. Communists were a strictly money party. They didn't have no money—I mean capitalizing, they're fighting for you, and they would have fundraisers.

Communists did try to recruit a lot of blacks; they did that. I don't think they got too many. I know a couple of my friends got in there, then I know a girl I used to hang around, she started to get in there, and we got after them and told her the government was strictly—they were after them, because that's when they were strong. The FBI man, he came by here. They came by and checked to see if we was Communists and [my wife], she was pretty active. They checked her out, phones were tapped and all. But he was nice. He talked about everything; talked to us and told us he was an FBI man.

[A] couple of friends of mine, they leaned toward the Communists. One of them was going with a girl, but this is how they were roping the Negro into the Commie Party, send the white girls in to the Negro boys. Make the white girls become acquainted with them, go out and around with them. I don't remember not one of the white girls. I remember the two boys that were going around, Jasper

Williams and his brother Jimmy were staunch commie; their older brother Jimmy Williams was really staunch Communist, and we used to get after him. Johnson, he was going with a white girl but he was kind of shy about it, but Jimmy wasn't.

Johnson told us [the girls were Communists]. To tell you the truth, I did see the girls around union hall, hall down around Erie Boulevard where the commies had a meeting place. We would see these girls. Johnson had a store on Erie Boulevard, a shoeshine parlor, and they used to come in. I used to get after Johnson. I heard so much about commies, that the Communist Party—this probably goes back, this is related to my wife's family. The Scottsboro [boys], that was part of my wife's family. See the Communists used that thing; they made a lot of money on that Scottsboro case. They got very strong on that Scottsboro case. They followed it up. I know it was a commie outfit, that's what made me suspicious, I knew it was a Communist outfit. The commies claim they are helping the blacks. They were capitalizing on the blacks; they make money, they were supposedly helping the blacks. At the beginning one of the fellows you interviewed, one of his sisters got ties in there and I told [his wife], because I hung around that family all the time, I told her to get after her daughter. She got her daughter away and out of there. Her daughter went to Washington; she's lived there ever since. She had an interest in the Communists; they were really good calm people. They go out of their way to help the Negro.

It wasn't my line. I told you, I grew up in the white world; I had nothing to worry about. That was not my line. Wherever these boys all went I went. I wasn't [concerned about Communists, but] because the government was after them, that's why. The government was strongly after them. The government was after Jimmy and all of them. They were after them strong; they were after them. I made it my business not to know any of them! Because I think this Jandreau was a leader, I think he was partly a head of the Communist Party, Leo Jandreau. I think he was part, that's the only one I can name. Jandreau, and no one else, could have done anything for you at that time. Get them a better job—union wasn't interested in getting [blacks] a better job.

They [the Communists] couldn't do, I don't think they could do too much for blacks, they were fighting for them but they couldn't do too much for them because the government was strong after the commies. They would test—I think some of them would test places where they didn't hire Negroes. Well they broke up the commie party. The government got on them pretty strict. They were following them all over, check you right out all the way.

☼

Ruth Young was an officer in the UE and a significant force in the Communist Party from 1936 through the late 1940s. She was the first woman on the national UE Executive Board. In 1950, she married Local 301's business agent, Leo Jandreau, and left her position in the UE. This came a year or two after her withdrawal from the party. Here, her daughter by her first marriage (to Charles Velson, a CP activist), Karen

J. Clark, recalls the events preceding and following her mother's arrival in Schenectady as Leo Jandreau's new wife. Her recollections capture the trauma experienced by a child growing up both inside and outside the left during the tumultuous decades of the 1940s and 1950s. Clark recalls her mother's and father's attempts to navigate between old and new loyalties—to the Communist Party, their union, and their families and friends.

It's easier for me to speak first about my mother because I am her biological child. I'm not Leo's biological child. So I remember in the pre-kindergarten years going with my mother to work when she was giving speeches. We were living in Brooklyn and we were going into New Jersey; it must have been District 4 [of the UE], I guess. I don't think that I even realized that my mother was particularly unusual when I was a little girl. I remember picket lines. I remember meetings. I also remember Peekskill. I was at Peekskill. . . . I knew my mother was important. She also took me to Best and Company to buy me straw hats and fancy clothes, took me on Fifth Avenue for Easter parades, to Radio City Music Hall, so I was really a very privileged child until we came to Schenectady. So yes [I was] the daughter of a leading woman of the left, but when she was home and we did her work things, we also did other things that I would think wealthy women did, or upper-middle-class women.

I have no sense of red diapering; I don't have any sense of that. I felt much more the child of a left leader when I was with Charlie, with my natural father, than I ever did with my mother. When the Rosenbergs were executed—this I will never forget—I was ten years old. I took the train down by myself. My father met me, we got in the car and he wanted to know, first question, what did mother say when the Rosenbergs were executed. He was much more aggressive. I remember not wanting to be asked, because there was a part of me that knew that he didn't approve of my mother anymore. My mother wasn't a Communist, and my mother really was trying to stay home and sort of bake cookies and she really did—it's funny, it took her years to learn how to bake a pie. My mother worked very hard at being a housewife and I cherished that, and I would go down there and it was his world, and I think there was a lot of pressure put on me. He would ask me stuff about her. There was a lot of pressure on me when Leo decided to pull out of the UE when I would go down there.

I wanted normalcy, but I don't know if I wanted normalcy as much as it was given to me, or whether I was just . . . they tried to give me a normal life. I think I would have liked to have squared my relationship with my father. When I was eighteen I wrote him a letter after Leo had adopted me, in which I said that I was being adopted, that essentially Leo really was the only father that I knew in the sense of typical father, and I think that it's really true. He was sort of much more normal in the small town of Schenectady, and I really didn't see the need to continue a relationship. Now I know [I felt] a lot of pressure to write that letter from my mother, never from Leo, but I think he pressured her and she pressured me, because he would never have pressured one of his children directly. He didn't do that. He always gave it to my mother to do—also typical of men of that generation. But I knew it was mean-spirited. He was in California. I was going to college. I really didn't want him in my life but I didn't think I needed to do that, and I regret very much that I did. And then when I found out that he had died, which my mother had known for several months and hadn't told me, I was furious with her.

I guess to sum it up is that I have all the picket line stuff memories with her and her meetings and her big hats that she wore. I knew she was important because people would be deferential to her. And then going back to that left world [of] my grandmother—my [paternal] grandmother was a real star, Clara Lemlich,[21] and she's very special. I really liked my grandmother. Most ten-year-olds didn't know about McCarthy the way I did, or McCarran, or the Smith Act, or the Rosenbergs, or all of this stuff. Most children of my age didn't know about those things. I probably knew about them much more than the average American. In retrospect, I think it's a very rich heritage to have. I'm very proud of it, but it was hard, it was heavy, and I also knew it was secret. I knew we didn't talk about it. . . .

[My mother] cried about it a lot when Leo made the decision—which was clearly the right decision—to move from the UE to the IUE. We were living on State Street, and Roseanne [my half-sister] was quite young. My mother's dearest friend in the world, Esther Matles [wife of UE founder James Matles], wrote her a letter saying they couldn't be friends, and my grandfather, and this was like the final touch—one of the few people I ever hated—wrote her a letter in which he was also disowning her, signing it, "Once a proud and happy pa and grandpa." He was a writer; he was very good with words. I think he was a man of no substance whatsoever. They disowned her, and she was hysterical. And Leo was very supportive, but he was also leading a battle, and she stood by his side. They always stood by each other's side. But I was aware I sort of had to be there, because Esther Matles was her best friend, not his best [friend]. She lost everything in many ways when she, in order to be Ruth Jandreau, she had to give up everything she ever was. Now maybe that's good. I'm certain she left the Communist Party. I understand why women like my mother, or like Leo, or like Charlie—caring, committed people of the working class—I certainly understand what the attraction of the American Communist Party was [to them], especially in the Depression and the war years. I can understand that intellectually without any problem, but I'm also sure that it was very misguided idealism; and certainly they didn't want you to have a family. It was principle before person, and those kinds of things. But it was a shame. She made a clean break, and probably had to, but she buried a part of herself. . . . I wouldn't want to bury any part of myself. There are parts of me I don't like, but I wouldn't want to give up any part of myself for anybody, because it is what I am. She did that. I can't imagine doing that. But this is also 1991, so it's different.

We were still on State Street. I was very aware. The radio . . . they were on the radio. There was something like—I was in seventh grade—and there was some commentator on, like maybe an Albany radio station, who was really red-baiting my mother. I knew that word red-baiting, too. I knew what it meant. I don't remember the rest of it. But it had to do with the split, and I think trying to paint Leo as a Communist. He was not a Communist at that time, and he had not been in quite a long time. [He dropped out] very early, compared to many other people. I think that's a real example of what I think was his basic instinctive intelligence. He was not a very educated man, but he was an extremely bright man, and Leo could really see the sham in anything. Much sooner than some people, I think. He and I only discussed it once. I think he was upset that I even knew. . . . I know what my mother told me, which is he felt that it [the Communist Party] was self-serving, and being used to exploit workers. He was a trade unionist. Actually, I think it's important to understand, my mother—despite having been active longer—in her heart was much more a trade unionist. They were trade unionists in that wonderful old sense, to me, very honorable sense, and I think he thought that he was being used, and his position was being used.

I'm guessing [my mother] left maybe '48, '49. She left the Communist Party before she left the union; it was not a simultaneous act. She married Leo. Leo had not been a Communist for many years. I mean, in relative terms, there aren't that many years, but compared to her. I'm guessing that he left probably before the war. When they got married in 1950 and they moved up here, they were both friends with Esther and Jim Matles.[22] The personal friendship was because Esther Matles was my mother's best friend, and I have pictures of them with their daughter and my mother and Esther on Brighton Beach. We spent a lot of time together and they visited in Schenectady and they saw Roseanne, and so forth. My mother was a wonderful letter writer and she and Esther must've written several times a month. I'm talking about very close friendship. I have one letter from Esther. I have the horrible letters. Esther wrote a letter and pretty much said if you don't do this [persuade Jandreau not to leave the UE], I can't be your friend; and I don't know whether Esther's letter preceded my grandfather's letter, or whether my grandfather's letter preceded Esther's letter. I just know that my mother was devastated. I know that my mother was devastated, she cried a lot, and for a long time.

He was very concerned about protecting my mother because of McCarthy. She could've been—I have no idea why she wasn't called, but I remember worrying that she would be. I never expected him to be called, and I know there was a grand jury up here, but he was never called to McCarran. They would've asked her to name names. She would not have named them; she would have been in contempt, and she would have gone to jail. She would have taken the Fifth, but she was out. I know that I was very worried that she was going to go, and I also knew that in Schenectady, New York, if you would take the Fifth Amendment, you had to be guilty. And I knew she would never name names. I knew she was pressured to name names after we were in Schenectady. I know that she was. In fact, an FBI agent did come to the house. I remember that. The FBI agent came to the door, to Pierce Road, because I'm the one who opened the door. So I think I was thirteen, must've been about '55 that an FBI agent came to the house, but I think that [they] also came on State Street. I'm sure it was more than once.

My evaluation of why Leo would have made a switch—now this is a daughter's evaluation—would have been threefold. The primary reason would have been because he thought it was best for the union, and for the workers, because he took his position and his responsibility very seriously. That would be number one.

Number two would be to protect my mother. That wouldn't have been his first reason. And number three would have been to sort of make a stand against the far left. I mean, if the far left had served the union so that he could have done his job and had not exploited, I think he ultimately would have left, but probably not when he did. I don't think that the Catholic Church [as some have claimed] had anything to do with it. I think he probably hated them so much it could have been a reason to stay [in the UE]. He was very upset when I was marrying for the first time. I was marrying a Catholic. He was beside himself. He was more upset than my mother was. "How could you marry a Catholic?" And I remember saying to him, what did he care? My father held the Catholic Church in contempt. Consistently. He held the church in contempt. I wouldn't say he didn't like Catholic people, but the institution, I mean the local Catholic Church he held in contempt. He certainly did, because they had—particularly [Father] Lamanna had talked against him.

He was a trade unionist. He told me that he dropped out of school in the eighth grade, that he always wanted to be a leader of men. He really was an incredible, unbelievable—its too bad he's not alive. He was a remarkable man. Remarkable.

☼

In 1953, Manuel Fernandez, born in the U.S. in 1917 to left-wing Spanish immigrant parents, was one of seven GE employees laid off for failure to testify before the McCarthy Committee in Albany (by taking the Fifth Amendment). In the mid-1930s, he entered the Communist Party and joined his father in vigorous support of loyalist Spain. During the Depression years, he worked in the Adirondack Mountains of New York for the Civilian Conservation Corp (CCC), and in the steel mills of Gary, Indiana—before obtaining a job at Schenectady GE in the late 1930s. At GE, he quickly got involved in union affairs and was soon elected shop steward, then an executive board member of the Union. Here he talks about his activities as a Communist unionist and the events that led to his expulsion from GE.

Well I started having meetings in '48. But I didn't bring the politics into the union until, oh, '48, '49. Forty-nine is when we started. . . . I remember Wallace was running against Truman. So this time I went out on the limb, my own. I had a meeting at noontime; I said, "This is going to be a serious meeting—has nothing to do with grievances." Everybody said, "What the hell was going on?" I said, "Do you remember in '46 that Truman told this union that if we accept the 18 cents-an-hour raise he would guarantee the company would not be allowed to raise prices?" And everybody said, "Well, you tell us about it." I said "Well it was true. But what did Truman do? The next day he told the company to raise prices, not the 18—but 36 percent." So I said, "You see how the union works against the company and the politicians in the company? So what is our chance? Our chance is to get a guy—not Truman, because he's a faker, he's owned by the corporations—we need a guy like Wallace that's going to tell us and tell the company to go to hell. And until we do that, these unions don't mean a goddamn thing. Let's face it. We got a union, and we get a few things, a few crumbs, but they make the big money because the politicians are in cahoots with these guys. So it's our job to distinguish between one and the other. I know 90 percent of you going to vote for Truman. That's your opinion. I respect that. But don't come tomorrow and say we made a mistake to me. Tell it to somebody else. Because tomorrow I know you're going to come and say you made a mistake, don't wait in the line. What can I tell you? Not only that he did that, he also broke the Taft-Hartley law. He broke the Wagner Act. Nobody did it but Truman. And the Wagner Act, when it was broken it was working against who? Not the company—you, and in favor of the companies. So don't tell me that Truman is a good man. Generally he's good, he's good for GE, but if you want my opinion you vote for Wallace." So like I say, 90 percent voted for Truman.

I did that on my own about Truman and Wallace . . . [Jandreau], he didn't like that. He didn't like what I told the people. Because he said, "Well, what were you trying to do? We don't want to get [into politics]." I said, "Leo, you don't want to get into politics? What are you talking about? You don't want to get into politics? We're in it, whether you like or not. You supported the Democratic Party again for mayor, but you tell me you're not into politics? What the hell is this?" I said, "Hey come on." Well, I don't know who told him; maybe the company called him up and told him. See, Sid Friedlander never went that far. He went around it. He went and ran in a different way. I took it right on, head on, I say, "Look, don't blame anybody, blame the politicians and the corporations. They're together." I told him right out. I say, it's no if or but. Just it, they're all against us.

They knew [I was a Communist]. Everybody in the plant knew me. They said that I was sick, really. Everybody knew me. Everybody. From the superintendent down to the mayor of Schenectady, everybody knew it. All my life. I never hide it. I didn't care. . . . That's what I believe in, and that's what I'm going to do. If I go underground the first thing they say [is] "another faker." You see what I mean? If you don't go on one level, you stay on that level no matter what happens. Yeah, I was open, open.

The biggest mistake the party ever made—because that was during the Korean War, and they voted against Leo—they voted against the war in Korea, which Leo was in favor, and the whole union was in favor. They . . . should have stayed out completely. If they wouldn't go along with, should have stayed out completely. See what I mean? And they voted against him . . . against the war, and that's when Leo got a chance. He said, "Get rid of them." The district [decided] to support the war, and we voted against it. Perlman, Lake, and them—they all got thrown out. That was the excuse that you needed to get rid of them, upon the pretense that Perlman was trying to take over the union. [He was the UE] lawyer. We needed him locally. Leo was already leaning the other way, but at that time, like I said, the party made mistakes that should have never been made. . . . [Charles] Rivers[23] was wrong [to leave the UE on the Korean War issue]. Because what good would it do if the UE was the only one on record in the labor movement [against the war]? You see what I mean? Isolate it, when it was already [isolated]. See, we are not in the majority; we're in a minority, let's face it. There are certain things you cannot do, because maybe that guy over there will support you on some issues, but on that one he will be against you. And after that he can't be seen with you, because you're labeled. You know what I mean?

Sometimes on a contract issues I had to compromise a lot of times—not for me; compromise for the worker, not for me . . . for the worker. Because, if you don't compromise at all you're going to be dead, because no matter what you do the company is going to throw you down.

I used to have the political affairs, the *Daily Worker,* all those papers. I had it right in the open, everybody used to read it. The women used to go to the bathroom and they took the paper, and they used to bring it back. And the superintendent used to take the paper; he used to hide it, but he used to take it. Oh, yeah, and he used to read it . . . Neil Dunne. I didn't distribute it; I just put it on the table. That's all. I had the [Schenectady] *Gazette.* I had the Bible—yeah, on the desk. Well now they can't say I only read one. You see what I mean? I read everything. I used to tell everybody. I read everything, even though I didn't read it. But look, one Bible, big one. I had the *Readers Digest.* I had three or four, I had the one from the IUE, a magazine from the IUE. I read everything.

One guy asked, one engineer—he was for Wallace, him and I, the only two guys with a Wallace button. He was an engineer; they threw him out. They threw him out of the company—fired him. Well this guy, he didn't go on McCarthy, no. He was an engineer, they could fire him any time they wanted to. But they brought him back, he was such a genius that they couldn't do without him, and they brought him back. So one day I'm going to the bathroom and I see him, I say, "Well what the hell are you doing here?" I said, "They can't get rid of us bastards." He said, "They depend on us, let's face it, without us they're nothing." And everybody heard him. So I told one lady I say, "You see, the company needs him, no matter what he is. He's going to work, because they need him. Without him you won't be working on those tubes. He's the brain." And he was. He was a brainy guy. Finally [he] quit himself. Told 'em to go to hell.

That's why I became openly [a Communist]. So I can be both forward and show—like the people in my job, they all voted for [me because] they knew me, and they vote for the right-winger for shop steward. They know him, and they knew me. . . . I want my people to know. If they want me like that all right, if they don't, hey. And I was there for years in the shop, and they all knew it. Management knew it. Personally [we got along, but] not when it came to . . . business, they take the company side. And all at once when McCarthy came they wanted me to sign the paper—"are you, or are you not?" And I told them to go to hell.

Notes

1. *Schenectady Union-Star,* 26 February 1954.
2. For an example focusing on the UE, see Ronald L. Filippelli and Mark McColloch, *Cold War in the Working Class: The Rise and Decline of the United Electrical Workers* (Albany: State University of New York Press, 1995).

3. I constructed the following narratives from over a hundred interviews conducted between 1991 and 1999 that now comprise the "Schenectady General Electric in the 20th Century Oral History Project." Most of those selected date to 1991 and 1992. I eliminated my own questions, and all hesitations, gaps, false starts, and repetitive answers (except when uttered for emphasis). I also occasionally re-arranged paragraphs and sentences. My editing decisions were made with the goal of constructing logical and linear narratives that would be easy to follow yet would also preserve the tone, language, "feeling," and context of the original dialogic exchanges. Occasional footnotes and bracketed comments were added where I felt elaborations or clarifications of terms, organizations, or individuals would be helpful. For the most part, I have relied on my interviewees to introduce the readers to the main characters and organizations that comprise the core of the story of McCarthyism in Schenectady, and specifically at Schenectady GE—with their various and often contradictory perspectives. Elsewhere, I have offered my own interpretation on certain facets of these events. See Gerald Zahavi, "Passionate Commitments: Race, Sex, and Communism at Schenectady General Electric, 1932–1954," *Journal of American History*, 53 (September 1996): 514–548.
4. Testimony of Salvatore Vottis, House Committee on Education and Labor, *Investigation of Communist Infiltration of UERMWA: Hearing Before a Special Subcommittee of the Committee on Education and Labor, House of Representatives*, 80th Cong., 2d sess., 1948, pursuant to H. R. 111, 213.
5. Max Gordon was regional CP organizer in the Albany and Schenectady area in the late 1930s. For more on his organizing work in Schenectady and elsewhere, see Max Gordon, interview by Fraser Ottanelli and Winifred Wandersee, 13 June 1985, audiotape in Zahavi's possession.
6. The NLRB votes were not company- or industry-wide, but were held plant-by-plant. In Schenectady all NLRB votes, except the final June 1954 vote (which took place after Jandreau had announced his decision), went squarely for the UE.
7. Carey Estes Kefauver, Senator from Tennessee between 1948 and 1963, made his reputation as chair of the Special Committee on Organized Crime in Interstate Commerce (the 'Kefauver Committee') between 1950 and 1953. For more on the committee, see William Howard Moore, *The Kefauver Committee and the Politics of Crime, 1950–1952* (Columbia: University of Missouri Press, 1974).
8. Marshall Perlin was the local UE lawyer. Marshall Perlin, telephone conversation with author, 3 September 1992; "Leo Eugene Jandreau" report, 19 August 1949, FBI file 100-290802, Federal Bureau of Investigation, FBI-FOIA.
9. Altogether, the "Cordiner Memo," which established GE's new policy, was responsible for seven lay-offs at Schenectady GE. Westinghouse and other firms also adopted similar policies—leading to the firing of over fifty UE activists. See Filippelli and McColloch, *Cold War in the Working Class*, 155.
10. Lemuel R. Boulware was GE vice-president for Labor and Community Relations. Boulware became synonymous with the firm's new labor-management philosophy, which came to be known as "Boulwarism." Boulwarism relied on public relations and community propaganda to communicate and "sell" GE's contract offers directly to the workers, bypassing union representatives.
11. On the expulsion, see Albert J. Fitzgerald to Leo Jandreau, 7 November 1947, ff. 156, District 3, District/Locals Series, 1975 Accession, United Electrical Workers National Office Records, United Electrical, Radio and Machine Workers of America Archives (Archives of Industrial Society, University of Pittsburgh, Pittsburgh, Pa.). The letter includes a 24 October 1947 telegram received from Martin Stanton, Frank Fiorello, and

Carmen DiGirolamo of Local 301 which deals with the expulsion of these three men for making statements through the press "affecting Union business other than authorized Union officials." The three men protested this as violation of free speech and noted: "Our statements were barred from the Union press which was only open to the opposing faction in control of the administration and we were compelled in the interest of free speech to make our views known through the only available source.... The action against us resulted from pure factionalism since we are and will continue to be active in the coming December elections in the Local."

12. Friedlander was one of the oldest and most widely respected of the CP members active in the GE plants. He was a publicly admitted Communist and party meetings often took place at his home.
13. Jandreau's left-wing slate of officers went down to defeat in 1948, but Frank Kriss, leader of the right-wing coalition, did not remain in power long. He and the rest of the right-wing opposition bolted the UE in 1949 to found a local CIO-backed IUE Local; this was after the expulsion of the UE from the CIO.
14. The phrase "pipe line to Moscow" came from an article published in 1952 in the *Saturday Evening Post*. See "Red Pipe Line into Our Defense Plants," *Saturday Evening Post*, 18 October 1952, 18–21, 106, 108, 110.
15. In 1944, the only World War II year I have figures for, Local 301 had approximately 25,000 members—not quite the numbers recalled by Carey. It is probable that a year or two earlier the numbers might have reached 30,000+. Vincent Maloney, Pres. UE Local 301, to Philip Murray, 5 March 1944, ff. 194, 1975 Accession, United Electrical Workers National Office Records.
16. I should add that Horowitz's narrative was constructed not from the answers of an interviewee at a formal interview, but from remarks that emerged in the course of a session with a group of former CP members (and "fellow travelers") who visited me at my Schenectady home back in July of 1999. They came, accompanied by two close acquaintances, to criticize an article I had written in the *Journal of American History* (see footnote 3) about racial and sexual themes in the Cold War union battles in Schenectady. Though several individuals spoke during the course of the two-hour discussion, Irving Horowitz's recollections were exclusively utilized to produce this edited account.
17. Marshall Perlin was a Columbia University Law School graduate and a radical attorney who specialized in labor and civil rights law. He represented Local 301, and later the UE, for much of his career. In addition, he worked with attorneys Arthur Kinoy and Frank Donner, and served as part of the legal defense team on the Rosenberg case, and also represented the Rosenberg's co-defendant, Morton Sobell. Perlin died 31 December 1998. *UE News,* January 1999; Marshall Perlin, telephone interview by author, 3 September 1992.
18. It's not clear which of two informants Horowitz was recalling. Both John Patrick Charles and Jean Arsenault Jr. revealed the names of local Communist Party members. The former worked for the FBI and the latter for McCarthy's Senate Investigation Subcommittee. Charles was vice-president and organizing secretary of the eastern upstate New York section of the CP; Arsenault was former Albany correspondent for the *Daily Worker*. Stenographic Record, U.S. House of Representatives, *Deposition of Jean Amedee Arsenault Before Executive Session of the [House] Committee on Un-American Activities*, 11 July 1953, 9–26, case file 539, box 11, Non-criminal Investigation Case Files, Bureau of Criminal Investigations, New York State Division of State Police; "Confidential," list of Communist Party members, 11 May 1950, file 6, box 153, J. B.

Matthews Papers, William R. Perkins Library, Duke University, Durham, N.C.; see also *Schenectady Union-Star*, 19 February 1954; *Schenectady Gazette*, 20 February 1954; and *Albany Knickerbocker News*, 7 April 1954.

19. Horowitz added the name "Jerry" later, upon reviewing a transcript of the edited interview. He had forgotten the name originally. Irving Horowitz, e-mail to author, 17 July 2000.
20. Actually, it was around 39 percent. Approximately 5,400 out of around 14,000 workers voted for the UE over the IUE. *Schenectady Gazette*, 1 July 1954.
21. Clara Lemlich was one of the more famous female trade union activists of the early twentieth century. She served as an executive board member of Local 25 of the International Ladies' Garment Workers' Union. In 1909 she was at the forefront of a walkout of shirtwaist makers, a walkout that led to the famous "Uprising of the 20,000." For more on Lemlich, see Carolyn Daniel McCreesh, *Women in the Campaign to Organize Garment Workers, 1880–1917* (New York: Garland, 1985).
22. James Matles was one of the founders of the UE and first director of organization of the union.
23. Communist Party member Charles Rivers helped organize the original group that went on to form Local 301 of the UE back in the early and mid-1930s. He was trained at the Lenin School in the Soviet Union and was assigned by James Matles, then active as an organizing director of the Trade Union Unity League (TUUL) in New York State, to organize a left-wing union at the Schenectady plants. For more on Rivers, see Charles Rivers, interview by Debra Bernhardt, 29 April 1991, audiotape, Oral History of the American Left, Tamiment Institute Library; Charles Rivers, interview by Ronald Schatz, 9 July 1976, audiotape, tape in Schatz's possession; and Charles Rivers' autobiographical manuscript, "Random Thoughts," typescript [1993], in Ron Rivers' possession.

Mixed Melody

Anticommunism and the United Packinghouse Workers in California Agriculture, 1954–1961

☼

Don Watson

Varieties of labor anticommunists emerged during the Cold War. Leaders as diverse as George Meany, Philip Murray, Walter Reuther, Father Charles Owen Rice, and Roy Brewer, plus thousands at shop-steward level played roles. Many had concerns about Stalin. Many fought over political and religious ideology and union turf. Where was the line to be drawn between concern about the role of Communists and harassment? The expulsion of eleven unions from the CIO in 1949 and 1950 did not end this question.

The United Packinghouse Workers of America (UPWA) was unique among CIO unions during the Cold War. While other CIO unions in the late 1940s and early 1950s purged their ranks of Communists, the UPWA, led by non-Communist officers, continued to allow Communists, a minority group, to participate in union affairs. President Ralph Helstein later told Sanford Horwitt, biographer of Saul Alinsky, "We were in trouble with other unions, on the verge of being thrown out of the CIO, all the time. We were investigated more than any other union in the CIO by the CIO."[1] The UPWA survived the CIO purge of 1949–50, another CIO Communist investigation in 1953,[2] and an AFL-CIO investigation in 1959–61 to become a force for civil rights and civil liberties during the Cold War. The UPWA's survival owed much to the work of Helstein, who welded a workable coalition within the union and won acceptance, if not always full approval, from the CIO and later the AFL-CIO.[3]

National CIO leaders encouraged the UPWA in early 1954 to take over the CIO Local 78 vegetable shed workers of California and Arizona before the pending merger of the CIO with the AFL. These workers were "fruit tramps." Their local was a CIO-chartered holdover from the defunct Food, Tobacco, Agricultural and Allied Workers (FTA), expelled by the CIO in 1950 for Communist domination. The UPWA needed a new home. Les Orear, then in charge of public relations for the UPWA, recalls, "The UPWA came to California in 1954 because the meatpacking was stagnating . . . when the CIO offered the chance—they took it. Perhaps they didn't realize what they were getting into."[4]

The shed tramps wanted the UPWA to carry their battle into the fields.[5] Thousands of them were being laid off. Grower-shippers using the technology of vacuum cooling instead of ice were sending lettuce and celery shed jobs to the fields, using less-expensive Mexican nationals working under the bracero program. The CIO staff set up meetings of the Local 78 shed workers to vote for affiliation with the UPWA. In April at Salinas, the summer lettuce capitol, the tramps readily voted to join the UPWA. However, tramp shed workers needed to vote during the next five weeks in other vegetable regions of California and Arizona.

While the voting proceeded, the UPWA's maverick Cold War position came into focus. The UPWA international convention at Sioux City, Iowa, on 7 May 1954, voted down a constitutional amendment to bar Communists from running for union office, rejecting the plea of a southern district director to "Give 'em a fair trial and hang 'em."[6] The UPWA was alone among mainstream unions in taking this position. California newspaper reports on the action shook up the tramps, according to CIO staff member Ken Gillie, who wrote to CIO executive vice-president John Riffe (in charge of CIO organizing); "much damage has been done."[7] However this unique position didn't prevent the tramps from voting for the UPWA at meetings in San Joaquin Valley, Oxnard, Imperial Valley, and Arizona, giving the UPWA a base for farm-labor organizing.[8]

Helstein relished stepping into the small, growing farm-worker movement in California. Orear recalled, "The leadership was socially ambitious. They wanted to be known as a force for human justice. They were strong in support of Black civil rights and also wanted to support Hispanic rights."[9] Helstein was close friends with both Carey McWilliams, author of the farm labor classic, *Factories in the Fields,* and Saul Alinsky, the community organizer.[10] Helstein flew to California in May for a three-day UPWA farm labor staff retreat at the Asilomar conference grounds at Pacific Grove.[11]

The UPWA found potential allies in small farm-worker movements. One was a group of Roman Catholic priests, led by Fathers Donald McDonald of San Jose and Thomas McCullough of Stockton, known as "The Mission Band." They had asked the church for permission to minister to farm workers, and they performed masses for domestic farm workers and braceros (one parishioner at McDonald's San Jose church was Cesar Chavez). They believed farm workers deserved a union and welcomed the entry of the CIO, although a concerned bishop from the Monterey-Fresno Diocese did ask for assurance the CIO union would effectively steer a course between collectivism and extreme private ownership. Fathers McDonald and McCullough remained allies during the next seven years.[12] Another ally was the Alinsky-sponsored Community Service Organization (CSO), an organization devoted to work with Mexican Americans that was setting up chapters in farm communities in California. The parent of CSO, the Industrial Areas Foundation, of which Helstein was a board member, had Fred Ross and Cesar Chavez on their payroll.[13]

Another potential ally was the AFL National Agricultural Workers Union (NAWU) of H.L. Mitchell and Ernesto Galarza. The NAWU was the successor to the Southern Tenant Farmers Union of the 1930s. After leading a series of agricultural strikes in California between 1946 and 1952, it had declined to only two full-time officers nationwide: Galarza, working out of his home in San Jose, California, and Mitchell, who had a small office in Washington, D.C. At this point, the NAWU no longer organized picket lines, demonstrations, or public meetings in California. Its last statewide conference had been in 1952. They surfaced mainly through press releases and testimony at state and federal congressional hearings. Galarza researched and produced works on farm labor and the bracero program while Mitchell lobbied to keep the NAWU alive, vainly hoping for a massive cash infusion from the AFL.[14]

Their main financial support came from the New York–based Sharecropper Fund, inspired by the socialist, Norman Thomas, plus a small subsidy from the AFL through former president William Green. The current president, George Meany, was ready to stop the subsidy; he had already shunned an organizing request from Mitchell for $500,000 in 1953. (Meany felt that subsidizing unions was against AFL principles.)[15]

The UPWA saw no jurisdictional conflict with the NAWU, which was not visibly organizing on a field level in California. Nothing in the minutes, staff reports, or letters in the UPWA files at the State Historical Society in Wisconsin mentions an attempted war with the NAWU.[16] The UPWA did approach individual NAWU members to help the UPWA's efforts, but not as part of a conscious strategy to end the NAWU.

Mitchell and Galarza, however, treated the UPWA's entry as an encroachment on their territory. They believed the 1946 AFL charter gave them the exclusive right to organize farm workers, and in letters to selected AFL leaders they warned that the UPWA would bring Communists into the farm labor movement. These targets included Meany, AFL secretary-treasurer William Schnitzler, Amalgamated Meatcutters secretary-treasurer Pat Gorman, and CIO president Walter Reuther. In addition they lobbied Neil Haggerty, secretary of the California Labor Federation.[17] Their continuous message was that the UPWA was a Communist infiltrated or dominated union, trying to take over the NAWU. Galarza described the UPWA to Meany as "the most heavily armored corporate machine west of the Mississippi River."[18]

Meany wasn't anxious to get into a quarrel with the CIO. Split since the 1930s, the two organizations were getting ready to merge. Meany rejected Mitchell's claim that the UPWA was violating the no-raiding pact, saying that the UPWA already had jurisdiction from the CIO before the pact was signed in June 1954. He also said the no-raiding pact only applied to union members under contract, not unorganized farm workers. Although himself anticommunist, he refused to comment on Mitchell's Communist charges. Meany did offer to talk to CIO president Walter Reuther about opening unity meetings between the two unions.[19]

Unity meetings began at CIO headquarters on 1 July 1954, with Mitchell unhappy about being forced into the talks. However, the meetings opened with CIO hopes for success. Victor Reuther, Walter's brother, and R.J. Thomas, assistant to CIO vice president John Riffe, helped the two unions plan a jointly-funded AFL and CIO agricultural drive. Although the UPWA was ready to pay for half the expenses, neither the NAWU nor the AFL could or would pay for the other half. Victor Reuther then told Galarza that if the NAWU made a deal with the UPWA, he would ask the CIO to pick up the NAWU's share.[20]

However, after two months of talks Mitchell advised Galarza to stop meeting with CIO leaders, whom he feared only wanted the NAWU to merge with the UPWA. Mitchell warned that getting involved with the UPWA-CIO "would put us right back where we were in 1939 when we (the Southern Tenant Farmers Union) pulled out of UCAPAWA-CIO (United Cannery, Agricultural, Packing and Allied Workers of America)." Mitchell constantly told people in the labor movement how the Communists, led by UCAPAWA-CIO president Donald Henderson, destroyed STFU in the 1930s.[21] Mitchell considered the UPWA-CIO the direct successor of the UCAPAWA-CIO."[22]

Unable to convince labor people that Helstein was a Communist, Mitchell targeted UPWA vice president Tony Stephens as the chief UPWA Communist and warned Galarza he could end up "pulling chestnuts out of the fire for commies like Stevens [sic]."[23] Mitchell, lacking hard evidence, sought information on Communist activity by Stephens.[24] In a confidential memo in 1955, he argued "A.T. Stephens is the top man . . . Helstein . . . maintains his position in UPWA only by cooperating at all times with Stephens and his machine."[25]

Mitchell did have the ear of Patrick Gorman, secretary-treasurer of the Amalgamated Meat Cutters and Butcher Workmen of America (AMC), who was Mitchell's most reliable supporter among the larger AFL unions. Gorman was a nonideological maverick, who took unusual but firm stands on certain issues. His important ally in helping Mitchell was the AMC vice president, Leon Schachter, an old Socialist friend of Mitchell. Schachter had organized the big New Jersey Seabrook Farm for AMC. Gorman, with help from Schachter, had been key in obtaining the NAWU's AFL charter at the end of World War II. Although Gorman knew little about the problems of California agriculture, he championed Mitchell's crusade.[26]

Like Mitchell, Gorman was also trying to locate data on alleged direct Communist ties of UPWA officers. He wanted this information while attempting an AMC merger with the UPWA—a long sought dream for meat industry solidarity. Gorman spent months vainly trying to obtain incriminating documents from Meany's office. He told Meany that if he could get these documents he would "blast the whole merger plan to Hades."[27] However, these documents, if they existed, never appeared.

Charges of Communism greeted the UPWA when they opened an agricultural drive during the 1955 Imperial Valley winter lettuce season. This was a continuation of the agricultural program drafted by the Asilomar conference in 1954. Rosalee Widman, in charge of the campaign, was accused of being the lead Communist. She was a former bacon slicer from St. Joseph, Missouri, who had become a UPWA leader in the Midwest and a champion of civil rights and women's rights. Widman complained, "Down here in the valley, the charges come that I'm 'red' . . . (they) just happen to come during the *only* time UPWA, CIO has put our A-D (Anti-Discrimination) program into effect!"[28]

The AFL Teamsters raised the Communist issue. Former Local 78 president Jim Smith, who defected to the Teamsters, called the El Centro hall a "nest for all the Communists who used to run F.T.A."[29] The Teamsters filed an NLRB petition to take over all of Local 78's vegetable sheds in California and Arizona. However, they were defeated by the vote of the tramps in the ensuing elections, 1,382 to 725.[30]

Some unusual Communist charges hung on in Imperial Valley. The UPWA was accused of coordinating with Mexican Communists allegedly infiltrating the bracero stream. Widman was supposedly hatching this plot in Mexico with the leftist labor leader Vicente Lombardo Toledano. Another charge was that the Mexican American CSO in Imperial Valley, which was cooperating with the UPWA drive, had been taken over by Communists.[31] Galarza sent out an internal NAWU newsletter on the charges, and Mitchell, at a farm labor committee meeting in Washington, D.C., threatened to go public. CIO lobbyist Milton Plumb, however, insisted that Mitchell meet with Victor Reuther before going further.[32]

The Reuther brothers continued their involvement with the UPWA-NAWU matter. In late 1955, when the CIO merged with the AFL, the Reuthers did not want to be buried in old-line AFL business unionism. Walter became chair of a newly created AFL-CIO Industrial Union Department (IUD). In 1957 the IUD gave the NAWU a $25,000 grant for farm labor organizing. Galarza was able to do some modest organizing in the Stockton region of California and hire an organizer in Yuba County. However, Victor Reuther, realizing that the IUD would probably not give a second grant, suggested to an October meeting of the NAWU Executive Board that they merge with the UPWA. Mitchell responded with a letter to Walter Reuther stating they wouldn't go into a union influenced "by forces subversive to all we stand for."[33]

Others besides the Reuthers were interested in bringing the NAWU and the UPWA together. Father Thomas McCullough, who helped Galarza in Stockton, and organizer DeWitt Tannehill, who worked for Galarza in Yuba County, asked the UPWA to help. They wanted to save the work of Galarza. They knew the UPWA was the only union willing to spend money for farm-labor organizing at that time while Galarza was the most knowledgeable educator on farm labor issues. The UPWA requested 200 copies of Galarza's excellent 1956 tract "Strangers in Our Fields" for use in UPWA organizing. However, closer organizational ties didn't happen.[34]

The UPWA farm labor program gained focus in 1958 and 1959, when Clive Knowles arrived in California. Knowles, a graduate of Harvard Divinity School and a former Unitarian minister, had worked for the UPWA since the late 1940s and was skilled at dramatizing campaigns. He believed in field-level confrontations, picket lines, and demonstrations to make the farm labor movement visible. Helstein and the UPWA wanted this kind of activity. They were already involved with the civil rights movement of Martin Luther King, Jr. and wanted similar involvement in California.

The union's meatpacking base was eroding. New plants were opening in the Mid-west and South, while UPWA packinghouses were beginning to close in the traditional packing centers of Chicago, Omaha, Kansas City, and other cities. The union needed new members in new places.

The UPWA's renewed agricultural activity disturbed Mitchell and Galarza. UPWA organizers renewed their sanitation-in-the-fields campaign, leading to a major conference of state agencies at the State Department of Health in Berkeley in June 1959. They spent $20,000 to bring in the CSO and Cesar Chavez to organize at Oxnard in collaboration with lemon shed workers. They led carrot worker strikes at the fields of vegetable shipper Bud Antle in the Imperial Valley and Watsonville. They also led hundreds of farm workers from Imperial Valley and Oxnard to picket a speech by Secretary of Labor James Mitchell at the Biltmore Hotel in Los Angeles. To the dismay of Mitchell and Galarza, these activities gave higher visibility to the UPWA on the farm labor scene.[35]

In the spring and summer of 1958, AFL-CIO Secretary Schnitzler, following settlement of a Louisiana NAWU-UPWA sugar dispute, successfully prodded Mitchell to cooperate with Helstein on a joint AFL-CIO California agriculture program. Thus Helstein, Mitchell, and Jack Livingston, director of the AFL-CIO department of organization, met and drew up plans for a joint field-shed program to be approved by the AFL-CIO executive council in August. Both the UPWA and the AFL-CIO would fund the program. Although the NAWU couldn't furnish money, Galarza would furnish organizers. The NAWU would work mainly in the north, and the UPWA in the south. The plan concluded: "On the basis of cooperation between the two unions and experiences gained in such an organizing campaign, it will be possible to determine whether a union of farm workers and a union of processing workers, or a single united union is required to service the interests of all agricultural workers."[36]

This cooperative atmosphere soon collapsed. Meany, who was cautious about stepping into agriculture, blocked taking up the plan in the executive council for six months and Mitchell decided to forge ahead without the UPWA. He now had on his side a powerful new lobbying force: the National Advisory Committee on Farm Labor (NACFL), formed by the Sharecropper Fund people who had been friends of Mitchell since the 1930s. The chief NACFL organizer was the dynamic Fay Bennett, and it included liberals such as Eleanor Roosevelt and co-chairs Frank Graham and A. Philip Randolph. Randolph led a pro-NAWU delegation, including Mitchell, to Meany's office in January 1959. Meany, however, insisted that the UPWA be included in any AFL-CIO farm drive. This forced Mitchell back into discussions with Helstein and Reuther to draft a joint program for the February AFL-CIO executive council meeting in Puerto Rico.[37]

The Puerto Rico executive council plan bypassed both unions. Instead, the AFL-CIO Department of Organization, directed by Jack Livingston, was to set up an Agricultural Workers Organizing Committee (AWOC). Livingston appointed as drive director a retired UAW warhorse from the 1930s, Norman Smith, a man unconnected with either union. Meany, according to Reuther and Randolph, insisted that Mitchell be kept out of the drive, but reluctantly agreed to allow Galarza to serve as assistant director.[38]

As the UPWA got ready to assist the AWOC drive, it was hit with new Communist charges. Former UPWA vice-president Tony Stephens (whom Mitchell had called the leading Communist) sent charges to Meany that the UPWA violated the non-Communist clause of the AFL-CIO 1957 Ethical Practices Code. Meany handed the Stephens charges to an executive council sub-committee of Walter Reuther and George Harrison, president of the Brotherhood of Railway and Steamship Clerks. At the same time, the House un-American Activities Committee opened hearings in Chicago on May 5–7 on alleged UPWA Communism.[39]

The Ethical Practices Code had been devised by Meany to meet congressional labor corruption charges, but he also added a non-Communist pledge that affected union staffs. As a result, some UPWA staff quietly resigned from the party. By 1957 the Communist Party was already a shadow of itself; many thousands of CP members had left the party in 1956–1957 following the Khrushchev anti-Stalin speech. The party was no longer a force in the UPWA, as it had been. As the leading Chicago UPWA Communist Herb March later remarked, "(The) McCarthy period just withered the Communist Party away."[40]

Helstein, anxious to move ahead on UPWA programs, acted quickly to stem damage to the union. He announced the appointment of a Public Policy Review Board that included Martin Luther King, Jr., and other prestigious religious and labor law figures, to monitor the UPWA's compliance with the code. Although the AFL-CIO ultimately cleared the UPWA, the charges hovered over the union for two years.[41]

The AFL-CIO Agricultural Workers drive opened at Stockton, California, in May 1959. Mitchell (in Washington D.C.), although denied a direct role by Meany, nonetheless monitored the drive by mail with Smith and Galarza. He feared that the bigger, more active UPWA would pluck the fruits. To prevent this, Mitchell wrote to Galarza, now an AWOC insider, to save what he could of the NAWU's mostly defunct locals and establish an NAWU presence. Smith thought a signed jurisdictional agreement between Mitchell and Helstein would help to prevent friction during the drive.[42]

Mitchell and Helstein did sign such a pact, in Livingston's Washington office, on 21 May. This pact applied only to workers signed by AWOC organizers, freeing both unions to organize agricultural workers elsewhere. The UPWA would get all the processing workers, shed or field, signed by AWOC. This included any work formerly done in sheds. The NAWU would get harvesting, pre-harvesting, and other fieldwork. The fuzzy part of the formula was field packing.[43]

Smith was not happy with this formula because field workers shifted back and forth day-by-day, and sometimes hour-by-hour, between harvesting and packing. Smith and the AWOC staff would have to decide whether a dues-paying field worker was a "processor" or a "harvester." Smith decided to put the dues money into escrow, pending an AFL-CIO decision on the proper union, or unions, to take the money. The UPWA had no objection, but Mitchell insisted that dues collected from field workers go directly to the NAWU, and he prodded Galarza to demand this. Mitchell saw Smith's delay as a gimmick to hand the jurisdiction over to the UPWA.[44]

Smith saw merger as the solution. He wrote to Livingston on September 28, "In my opinion, I think you should work toward getting a merger of this whole movement into one organization because the field operation, especially on these machines, cannot be separated in a logical manner." Mitchell, though, saw merger suggestions as a Smith-Knowles conspiracy to put the UPWA in and shove the NAWU out. No records exist in the UPWA archives, however, that reveal a master plot by the UPWA to take over the AWOC or to promote a merger.[45]

Mitchell then attacked Smith for hiring Lou Krainock as AWOC public relations director in August. Mitchell labeled Krainock a UPWA agent and a "Commy newsman." Krainock had been UPWA educational director in 1950-51 and had worked for the Highlander Folk School of Tennessee in 1948-49. The school was now under attack in the South as a "Communist training school." Mitchell charged that Smith was allowing Krainock to take over the AWOC Stockton headquarters office in behalf of the UPWA. Although Krainock was friendly to the UPWA, no records show UPWA complicity in Krainock's hiring.[46]

Mitchell's charges hit Smith's sensitive nerve. In October, Smith demanded Livingston halt the letters; he felt they were sabotaging his campaign.[47] Livingston and his assistant, Franz Daniel, along with Walter Reuther and Randolph, met with Meany on this issue on 11 January 1960. They asked his support to give Mitchell a new job either as an AFL-CIO farm labor lobbyist or as a farm labor committee secretary, on the condition that Mitchell get out of AWOC affairs and that the NAWU merge with the UPWA.

With Meany's presumed support, Reuther and Randolph met the next day with Mitchell for his approval. Mitchell balked, however, and said the NAWU would rather go to the Meat Cutters (where Mitchell had friends).[48] When he called an emergency NAWU board meeting on this issue, Victor Reuther came to urge that they merge with the UPWA who, unlike the AMC, had shown a genuine interest in farm labor. However, board members raised again the Communist issue, and voted to instead enter merger talks with the AMC.[49]

Meany, in a split with Reuther, Randolph and Livingston, came out in favor of the idea. He told both Gorman and Mitchell that the NAWU had the full right to merge with the AMC if they desired. He may have seen this as the best solution to his long-standing problem with Mitchell. Meany privately warned Gorman that the federation would look with disfavor on using Mitchell "as a spearhead for any organizational drive." In effect, he wanted the AMC to take over the NAWU's farm labor jurisdiction without the further major involvement of Mitchell.[50]

The NAWU-AMC merger took six months to consummate. In the meantime, Mitchell persuaded the AMC to hire the unemployed Galarza as a California organizer. He had quit the AWOC earlier in the year, in solidarity with Mitchell. Mitchell believed that Galarza, holding credentials from a major union instead of the minor NAWU, could now stand tall to Smith. Galarza complained to Mitchell, however, "You are going to need a Paul Bunyan to accept such an assignment. I would have to face Smith's organization—himself and 12 staff members. Every one of the key organizers are working for him, not us . . . It is Smith who has the mandate, the money and the accredited authority of the AFL-CIO, not I." The hiring in effect placed Galarza and the AMC at war with the AWOC organizing program.[51]

The May AFL-CIO executive council meeting reacted with fury on what they saw as an attack on the official farm labor program. After extended discussion, the council handed the issue to an executive committee composed of Meany, Schnitzler, Harrison, James Carey, and Reuther. The actual minutes of this inner meeting, if there were any, are not available, but after the meeting Meany called Mitchell to say they had decided to withdraw the charter of the NAWU. They instead decided to charter the AWOC, giving it the ability to collect and spend dues, supervised by a steering committee of California labor officials.[52] Mitchell and Galarza then assailed the AFL-CIO leadership for chartering the AWOC, terming it a "dual union." On this issue Mitchell lost the support of old friends like Norman Thomas and Fay Bennett of the Sharecropper Fund, who implored him to call off his war.[53] The Meat Cutters were also concerned about the rift. Gorman and Schacter drafted a conciliatory telegram to Meany and then demanded Mitchell sign it. This cleared the air for Meany, who still wanted the AMC to step in.[54]

Meany then met with Gorman and another AMC officer for a social luncheon on 21 July at the Drake Hotel in Chicago. According to Gorman, Meany told them that if the NAWU merged with the AMC, *they*, not the UPWA, would enroll all the members signed by the AWOC. He wanted the AMC not to otherwise interfere with the AWOC operation. Following this the NAWU-AMC merger was approved at the August executive council meeting. After the meeting Meany wrote to Thomas Lloyd, AMC president, "the jurisdiction of the Amalgamated Meat Cutters and Butcher Workman of North America will not be more, nor less than the jurisdiction held heretofore by the two organizations." That this was to be *exclusive* jurisdiction for the AMC wasn't stated. But it was Meany's Drake Hotel oral pledge, implying exclusive jurisdiction, that would stay in the memory of Mitchell and Gorman over the coming months.[55]

With Galarza soon departing from the AMC, all that was left of the old NAWU after the August merger was a title and desk for Mitchell in Memphis, Tennessee. Unable himself to go to California, he prodded the AMC leadership to enter the California fray. On Mitchell's suggestion Gorman asked Meany to hire laid off AMC organizers onto the AWOC staff. Meany told him not to bother, because he was thinking about closing out the AWOC.[56]

But Mitchell saw with dismay continuing AWOC-UPWA cooperation in California. A solid AWOC-UPWA alliance had blossomed. He sent a letter to Gorman (evidently to frighten him) stating that *"Nearly all of the organizers (in AWOC) have at one time been in the UPWA."* [italics added] Gorman told this to Meany, who ordered an investigation. Investigator Franz Daniel soon reported back to Meany that only *two* out of sixteen staff members, as of 9 December, had ever been connected with the UPWA.[57]

Caught in a gross overstatement, Mitchell roared back with a new letter to Gorman zeroing in on Krainock, the proven ex-UPWA staff member. Mitchell stressed Krainock's connection with the Highlander Folk School, which "was used as a center for the old CIO unions and later ousted by the CIO as Communist dominated." Gorman relayed Mitchell's new charge to Meany.[58]

Gorman's continuing involvement with Mitchell's crusade led to the next step when the AMC intervened in a UPWA-AWOC supported 1961 Imperial Valley lettuce strike. This strike was officially certified by the California Department

FIGURE 3.1 In 1961 domestic field workers in the Imperial Valley struck sixteen ranches. The strike was supported by the Agricultural Workers Organizing Committee, AFL-CIO, and by the United Packinghouse Workers of America. *Credit: Illinois Labor History Society.*

of Employment at sixteen ranches. The strikers were asking for $1.25 an hour, plus restoration of lost piece rates.[59] The Mexican government demanded that the Imperial Valley Farmers Association and the Department of Labor remove all braceros from the struck ranches.[60] During the strike, Gorman and California AMC official Max Osslo sent letters to Smith and the California Labor Federation leadership asserting that the involvement of the AWOC and the UPWA in the strike was an infringement on AMC farm labor jurisdiction. Because of this jurisdictional charge, the California Labor Federation and the Los Angeles Labor Council withdrew promised financial aid for the strike.[61]

It seems that the only motive of the AMC to intervene in the strike was to assist Mitchell's private crusade to kill AWOC-UPWA cooperation. AMC leaders had made no plans of their own to organize farm workers in California. They gave the idea up entirely during the summer when Gorman and Lloyd announced to their staff, "We are certainly in no position to spend two million dollars on a campaign in California which does not have too much hope of being successful."[62] To be fair to Gorman, he did take some maverick stands during the Cold War, including support for the suppressed movie *Salt of the Earth* and support for the Labor for Peace movement, coining the phrase "Co-Existence or Non-Existence."[63]

This episode in farm labor history shows how sincere anticommunists could be led to excess during the Cold War. An AFL-CIO farm labor program was attacked because it was too closely associated with the UPWA. Father Charles Owen Rice, the crusading Pittsburgh labor priest who fought in the 1940s against Communists in the United Electrical Workers, later reflected: "McCarthyism was an era and a malignancy and it had an effect on liberals of a certain type who became ultra anticommunist; even some, who had been sensible and tolerant, began proclaiming that their anticommunism was as strong as anyone's . . . It is only a step from regarding the enemy as superhuman to regarding him as unhuman."[64]

Notes

Don Watson acknowledges his fruitful exchange with H.L. Mitchell during his declining years and wishes to thank Henry Anderson and Anne Loftis for their assistance.
1. Sanford D. Horwitt, *Let Them Call Me Rebel: Saul Alinsky, His Life and Legacy* (New York: Alfred A. Knopf, 1989), 242.
2. See Minutes of CIO Executive Committee, 27 October 1953, Washington, D.C., reel 18, Archives of Labor History and Urban Affairs, Wayne State University (hereafter cited as ALHUA).
3. Although none of the top officers were Communists, either organizationally or ideologically, Communists in the UPWA had 1930s roots in District One that included the Chicago stockyards. For background on the politics of the UPWA see Rick Halpern, *Down on the Killing Floor: Black and White Workers in Chicago's Packinghouses, 1904–54* (Urbana: University of Illinois Press, 1997), and Roger Horowitz, *Negro and White, Unite and Fight": A Social History of Industrial Unionism in Meatpacking, 1930–90* (Urbana: University of Illinois Press, 1997). Both books are based on extensive interviews by Halpern and Horowitz for the UPWA Oral History Project at the State Historical Society of Wisconsin. For how the UPWA saw itself, see Leslie F. Orear and Stephen H. Diamond, *Out of the Jungle; the Packinghouse Workers Fight for Justice and Equality* (n.p.: Hyde Park Press, 1968); For a different view, see David J. Saposs, *Communism in American Unions* (New York: McGraw-Hill, 1959), 202.
4. UPWA Executive Board Minutes, 26 January 1954, box 108-9, Papers of the United Packinghouse Workers of America, Wisconsin State Historical Society, Madison, Wisconsin (hereafter cited as UPWA); Les Orear, interview by author, Chicago, 22 October 1996.
5. Local 78 leader Jerry Breshears recalled, "The bracero program had never been of interest to the shed workers until they had lost the work." Jerry Breshears, interview by author, El Centro, Calif., 8 January 1980.
6. *Des Moines Register*, 5 May 1954.
7. Ken Gillie to John Riffe, 19 May 1954, box 434-5, UPWA.
8. Irwin DeShetler to Riffe, 15 June 1954, box 434-5, UPWA.
9. Orear, interview.
10. The McWilliams connection was built around his editorship of *The Nation*; for the Alinsky connection, see Horwitt, *Saul Alinsky*, 212–13, 236–8.
11. Helstein to Stephens, memo, 1 July 1954, box 143-15, UPWA.
12. Virgil Mitchell report, 6 July 1954, box 434-8, UPWA.
13. The fullest study of the Community Service Organization and the Industrial Areas

Foundation is Carl Tjerandsen, *Education for Citizenship: A Foundation's Experience* (Santa Cruz: Emil Schwartzhaupt Foundation, 1980).

14. The best source on the NAWU is the Southern Tenant Farmers Union papers on microfilm. Reels 32 through 43 cover the NAWU's birth until merger into the AMC. Papers of the Southern Tenant Farmers Union, available on microfilm at various sites (hereafter cited as STFU).
15. For Meany's viewpoint on subsidies, see Archie Robinson, *George Meany and His Times* (New York: Simon and Schuster 1981), 181.
16. Les Orear, staff member close to Helstein in Chicago, said, "I was not aware of any problem with Mitchell and his union. Nobody told me about it." Orear, interview.
17. John Henning, former assistant to Haggerty, interview by author, San Francisco, 7 December 1997.
18. Galarza to Meany, 10 June 1954, reel 38, STFU.
19. Mitchell to Galarza, 4 June 1954, reel 38, STFU; Meany to Mitchell, 9 February 1955, box 3-5, Schnitzler Papers, George Meany Memorial Archives, Silver Spring, Maryland (hereafter cited as GMMA).
20. R.J. Thomas to Walter Reuther, memo, 14 July 1954, box 62-15, CIO Washington Office, ALHUA; Mitchell to Meany, 3 August 1954, reel 38, STFU. For Victor Reuther's role, see Galarza to Mitchell, 6 November 1954.
21. As he warned Louisiana AFL attorney Paul Barker, "The CIO Packinghouse Workers, Communist influenced if not dominated, is moving in," Mitchell to Barker, 13 October 1954, reel 38, STFU.
22. For Mitchell's version of problems with UCAPAWA, see H . L. Mitchell, *Mean Things Happening in this Land* (Montclair, N.J.: Allenheld Osman, 1979), chaps. 13 and 14.
23. Mitchell to Galarza, 22 November 1954, reel 38, STFU.
24. Mitchell to Lloyd, 6 January 1955, reel 38, STFU; Mitchell to Twomey, 25 January 1955, reel 38, STFU.
25. Mitchell, memo, undated 1955, reel 39, STFU; For Helstein's viewpoint on Stephens, see Helstein, interview by Elizabeth Balanoff, box 7-5, Helstein Papers, Wisconsin State Historical Society.
26. See Hilton E. Hanna and Joseph Belsky, *The "Pat" Gorman Story . . . Picket and the Pen* (Yonkers, N.Y.: American Institute of Social Sciences, 1960), 295–97.
27. Gorman to Meany, 14 September 1956, reel 140-316, Papers of the Amalgamated Meatcutters and Butcher Workmen of North America, Wisconsin State Historical Society, Madison, Wisconsin (hereafter cited as AMC).
28. Widman to Stephens, 2 April 1955, box 126-9, UPWA.
29. Joe Ollman, weekly report, 8 January 1955, box 126-9, UPWA.
30. *Salinas Californian*, 29 February 1954, 6 October 1954.
31. Spangler and Santiestevan to De Shetler, 18 February 1955, box 126-9, UPWA; for a detailed reply to various charges, see Widman to Stephens, 2 April 1955, box 126-9 UPWA.
32. Galarza, Report to NAWU, 4 May 1955, box 12-11, Papers of Ernesto Galarza, Department of Special Collections, Green Library, Stanford University, Stanford, California (hereafter cited as EG Papers); Minutes, U.S. Section, Joint U.S.-Mexican Trade Union Comm., 1 June 1955, box 22-1, EG Papers.
33. For Victor Reuther's reasoning on not giving another grant, see Mitchell to Galarza, 8 March 1957, reel 40, STFU; for the "subversive" quote, see Mitchell to Reuther, 5 November 1957, reel 40, STFU.
34. Joe Ollman Field Report, 16 February 1958, box 149-1, UPWA; Tannehill to Stephens,

24 July 1958, box 149-1, UPWA; Minutes, U.S. Section, Joint U.S.-Mexican Trade Union Comm., 30 October 1957, box 22-1, EG Papers.
35. For Knowles' field activity philosophy, see Knowles to Helstein, 30 January 1959, box 144-1, UPWA; for overview of UPWA farm labor activity, see 1958–60 issues of *Packinghouse Worker*.
36. Mitchell to Livingston, 24 October 1958, box 46-12, Dept. of Org., GMMA.
37. Mitchell, memo, 8 January 1959, reel 42, STFU; Reuther to Mitchell, 9 January 1959, reel 42, STFU.
38. Ex. Council Minutes, 23 February 1959, Coll. 37, GMMA; on keeping Mitchell out of the drive, see Mitchell, memo, 12 January 1960, box 8-1, EG Papers.
39. Ex. Council Minutes, 21 May 1959, Coll. 37, GMMA; UPWA Officers Letter, 18 May 1959, reel 42, STFU.
40. Herb March, interview, United Packinghouse of America Oral History Project, Wisconsin State Historical Society, Madison, Wisconsin (hereafter cited as UPWAOHP).
41. Reuther to AFL-CIO Executive Council, 5 April 1961, box 306-3, Reuther Coll., ALHUA.
42. Galarza to Mitchell, 18 May 1959, reel 42, STFU; Smith to Livingston, 21 May 1959, box 46-3, Dept. of Org., GMMA; Mitchell to Galarza, 8 June 1959, reel 42, STFU.
43. Memorandum of Understanding, 21 May 1959, box 9-10, EG Papers.
44. Galarza to Mitchell, 14 July 1959, reel 42, STFU; Mitchell to Galarza, 20 July 1959, reel 42, STFU.
45. Smith to Livingston, 28 September 1959, box 46-12, Dept. of Org., GMMA.
46. Mitchell to Smith, 26 October 1959, box 59-10, Dept. of Org., GMMA.
47. Knowles to Helstein, 16 November 1959, box 144-1, UPWA.
48. Mitchell, memo, 12 January 1960, box 8-1, EG Papers.
49. NAWU Ex. Board Minutes, 5–6 February 1960, reel 43, STFU.
50. Lloyd-Gorman to Meany, telegram, 15 January 1960, reel 43, STFU; Gorman to Lloyd-Poole, memo, 18 January 1960, roll 140-707, AMC; Meany to Mitchell, 15 February 1960, box 8-1, EG Papers.
51. Galarza to Mitchell, 16 April 1960, reel 43, STFU.
52. AFL-CIO Ex. Council Minutes, 3–6 May 1960, Coll. 37, GMMA; Mitchell, memo, 6 May 1960, reel 43, STFU.
53. Bennett to Mitchell, 18 May 1960, reel 43, STFU; Thomas to Mitchell, 25 May 1960, reel 43, STFU.
54. Gorman to Mitchell, telegram, 26 May 1960, reel 43, STFU; Mitchell to Meany, telegram, 27 May 1960, reel 43, STFU.
55. Gorman to Mitchell, 21 July 1960, reel 44, STFU; Meany to Lloyd, 6 October 1960, roll 140-712, AMC.
56. Gorman to Meany, 16 November 1960, roll 140-693, AMC; Meany to Gorman, 23 November 1960, roll 140-692, AMC.
57. Gorman to Meany, 16 November 1960, roll 140-693, AMC; when Mitchell learned Meany was investigating the charge, he wrote to Galarza and asked how many organizers from UPWA were actually on the AWOC payroll. Galarza, who had been off the staff for nearly a year, replied that he didn't know. For this exchange, see Mitchell to Galarza, 3 December 1960, box 5-1, EG Papers, and Galarza to Mitchell, 12 December 1960, reel 44, STFU; for the report from Daniel back to Meany, see Daniel to Meany, 9 December 1960, roll 140-679, AMC.
58. Gorman to Meany, 9 January 1961, roll 140-676, AMC.
59. The strike was covered almost daily in the *Imperial Valley Press* from mid-December

1960 until the first week of March 1961. The *New York Times* carried six stories on the strike.
60. Secretary of Labor Arthur Goldberg statement, 4 March 1961, box 460-2, UPWA.
61. Gorman to Smith, 26 January 1961, private papers, Henry Anderson; Gorman to Pitts, 6 March 1960, box 460-2, UPWA. See remarks of Knowles in minutes of UPWA educational conference, Stockton, 7 April 1960, box 395-2, UPWA.
62. Lloyd, Gorman to AMC leaders, undated (circa July 1961), reel 140-664, AMC.
63. For Gorman's role on *Salt of the Earth*, see James Lorence, *The Suppression of "Salt of the Earth," How Hollywood, Big Labor, and Politicians Blacklisted a Movie in Cold War America* (Albuquerque: University of New Mexico Press, 1999), 129, 199. For the "Coexistence" quote, see Helstein, interview by Halpern and Horowitz, box 7-9, Helstein Papers, UPWA.
64. Charles McCollester, ed., *Fighter With A Heart: Writings of Charles Owen Rice Pittsburgh Labor Priest* (Pittsburgh: University of Pittsburgh Press, 1996), 108.

The United Packinghouse Workers of America, Civil Rights, and the Communist Party in Chicago

Randi Storch

When the United Packinghouse Workers of America (UPWA) formed in 1943, workers in Chicago's meatpacking industry supported interracial and militant unionism. This union culture was characterized by a largely white ethnic leadership that openly reached out to black and white ethnic workers, who in turn promoted racial equality as one part of a larger agenda for workers' rights. Chicago meatpackers' vote for Herb March, a Jewish Communist trade unionist, to lead their district and to represent their locals on UPWA's international executive board symbolized this spirit. In the early 1930s, when the AFL and independent unions focused more directly on white skilled and semi-skilled workers, March began organizing black and white ethnic packinghouse workers into revolutionary dual unions. Through union defeats in the 1930s, many AFL unionists learned the unfavorable consequences of racial division among stockyard workers, and during World War II they joined March in building a strong interracial, industrial union.

Yet by 1953, the UPWA and the Communist Party had fully developed a new approach to race, characterized by a shift from an interracial focus to one centered on black workers and their civil rights. Blacks replaced whites in high-ranking union positions, the district union hall moved to a black neighborhood, and the union's business focused even more strongly on issues of civil rights. Herb March and his interracial ideals quickly fell out of favor with both his fellow leading unionists in Chicago's stockyards and with leaders of the Communist Party's national board. Fellow Communist and non-Communist unionists began to characterize March's insistence on an interracial approach to leadership as racism. Accused by fellow Communists and unionists of being a "white chauvinist," March

FIGURE 4.1 Herbert March speaking at the "Negro and White, Unite and Fight" rally, in minus eight-degree weather, January 1952. *Credit: Wisconsin Historical Society, Image Number Whi-6670.*

became demoralized and disgusted. He left Chicago, the stockyards industry, and the party. March's story is not an isolated one. In the early 1950s, the Communist Party revised its approach to race and encouraged the UPWA's shifting racial policies. The result was not only the UPWA's loss of many white ethnic Communist leaders, but also the alienation of its historic base among white ethnic workers. This chapter contextualizes the postwar changes that encouraged such new racial agendas, and seeks to explain some aspects of the relationship between the UPWA and Chicago's Communist Party.

By the 1940s, the Union Stockyards filled one square mile, five miles southwest of Chicago's downtown Loop. Forming one of the largest industrial concentrations in the nation, the stockyards were the home not only to the "big three" packers—Armour, Swift, and Wilson, each employing five to seven thousand men and women—but also to smaller houses such as P. D. Brennan, Roberts & Oake, Miller & Hart, Agar, Reliable, and Illinois Meat, each employing between one and five hundred workers. By the late 1940s, around 30,000 workers labored in the Union Stockyards' slaughterhouses, processing mills, and livestock pens.[1]

The Back-of-the-Yards neighborhood that joined the yards, and the neighborhood just over a mile to its east, Bronzeville, allowed stockyard employers to draw on a heterogeneous workforce. Several Slavic groups (with Polish most numerous), a scattering of other European immigrant groups, and Mexicans, living in the Back-of-the-Yards neighborhood, had worked in the stockyards since the turn of the century. African American workers living in the city's black belt, however, began working in the yards in significant numbers only during and after World War I.

World War II changed the racial composition of Chicago's packinghouse workers. Wartime labor shortages allowed many white workers to leave the stockyards for more lucrative employment, creating opportunities for thousands of new African American migrants from the South. By the end of the war, black employment in Chicago's stockyards reached 40 percent of the total workforce.[2]

Communist trade unionists, who had earned leadership positions throughout Chicago's UPWA locals, set out to integrate these new black workers into the stockyards' militant culture. Communists supported black workers' notion that the union could be used for both racial equality and economic security. In using the union to better their position at work and in the city, African Americans increasingly came to respect Communist unionists. One African American, who came to work at Wilson's packinghouse at the beginning of the war, remembered why the Communist Party was so appealing: "I was interested in the black masses and I thought these guys had the right answer." Another recalled, "We wanted to get free from where we were . . . I didn't care who helped us. Help us, you know, that was the general attitude."[3]

Throughout the war, Communists pushed these new black recruits into leadership positions where they worked in coalition with white leftists and centrists in the union. Herb March, district director of the UPWA, put new black militants such as Sam Parks and Charles Hayes in touch with white Communists in Wilson's plant. Carl Nelson worked as a pipe coverer, Joe Zabritski was a pipe fitter, and Anton Pasinski worked in the beef-cutting department. Together with Parks and Hayes, this group challenged conservative unionists' control in the plant and offered their own militant leadership to Wilson's workers. Sam Parks remembered how this interracial coalition succeeded in forcing the integration of an all-white sliced bacon department. Hog and beef kill workers walked off the job. In their bloody overalls and with their knives, they marched into the company's office, sat on the desks, and demanded integration. Parks recalled that the secretaries were frightened and "thought the revolution had come."[4] John Wrublewski, a worker who was not a Communist, supported this aggressive coalition of black and white Communists and non-Communists even though they were (in his words) "kind of out there" because, he explained, they "were a hell of a lot better than what we was used to having. . . . These guys were ready and willing to fight."[5]

Certainly not all new African American workers became Communists, but in the 1940s Communists believed that their greatest number of recruits were from these new packinghouse laborers, who tended to be more committed to racial equality than the generation of African American packinghouse workers who had entered the yards during and after World War I. In fact, many willingly joined with white Communists to fight in-plant (and later community-wide) racial discrimination. In several important cases, black unionists allied with white Communist unionists and won control of UPWA local leadership positions by pushing militancy and bringing attention to racial grievances.[6]

By the late 1940s, local conditions in Chicago's stockyards combined with international events to change the racial focus of the UPWA and the role of its Communist leaders. In 1947 the Taft-Hartley Act attempted to silence the UPWA's left leadership. When UPWA international officials refused to sign non-Communist affidavits required by the act, AFL unions launched raids on some UPWA locals. Alongside this grim domestic scene, the Cold War brewed abroad, turning wartime allies into bitter enemies. In this context, the UPWA launched its second postwar strike for wage increases. The Taft-Hartley Act's provision for a sixty-day strike notification hurt workers' ability to act spontaneously and allowed packers to prepare for a production stoppage. The law's injunctions, moreover, severely limited picket activity and created significant court costs for the union. To make matters worse, packinghouse workers did not unify around this 1948 strike as they had in 1946. This time the AFL's Amalgamated Meat Cutters secretly settled with the packers, creating dissension among workers and allowing meat production to continue at a limited rate. Although Chicago's showing was strong and a number of community organizations supported the union, after thirteen weeks strikers trickled back to work, forcing UPWA leaders to settle for the company's nine-cent offer.[7]

Rather than give in to this defeat, the UPWA rebuilt its locals around a civil rights program focused on racial equality at work and in the community. Following the 1948 strike defeat, UPWA leaders noted decreased union support, particularly from white unionists. In Swift Local 28, union membership fell from a high in 1948 of 86 percent to an all-time low, just one year later, of 45 percent.[8] In order to revive shop-floor organization and build bridges between whites and the increased number of black workers on the shop floor, the UPWA's executive board arranged for Fisk University's Race Relations Institute to conduct a series of surveys of racial attitudes among its union members. Ralph Helstein, UPWA president, recalled his motivation for the surveys: "I felt there had to be something affirmative going on outside of an area in which the companies could screw us."[9] The surveys not only documented the high level of African American activism in the union and the continuation of discriminatory practices in the plants, they sparked a number of anti-discrimination activities that the union began to champion in 1949. By 1950 Chicago's UPWA district had an Anti-Discrimination department charged with the goal of eliminating discriminatory practices in plants and in the communities where their workers lived. In addition to integrating all-white departments in the plants, training blacks so they could qualify for apprenticeships in the mechanical gangs, and using grievance procedures to push against racist shop floor practices, the locals' Anti-Discrimination departments worked to stop employer discrimination against applicants. Its leaders fought various forms of discrimination in the city, thereby broadening their attack against discrimination at work and in workers' communities.

Black and white Communists were central to the promotion of this new UPWA agenda. Despite the provisions of the Taft-Hartley Act and the resignations of some Communists from union offices, party unionists did not become isolated in the union. Instead, several Communist union leaders resigned from their local offices, only to be replaced by other Communists, who formally resigned from party membership and signed Taft-Hartley affidavits, but who remained close to Communist circles. Herb March relinquished his post as Chicago's UPWA district director but continued to advise Armour's Local 347 until he was put on as a union organizer by an overwhelming vote of the membership.[10] Communist trade unionists seemed impervious to right-wing attacks, even in their own union, because they successfully negotiated left-center coalitions and because, after the failed 1948 strike, they too looked to civil rights as a constructive area in which to rebuild their union. This focus on civil rights represented a return to an agenda that Communists had long pushed.

As early as 1928, the Communist Party articulated its position for black self-determination. The position, modeled on developments in czarist Russia, was designed to organize African Americans in both the North and the South. In the South, the argument went, African Americans composed a dispossessed nation, with unfulfilled rights to land and self-government. Thus the fight for self-determination in the South was a fight for black nationhood. In the North, however, rather than push for nationhood, party leaders directed activists to work for interracial solidarity, which Chicago labor and community leaders did with vigor. They organized protests on behalf of the black men falsely accused of attacking a white woman in Scottsboro, Alabama, formed councils of unemployed black and white workers, and tried to form racially integrated unions. Chicago's Communists prided themselves on interracial action and programs.[11]

During World War II, however, the focus of the party shifted to winning the war and defeating fascism. Even in their struggle for the establishment of a Fair Employment Practices Commission to end discriminatory hiring on government contracts, some Communists, such as African American party leader Harry Haywood realized that most party leaders were distracted with the war. Although packinghouse party members worked to recruit black members, national party struggles for racial justice took a back seat to the defeat of Germany. Haywood found that instead of the party keeping its leading role on civil rights, it fell behind the leadership of the National Association for the Advancement of Colored People (NAACP) and A. Philip Randolph.[12] Moreover, in the glow of the wartime alliance between the United States and the Soviet Union, party leaders in 1944 followed the lead of party secretary Earl Browder and voted to dissolve the party and replace it with the Communist Political Association. Some Communists thought that by dissolving the party, leaders were also planning to permanently dilute their active and militant positions, particularly as they related to race.

Emerging from the war, the American Communist Party underwent a crisis in its leadership that resulted in a shift away from the party's moderate wartime policies of cooperating with industrial capitalists and working within the Democratic Party.[13] As a result, the party rejected Browder and his wartime approach and restored the party's status as a revolutionary organization. The party also returned to a more militant posture on racial issues. Communist Party trade unionists' interest in revitalizing civil rights activity coincided with both the agenda of newly politicized African Americans in the UPWA and with the new focus of the American Communist Party. Consequently, the divisions that emerged within Chicago's UPWA in the late 1940s and early 1950s, due to its new focus on black workers, were reflected in debates within the Communist Party as the party developed its own program on race.

Within the national party leadership, Claudia Jones, a black Communist from the West Indies, called for a change in the party's position on race, and Harry Haywood, a black Communist from Chicago, demanded that the party reestablish its program for black self-determination. This policy, supported by young black Communist members, saw black self-determination as a key to a newly revitalized revolutionary program for African Americans.[14]

The party's leadership though, led by Eugene Dennis, articulated a watered-down version of this position. Instead of self-determination for African Americans being central to the realization of socialism, party leaders saw a program of electoral reform and coalition building as more important to the party's future. Dennis remarked:

> If the American people, the labor movement in alliance with the great Negro People and all progressive and democratic forces, can check and defeat the onslaught of pro-fascist monopoly reaction, and bring into power, as an important phase of that struggle, a progressive presidential ticket and Congress in 1948, with all that this would entail, many things would be possible, including, at least, tremendous strides toward the full realization of equal rights of the Negro People in the Black Belt.[15]

As national party leaders struggled over a race policy, Chicago's Communists witnessed an overall decline in their black membership. By 1949, Chicago's Communist leaders believed that the party had lost the vanguard role it once held in Chicago's Black Belt. Competition with the NAACP, the Urban League, and community groups meant that the Communist Party was no longer the most visible proponent of black and white unity. And even more egregious to party leaders was the fact that reformist groups altogether barred Communists from some race-based coalitions such as the Illinois Fair Employment Practices Commission.[16]

Communist leaders feared that the success of these moderate civil rights groups in the African American community would lead blacks in general to continue to exclude Communists from their racial reform activities. Chicago's party leaders therefore advocated united front activity whereby Communists would join with reformist groups to lead the further organization of African Americans. Chicago's party leaders encouraged their rank and file to join the NAACP, the black Elk fraternal organization, and African American churches. The party's new stage in black liberation, announced in 1949, emphasized Communists' need to "appreciate . . . unity as indispensable."[17]

This new phase of party activity fit neatly with increased activism that was occurring among Chicago's newly expanded black community and with the priorities that UPWA leaders developed after their 1948 strike defeat. With their central focus on anti-discrimination, Communist trade unionists and their allies now took the lead in revitalizing their union and in bringing race issues to the community. In Armour's Local 347, party leader Herb March coordinated the local's attack against Armour's unwillingness to hire blacks as clerical and sales representatives. The success of noontime rallies, letter writing campaigns, and newspaper publicity reinforced black workers' support of the union, the union's commitment to race, and the centrality of unionists (many of whom were Communists) who cared about civil rights.

While making strides in their stand against racism in the workplace, the UPWA's District Anti-Discrimination Committee still considered the "elimination of discrimination in the communities where its members reside" as one of its most important mandates. They therefore continued a program of ending discrimination in housing, taverns, restaurants, theaters, and hotels.[18]

Particularly important were the union's efforts in fighting racial violence that resulted from housing controversies in Chicago's neighborhoods. When some blacks, including Frank Brown, a UPWA program coordinator, moved into Trumbull Park, a government-owned housing project, violent white protests ensued. Charles Hayes, newly elected district director of UPWA, and other union leaders marched in an official capacity against the violence in the project. Party unionists and their supporters made persuasive arguments to UPWA convention delegates and convinced the international union to formally denounce the attacks. While other unions backed down from taking a firm stand on civil rights, the UPWA solicited its members in their homes and encouraged them to support interracial housing.[19]

Though the UPWA's leaders sanctioned most of its members' anti-discrimination activity, some Chicago leaders acted independently of the international. Much of this action centered around Sam Parks, who remained a very close ally of the Communist Party after formally resigning from it and who used his role as chair of the district's Anti-Discrimination Committee as a base for action. Parks allied himself in the community with the Communist-led Civil Rights Congress and with the Negro Labor Council, where Communists actively sought to promote united-front activities. Parks also worked closely with Communists and other supportive packinghouse workers in the Anti-Discrimination Committee's activities. For example, by leading a mass mobilization of automobile and packinghouse workers, Sam Parks joined with other left-wing Chicago trade unionists to win control of the local NAACP branch from moderates. Local stewards in meatpacking and auto encouraged active unionists to join the NAACP by recruiting in their shop departments. Such organizing resulted in the election of UAW militant Willoughby Abner to leadership.[20] Parks also used his leadership skills to campaign against discrimination in black belt businesses that refused to hire African Americans. Joining with three other packinghouse workers, Parks sat in at Goldblatt's lunch counter over the store's discriminatory policy against allowing blacks and Mexicans to eat there.[21]

Such activity also influenced anti-discrimination activity among Mexican workers. Communist Party members and union veterans Refugio Martinez and R. Ramirez organized against immigration agents' random attacks on the Mexican American community in their search for undocumented immigrants. A delegation from several Chicago locals visited the head of the immigration department in Chicago to protest these actions and reported a decrease in the attacks after their visit. At the same time, they coordinated with members of other unions a labor committee in defense of Mexican Americans.[22]

By 1952 the union and the Communists within it had proved they were able to withstand the political turmoil of the late 1940s and early 1950s, including Henry Wallace's 1948 campaign, the Congress of Industrial Organization's (CIO) expulsions, and Joseph McCarthy's witch hunts. Together they showed that their dedication to racial equality and workers' democracy could successfully challenge the increasing bureaucracy and political narrowness that was developing in other CIO unions during this period.

Yet while this direction created new activism against racist practices at work and invigorated networks of racial activists in Chicago, the UPWA's new emphasis on civil rights created internal conflicts. The union's decision to rebuild around its black membership discouraged many in its white membership, and growing black insurgency in the union increasingly concerned moderate white unionists. This tension came to a head when the union hall was relocated from Marshfield, a Polish neighborhood, to a new location in the African American community, at Forty-ninth street and Wabash, where the former International Workers' Order building became available for purchase. White workers then stopped attending meetings. Ford Bartlett remarked, "The reason I don't go is all the meetings are at 48th and Wabash and it's all colored there." Anthony Masiello, a semiskilled butcher from Swift, stated, "when you go to meetings there are just four or five white and 200 colored. Well . . . the majority in the plant are colored, by far . . . the colored talk 'colored troubles,' so the whites don't want to go to the Hall."[23] With the continued decline in numbers of white workers in Chicago's meatpacking plants, blacks increasingly filled the union and the positions in it, reinforcing whites' conviction that the union was no longer concerned with them.

Within the divisive climate of the Cold War, some disgruntled white workers associated the UPWA's racial agenda with Communism. Rentals of the union's new hall seemed to confirm this notion. By continually renting its space to Communist-supported groups and activities such as a birthday ball committee for William Z. Foster (who replaced Browder as national head of the Communist Party of the USA), a dinner for Claude Lightfoot, who was a new black member of the Communist Party's national committee, and a concert-rally by black singer Paul Robeson, district leaders of the union promoted the close association of black rights and Communism. The white members of Chicago's UPWA locals were not alone in identifying such a relationship. Even earlier than Chicago's locals did, white packinghouse workers in Nebraska, Kansas, Missouri, and Iowa conflated the UPWA's anti-discrimination work with Communism.[24]

Such connections between Communism and black rights were reinforced when the House of Representatives' Committee on Un-American Activities (HUAC) came to Chicago to interrogate suspected Communists in the UPWA. The *Chicago Tribune* gave front-page coverage to such stories as "Ex-Communist Tells of Union Infiltration" and "Charge Union Under Thumb of Kremlin Agents." Fellow unionists read the confession of Roy Thompson, black union leader, that he joined one of the party's three cells in the Armour plant because Communists promised that they would fight for black rights. In his testimony Thompson claimed, "I was sold on the idea that I should join the Communist Party, on the grounds that the Communist Party was interested in the affairs of the Negro and the advancement of all minority groups." While other union leaders were not as outspoken in their testimony, the presence of such leaders as Sam Parks and Leon Beverly before the committee simply confirmed to many white ethnic unionists that the union and its focus on black rights was due to the presence of Communists in their leadership. Although the *Daily Worker* tried to shrug off the effect of HUAC, its strains were felt at home.[25]

In addition to accentuating internal union divisions, the UPWA's racial agenda exacerbated conflicts that were occurring in Communist circles. In 1949, Pettis Perry, a member of both the party's national board and its Negro Commission, contributed an article to *Political Affairs*, the party's theoretical journal, in which he focused on racism within the party, a phenomenon he labeled "white chauvinism." The ensuing party campaign—the white chauvinism campaign—was targeted against party members in an effort to eliminate all racist elements and thereby to prepare the party to be the vanguard of racial activism. In the midst of the Cold War and the domestic red scare, however, this campaign turned former friends and allies against one another. Although the campaign exposed traces of racism within the party, its assumptions and tactics fostered hostility and suspicion between party members and thereby exacerbated the party's external problems.[26]

Such tensions escalated when a newly formed black caucus in Chicago's UPWA district, led by black Communists, pushed for more black union leadership. In the Armour plant, where the union had been built on interracial solidarity, black union activists tried to get rid of their local president Joe Bezenhoffer, who was white, and successfully replaced Harold Neilson, also white and Herb March's replacement for district director, with a black union leader, Charles Hayes. Members of the caucus did not always agree with each other (several of its members, for example, opposed Hayes's bid to serve as district director), but they were united in their desire for black leadership. White Communists, however, did not quickly or enthusiastically embrace such a perspective. Earl Durham, black party leader in Chicago, remembered that "some of them supported the idea but some of them weren't quite sure that the workers were ready for it." This hesitation alienated black caucus members from white Communists. Some felt betrayed. Durham explained that although white workers may never have been ready for black leadership, they also weren't ready for socialism, and that did not stop white Communists from trying to recruit them.[27]

In Chicago, Herb March's experience reveals the destructive path that the change in union culture had on the party's ranks. In 1951 party members asked March to pick up Leon Beverly, local UPWA president, and attend a meeting. There Sam Kushner and Claude Lightfoot, Chicago party leaders, informed March that in his absence he had been tried and found guilty of white chauvinism. They alleged that March prevented black women from taking leadership positions within his local union. March later recalled that he wanted to run for district secretary because, he argued, "I could take positions on all sorts of things that maybe other people can't, and the council presents black and white together."[28] Regardless, fellow party activists believed he was trying to prevent the political development of future black leaders. After consulting Abe Fineglass, Communist leader of the Fur and Leather Workers' Union, about the possibility of making an appeal, March took his case to party leader William Z. Foster, who promised March that he would publicly attack the charges against him in an article against the white chauvinist campaign. Although Foster's 1953 article on labor unity directed Communists to not use white chauvinist charges gratuitously and the national board directed March to go back to Chicago and to continue his work, local leaders continued to undermine March at home, paving the way for new UPWA leaders. Disheartened and discouraged, March and his family left Chicago's stockyards, the UPWA, and the Communist Party, the passions to which they had dedicated their lives.[29] The controversy within the party over March fueled the rise of black insurgency in the union. Both trends created conditions that effectively ended Communist trade unionists' push for an active interracial union agenda in Chicago's UPWA.

From the early 1950s until plant closings began in the mid-to-late 1960s, white workers became convinced that the union had gone too far in its racial program. It was one thing to work against discrimination as part of a larger union agenda when the union was largely composed of white ethnic workers, and quite another to push black issues and black leaders to the fore while whites remained a minority on the shopfloor. Thus while the left-center coalition of the UPWA could point to civil rights achievements at a time when labor more generally was turning its back to such moral stands, most of its white members were not converted into civil rights activists but instead became alienated from the militant interracial traditions and community of the UPWA.

Within the context of Chicago's changing demography, the Cold War's deleterious effects on American trade unionism, and UPWA's post-1948 union agenda, the American Communist Party developed a new line on race. In many ways, the combination of these forces saved the UPWA from moving to a bureaucratic and unresponsive union. Instead of moving in such a direction, the UPWA's international leadership encouraged its locals to focus on their own issues and to act against perceived problems affecting their members. In the case of Chicago's locals, unionists struggled for social justice and racial equality on the shopfloor and throughout the city. Other CIO unions' structure and politics, like those of the United Auto Workers (UAW), shifted in the opposite direction during the war and postwar years. With the UAW's purge of Communists from its ranks and the ascendance of a top-heavy administration maintaining a tight grip on its locals' leaders, support for social justice predominately came from top officials.[30] Yet while Chicago's UPWA's activism brewed from below, its political and social changes isolated Chicago's white ethnic workers and signaled the decline of militant interracial activism.

Herbert Hill has called for historians to expose the racism inherent in the labor movement in the postwar period.[31] In examining this question, however, it is not sufficient to describe white unionists opposing the goals of black unionists or black militants, or to reveal that the attitudes of white unionists in the 1940s and 1950s were different from the racial attitudes of academic liberals in the 2000s. Instead, we need to understand that racial attitudes were not inherent and unchanging among America's unionists, but complex and often conditional. The interracial, left-center coalition of Chicago's UPWA local leadership allowed its union to stand above the rest of the CIO in making a stand for social democracy. And yet in the tense years of the Cold War, anticommunism and black militancy reinforced white ethnic workers' racism and alienated white workers from those who pushed for black workers' equality.

Notes

1. "General Statistics For Standard Metropolitan Areas, By Industry," *Census of Manufacturers: 1947*, vol. 3 (Washington, D.C.: Government Publishing Office, 1950), 183; Rick Halpern and Roger Horowitz, *Meatpackers: An Oral History of Black Packinghouse Workers and Their Struggle For Racial and Economic Equality* (New York: Monthly Review Press, 1999), 27; Theodore Purcell, *The Worker Speaks His Mind on Company and Union* (Cambridge: Harvard University Press, 1954), 3–4; Rick Halpern, *Down on the Killing Floor: Black and White Workers in Chicago's Packinghouses, 1904–54* (Urbana: University of Illinois Press, 1997), 7–43.
2. Halpern, *Down on the Killing Floor*, 168.
3. First quote from interview with Sam Parks, 3 October 1985, United Packinghouse Workers of America Oral History Project (hereafter cited as UPWAOHP), State Historical Society of Wisconsin (hereafter cited as SHSW), Madison. Second quote from interview with Charles Hayes, 27 May 1986, UPWAOHP.
4. Parks, interview, 3 October 1985, UPWAOHP.
5. John Wrublewski is quoted in Halpern, *Down on the Killing Floor*, 179–180.
6. Ibid., 169, 180; For other examples in the Armour and Wilson plants see Carl Nelson's Affidavit, 12 February 1959, Box X-9, file 1934–1954, Chicago Police Files, Chicago Historical Society.

7. "Filing Requirements of Taft Hartley," n.d., Box 44, File 10; "Assessing the Strike," 9 June 1948, Box 452, Folder 14; "Anti-Reds in Packing Union Threaten Revolt," *Chicago Daily News*, 1 July 1948, Box 50, Folder 7; Letter from George Kovacevich to Ralph Helstein, 13 September 1948, Box 50, Folder 7, UPWA Papers, SHSW; Halpern, *Down on the Killing Floor*, 227–245.
8. Purcell, *The Worker Speaks His Mind*, 64; Halpern, *Down on the Killing Floor*, 237.
9. Helstein, quoted in Roger Horowitz, *"Negro and White Unite and Fight!": A Social History of Industrial Unionism in Meatpacking, 1930–1990* (Urbana: University of Illinois Press, 1997), 221.
10. Affidavit by Carl Nelson, 12 February 1959, Chicago Police Files, Chicago Historical Society; Affidavit by A.T. Stephens, 22 November 1958, File 287, Folder 3; International Executive Board Meeting, 3–4 June 1948, Box 29, Folder 3, UPWA papers, SHSW.
11. Randi Storch, "Shades of Red: The Communist Party and Chicago's Workers, 1928–1939" (Ph.D. diss., University of Illinois at Urbana Champaign, 1998), especially 12–77 and 155–195.
12. Harry Haywood, *Black Bolshevik: Autobiography of an Afro-American Communist* (Chicago: Liberator Press, 1978), 499.
13. James R. Barrett, *William Z. Foster and the Tragedy of American Radicalism* (Urbana: University of Illinois Press, 1999), 226–229; Edward Johanningsmeier, *Forging American Communism: The Life of William Z. Foster* (Princeton: Princeton University Press, 1994), 293–313; James Ryan, *Earl Browder: The Failure of American Communism* (Tuscaloosa: University of Alabama, 1997), 224–245.
14. Haywood, *Black Bolshevik*, 543–544.
15. Eugene Dennis quoted in Haywood, *Black Bolshevik*, 557.
16. G. Lightfoot, "Fluctuation Among Negro Members," *The Party Forum* (26 May 1949): 2, 4; "A New Stage of Negro Liberation Struggle," *The Party Forum* (22 October 1949): 4. For an explanation of the Communist party's influence in Chicago in the 1930s see Storch, "Shades of Red," especially 12–77 and 155–195.
17. "New Stage of Negro Liberation Struggle," *The Party Forum* (22 October 1949): 3.
18. UPWA Anti-Discrimination Program, 19 January 1951, Box 344, Folder 15, UPWA Papers, SHSW.
19. Anti-discrimination Report, 26 April 1952, Box 348, File 14, Proceedings of the 9th Convention of the UPWA; also see "Will the KKK ride in Chicago?" Box 447, File 6; "Council Against Discrimination of Greater Chicago," 1 July 1952, Box 347, File 8, UPWA Papers, SHSW.
20. Richard Sauders, Todd Tate, and Annie Collins Jackson, interview, 13 September 1985, UPWAOHP, SHSW; Christopher Robert Reed, *The Chicago NAACP and the Rise of Black Professional Leadership, 1910–1966* (Bloomington: Indiana University Press, 1997), 161–187.
21. Anti-Discrimination Committee Reports, 1952, Box 348, File 14, UPWA Papers, SHSW. Each year the Anti-Discrimination Committee gave reports to the district convention. See 1953, for example; Also, Halpern, *Down on the Killing Floor*, 241.
22. Anti-Discrimination Committee Report, 8 June 1952, Box 348, Folder 14; District Anti-Discrimination Report to District Convention, 1953, UPWA Papers, SHSW.
23. Ford Bartlett, quoted in Purcell, *Worker Speaks His Mind*, 210; Anthony Masiello, quoted in Purcell, *Worker Speaks His Mind*, 202.
24. Wilson Warren, "The Limits of Social Democratic Unionism in Midwestern Meatpacking Communities: Patterns of Internal Strife, 1948–1955," in *Unionizing the Jungles:*

Labor and Community in the Twentieth Century Meatpacking Industry, ed. Shelton Stromquist and Marvin Bergman (Iowa City: University of Iowa Press, 1997), 128–158.
25. "Ex-Communist Tells of Union Infiltration," *Chicago Tribune*, 5 September 1952; "Charge Union Under Thumb of Kremlin Agents," *Chicago Tribune*, 5 September 1952; House Committee on Un-American Activities, *Hearings On Communist Activities in the Chicago Area—Part 2*, 82d Cong., 2d sess., 1952; "Negro Unionist Tells Un-Americans to Hunt Un-Americans in KKK," *Daily Worker*, 5 September 1952.
26. Haywood, *Black Bolshevik*, 586–598.
27. Earl Durham, interview by author, Chicago, Illinois, January 2000.
28. Herb March, interview, 21 October 1986, UPWAOHP, SHSW.
29. Halpern, *Down on the Killing Floor*, 243–244; Herb March, interview, 21 October 1986, UPWAOHP, SHSW; see also Gerald Zahavi, "Passionate Commitments: Race, Sex and Communism at Schenectady General Electric, 1932–1954," *Journal of American History* 83 (September 1996): 514–548.
30. Robert Zeiger, *The CIO, 1935–1955* (Chapel Hill: University of North Carolina Press, 1995), 347; Martin Halpern, *UAW Politics in the Cold War Era* (Albany: SUNY Press, 1988), 246–248, 267; Nelson Lichtenstein, *Labor's War at Home: The CIO in World War II* (Cambridge: Cambridge University Press, 1982), 283, 237, 241; Harvey Levenstein, *Communism, Anti-Communism, and the CIO* (Connecticut: Greenwood Press, 1981), 330–340.
31. Herbert Hill, "The Problem of Race in American Labor History," *Reviews in American History* 24 (1996): 190. Also see the exchange between Herbert Hill and Nelson Lichtenstein in *New Politics* 7 (winter 1999): 133–163.

"An Anarchist with a Program"

East Coast Shipyard Workers, the Labor Left, and the Origins of Cold War Unionism

☼

DAVID PALMER

For East Coast shipbuilding trade unionists, the Cold War began before the end of World War II. A broad left-wing developed in the major Atlantic Coast shipyards of the Northeast during the early 1940s that became the target of anticommunist business, government, and union leaders. While the Communist Party of the United States (CPUSA) played a role in this shipyard labor left, other forces were equally significant even though they lacked the institutionalized organization of the CPUSA.

Labor historians often characterized Congress of Industrial Unions (CIO) unions as battlegrounds within which activists of the CPUSA "left" combated those of the anticommunist "right," with most workers consigned to being "supporters" of either the "left" or "right."[1] Some labor historians pit a presumably activist CPUSA against a trade union–oriented labor left that lacked political dynamism and diversity.[2] The experience of the Industrial Union of Marine and Shipbuilding Workers of America (IUMSWA) at the grassroots provides a different picture.[3] The World War II history of IUMSWA Local 16 at Federal Shipbuilding, Kearny, New Jersey illuminates both the complexities of the fierce anticommunism that characterized union and political life in America on the eve of the Cold War and the role of a broad labor left that was the target of this anticommunism. In the IUMSWA, the labor left went far beyond the rigid politics and practices of the CPUSA. Its essence was perhaps best captured by inside organizer Lou Kaplan, who explained his politics to Federal Shipyard workers with a very basic phrase: "I'm an anarchist with a program." The experience of this particular union local points toward a grassroots political explanation for American trade union decline in the second half of the twentieth century, a decline that was not reversed until a broad left was reestablished within the ranks of labor locally and nationally during the 1990s.[4]

Founded in 1933, the IUMSWA emerged from inside organizing, and it

85

dominated East Coast shipyard unionism by the end of the decade. Its first success, at New York Shipbuilding, Camden, New Jersey, preceded the formation of the breakaway CIO, and it was the earliest of the new industrial unions to become part of the CIO once it was formed. During the late 1930s, the IUMSWA's main organizing successes were concentrated in the Northeast, with major gains in the port of New York and North Jersey. In 1937, the IUMSWA won a union election at Federal Shipbuilding in Kearny, New Jersey. The yard was located between Newark and Jersey City, just across the Hudson River from Manhattan, a strategic location for the IUMSWA and the CIO.

By World War II, the shipbuilding industry employed more workers in America than any other, reaching a peak of 1,686,600 by 1943. Federal Ship, owned by U.S. Steel Corporation, had become one of the major shipbuilding employers in the Northeast and built more destroyers during the war than any other shipyard in the world. Given the industry's indispensibility during the war, the IUMSWA's ability to maintain production and worker morale made the union critical to an Allied victory. In this larger national drama, Federal Shipyard became a turbulent focus for the union when its earlier election victory seemed to vanish as tens of thousands of new non-union workers flooded into the two yards at Kearny and Newark.[5]

At Federal Ship, activists held a wide range of political views, reflecting in turn the varied outlooks of rank-and-file workers. On the right, anticommunists who identified with the Democratic and Republican parties, usually based in North Jersey urban machine politics, coalesced with socialists, often experienced shipbuilders from the River Clyde in Scotland. The left included leftwing Democrats, progressive Republicans, and Communist Party members and allies. Other independent leftists can best be described as highly pragmatic anarchists with philosophical roots in the American syndicalism of William Z. Foster's early years and the Industrial Workers of the World (IWW) of Bill Haywood and Eugene Debs.

John Green and Phil Van Gelder held the IUMSWA's first major offices and played key roles in organizing the union. They also shaped the IUMSWA's early political outlook and practice. Both of them belonged to the Socialist Party (SP), rather than the Communist Party, but were members of the SP's left faction, the Revolutionary Policy Committee, where they first met. Their politics and actions differed sharply with conservative SP trade unionists such as International Ladies Garment Workers Union (ILGWU) president David Dubinsky. Green and Van Gelder shared a similar socialist philosophy, but came from very different backgrounds.[6]

Green had worked as a shipbuilder on the Clyde during World War I, where he became involved in the militant shop stewards' upheaval then sweeping England and Scotland. He immigrated from Clydebank, Scotland to Philadelphia in 1923 and joined New York Ship in 1931. He coauthored the first preamble of the IUMSWA constitution, which reads like a classic summation of anarcho-syndicalism: "Through our Union we prepare ourselves for the Workers' struggle, not merely to win concessions of higher wages and shorter hours, but to abolish forever the system of exploitation that compels us to support with our labor an idle owning class."[7]

As the IUMSWA grew during the 1930s, Green became a close ally of James Carey, a native of South Jersey where Camden was situated.[8] During World War II, when Green became a vice president of the CIO, he dropped his socialist views and supported Carey's anticommunism. Green's shift reflected his alliances with anticommunist political forces that dominated significant parts of the Democratic Party in the Northeast, as well as his desire to limit the influence of those on the labor left who threatened his control over the IUMSWA.

John Green's Scottish heritage became his main identity within the shipyard union. He was not alone, for many Scottish shipbuilders found work in the American yards, retaining their brogue and culture but not always the radicalism of the Clyde. A number of Scottish shipyard union leaders identified with Green, including Peter Flynn of Federal Ship. Flynn had been a socialist in the old country like Green, but he rejected communism and he did not share Green's syndicalist past.[9]

In contrast to Green and Flynn, Phil Van Gelder believed in the American socialism associated with the tradition of Eugene Debs. Van Gelder also was drawn to the views of Norman Thomas, Debs's successor as leader of the SP. Much of Thomas's program, however, became the core of New Deal social policy, making it easy for Van Gelder to support the left wing of the Democratic Party when the SP fell apart in the late 1930s.[10]

Van Gelder assisted Green in organizing New York Ship in 1934 and became the IUMSWA's first national secretary-treasurer. Although Van Gelder accepted Norman Thomas's social democratic philosophy, he also advocated direct action in shipyard organizing. He stayed loyal to these sometimes contradictory political values his entire life and managed to maintain a pluralistic view of the left. Sometimes he worked in alliance with the Communist Party, and sometimes he openly opposed it. At no time, however, did he adopt the ideological anticommunism of leaders such as the United Electrical Worker's (UE) Carey of the CIO, or the ILGWU's Dubinsky, who initially was a leader in the CIO but then returned his union to the American Federation of Labor (AFL). Van Gelder advocated centralizing the IUMSWA after the disastrous 1937 New York Harbor shipyard strike, a position that shifted his outlook away from locally-focused direct action by the late 1930s. He had no "rank-and-file" experience like Green because he never worked in a shipyard. Nevertheless, his outlook reflected a perspective that could be found among many at the grassroots, which accounts for much of his popularity when he was a national officer in the IUMSWA. He represented one part of the spectrum of the IUMSWA's broad labor left during the pre-Cold War years. Appreciating his contributions to the IUMSWA is crucial to understanding the diverse left movement that succumbed to the onslaught of Cold War labor anticommunism.[11]

A majority of Federal Ship workers regarded themselves as New Dealers and supported the Democratic Party of Franklin D. Roosevelt. Some aligned themselves with the left wing of the union, but others included right-wing New Dealers who identified with Mayor Frank ("I am the law") Hague and his Democratic

Party machine in Jersey City. The political divisions that characterized Roosevelt's New Deal and that existed within the New Jersey Democratic Party under Hague's influence were mirrored in the IUMSWA's North Jersey union locals, including the Federal Shipyard local.

Hague ruled his city as an authoritarian with rabidly anticommunist politics. Because of his role as a power broker in the national Democratic Party, of which he was national vice chairman, he maintained dominance not just through local patronage and corruption, but also through his control of the distribution of Works Progress Administration (WPA) funds throughout New Jersey. From 1937 to 1939 the CIO, Norman Thomas, and the American Civil Liberties Union (ACLU) all challenged Hague's refusal to allow free speech, the right to assemble, and the right to organize unions within Jersey City. They sponsored demonstrations, meetings, and union organizing drives, all of which were met with vigilante mobs and police violence coordinated by Hague and his officials. The United States Supreme Court finally ruled against Hague in a major lawsuit involving freedom of speech. Within hours Hague invited the CIO into his city and welcomed one of the main organizations involved in opposing his rule: the IUMSWA. Green accepted Hague's invitation, and the IUMSWA became the first CIO union to hold a convention in Jersey City. Federal Ship's Local 16 became the sponsoring local, enhancing the power of anticommunist and pro-Hague union activists, while marginalizing those on the left within the local who continued to push for full political democracy and accountability in Jersey City and North Jersey generally.[12]

A surprising number of Federal Ship workers were registered as Republicans, but most supported the programs and spirit of the New Deal. One part of this group maintained local loyalties to the traditional urban machine-style Republican politics of Bergen County. Mayor Hague had to make deals with Republicans who dominated Bergen County, even as he controlled Jersey City within the county. Then there were those who believed in the Progressive Republican tradition more to the left, which was compatible with pro-New Deal views.[13]

John Dempsey stands out as the most prominent Local 16 leader identified with the Republican urban machine right wing. Mayor Hague's apparent moderation toward the IUMSWA may have come partly from political ties that his machine had with Local 16 officers such as Dempsey. Elected Local 16 president in July 1938, Dempsey believed in local union autonomy, but he also had major policy differences with left-wing leaders such as Nat Levin. As a Jersey City Republican in the midst of Hague's Democratic Party machine, Dempsey learned to work with political bosses. Hague found it advantageous to allow a small, if ineffective, minority of Republicans to operate in Jersey City, because some county jobs, such as those on the election board, required representation from both parties.[14]

Left-wing Local 16 welding steward Nat Levin considered Dempsey to be part of the forces that made it "very difficult to maintain a strong and decent organization." Lou Kaplan later became convinced that Dempsey built a corrupt political machine inside Local 16, using a patronage system among stewards and committeemen: "Dempsey [was] emblematic of what I considered a thief within the labor movement, because he was building his machine on the basis of lost time. That was the biggest dishonesty. But it was part of the labor movement as it was, part of the political movement . . . in Jersey City, Newark, and the area—how many pork choppers were on." Hague's machine clearly served as a model for Dempsey's organization in the yard.[15]

Dempsey surrounded himself with "strong arm guys," as Kaplan called them, to get his way in union meetings, but he also enjoyed a popular following as a local leader. Both the broad spectrum of local-level progressives and the IUMSWA national officers viewed Dempsey's potential power as a menace. Green was suspicious of Dempsey's independence on the right, just as he feared Nat Levin's on the left. Welder and union activist Terry Foy recalled that Dempsey "had a lot of stature. He was a very impressive . . . tall guy, heavy set, ruddy complexion, and spoke rather well. He handled himself well, and [was] tough." Besides ruling with an iron hand, Dempsey was a superb parliamentarian. Many workers, including rank-and-file welder Joe Peters, liked Dempsey's personal style, which symbolized union power to them. Dempsey built this following not just through dubious "lost time" payments, but also by personally encouraging workers like Peters to attend their department shop meetings. His greatest weakness, according to Foy, was that he surrounded himself with corrupt and self-serving men.[16]

Dempsey also won support as a local leader through his skill in making alliances. He got the backing of those who wanted more independence from the national union, but also cultivated ties with a number of loyalists in the national office. Green must have realized this when he helped promote Dempsey to IUMSWA national vice president at the 1939 Jersey City convention, the first CIO-affiliated event that Hague allowed in his city.[17]

The labor left also included Republicans. Terry Foy was the most significant labor left leader to emerge from the Republican pro-New Deal group. Like Dempsey, he had connections with Republican politicians in the area and understood how the Democratic Party machine of Mayor Frank Hague operated in Jersey City. Foy found employment at Federal Ship through Fred Hartley, the anti-labor Republican congressman who later co-authored the Taft-Hartley Act.[18]

Foy had never been in a union, but his father had been a LaFollete Republican, which made him receptive to the organizing then underway at Federal Ship. "I didn't know from unions . . . other than that you were supposed to work and get wages and make a living." When he first started, he saw workers around him wearing union buttons and decided to talk to the pipe shop steward about joining the CIO. "The CIO was in an organizing campaign all over Jersey at that particular time [1939]. . . . I figured it was to my best interests to be in the union." When Foy transferred to the welding department, shop steward Nat Levin encouraged him to become active in Local 16. Foy's natural leadership abilities soon emerged, and by 1943 he became night shift spokesman, joining Kaplan and the others as a leader of the left wing progressives.[19]

Local 16 was considered by many to be a stronghold of the Communist Party within the IUMSWA. At the grassroots level, however, the picture looked somewhat different. Most of those who were either in or identified with the CPUSA focused mainly on trade union activity in their daily contacts with workers. Nat Levin was the most prominent of these people. He entered Federal Ship as a volunteer organizer to assist with the organizing drive of 1936–37. His egalitarian outlook stemmed in part from early experience working in his father's carpentry trade, where he encountered workers of many different European backgrounds. He also had a strong commitment to combating racial prejudice against black and Hispanic workers. During World War II, he did not play as prominent a role in the left-wing opposition to Local 16's right-wing leadership as he had in the late 1930s. This was partly because his strong adherence to the no-strike pledge led him to focus his efforts on committees that aimed to increase production for the war effort. He continued to informally train leadership within the local, and was instrumental in recruiting workers like Terry Foy to the left-wing movement.[20]

Not all radicals were allied with the labor left. Mendy Mendelson, a very sectarian Trotskyist, was so anti-CPUSA that he worked actively for the Local 16 right-wing faction. He ran on Dempsey's anticommunist election slates and even provided secret information to Green about alleged CP activities at Federal Ship. Generalizing about Trotskyist organization—beyond Mendelson's activity—is difficult, because its presence at Federal was very small. There were also those in the CP who falsely accused some activists of being "Trotskyist" because they refused to adhere strictly to the Party line and discipline—an accusation made, for example, by Henry Tully against independently minded Lou Kaplan.[21]

Federal Ship's black union leaders at the grassroots were almost universally in the labor left and identified with the left wing of the New Deal. At the same time, most allied themselves with the CPUSA. Bob Monroe emerged as an important leader among the black trade unionists in the plate shop, one of Federal Ship's largest departments. Monroe had served as a precinct captain for the Jersey City Mayor Hague's machine, where he gained a rough education in corrupt urban politics. The progressives' stand for equality in the union later drew him to their ranks, and eventually he allied with the Communist Party. His powerful physical build made him valuable when Local 16 president John Dempsey's "goons" threatened the leaders of the progressives. He had excellent rapport with people and was an able speaker, which earned him the respect of many white workers and helped to reduce racial prejudice among the rank-and-file.[22]

Black workers were a critical group to organize, especially in the plate shop, one of the most militant locations in the yard. In contrast to other major shipyards in the Northeast, blacks worked at Federal Ship since the yard opened during World War I. They continued to occupy the lowest-paying, dirtiest, and physically most demanding positions, such as laborers, porters, reamers and drillers, red lead painters (done in the ships' inner bottoms), and helpers to skilled tradesmen. In the plate shop, blacks worked as "slingers," using heavy hammers to shape plates after they had been bent by machines. When Lou Kaplan first met these men, many of them belonged to the union but had no use for the current leadership. He sought to unite them with other progressives in the yard, arguing that the status of black workers would remain low if they stayed isolated.[23]

Al Elliot, another key black worker from the plate shop who joined the opposition, became active in left wing politics and was identified with the Communist Party. When the labor left openly challenged those who held power in Local 16 during 1943 and 1944, Elliot became the leading spokesman and candidate of the black workers. A third leader in this group, Antonio ("Tony") Tully, worked in the riveting department. Tully was born in Jamaica and then moved with his family to Panama. His father was Irish and his mother was Jamaican, but the family spoke fluent Spanish. He had several brothers at Federal, including Henry, his twin. While both Tony and Henry were active in Local 16 politics, Tony was the one most widely recognized as a rank-and-file leader. The Tully brothers also identified with the politics of the Communist Party, as did a number of black and Hispanic shipyard workers, because of the CP's stand against racial discrimination. They respected the leadership of Benjamin Davis, the black Communist city council member from Harlem who was outspoken on the needs of black people and the poor.[24]

Organizing Federal Ship's black workers into the union was critical for several reasons. First, they represented a major bloc of workers. At the height of the war, some 7,000 of the 40,000 workers at Federal's Kearny and Port Newark yards were black. Henry Tully, shop steward in the drilling and reaming department, maintained records indicating that 49 percent of that department's workers were black (African American or Caribbean), while 30 percent were Eastern European, 8 percent of Italian descent (mostly Sicilian), and only 11 percent were from English-speaking backgrounds (American-born, English, Scots, and Irish). Tully appreciated the extent of discrimination against those who did not speak English because of his mixed Jamaican-Panamanian background, and he saw a connection between prejudice against immigrants (European and non-European) and non-whites. He believed it was no coincidence that in his department, where the work was particularly difficult, noisy, and dirty, almost all of the department's workers were black or either non-English speaking Eastern Europeans, while only a handful were English-speaking white workers.[25]

Bringing black workers into the union became a matter of principle for those on the left, particularly Lou Kaplan and Nat Levin. In their view no democratic organization could sustain itself without justice and equality for all of its members, including non-whites. Levin was the first person at Federal to fight for the right of racial minorities to hold welding jobs. In the face of fierce verbal opposition from some white workers, especially those in the welding department, blacks gradually started to fill the new jobs. For some white union activists with more traditional politics, such as Terry Foy, racial equality became an entirely new experience when seen in these personal terms and explained by Nat Levin in his patient but uncompromising manner. For Levin, racial equality and unity gave expression to "the beautiful words of the preamble to the Constitution of the Union" with its non-discrimination declaration. It "was the guide for all of us in trying to build the organization."[26]

Flynn, Dempsey, and other Local 16 officers provided little support for the fight for equality, despite the fact that the IUMSWA officially, if not in practice, opposed discrimination. Green and Van Gelder had endorsed black participation in the labor movement as early as the 1935 New York Shipyard strike in Camden.

However, racial discrimination continued in most shipyards. The AFL had the worst record, but the IUMSWA also had its problems. Nationally the IUMSWA did not keep segregated seniority lists like the AFL, but a major push from progressives was needed to get the IUMSWA to take a stand against segregation in the workplace. In contrast to Federal Ship, virtually all skilled jobs at New York Ship (John Green's home local) remained exclusively white during World War II.[27]

White welders' resistance at Federal to blacks in their department broke down once blacks and whites got to know each other on the job. Joe Peters, a rank-and-file welder of second generation Lithuanian background and a Dempsey loyalist who never held a union post, remembered the development of camaraderie among white, black, and Hispanic workers. He favorably recalled memories of socializing at the end of the shift, when fellow workers visited each other's homes and learned about new customs, foods, and drinks. Problems of racial and ethnic prejudice at Federal Ship certainly were present during World War II, but racial discrimination and violent opposition to workplace integration did not dominate the union culture to the extent that it did in places like the Detroit auto plants or the Philadelphia transit system, where bitter race riots broke out.[28]

The link between Spanish-speaking and black workers provided another means of building labor left unity in Local 16. The Tully brothers, with their Panamanian background and fluent Spanish, brought Latin American workers into the ranks of the progressives. Their Jamaican roots, in turn, made it easy for them to develop strong ties with African Americans. There were many informal social networks linking these groups, which might best be described as Afro-Caribbean.[29]

The Tully brothers had a particular affinity with "Spanish" workers. Many were Cuban and Puerto Rican, but a number also hailed from Galicia, the Spanish province where shipbuilding dominated the economy. Henry Tully discovered, to his surprise, that he could not communicate with these men in Spanish, since they spoke Galician—a separate minority language. As a fellow immigrant, he identified closely with the Galicians and socialized with them in their neighborhood just east of Manhattan's Chinatown.[30]

However, the main leadership among the Hispanics came from one of their own—Victor Garcia, who was Puerto Rican. His left wing outlook gave him political connections to Tony Tully, Levin, Kaplan, and others in key areas of the yard. Although he worked as a lowly cleaner, his organizing skills enabled him to lead the smaller but very vocal group of Spanish-speaking workers, exerting an influence among them that matched the leadership of Elliot and Monroe among black workers. A popular speaker, Garcia regularly voiced his opinions at union meetings. He spoke English well, with a heavy accent. Henry Tully remembered how Garcia used these occasions to forcefully combat the prejudice of English-speaking union members and to educate them to change their attitudes.[31]

Independent leftists, perhaps best characterized as anarcho-syndicalists, sought to bridge the gap between the majority of white workers who identified with New Deal politics of the Roosevelt administration and a minority who identified with the Communist Party, including many black and Hispanic workers. Historian David Milton has described a syndicalist wing within the CPUSA during the 1940s and 1950s, which accounts for the remarkable independence of a number of labor leaders identified with the party. These included many leaders and staff organizers in the UE who refused to go along with the CPUSA directive to dissolve the union during the 1950s. Lou Kaplan was among these UE staffers who opposed CPUSA interference in the UE, even though he supported many of the party's political objectives. In the East Coast IUMSWA a decade earlier, Kaplan was without a doubt the union's most outstanding organizer, and he exemplified this independent left wing approach in his organizing.[32]

Kaplan grew up in New York City, where he was raised in a Jesuit Catholic orphanage and learned how to survive on the streets. His unusual upbringing and remarkable intellectual talents opened doors, allowing him to study at UCLA, where he got a B.A. in 1936 and an M.A. in journalism in 1938. That year he visited San Francisco, got swept up in the shipping strike then in progress, and began organizing with Harry Bridges' International Longshoremen and Warehousemen Union (ILWU). After a year he returned to the East Coast and worked at the Brewster Aeronautical plant in Port Newark, New Jersey, as a final inspector on the PBY Catalina bomber assembly line. There he worked as a volunteer organizer for the plant's UAW local, which sought to consolidate by increasing membership and participation. North Jersey UE activists convinced Kaplan in late 1941 to move to the Federal Shipyard, where his talents were more urgently needed.[33]

Kaplan worked initially as a rank-and-file ship fitter, organizing on the inside, and later as a full-time staff organizer for the IUMSWA between 1942 and 1946. He allied with the Communist Party, but disagreed with much of their national trade union line. While he upheld the World War II no-strike pledge, he did not do so in the rigid manner demanded by CP leaders. He believed that CP national trade union director Jack Stachel did not understand how to connect left-wing politics with rank-and-file workers' concerns and characterized Stachel as little more than "a tie salesman." In contrast, Kaplan adopted an intensely pragmatic approach that proved the key to his success as a trade union organizer.[34]

He routinely explained to shipyards workers that he was "an anarchist with a program" and denied that he was a party member, even though he was sympathetic with many of the objectives of the CPUSA. His political language tended to deflect anticommunist attacks from workers, though not from his enemies within the IUMSWA leadership. It also reflected the reality of shipbuilding's complex rank-and-file politics. Kaplan called himself an anarchist because he believed in radical politics and, at least in principle, supported socialism and workers' control of the economy. Above all, he encouraged direct action and defiance of illegitimate authority. All the while, his "program" stressed trade union democracy and on-the-job representation, decent wages and working conditions, and a range of very specific "straight" trade union objectives. Kaplan supported President Franklin D. Roosevelt and much of the New Deal, not unlike many on the left who also led militant strikes. Kaplan believed in radical socialism in the long-term, but he adopted realism tactically for the short-term. The main non-communist radical influences on him were the syndicalist socialism of immigrant shipyard workers from the Scottish Clydeside whom he encountered at the Kearny yard. The "anarchist" part of his politics was most influenced by the direct-action tactics of the Industrial Workers of the World (IWW), who had been strong among Philadelphia area port workers during World War I but whose influence continued through the early 1930s.[35]

If Kaplan can be regarded as the "anarchist with a program," Andy Reeder exemplified the direct action tactics of the IWW in practice. Reeder did not start out with progressive politics. He came from a conservative Republican working-class family in Philadelphia and as a teenager joined the local Ku Klux Klan because of his hatred of Catholics. He soon quit the KKK because he came to dislike their program as narrow and no answer to the unemployment and poverty of the 1930s. As the Depression deepened he left home, encountering the Wobblies and their direct-action tactics while riding freight trains in search of work. He later used these tactics when he got jobs in a number of non-union East Coast shipyards, including Bath Iron Works in Maine, Fore River in Quincy, Massachusetts, and Sun Ship in Chester, Pennsylvania. When he got a welding job at Federal Ship in the late 1930s, the radical organizers there were not Wobblies, but Communist and Socialist Party members and sympathizers who routinely used IWW direct-action tactics. He became an inside organizer for the IUMSWA because of his anger at the bad treatment of workers by yard supervisors and was fired from a number of locations, including Federal Ship. By this time, New York Ship had a very strong IUMSWA local, which made it possible for him to maintain his job with dignity. Like other shipyard union activists, he continued to assist organizing efforts beyond New York Ship.[36]

Reeder played a major undercover organizing role for Kaplan in the second Sun Ship drive during World War II and was elected president of IUMSWA Local 1 at New York Ship, by 1944 the union's largest local nationally. He had little use for intellectuals in the labor movement and never joined a left-wing organization, but he greatly admired Van Gelder, who workers called the "shipyard philosopher" (Van Gelder had briefly taught at Brown University before his involvement with union organizing), and Kaplan, whom he considered the finest organizer he had ever known. Reeder's perspective speaks to the breadth of the labor left in the East Coast shipyards during World War II and provides another illustration of the heterogeneity of the labor left beyond the CP.[37]

By 1940, Federal Ship had become the nation's most important builder of destroyers. Its significance to organized labor also derived from its location in the metropolitan region with the greatest number of shipyard workers: the New York–Newark area, with 90,900 workers out of 556,100 nationally. By 1942 the San Francisco area employed more shipbuilding workers, but on the East Coast, the New York–Newark area continued as the hub of shipbuilding, with the Federal Shipyard at its center. IUMSWA Local 16 had demanded a union shop at Federal Ship since its organizing victory and first contract negotiations in 1937. By 1941, Local 16 found it increasingly difficult to sign up new members and collect monthly dues on a person-to-person basis, so the local decided that survival depended on making union membership a condition of employment.[38]

The expiration of Local 16's contract with Federal Shipbuilding on 24 June

24 1941, took place in the context of a temporary agreement on new Atlantic Coast Zone Standards between the IUMSWA and the Atlantic shipbuilding industry, which included Federal. The IUMSWA hoped to avoid a strike because it wanted to assist with the national emergency President Roosevelt had declared in May in response to the expanding war in Europe. The IUMSWA's renunciation of strikes in the industry-wide shipbuilding agreement set the stage for the CIO's later acceptance of the no-strike pledge.[39]

Although Federal Shipbuilding agreed to pay the new wage rates, the IUMSWA appealed to the newly formed National Defense Mediation Board (NDMB) when the company refused the union shop demand. The NDMB recommended acceptance of a "maintenance of membership" clause requiring all who joined the union to remain members for the life of the contract, but it had no power to enforce the decision. U.S. Steel, which directed Federal Ship's policy, refused to comply, fearing implications for the steel industry. The NDMB decision and U.S. Steel resistance to it tested the federal government's power to regulate management-labor disputes, and it highlighted the centrality of the union security issue for trade unions.[40]

John Green and other IUMSWA leaders saw this decision as a victory, but many Local 16 members regarded the maintenance-of-membership compromise as a sell-out and no substitute for the closed shop. In July 1946, union members voted down the NDMB maintenance-of-membership recommendation by 1,422 to 1,203. By this time, however, the yard employed over 17,000 workers who would be affected by the decision. The union vote represented the preference of only a minority of Federal Shipyard workers, and Local 16 struggled for the next three years to involve the rapidly increasing non-union majority in the yard's union movement.[41]

Local 16 vice president Peter Flynn, with executive board approval, advocated membership endorsement of the NDMB proposal, and also called for a strike within forty-eight hours, if Federal Shipbuilding refused to agree to binding arbitration on the maintenance-of-membership clause. On 6 August, 12,000 workers went on strike, with a highly-disciplined mass picket over ten-deep and stretching a mile long, that blocked the yard's single entrance during shift changes. In response to this threat to a vital war industry, American Clothing Workers of America (ACWA) president Sidney Hillman, now Associate Director General of the Office of Production Management (OPM), convened a group for two weeks in Washington that included Federal Shipbuilding president Lynn Korndorff, IUMSWA president John Green, and various NDMB and Navy Department officials. When some officials raised the possibility of Naval seizure of the yard to break the impasse, Korndorff endorsed the idea to counter management's bad public image, while the IUMSWA supported a takeover, as long as there would be "guarantees that our collective bargaining rights will not be impaired by the transition."[42]

On 23 August, the eighteenth day of the strike, President Roosevelt finally ordered the Navy Department to assume full control of the Federal Shipyard. The IUMSWA's leadership believed that seizure would expedite enforcement of the NDMB's recommendation, but Secretary of the Navy Frank Knox did not concur with the NDMB on maintenance-of-membership. He instructed Admiral Harold Bowen, the officer who took charge of the yard, to follow standard Navy yard policy by maintaining prevailing wages, hours, and working conditions, but gave no concessions to the union. Bureaucracy soon bogged down Local 16 in its efforts to process mounting grievances and to collect dues. Daniel Ring of the Maritime Commission was installed as Admiral Bowen's assistant covering industrial relations and held ongoing discussions with Local 16 representatives, but little progress was made.[43]

In October elections, Local 16 members voted in Peter Flynn as the new president, and John Dempsey, who had been president two years earlier, as vice president. George Wright, the IUMSWA's national vice president, was re-elected to his third term as financial secretary. Al McNulty defeated Nat Levin for treasurer, creating a solid anti-left local executive. For the first time, John Green appeared to have a group of Local 16 officers who were loyal to the national office and his own increasingly anti-left views. Flynn's relationship with Green became strained, however, because of Flynn's inability to implement a clear plan for consolidating the local. After the election, Green contacted financial secretary Wright about the local's declining dues and low membership, and demanded that the local "force a complete showdown on the maintenance of membership clause." In reply, Flynn admitted to national Secretary-Treasurer Van Gelder that the local was "plodding along an endless road thru a wilderness of bureaucracy," but vowed to "do the best we can to keep the flag flying."[44]

After the 7 December Japanese bombing of Pearl Harbor and United States entry into World War II, Federal Shipyard's interim manager, Admiral Bowen, and Navy Secretary Knox recommended return of the yard to U.S. Steel because top Naval personnel were in short supply. President Roosevelt returned the yard to private management on 5 January 1942.[45]

By 1942, Local 16's financial troubles were worse than ever. The union encouraged department stewards to be more aggressive in enrolling new members and collecting dues, but the traditional person-to-person method failed to keep pace with the yard's hiring rate. Employees doubled between January 1941 and January 1942, from 10,000 to 20,000, but members in good standing remained stagnant at only about 10,000. New union members averaged only 700 per month over this period, with many falling behind in dues payments. By March 1942, fewer than half of the yard's 23,000 employees belonged to the union. Support for the August 1941 strike had been very strong, but afterward Local 16's expenditures increased sharply, running almost triple to what they had been at the start of 1941. Flynn and Dempsey made the problem worse by giving excess "lost time" payments to their favorite stewards and committeemen as a reward for supporting their faction within the union local.[46]

When private management resumed control of the yard, the ritual of negotiations with the union continued. President Roosevelt authorized the formation of the National War Labor Board (NWLB) on 12 January 1942, which provided some hope for Local 16. At public hearings two months later, national IUMSWA attorney M. H. Goldstein used genuine membership and expenditure figures (rather than the inflated numbers printed in the *Shipyard Worker*) to illustrate why Local 16 needed maintenance-of-membership. He described a pattern of local union decline and increased industrial relations instability, thus revealing the truth about the mess in Kearny. Federal Shipbuilding president Korndorff countered that "since the return of the yard to the Company there has been no agitation, no dissension, no dissatisfaction on the part of the employees discernible to the management." He made his usual plea for the "right to work," but NWLB members were not convinced.[47]

While the NWLB deliberated, President Roosevelt convened a special conference on shipyard labor at the White House attended by Secretary of the Navy Knox, Sidney Hillman, NWLB head William Davis, Judge Stacy (the public representative for the original NDMB recommendation), and John Green. Roosevelt made it clear that he no longer advocated neutrality in the Federal Shipyard case. America needed ships, and this was no time for a labor dispute in the nation's most important destroyer yard. When John Green asked Roosevelt for his view on maintenance-of-membership and whether "a man ... delinquent in the payment of his dues and not in good standing . . . could be discharged. . . . The President replied 'Categorically, yes.'"[48]

With the president now firmly behind the original NDMB decision and its rigorous enforcement, the final decision of the NWLB was a foregone conclusion. The representatives of the public (William Davis, Frank Graham, Wayne Morse, and George Taylor) and of labor (Thomas Kennedy, George Meany, Emil Rieve, and Martin Durkin) believed that the company had created conditions detrimental to the war effort. The four employer representatives held to U.S. Steel's anti-maintenance position. Writing for the majority, Graham dismissed Federal Ship's allegation that the NWLB had no jurisdiction in the case and delivered a scathing criticism of U.S. Steel: "In the momentous struggle between the United Nations and the Axis Powers, let us have no defiance of the nation, no mustering of disunity, no measuring and testing of the comparative sovereignty of the United States Steel Corporation and the United States of America. . . . Failure to settle this dispute would reveal both a lack of the acceptance of the democratic process and a lack of understanding of the decisive role of ships in the world strategy of the United Nations against the long gathered might of the Fascist-Axis Powers." As a result of this pressure, Federal Shipbuilding signed an agreement with the union on 29 May incorporating the maintenance-of-membership clause as written by the NWLB.[49]

The union seemed to be winning the legal battle, but during the summer little had changed at the grassroots level in the yard itself. All new members still had to sign up by hand, which meant that over 10,000 non-union workers at the yard had to be organized into the union. Members had to be buttonholed at the gates each month, because stewards could not collect dues on company property. The problem of new members who failed to pay dues continued to grow. Worst of all, as the union fought to obtain maintenance-of-membership, it neglected other pressing issues, including job-related concerns that were far more important to the average worker than dues and membership figures. Flynn's incompetence and

Green's reliance on government proceedings to the neglect of grassroots organizing created a chasm between union officials and the rank-and-file. This crisis opened an enormous gap between the union's increasingly right-wing leadership and an emerging left wing committed to mobilizing workers and carrying out limited direct action.

Flynn's inaction created a leadership vacuum that was filled by a new group of young union activists who ranged from liberal Democrats and Republicans to Communists and other left-wing radicals. The main leaders of this left progressive group included Lou Kaplan, Terry Foy, Vic Johnson, Victor Garcia, Antonio Tully, and Al Elliot. In early 1942 they pushed for a new organizing drive to rebuild the local and attacked the "business as usual" complacency of Local 16's officers. They committed themselves to unity across all social barriers, especially racial and ethnic ones. Nat Levin continued to assist them, but more as a union "teacher" than a spokesman, devoting most of his time to the labor production committees for advancing the war drive.[50]

Most of those who became part of the broad labor left originally came to Federal Ship just to get a good job, but a few, such as Lou Kaplan and Vic Johnson, deliberately entered the yard to advance the CIO. Kaplan started recruiting for the union almost as soon as he was hired. He quickly got to know Levin, Elliot, and other key leaders on the left, as well as independently-minded workers like Terry Foy. By spring of 1942, Kaplan won an elected position on the union negotiating committee and became its main spokesman. The left progressives had a wide range of workers in their ranks, including men from white, black, and Hispanic backgrounds. For the most part, women worked in the Port Newark yard, built as a World War II auxiliary to the larger Kearny yard. As of 1943, the progressive group lacked women leaders, but a year later a few women had become involved as candidates aligned with it.[51]

By early 1943, many progressives believed that the union functioned as little more than a "dues collection agency," in Kaplan's words. The company still refused to discipline union members not in good standing, making the union security provision useless. It also refused to meet with Flynn and Dempsey, claiming that they had not worked in the yard for over a year, and so could no longer serve as legitimate Local 16 representatives.[52]

With the local continuing to lose members and money, national IUMSWA Secretary-Treasurer Phil Van Gelder ordered Financial Secretary George Wright to send a complete report on Local 16's indebtedness. Flynn replied on Wright's behalf that the prolonged legal wrangling after the 1941 strike and huge employment numbers from Federal Shipyards' turnover—then the highest on the East Coast—had drained Local 16's resources. Van Gelder rejected Flynn's excuses, having dealt with this type of problem many times before, but viewed the developing crisis at Federal as a particular threat to the national union.[53]

On the eve of World War II, Local 16 was the union's second largest local, in terms of dues-paying members. Together, Local 16 and Local 1, at Camden, New Jersey's New York Shipbuilding, formed the IUMSWA's core membership. The combined employment at Federal's Kearny and Port Newark yards (both under a single Local 16 contract) was approximately 40,000 in 1943, some 8,000 more than New York Ship, making Federal Ship the largest employer covered by the IUMSWA—and potentially the largest local. The problem at Federal therefore threatened the financial position and morale of the entire national union.[54]

Tom Gallagher, Green's special assistant in the national office, made a preliminary investigation that revealed disturbing evidence of union mismanagement and possible corruption. Van Gelder then ordered a full audit. He concluded from the results that Local 16's problems derived from the "large sums of money spent by the Local to reimburse officers and committeemen for lost time"—lost time supposedly connected to grievance handling and dues collecting.[55]

With a solid base among the shop stewards, the progressives decided to take the initiative. Nat Levin, Ramsey MacDonald, and others declared that Local 16's difficulties involved not just financial mismanagement but also union democracy. They insisted that the national office intervene, charging that there were "many irregularities on the ballot" for the positions of trustee and the negotiating committee, which were elective positions tied to Flynn's "lost time" system.[56]

Peter Flynn rapidly lost control of the organization. The Army drafted him in the spring, after the company refused him reentry onto Federal Ship's employee list. Dempsey and Wright, older men, fared better. The company agreed to work with Dempsey, and he assumed the Local 16 presidency in Flynn's absence. Dempsey could not immediately consolidate his position, which gave a temporary advantage to the progressives, under Kaplan's leadership.[57]

Dempsey faced an extremely difficult situation. The net worth of Local 16 had declined from $23,336 in January 1941 to $596 by February 1943. As of 14 April there were 12,589 members "technically" in good standing and a staggering 16,057 delinquents. Local 16 members in good standing now represented little more than a fourth of the workers at Federal's yards. Local 16 officers had neglected to issue delinquent lists to the departments, making it impossible for stewards to collect back dues. They also had failed to submit delinquent lists to the company, so the contract's maintenance-of-membership clause had not been enforced.[58]

The issue of corruption became a rallying point for the progressives. With the IUMSWA sitting on a powder keg, Green sent in Charles Brecht, regional director for North Jersey–New York Harbor, to conduct a full-scale investigation. The local's members gave their approval at the 2 May meeting and unanimously authorized a progressive-initiated motion for an investigating committee within the local itself. Those elected to the committee included Al Elliot, Lou Kaplan, Ramsey MacDonald, Terry Foy, and Tom Damato.[59]

Flynn and those around him had viewed the local conflict as one between anticommunists loyal to Green versus Communists and "fellow travelers." Now, however, the local's right-wing leaders faced an investigation of union corruption that could completely undermine their position. Kaplan was aware of the ideological dimensions of the struggle and later came to view it as part of the general development of the left-right split in the CIO, not just a battle against dishonest and incompetent officers. Nevertheless, he conducted the fight in Local 16 on a trade-union basis comprehensible to any worker, rather than along ideological lines.[60]

In contrast to Kaplan, Van Gelder disliked characterizing this type of local conflict as left versus right, or progressive versus conservative. For Van Gelder, the problems within Local 16 stemmed from corruption, factionalism, and personal abuse of power not related to ideological differences. He did not perceive the political ramifications of the local battle. Part of the reason for Van Gelder's and Kaplan's differing perceptions came from the fact that Kaplan worked inside the shipyard, while Van Gelder saw things at a distance from the Camden office. Van Gelder's failure to understand this emerging left-right split within the IUMSWA later caught him off guard when he left his elected union position to join the Army near the end of the war and was pushed out of leadership by Green and his right-wing faction.[61]

The local investigating committee presented its report at the June 1943 membership meeting, with Kaplan as the spokesman. He described the disappearance of receipts and vouchers, as well as check forgeries. He charged Flynn, Dempsey, and their allies with responsibility for the long, detailed list of misdeeds. Several months later the IUMSWA auditor discovered a secret bank account, shared by Flynn and Wright, into which union funds had been channeled. President Green, however, made no charges against the two and instead had all the local's funds put under the jurisdiction of the national office.[62]

In his investigation committee report, Kaplan questioned the integrity of the local officers and attacked their "Communist" allegations: "Those who cry disruption! Or scream Communism! When the Union membership demands an investigation when it finds that it hasn't a reserve to carry on this political battle for the protection of labor's interests and the war effort, are actually, working against labor and our union. They are destroying the main base of support to our President, which is the C.I.O."[63]

Kaplan listed specific recommendations for reforming Local 16, including regular auditing, opening the union local's financial books to the membership, and requiring that officers work in the shipyard. He then called for a renewed organizing drive at Federal, based on honest trade unionism, to make it "a 100% C.I.O. yard" and to "free the local of those forces who, by their parasitic activities act as a weight on the growth of our union." He concluded with an admonition for trade unionism with a broader vision, a perspective that proved to be tragically prophetic during the transition from World War II to the Cold War: "The union is our most potent weapon to see that we win the peace as well as the war. We must build it into the strong, agile, fighting force capable of handling the complex situations which we will face in the post-war world. . . . But—if we fail to acknowledge our weaknesses and fail to eliminate them, we shall become diseased, we shall slowly decay, and we shall finally die."[64]

In May 1943 the union began negotiations for a new contract with the company, but when the agreement expired many issues remained unresolved. The union negotiating committee had to continue talks with management because of the no-strike pledge. Inside the yard, however, workers expressed impatience with wages that lagged behind wartime inflation; long overtime hours and seven-day weeks without adequate vacation relief and pay; and failure to enforce the maintenance-of-membership provision. In an effort to break the deadlock, the progressives drummed up local and national publicity, and sent a union delegation to Washington to lobby for NWLB resumption of hearings on their case. Sympathetic board member Wayne Morse, who met the delegation personally, proved instrumental in convincing NWLB director William Davis to act immediately.[65]

Meanwhile, IUMSWA president Green sought to reestablish order in Local 16 without allowing the progressives, and particularly the left, to assume control. Within the national General Executive Board (GEB) he created a special committee of Ross Blood, John Grogan, and Herbert Moyer to deal with the situation in Kearny. Blood and Grogan became key players in the political realignment then developing within the national IUMSWA.[66]

The showdown between the progressives and Dempsey's group came during the July campaign for national convention delegates. This year the contest developed into a highly partisan ideological fight between two slates, each with forty-one candidates. The progressives called themselves the "CIO Builders Committee," and they attacked the Dempsey regime's slate for its corrupt practices and for being "phonies . . . trying to save the Union from Communism . . . By squandering Union funds." Dempsey's "American Trade Unionists" slate pledged to "fight as one to see that not only Local 16 shall be cleansed of Communism," but to support union leaders "who will . . . keep their eyes on one world capital, Washington, D.C." The "CIO Builders Committee" had a straightforward program: end union corruption, secure a new and better contract, and improve production to help win the war. It supported militant action, within the confines of the no-strike pledge. In contrast, the "American Trade Unionists" had no program or basis of unity except anticommunism, and it was divided on the no-strike pledge.[67]

John Green intervened when the "CIO Builders Committee" slate won the Local 16 delegate election. His attitude may have been fueled in part by the information he received from informants in the yard. They included rivals on the left, not just the right. During the height of the Flynn-Wright-McNulty scandal, Green received a phone call from Mendy Mendelson, the particularly sectarian Trotskyist, about "a rump meeting of the Commies and the Local 16 Investigating Committee." Mendelson provided information at other times, but Green was reluctant to establish permanent ties with him. Other informers included shipyard workers who were recruited by the FBI through the Catholic Church in Jersey City. While this surveillance network was separate from the union, some IUMSWA officers, such as Hoboken Local 15's John Grogan, had ties with the Association of Catholic Trade Unionists (ACTU), which promoted these activities. Van Gelder, who was never in the CPUSA, was under surveillance by the FBI at this time because he was willing to work with Party members in the labor movement and on occasion attended meetings where Communists were present.[68]

Green found it advantageous to promote a growing anticommunist union bureaucracy in North Jersey, with John Grogan emerging as one of the main leaders. Grogan headed Local 15 in Hoboken, north of Jersey City. He was a machine-style trade unionist, but with more sophistication and connections than Local 16 leader John Dempsey, who was tied to the Hague machine. Grogan had little experience as a shipyard worker, having moved quickly from a non-production job to a full-time officer. He soon built a power base in the North Jersey–New York City harbor region and played a key role in the national IUMSWA officer's moves against the left wing in Local 16. The special committee set up by Green to deal with Local 16 problems provided Grogan with the opportunity to expand his trade-union influence in North Jersey, which eventually rivaled Green's own New York Ship constituency. In later years, Grogan used his local union base to move into national IUMSWA leadership.[69]

Green's effort to both rebuild Local 16 and contain the left also required renewed organizing. In early August he assigned IUMSWA staff organizer Gavin MacPherson to the organizing drive at Federal's Port Newark yard. MacPherson's chief task, however, was to deal with Local 16's problems with the Kearny workers. He originally ran Local 22, the Chelsea "shore gang" (dock workers) in Manhattan, which he had organized from the inside. He knew how to handle men on the shape-up, the mob-connected ILA (International Longshoremen's Association) bureaucrats on the docks, and waterfront racketeers such as the Anastasia gang. In the late 1930s he allied with the left in New York Port. Later he earned a reputation as a hard-core anticommunist when he purged left-wing staffers in the disastrous 1941 Fore River Shipyard organizing defeat in Quincy, Massachusetts. At Kearny, however, he confronted a very different, far more established group of progressives than at Quincy.[70]

The continuing deterioration of workers' morale and their anger over delays in expected wage raises and vacation days under endless overtime ignited a rank-and-file rebellion in September. Even the militant left could no longer contain workers who had lost confidence in government boards and distrusted the union's reliance on government-sponsored conferences. The unrest started among workers who were not union members but who now numbered in the tens of thousands. As Vic Johnson related: "Our problem was the unorganized, those who did not know what was being done, or what the situation was in Washington. . . . Non-unionists baited us for 'being afraid to strike' … . Around the yard appeared the slogan 'No dues till we get action!'. . . . Even sober old-time trade unionists . . . spoke bitterly of 'teaching that War Labor Board crowd a lesson.' Spontaneous work stoppages, slowdowns, sitdowns multiplied. Finally, we got a sitdown that we couldn't keep from the public or from the WLB. The hookers-on in the steelyard and plateshop sat down and refused to budge. The company tried to break it up by sending the men home. They went home, to return the next day and sit down again."[71]

John Green came to Kearny to end the strike, but he met with "a respectful, deadly silence," according to Johnson. "The men were still sitting when he left the yard forlornly." On the swing shift, Johnson and other union leaders called a meeting to try to keep the strike from spreading. Nine hundred men crowded around Johnson and his colleagues, who stood on a pipe-bench and argued for holding off another week until the NWLB's Shipbuilding Commission made a decision. They managed to convince the swing shift. On the following day the first shift hookers-on and welders also decided to go back to work. When an NWLB "strike wire" arrived demanding an end to the job actions, the yard was running again, but the workers had made their point. As Johnson put it, "Unless there was action in the capital there was going to be action in the shipyards—plenty of it." A breakthrough finally came on 15 September, when the Shipbuilding Commission handed down its decision. It ruled in favor of an automatic dues check-off for Federal Shipbuilding. To the average worker, however, the ruling's stipulations for retroactive wage increases and longer vacations were the real gains.[72]

On this same day Green suspended Local 16's autonomy in an effort to contain the chaos. He assigned staff organizer Charles George as the local's interim director. MacPherson and several other staff members continued to work at Kearny and Port Newark, adding to the power of the national office over the local. Green prohibited all distribution of leaflets or newspaper releases unless sanctioned and signed by administrator George. Within days, Green also nullified the results of the Local 16 delegate election for the IUMSWA national convention in late September, replacing elected representatives from the "CIO Builders Committee" with Dempsey's defeated "American Trade Unionists" candidates. Dempsey's factions now lined up behind MacPherson, who took over as administrator, while the progressive-left faction supported George, whom Green demoted to staff organizer. John Grogan chaired a peace meeting between the factions, winning a temporary truce. Both sides agreed to end distribution of unauthorized leaflets, but Dempsey remained president with the blessing of the national office. Green then established a provisional board under MacPherson, with a new grievance committee made up of MacPherson, Wright, and Levin, reducing the progressives to minority status once again. Despite clear evidence of extensive wrongdoing by Local 16 officers, particularly Wright, Green removed only treasurer McNulty.[73]

Federal Ship ignored the NWLB's Shipbuilding Commission maintenance-of-membership decision until workers mounted more protests like those of early September. Acting independently of the union, however, workers were mainly protesting delays in pay increases rather than dues-related issues. Their anger surfaced again in October. Many workers saw a connection between management's wage increase delays and the reinstatement of the corrupt leaders Wright and Dempsey, especially when MacPherson put Dempsey back on the grievance committee.[74]

For the first time since the union had come to Kearny, left-wing activists found themselves in the middle. They opposed national office autarchy but could not agree to support outright strike protests by the rank-and-file. In the words of Nat Levin, "It was a time of great stress for many of us, caught between company and national (patriotic) pressure for production. Press and radio . . . told us every day, 'You are war workers, safe from the war, and getting rich on the sacrifices of others.'"[75]

According to Vic Johnson, some of the rank-and-file unionists decided it was time to physically eject "Dempsey and his goons he usually keeps hanging around the office." Johnson and Blackie Nemitoff persuaded the rank-and-filers not to do this; they were afraid that the union's reputation would be ruined if the hall was wrecked. Instead, they proposed having "another demonstration" combined with a one-hour work stoppage. To Johnson, "this was playing with dynamite—how explosive we have since learned. Still, it seemed better at the time than letting our tough boys loose on Dempsey and the union hall." Johnson and the others tried unsuccessfully to reach Green to get his approval of the alternative protest, even though Green certainly would have vetoed the idea.[76]

Johnson already knew that "the die was cast." At 2 P.M. during the Kearny yard's shift change, "hundreds of men began to pile up in front of the gates" to protest the fact that the board-authorized wage increases had not been put in their checks. Union activists circulated in the crowds, speaking in low voices to avoid being overheard by company officials. The press had been notified of the job action ahead of time, so reporters were there with their cameras. Police quickly removed Johnson from company property at Industrial Relations Manager Love's request, and then ejected other leaders. When the shipyard's starting whistle blew, every worker managed to get through the gates. Technically, the action had not violated the no-strike pledge. After Johnson managed to sneak back into the yard, he marched with fifty pipe fitters down to the superintendent's office to demand that steward Artie Knight, one of the leaders removed from the yard, be allowed to return. Management refused and fired Johnson, Knight, Joe Agata, Nemitoff, and one other steward.[77]

Demonstrations later erupted on the swing shift when workers learned of the firings. The grievance committee and a rank-and-file committee met with Love, to no avail. Yard meetings among workers continued. On the following morning, when Love publicized his decision to fire the leaders, the outside machinists massed in a solid group to support Vic Johnson, their steward. Johnson, Ramsey MacDonald, who worked in the department, and Local 16 Administrator MacPherson tried to defuse the situation, but "the machinists were steamed up by this time so nobody could keep them in," according to Johnson. On the swing shift some stayed outside the gates, while others went in, worked two hours for their time-and-a-half pay, and then left. The midnight shift did the same.[78]

Staggered walkouts by machinists and then second shift welders continued over the next two days. Inside, Lou Kaplan kept the painters from going out. Although he agreed action had to be taken, he was concerned that walking out of the plant would be seen as a violation of the no-strike pledge. As an alternative, he organized a demonstration inside the plant. He and the painters marched around the yard and then blocked the doors to Love's office with him inside.[79]

The union's yard leadership, supported by Johnson and his fired colleagues, finally persuaded protesting workers to return to their jobs. These protests eventually got results. For the first time the company indicated that it would abide by the NWLB decision on wages and vacations, after the full NWLB ruled favorably on the Shipbuilding Commission's earlier decision. The risks were too high on either side for the confrontation to continue. A total of 13,000 workers took part in the wildcat walkouts and demonstrations at one point or another during the second week of October. This massive show of strength openly defied Green's and Dempsey's conservative interpretation of the no-strike pledge. The company did not reinstate the five fired men, but it did institute the automatic dues check-off by mid-November.[80]

The broad left had pushed the no-strike pledge to its limits, combining short walkouts with demonstrations, and had won progressives and many rank-and-file workers to its side. Top leaders in the Communist Party opposed these types of tactics, but many rank-and-file party members and the independent left ignored their advice by initiating new forms of direct action at Federal Ship. This attested to the difference between the official CP line and the reality of working-class experience inside the shipyards. The Trotskyist position of complete opposition to the no-strike pledge also would have been unrealistic, because workers overwhelmingly supported the war effort and its production needs, regardless of their immediate grievances. Most workers in this industry simply would not have supported lengthy full-scale strikes that jeopardized the lives of family members and friends fighting overseas.[81]

In June 1944 an arbitrator finally settled the long-standing controversy over enforcing maintenance-of-membership, ruling that certain employees charged by the union with nonpayment of dues had to be fired. The legal fight by IUMSWA attorney Goldstein had dragged on for over three years, and had involved not only the NWLB but at various points the U.S. Navy, cabinet-level officials, and even the president of the United States. Federal Shipbuilding management accepted maintenance-of-membership and the check-off, in part to alleviate the chaos caused by the breakdown of union leadership in 1943. This did not automatically solve Local 16's problems.[82]

To consolidate its gains, the local union needed to elect new leaders and build a solid organization based on full membership involvement. This was accomplished by 1944, with a massive victory for the broad labor left, led by Terry Foy. He was elected Local 16 president, finally defeating those around Dempsey.[83] This victory, however, proved short-lived and never extended beyond the local level. Green had amassed power at the national level and in other sympathetic locals. With the end of World War II, he was ready to move against the labor left, which he knew planned to remove him as national president.

The left labor challenge to Green and the right wing came during the IUMSWA national convention in January 1946. A majority of the left-wing candidates at Federal Ship had been elected as convention delegates, but when they arrived at Atlantic City, Green's faction refused to seat them. One of those elected to the left-wing delegation was Lou Kaplan, who had become a full-time IUMSWA staff organizer in 1944 and had left Federal Ship. In 1945 he directed the IUMSWA's successful Fore River organizing campaign, but after the July NLRB election win Green refused to let Kaplan lead negotiations for the new contract. In protest, Kaplan went back to work at Federal Ship to fight on the inside. The left labor campaign leading up to the January 1946 convention became national, with Phil Van Gelder running against Ross Blood for his old position as national IUMSWA secretary-treasurer. Andy Reeder, as president of New York Ship Local 1, led the revolt against Green from inside Green's home local and original base of support.[84]

Ross Blood proved an ideal candidate against Van Gelder. He had been a right-wing New Dealer who originally worked at New York Ship, Green's home base. He knew Local 16's left-wing group well, having become involved, along with John Grogan, in overseeing Local 16 when it was torn by factionalism and financial mismanagement during 1943. Blood became temporary secretary-treasurer of the IUMSWA when Van Gelder joined the Army in late 1943, which allowed him to establish a national network and extensive union patronage. On returning from the European war in 1945, Van Gelder discovered that Blood had replaced him permanently. Green grew suspicious of Van Gelder's loyalty when Van Gelder refused in 1941 to attack left-wing trade unionists, including those in the Communist Party, who sought positions at the national level of the IUMSWA. Blood, on the other hand, was a dependable anticommunist and an avowed loyalist who appeared not to threaten Green's leadership.[85]

When Green's faction refused to seat the duly-elected Federal Ship delegates, Kaplan and others excluded leaped out of the balconies onto the main floor and tried to physically take over the stage. Fistfights broke out everywhere, but the rebels were eventually evicted from the hall. Van Gelder was defeated in the convention vote, and the broad labor left within the IUMSWA collapsed. CP members remained active in the union, but became totally marginalized.[86]

Green's triumph over the left within the IUMSWA came at a terrible cost. The shipbuilding industry went through massive downsizing as all wartime auxiliary yards closed and major established yards sharply cut back employment. By the late 1940s even Federal Shipbuilding at Kearny closed its doors, never to reopen. Green's response to the deindustrialization crisis in shipbuilding was to raid other unions for members, in particular AFL railroad locals. He tried to push a conversion program for shipbuilding by lobbying Washington politicians. The Truman administration, however, preferred to focus on the development of airpower to meet challenges from the Soviet Union, rather than on building naval ships, of which a huge surplus existed from World War II. IUMSWA rank-and-file shipbuilders believed that Green was losing interest in their concerns and in response turned to the AFL Boilermakers Union. By the early 1950s two of the IUMSWA's largest locals—New York Shipbuilding in Camden and Electric Boat in Connecticut—had disaffiliated from the IUMSWA and joined the AFL. Green's power deteriorated along with his personal health, and John Grogan, his old ally from North Jersey, displaced him as national president. Grogan later ran unsuccessfully for mayor of Hoboken, New Jersey, but he retained his power base within a now virulently anticommunist and thoroughly bureaucratic IUMSWA.[87]

The former leaders of IUMSWA's labor left became dispersed, some remaining with the labor movement, others abandoning it altogether. Van Gelder left the IUMSWA to organize with the Machinists Union, joining his old nemesis the AFL. He remained with the Machinists for the remainder of his working life, and in retirement saw the merger of the Machinists and the remains of the IUMSWA in the 1980s. At the local level, however, not much changed. Four decades after the destruction of the left in the IUMSWA, Fore River Local 5 union officers still falsely referred to Van Gelder as a Communist, even though the Fore River local charter on their office wall had Van Gelder's and Green's signatures.[88]

Andy Reeder lost all interest in the union after the 1946 convention defeat and one afternoon he just walked out of New York Ship, never to return. He left the labor movement entirely and remade his life as a small businessman, spending most of his leisure time organizing and coaching recreational baseball teams for boys from lower-income families. He also lost all contact with people he had known in the labor movement, and transformed himself from a Roosevelt Democrat with IWW sympathies to a Reagan Republican.[89]

Terry Foy left the IUMSWA in the late 1940s, after the second 1946 convention. He stayed in the union movement for a number of years, organizing with the Mine, Mill and Smelters Union under its Communist leadership following the union's expulsion from the CIO. As the anticommunist movement gained momentum in the early 1950s, however, Foy left the union movement and became a bail bondsman in North Jersey. Eventually he made a small fortune from what he described as "the crime boom" of the 1960s and 1970s in the region. By the late 1980s he lived in a quiet North Jersey suburb, drove a gold Mercedes, and had no contact with his former colleagues.[90]

Nat Levin left the Federal Shipyard in the late 1940s. By the early 1950s he became a major target of anticommunist government investigations, even though he never posed any type of security threat; if anything, he proved himself to be one of the most patriotic shipyard activists during World War II. After he retired, he lived in public housing with little money and lost contact with all his former shipyard colleagues except Henry Tully.[91]

Some former Federal Ship left-wingers remained active in the union movement. Vic Johnson continued as a union organizer on the West Coast with Bridge's ILWU after leaving the IUMSWA. Henry Tully left Federal Ship after World War II to take a more secure job with the U.S. Post Office in New York City. He also became active in the postal union at the local level. When he retired, he continued to live where he had since the 1940s, an apartment complex in the center of Harlem. When interviewed, Tully made of point of the fact that Langston Hughes had lived in the next apartment tower, and that both the Apollo Theater and the church where Reverend Adam Clayton Powell, Jr. had been minister were a few blocks away. Tully's world symbolized the sense of African American history that many Harlemites retained and which was central to his own worldview.[92]

Kaplan quit his job at Federal Ship immediately after the January 1946 IUMSWA convention but remained in the union movement. He had three opportunities to organize with other unions. Harry Bridges, head of the ILWU, asked him to go to Hawaii, which was rapidly becoming the ILWU's stronghold. Kaplan turned Bridges down because his wife June thought Hawaii was too far from their New Jersey-based family. Jimmy Hoffa, a rising force in the Teamsters, had earlier offered Kaplan a lucrative position in the union's organizing department. Hoffa got to know Kaplan when Kaplan was providing IUMSWA shipyard-worker support for striking UE Westinghouse workers in Philadelphia. Hoffa wanted to get trucks into the plant, but Kaplan argued with Hoffa that the truckers' business agent Cohn was "a crook and sellout artist." Kaplan brought in some very tough shipyard workers from New York Ship, Federal Ship, and Sun Ship, making it impossible for the truckers to break through the UE lines. Hoffa had Cohn removed and brought him up on charges, in part as a favor to Kaplan because of his support for Teamster pickets. Hoffa later arranged to meet Kaplan in a local Philadelphia hotel. "Why are you wasting your time for peanuts?" Kaplan recalled Hoffa asking him. "I'll pay you more money than you've ever made in your life." Kaplan replied, "Jimmy, there are guys who do it because they believe in it," and he turned down the offer. The offer that Kaplan did accept came from the UE's James Matles. In the UE, Kaplan went on to lead major organizing efforts to defeat challenges from the rival International Union of Electrical Workers (IUE) and the Machinists. He even faced his old ally, Phil Van Gelder, in several Machinist raids on UE shops and consistently defeated Van Gelder.[93]

Kaplan was on the UE staff from 1946 to 1970, representing workers at GE, Westinghouse, and many other companies. In the 1950s he was summoned and testified before the House Un-American Activities Committee, but he refused to turn on anyone in the left. During this time he and his family were under constant FBI surveillance. In the 1960s Van Gelder and Kaplan met again, this time as friends at a meeting of major union officials opposed to the Vietnam War. By the end of the decade, Kaplan moved to the American Federation of State and County Municipal Employees (AFSCME) where he organized public sector workers. He also actively organized union support for civil rights protests, and was assisting the AFSCME garbage workers in Memphis when Martin Luther King, Jr. was assassinated there while championing their struggle. In 1971 Kaplan's public sector connections led New York Governor Nelson Rockefeller to call on him to serve as a negotiator during the prison uprising at Attica, an event that spurred prison reform across the nation. Kaplan's last position was as Secretary of Workmen's Compensation for Pennsylvania under Governor Milton Schapp, whom Kaplan had known many years before, having organized workers at one of Schapp's factories into the UE. The compensation reforms Kaplan initiated had a substantial influence on improving other systems around the country.[94]

By the 1980s Kaplan had retired, but he began to meet on a number of occasions with former IUMSWA colleagues and retired workers in public reunions, forums, and private interview sessions.[95] Many of those who had completely lost touch with the labor movement, including Reeder, Foy, and Levin, now had contact with those who had once been part of a common struggle in the shipyards. Others who had remained active but had lost contact with each other, such as Van Gelder and Kaplan, could renew ties with these former activists. This was only a brief moment at the end of their lives, however, and was a time for remembering, rather than taking action. Had these former IUMSWA grassroots activists of the broad labor left, and thousands like them from other unions, not been separated by the anticommunist storm that swept America in the 1940s and 1950s, we can only wonder how different the U.S. labor movement might be today.

Notes

1. See, for example, Walter Galenson, *The CIO Challenge to the AFL: A History of the American Labor Movement, 1935–1941* (Cambridge: Harvard University Press, 1960); and Bert Cochran, *Labor and Communism: The Conflict that Shaped American Unions* (Princeton: Princeton University Press, 1977).
2. See, for example, Irving Bernstein, *Turbulent Years: A History of the American Worker, 1933–1941* (Boston: Houghton Mifflin, 1969); Steve Rosswurm, "Introduction: An Overview and Preliminary Assessment of the CIO's Expelled Unions," *The CIO's Left-led Unions*, ed. Steve Rosswurm (New Brunswick, N.J.: Rutgers University Press, 1992); and Robert H. Zieger, *The CIO, 1935–1955* (Chapel Hill: University of North Carolina Press, 1995).
3. For an overview of the Industrial Union of Marine and Shipbuilding Workers of America (IUMSWA) that focuses on local organizing during its first decade, see David Palmer, *Organizing the Shipyards: Union Strategy in Three Northeast Ports, 1933–1945* (Ithaca, N.Y.: Cornell University Press, 1998).
4. Evidence of the resurgence of the union movement includes the first percentage increase since the mid-1950s in total membership of the AFL-CIO, in 1999. This change occurred in large part because of left-led reform movements inside many unions, including the Teamsters, United Mine Workers (UMW), United Automobile Workers (UAW), International Union of Electrical Workers (IUE), and Steelworkers. The election of Sweeney to AFL-CIO president over Lane Kirkland's successor-designate became possible in part because Sweeney had built his own union, the Service Employees International Union (SEIU), into one of the fastest-growing and most dynamic unions in the country, through hiring left-wing labor activists for top SEIU staff positions. This echoed John L. Lewis's hiring of Communists within the CIO.
5. U.S. Dept. of Labor, "Wartime Employment, Production, and Conditions of Work in Shipyards," Bulletin No. 824 (Washington, D.C.: GPO, 1945), 5.
6. For detailed background on John Green and Van Gelder, see Palmer, *Organizing the Shipyards*.
7. Palmer, *Organizing the Shipyards*, 24–35; Phil Van Gelder, telephone interview by author (handwritten notes), 11 October 1987; First IUMSWA Constitution, Preamble, RG 9, Box 5243, (file) "Compliance" (in April 1935 section), National Archives (hereafter cited as NA). David Palmer conducted all interviews. Unless otherwise indicated, they were taped.
8. Ben Maiatico, interview by author, Mount Laurel, N.J., 13 September 1987. Maiatico remained a John Green loyalist his entire life and retired as a full-time staff representative of the IUMSWA. Nevertheless, he exhibited none of the autocratic characteristics of Green and retained the non-prejudiced views enshrined in the first IUMSWA constitution of 1934. He met Green at New York Ship in 1933 during initial organizing there and was a founding member of the national union. Maiatico knew James Carey, as well, and so had a very close understanding of Green's relationship with Carey.
9. For the relationship between Peter Flynn and John Green, as well as Flynn's anticommunism, see *Shipyard Worker*, 10, 24 March, 7, 21 April 1939, and 23 February, 12 April, 2 August, 1940; Flynn to Green, circa January 1940, Green to Flynn, 18 January 1940, Box 50, file "Jan.–Apr.", IUMSWA Archives, McKeldin Library, University of Maryland, Suitland, Maryland (hereafter cited as IUMSWA Archives); Flynn to Green, 28 July 1940, Series II, Box 48, file 13, IUMSWA Archives; IUMSWA, *Proceedings, 6th National Convention*, Baltimore, Md., 13–15 September 1940, 24–58.

10. For detailed background on Van Gelder, see Palmer, *Organizing the Shipyards*. The author conducted interviews with Van Gelder, corresponded with him, and taped his public speeches between 1983 and 1987, which are the basis of this analysis. For very positive assessments of Van Gelder by union activists who originally were New York Ship workers with widely varying political views, see Andy Reeder and Lou Kaplan, interview by author, Wilmington, Del., 3 September 1986; Andy Reeder, interview by author, Wilmington, Del., 30 May 1987, 21 May 1988; Maiatico, interview; and George "Chips" De Girolamo, interview by author, Marlton, N.J., 14 June 1987.
11. Ibid.
12. *Frank Hague v. Committee for Industrial Organization*, 307 U.S. 496–533 (1939). For the history of the relationship of the IUMSWA and Local 16 to Hague and Jersey City politics, see David Palmer, "Organizing the Shipyards: Unionization at New York Ship, Federal Ship, and Fore River, 1898–1945," (Ph.D. diss., Brandeis University, 1990), 639–675. Harold Ickes, Roosevelt's Interior secretary who theoretically controlled WPA funds, considered Hague to be a prototypical American fascist, but Jim Farley, Franklin D. Roosevelt's campaign manager and the postmaster general, had the final say regarding WPA money funneled through Hague for distribution locally.
13. Lou Kaplan, interview by author, Collingswood, N.J., 8 January 1983; Kaplan (with Reeder), 3 September 1986; Kaplan and Terry Foy, interview by author, Union, N.J., 6 April 1988; Terry Foy, interview by author, Union, N.J., 20 May 1988.
14. Nat Levin, letter to author, 11 March 1988; Foy and Kaplan, interview, 6 April 1988. For an account of how the Republican Party operated in Jersey City under Hague, see Richard J. Connors, *A Cycle of Power: The Career of Jersey City Mayor Frank Hague* (Metuchen, N.J.: Scarecrow Press, 1971), 106–139.
15. Levin, letter to author; Kaplan (with Foy), interview.
16. Levin, letter to author; Kaplan (with Foy), interview; Joe Peters, interview by author, Kearny, N.J., 26 June 1987. In contrast to Kaplan, Foy believed that Dempsey was not entirely bad, because after the war the left built an alliance with him against Green.
17. Foy, interview, 6 April 1988; IUMSWA, *Proceedings, 5th National Convention*, Jersey City, N.J., 8–11 September 1939.
18. Foy, interview, 6 April 1988; Nat Levin, letter to author, 18 November 1988.
19. Foy, interview, 6 April 1988.
20. Levin, letters to author; Foy, interview, 6 April 1988.
21. Foy, interview, 6 April 1988; Henry Tully, interview with author, New York City, 4 April 1988; "Excerpts of a telephone conversation between John Green and Mr. Mendelson of Local 16," 3 June 1943, Series 5, Box 51, IUMSWA Archives. It was not possible to identify the Trotskyist organization to which Mendelson belonged. Tully's "Trotskyist" characterization of Kaplan, even though Kaplan worked closely with the CPUSA and defended it against anticommunists, typified internal Party politics during the 1930s and 1940s.
22. Kaplan, interview, 8 January 1983; Tully, interview; Foy, interview, 6 April 1988.
23. Kaplan, interview, 8 January 1983; Tully, interview; Foy, interview, 6 April 1988.
24. Kaplan, interview, 8 January 1983; Tully, interview.
25. Bert Walters and Al Elliot leaflet, "We Repudiate," circa June–July 1944; Department list (Federal yard only) of union members paid up through June 1942, as of September 1942 (with September 1943 documents), Series 5, Box 51, IUMSWA Archives; Tully, interview (ethnic percentages on drilling department workers are drawn from Henry Tully's Dept. 40 steward book, read by him onto tape); Kaplan and Foy, interview; Levin, letters to author, 11 and 31 March 1988, and 8 January 1989. It is difficult to de-

termine how many of Federal Shipyard's workers were black because of the absence of documentation in union and government documents, but an estimate can be made using information from the "We Repudiate" leaflet above, put out by the labor left's "Unity Slate."
26. Kaplan and Foy, interview; Levin, letters to author, 11 and 31 March 1988, and 8 January 1989. Levin's reference to the preamble was in part a recollection of the inspiration Mike Smith (a socialist) had been to him as a union "teacher."
27. Kaplan, interview, 8 January 1983; Maiatico, interview. The IUMSWA generally had a very weak record regarding black workers, and in the South often acquiesced to white workers' racism. Wherever racial discrimination was opposed in the shipyards, it was local activists, not national officers, who apparently took the initiative. Among those with the best record in this struggle were left-wing trade unionists. The new movement at Federal Shipyard led this drive for equality on the job. Lou Kaplan was instrumental during the second victorious Sun Ship union election campaign in getting the organizing drive to push for an end to the company's segregated yards. To assist with this part of the campaign, Kaplan recruited Monroe and Elliot, who mobilized not only black shipyard workers but also the Philadelphia black community. For a very different assessment of IUMSWA left-wing activists' approach to racism in the shipyards, see Bruce Nelson, "Organized Labor and the Struggle for Black Equality in Mobile during World War II," *Journal of American History* 80 (1993): 952–988.
28. Tully, interview; Peters, interview. For background on the Detroit race riots, black-white relations in the auto industry, and the racial policies of the UAW at this time, see August Meier and Elliot Rudwick, *Black Detroit and the Rise of the UAW* (New York: Oxford University Press, 1979), 108–222. For the AFL's involvement in the Philadelphia transit strike against blacks, see Herbert Hill, *Black Labor and the American Legal System* (Madison: University of Wisconsin, 1985), 274–308. For the racial policies of the Boilermakers' Union (AFL) in shipbuilding, see Hill, 185–208.
29. Tully, interview.
30. Ibid.
31. Ibid.
32. Kaplan, interviews, 8 January 1983 and 6 April 1988; David Milton, *The Politics of U.S. Labor* (New York: Monthly Review, 1982).
33. Lou Kaplan obituary (1916–2000), written by June Kaplan, letter to author, 9 May 2000; Louis L. Kaplan resume, circa 1983; Kaplan, interviews, 8 January 1983 and 6 April 1988.
34. Kaplan resume; Kaplan, interviews, 8 January 1983, and 6 April and 19 September 1988.
35. Ibid.
36. Andy Reeder, interviews by author, Wilmington, Del., 3 September 1986, 21 May 1988; Reeder, interview by author, Cambridge, Mass., 17 November 1988; Reeder, letters to author, 4 August, 23 September, 4 December 1986; 9 January, 16 February, 3 July 1987; 31 October 1988; 13 January, 12 February, 29 March, 14 and 22 April, 29 June 1989; Reeder personal papers and documents given to author.
37. Ibid. For Reeder's undercover organizing at Sun Ship for the IUMSWA, see Sun Shipbuilding and Dry Dock Co. and IUMSWA, NLRB Case No. C-1899, Decision and Order, 16 January 1942; Sun Shipbuilding . . . and IUMSWA, Case No. IV-C-761, Intermediate Report, 14 June 1941, RG 25, Box 504, NA.
38. U.S. Dept. of Labor, "Wartime Employment, Production and Conditions of Work in Shipyards," Bulletin No. 824 (Washington, D.C.: GPO, 1945), 5; Harold G. Bowen,

Ships, Machinery, and Mossbacks: The Autobiography of a Naval Engineer (Princeton University: Princeton, 1954), 47–126; Deans to Korndorff, 24 March 1941, Series 5, Box 50, file "Jan.–April, 1941," IUMSWA Archives; De Girolamo, interview; *Shipyard Worker*, 15 August 1941.

39. "Chronological Statement of More Important Events Relating to Labor Situation at Federal Shipbuilding and Dry Dock Company, Kearny, New Jersey," Federal Shipbuilding, Kearny, N.J. (29 May 1942), 3-5.; Love to Deans, 28 June 1941, Series 5, Box 51, file "May–Aug., 1941", IUMSWA Archives; Nelson Lichtenstein, *Labor's War at Home: The CIO in World War II* (New York: Cambridge University, 1987), 48, 68–69; Joel Seidman, *American Labor from Defense to Reconversion* (Chicago: University of Chicago, 1976), 131–132.

40. "Chronological Statement," 3–6, 57–62, 67; *Shipyard Worker*, 25 July 1941; Seidman, *American Labor from Defense to Reconstruction*, 62–63, 108; National War Labor Board, *Termination Report: Vol. I, Industrial Disputes and Wage Stabilization in Wartime* (Washington, D.C.: GPO, 1947), 81. On the problem the NDMB faced regarding enforcement of the Federal Shipbuilding recommendation, Seidman comments: "Until this time it had not been clear whether the 'Mediation' board was in fact that or an agency of compulsory arbitration, since its recommendations had never before been flatly rejected. Yet it was evident that, should the Federal Shipbuilding concern successfully defy the board, its usefulness would be ended and the way might be opened for drastic congressional action. President Roosevelt met the challenge by ordering seizure of the company's plant." (p. 63) Emphasis in original.

41. Resume of the Federal Shipbuilding and Dry Dock Company Situation, Federal Employees Committee (FEC) leaflet, circa September 1941; Daniel Ring to Frank Graham (NWLB), Labor Relations at Federal Shipbuilding . . . (docketed) 7 May 1942. Both in "NDMB, Federal Shipbuilding, 2050(6)," RG 202, NA. "Chronological Statement," 5–7.

42. Kearny Observer, 9 October 1941; "Resume . . . ," FEC leaflet; "Special Mass Meeting at Mosque Theater," Local 16 leaflet, circa late July 1941, reprinted by FEC, "NDMB, Federal Shipbuilding . . . , 2050(6)," RG 202, NA; *Shipyard Worker*, 8 and 15 August 1941; "Chronological Statement," 9–11, 61, 62, 67.

43. Harold G. Bowen, *Ships, Machinery, and Mossbacks: The Autobiography of a Naval Engineer* (Princeton: Princeton University Press, 1954), 208–209, 212; Green to Franklin Roosevelt, 26 August 1941, Series 5, Box 51, IUMSWA Archives; Executive Order authorizing seizure of the Federal Shipbuilding plant, in "Chronological Statement," exhibit R, 78–79; *Shipyard Worker*, 19 September 1941. For a discussion of the Federal Shipbuilding takeover within the broader context of presidential seizures, see John L. Blackman, Jr., *Presidential Seizure in Labor Disputes* (Cambridge, Mass.: Harvard University Press, 1967).

44. *Shipyard Worker*, 24 October 1941; Green to Wright, 27 October 1941; Flynn to Van Gelder (original spelling), 5 November 1941, Series 5, Box 51, IUMSWA Archives.

45. "Chronological Statement," 14–17, 92.

46. National War Labor Board (NWLB), "Verbatim Transcript of Public Hearing . . . Federal Shipbuilding . . . and IUMSWA, Local 16," 30 March 1942, 102–103, 105, 106; *Kearny Observer*, 23 January, 21, 28 August 1941, 7 January 1942; *Shipyard Worker*, 8, 15 August, 14 November 1941.

47. NWLB, "Verbatim Transcript of Public Hearing . . . Federal Shipbuilding . . . and IUMSWA, Local 16," 30 March 1942, 15–18, 29, 102–106, 116; M. H. Goldstein to Green, 8 January 1942, Series 5, Box 51, IUMSWA Archives; "Chronological Statement," 19–23.

48. John Green, "Confidential Memorandum to Dr. Frank Graham of the NWLB," 21 April 1942, Series 5, Box 51, IUMSWA Archives.
49. NWLB, Federal Shipbuilding and Dry Dock Company v. IUMSWA Local 16, Majority Opinion (written by Frank Graham), 24 April 1942; "Chronological Statement," 23–32. For an example of union protests over the delay in implementing the NWLB decision, see Green to Davis, 27 May 1942, Series 5, Box 51, IUMSWA Archives.
50. Levin, letter, 8 January 1989. The assessment of Levin as a "teacher" is the author's, based on interviews with workers who knew Levin.
51. *Kearny Observer*, 24 July 1942 (for Kaplan's role on negotiating committee); Kaplan, interview, 8 January 1983; Tully, interview; comments by Kaplan at the author's seminar paper talk, "From the Clydebank to the Jersey Yards: Organizing at Camden and Kearny," Princeton University, 13 April 1989. The labor left at Federal Ship appears to have been less committed to employment rights for women than it was to improving conditions for black, Hispanic, and non-English speaking European men. This may have been due in part to the fact that during World War II most women worked in the auxiliary Newark yard, while the main activism in Local 16 came from the permanent Kearny yard. Kaplan, however, did push for women to be included on union election slates of the progressives.
52. Kaplan, interview, 6 April 1988. Green to Korndorff, 2 February 1943; Korndorff to Green, 5, 12 February 1943; Green to Davis (NWLB), 11 February 1943; Elaine Wright (NWLB) to Green, 19 February 1943; NWLB arbitration notification, 1 March 1943. All Series 5, Box 51, IUMSWA Archives.
53. Flynn to Van Gelder, 11 March 1943; Korndorff to Rothbard, 1 September 1942, both Series 5, Box 51, IUMSWA Archives. U.S. Dept. of Labor, *Wartime Employment, Production, and Conditions of Work in Shipyards*, Bulletin No. 824 (Washington, D.C.: GPO 1945), 8–14, 25–35. Bernard Mergen, "A History of the Industrial Union of Marine and Shipbuilding Workers of America, 1933–1951," (Ph.D. diss., University of Pennsylvania, 1968), 249–253. Report of Secretary Phil Van Gelder, IUMSWA, *Proceedings, 2nd National Convention*, Camden, N.J., 20–23 August 1936. Van Gelder, interview, 17 September 1988. Between 1934 and 1944, 34 out of 69 IUMSWA locals were either suspended (autonomy lifted) or dissolved, a number of these twice. Of the IUMSWA's 69 locals, 20 disappeared during this decade, including those at some of the country's largest shipyards. The majority of suspensions or dissolutions stemmed from locals that collapsed because of low membership. A small number of viable locals were disciplined for financial mismanagement (usually corruption) or insubordination to the national office.
54. For a comparison of the number of Local 16 members and total Federal Shipbuilding employees at the Kearny and Port Newark yards, see "Memorandum on Local 16" (unsigned, by the union), 1 May 1943, Series 5, Box 51, IUMSWA Archives.
55. Van Gelder to Local 16, 13 April 1943; IUMSWA Memorandum (unsigned), 1 May 1943. Both Series 5, Box 51, IUMSWA Archives.
56. Ramsey MacDonald, et al. to Green, 8 and 10 April 1943, Series 5, Box 51, IUMSWA Archives.
57. Flynn (from U.S. Army Camp Pickett, Va.) to Tom Damato, 5 June 1943; Dempsey to Green, 26 July 1943; IUMSWA Memorandum (unsigned), 1 May 1943. All Series 5, Box 51, IUMSWA Archives. Foy, interview, 20 May 1988; Kaplan, interview, 6 April 1988; Neil McMahon, interview by author, Kearny, N.J., 26 June 1987. Neil McMahon, a rank-and-file welder with no knowledge of internal union politics, recalled that he heard Flynn lost his job in the shipyard because he never came to work. This story,

which circulated among the workers, matches the correspondence from Korndorff to Flynn mentioned earlier.
58. IUMSWA Memorandum (unsigned), 1 May 1943; undated table in September 1943 records. Both Series 5, Box 51, IUMSWA Archives. *Shipyard Worker*, 23 February 1940.
59. IUMSWA Memorandum (unsigned), 1 May 1943; Charles Brecht reports, 21, 28 May 1943; Van Gelder to Wright, 7 June 1943; Local 16 investigating committee report, circa June, 1943. All Series 5, Box 51, IUMSWA Archives. Kaplan and Foy, interview.
60. On Kaplan's view of the Local 16 struggle as left versus right, see Foy and Kaplan, interview. In virtually every conversation with Kaplan since 1982, Kaplan repeated this left versus right scenario. Foy agreed with him on this, although he evaluated some personalities differently. Foy also noted that the left was only one part of the broad coalition of progressives opposed to Flynn and Dempsey. (Foy, letter to author, 16 December 1988.) Al Petit-Clair, on the other hand, saw the struggle as progressives versus bureaucrat-conservatives, and *not* left versus right. He believed that there were many among the progressives who were not necessarily "left," while the bureaucrat-conservative faction had Trotskyists who considered themselves "left." (Petit-Clair, interview by author, Toms River, N.J., 15 September 1987.) These various perspectives actually were not that far apart, except that Kaplan used the words "left" and "right" more explicitly.
61. Van Gelder, interviews by author, Catonsville, Md., 6 January 1983 and 11 June 1987. Van Gelder held this view of Local 16 factions even some forty years after the events. When Kaplan learned of this he found it incomprehensible, given that Van Gelder had been red-baited and pushed out of office by the IUMSWA's anticommunist right wing. (Based on conversations and correspondence with Van Gelder and Kaplan.)
62. Local 16 investigating committee report, circa June 1943; Roy Williams (auditor) to Green, 19 November 1943. Both Series 5, Box 51, IUMSWA Archives.
63. Ibid.
64. Ibid. Kaplan provided many examples of the severity of the internal conflict: "It was with a great deal of difficulty that we managed to gather this information ... The auditor's books were thrown out of the window, and George Wright threatened to throw the auditor out of the office. Brother McNulty threatened to 'suck my blood' for daring to ask him questions pertaining to a shortage in the change fund. Al McNulty boasted that we would never get to make our report, and that the membership here present doesn't care to know the truth."
65. J. Caldwell Jenkins, Preliminary Report, Department of Labor (DOL), 22 June 1943; Dempsey to John Steelman (DOL), 29 June 1943; Jenkins, Final Progress Report, 3 July 1943; NWLB, Arbitration Award, case no. NDMB-46 for 25 April 1942, awarded on 14 July 1943; NWLB, Opinion on Case No. 25-390 D, 13 September 1943, and Directive Order on same, 15 September 1943. All RG 202, Box 7750, (file) "Shipbuilding Commission–Dispute Files: 111–2546 to 111–2612", NA. Victor Johnson, "Why War Workers Strike," *New Republic*, 21 June 1943. Kaplan, Johnson, and Walters also met with John Steelman, Roosevelt's confidant in the Labor Department. Kaplan and Johnson also successfully lobbied Congressman Mary Norton, chair of the House Labor Committee, and Jersey City Mayor Frank Hague to send telegrams to NWLB head William Davis. Vic Johnson was convinced that Hague's intervention, carried out personally through one of the mayor's relatives, had special influence on Davis's decision to move more quickly. See Johnson and Kaplan to Davis, 14 July 1943, Mary Norton to

Davis, Frank Hague to Davis, both 23 July 1943, RG 202, Box 7750, (file) "Shipbuilding Commission–Dispute Case Files: 111-2546 to 111-2612," NA.
66. Green to Blood, Grogan, Moyer, 12 June 1943; Moyer to Green, 21 June 1943, Series 5, Box 51, IUMSWA Archives.
67. Campaign leaflets for convention delegate slates, "Extra! Extra! Extra! The biggest phoney in modern history is Hitler!" and "Election of 41 Delegates," circa August 1943, Series 5, Box 51, IUMSWA Archives. Trotskyist Mendy Mendelson ran on the Dempsey anticommunist slate and was adamantly opposed to the no-strike pledge.
68. Lou Kaplan, telephone interview by author (handwritten notes), 20 June 1989; "Excerpts of a telephone conversation between John Green and Mr. Mendelson of Local 16," 3 June 1943, Series 5, Box 51, IUMSWA Archives; Foy, interview, 20 May 1988; Jack Collins, interview by author, Gloucester, N.J., 13 September 1987; Arthur Boyson, telephone interview by author (handwritten notes), 18 July 1988.

While at Van Gelder's home in June 1987, he showed the author his entire FBI file (obtained through the Freedom of Information Act and now deposited at Walter Reuther Labor Archives, Wayne State University). His file started in 1943 and ended in the early 1950s.
69. Impressions of Grogan are drawn from interviews with Van Gelder; Foy, interview by author, Union, N.J., 20 May 1988; Foy and Kaplan, interview; Al Petit-Clair, interview; and Tully, interview. Evaluations of Grogan ranged from relatively positive (Petit-Clair) to very negative (Kaplan and Van Gelder).
70. Gavin MacPherson report, 14 August 1943, Series 5, Box 51, IUMSWA Archives; Kaplan, interview, 6 April 1988; Van Gelder, telephone interview by author (handwritten notes), 17 September 1988.
71. Johnson, "Why War Workers Strike."
72. Johnson, "Why War Workers Strike." Carl Schedler (NWLB) to Korndorff (strike wire), 9 September 1943; Shipbuilding Commission of the NWLB, Directive Order, Opinion, and Dissenting Opinion on Case No. 25-390-D (Federal Shipbuilding v. IUMSWA Local 16), 15 September 1943. Both RG 202, Box 7750, (file) "Shipbuilding Commission–Dispute Case Files: 111-2546 to 111-2612", NA; "Suspension of Local Autonomy Notice," circa September 1943, Series 5, Box 51, IUMSWA Archives.

Vic Johnson resembled Kaplan in his style and philosophy. Before working at Federal Ship, he had been a merchant seaman, serving as a chief engineer at sea. He became active in the National Maritime Union (NMU), led by Communist Party member Joe Curran. He had been friends with Blackie Myers, Curran's one-time ally and later rival, and had been an early skeptic of Curran. By allying with Myers, Johnson was also allying with the syndicalist wing of the CPUSA identified by David Milton, who also knew Myers well from the NMU. Johnson believed in rank-and-file direct action and was not afraid to challenge the CP hierarchy. He accepted the no-strike pledge, but like Kaplan believed that this did not mean refusing to fight the company for workers' rights. Kaplan, interview, 6 April 1988; Victor Johnson, "Why War Workers Strike: The Case History of a Shipyard 'Wildcat'" *The Nation*, 15 January 1944, 68–71. For a sketch of Blackie Myers' position within the trade union movement and the contest with Curran, see Milton, *The Politics of U.S. Labor*. For a profile of Joe Curran, see Charles P. Larrowe, *Harry Bridges, The Rise and Fall of Radical Labor in the U.S.* (New York: Lawrence Hill, 1972), 288–290.
73. Green and Van Gelder to Dempsey, 24 August 1943; "Suspension of Local Autonomy Notice," circa September 1943; Green to Charles George, 15 September 1943; Vivian

Shirley Nason (Local 16 Publicity Director) to Green, 17 and 29 September 1943; Green to MacPherson, 9 October 1943; John Grogan, minutes of meeting held on 1 October in Jersey City; "Memorandum of Understanding Reached at Conference Held in Office of John Green on 5 October 1943, Regarding Local 16 Situation." All Series 5, Box 51, IUMSWA Archives. Kaplan, telephone interview by author (handwritten notes), 20 June 1989; Foy and Kaplan, interview; Van Gelder, interview, 17 September 1988. IUMSWA, *Proceedings, 9th National Convention*, New York City, 21–24 September 1943, delegate list.

74. Shipbuilding Commission, Directive Order, 15 September 1943; Victor Johnson, "Report to President Green Re Dismissals of Five Committeemen," circa November 1943, Series 5, Box 5, IUMSWA Archives.

Some labor historians have strongly criticized the no-strike pledge. Every worker interviewed by the author, however, believed in the importance of this restraint as a way to support American soldiers and sailors overseas. This was true of those on the political left, center, and right. The real issue was whether the pledge was absolute, or whether infractions were justified at times. The CIO leadership, of course, completely opposed any strikes or slow-downs, at least in official statements. For a contrast in perspectives at the local level, see author interviews with Andy Reeder (30 May 1987 and 21 May 1988), and Ben Maiatico. Reeder claimed Maiatico was defeated for reelection as Local 1 secretary-treasurer in 1944 because he called striking shipyard workers "scabs." Reeder opposed the actions of these strikers, but he was measured in his response and considered their grievances to be just. Maiatico believed that they were completely wrong, regardless of their grievances, and that they were going against the cause of winning the war. Arthur Boyson, local IUMSWA rank-and-file officer at the Fore River yard, also took a tough stand against strikers in 1944, but was a popular figure in the 1945 election campaign. Boyson also defended John L. Lewis in front of other trade unionists, despite Lewis's role in leading the wartime coal strikes.

The situation at the local level was often more complex than portrayed by historians. For a critical view of CIO unions' and workers' positions on the no-strike pledge, see Lichtenstein, *Labor's War at Home*. For an alternative, positive perspective, see Joshua Freeman, "Delivering the Goods: Industrial Unionism during World War II," in Daniel J. Leab, *The Labor History Reader* (Urbana: University of Illinois, 1985), 383–406. Lichtenstein discusses the Federal Shipbuilding wildcats of 1943, but does not discuss the role of the left in Local 16.

75. Levin, letter to author, 8 January 1989.
76. Johnson, "Report to President Green Re Dismissals of Five Committeemen."
77. Ibid.
78. Ibid.
79. Johnson, "Report to President Green Re Dismissals of Five Committeemen"; Kaplan, interview.
80. NWLB "Strike Wire" to Korndorff, Abelow, and Green, 12 October 1943; MacPherson to Davis (NWLB), 20 October 1943. Both RG 202, Box 7750, (file) "Shipbuilding Commission–Dispute Case Files: 111-2546 to 111-2642", NA. Johnson and Joseph Agata to Philip Murray, 27 November 1943; Notice by Love on automatic check-off, 22 November 1943. Both Series 5, Box 51, IUMSWA Archives.
81. Kaplan, interview, 6 April 1988; Johnson, "Report to President Green Re Dismissals of Five Committeemen."
82. For the final part of the legal history of the union security issue at Federal Shipbuilding in 1944, see Shipbuilding Commission of the NWLB, Supplemental Directive Order

and Opinion, Case No. 111-2612-D, 28 January 1944; NWLB, Division of Field Operations, Section of Regional Case Review, Case No. 111-2612-D, 6 March 1944; Arbitrator's Award (by David Benetar), Federal Shipbuilding and IUMSWA Local 16, 14 April 1944; Arbitrator's Award (by Benetar), 15 June 1944. All RG 202, Box 7750, (file) "Shipbuilding Commission–Dispute Case Files: 111-2546 to 111-2612," NA.
83. For the 1944 Local 16 election, see Palmer, "Organizing the Shipyards" (Ph.D. diss.), 758–65.
84. Palmer, *Organizing the Shipyards*, 232–34; John Green obituary, *The Shipbuilder*, 28 February 1957; interviews with Kaplan, Reeder, Van Gelder, Reeder, Maiatico.
85. Around this time, some in the IUMSWA GEB were accusing Irving Velson (a GEB member and Brooklyn activist) of being a Communist. Van Gelder defended Velson as a good trade unionist and opposed the red-baiting. Velson never affirmed or denied membership in the party, but seems to have had an excellent record in the IUMSWA for union work. The September 1943 convention voted to expel him from office, over the objections of Van Gelder and others. Green never forgot Van Gelder's stance on the issue, which may have been one of the reasons he moved against Van Gelder later. Ross Blood, the man who eventually replaced Van Gelder as national secretary-treasurer, chaired the committee that accused Velson. See IUMSWA, *Proceedings, 9th National Convention*, New York City, 21–24 September 1943, 118–151.
86. Ibid.
87. Ibid.
88. Van Gelder, interviews; Fore River Shipyard IUMSWA Local 5 officers and members, interview by author, Quincy, Mass., 26 May 1987.
89. Reeder, interviews.
90. Foy, interviews.
91. The anticommunist persecution of Nat Levin was so severe that his family has never wanted him to meet with the author in person. Levin compromised with his family by talking with the author by phone, but mainly corresponding through detailed letters.
92. Kaplan, interview, 6 April 1988; Johnson, "Why War Workers Strike"; Tully, interview.
93. Kaplan, telephone interview by author (handwritten notes), 24 October 1999; and other Kaplan interviews.
94. Kaplan, interviews; Lou Kaplan obituary.
95. These forums included seminars with students at Harvard University, Princeton University, and Rutgers University; and New York Shipbuilding Welders' reunions (1986, 1987, 1988) organized by Andy Reeder in Camden, New Jersey. Van Gelder, Reeder, and Maiatico were featured speakers at the 1986 reunion. This particular event was attended by hundreds of shipyard retirees and their families, and was widely covered in local newspapers and television.

The Battle for Standard Coil

The United Electrical Workers, the Community Service Organization, and the Catholic Church in Latino East Los Angeles

☼

KENNETH C. BURT

In 1952, the United Electrical, Radio, and Machine Workers (UE) battled the newly chartered International Union of Electrical, Radio and Machine Employees (IUE) in East Los Angeles. The two unions struggled for the right to represent electrical workers at Standard Coil, a secondary supplier that provided parts for the Sabre Jet. The UE had been expelled from the CIO in 1949 for following the Communist Party line, and the CIO chartered the IUE the same day to bring electrical workers back into the CIO fold. A close look at this previously unexamined campaign demonstrates two important points in the evolving understanding of organized labor and the Cold War. First, the election was not fundamentally a conflict between the right and the left, but a bitter battle within the liberal left. Second, local conditions and alliances were the principal determinants of election results. While the IUE utilized anticommunist rhetoric and drew support from a range of anticommunist allies in its battle for Standard Coil, it was ultimately grassroots issues, and not the national red scare, that decided the election.

The rivalry between the UE and the IUE mobilized competing constellations of allied organizations. The IUE received aid from the CIO, the Catholic Church, the commercial media, and various federal agencies. The UE won assistance from the other unions similarly expelled from the CIO and from the Communist Party (CP) itself. As in many other representational elections involving UE, a majority of the workers at Standard Coil were ethnic Catholics. In contrast to the large General Electric and Westinghouse plants in the East and Midwest, the factory in Los Angeles was relatively small and the workforce was comprised overwhelmingly of young Latinas. In addition, the UE was not the largest electrical union in Los Angeles—Manufacturing Local 1710 of the AFL International Brotherhood of

Electrical Workers (IBEW) was larger. The most ironic twist in this case was that the UE was *not* nobly defending itself from a "raid" by another union. At Standard Coil, the *UE* was doing the raiding.[1]

The battle for Standard Coil took place amidst the sea change that transformed both labor and Latino politics in greater Los Angeles and especially on the east side, the heart of radical Los Angeles, between 1947 and 1952. In 1949 the Communist Party and its allies lost control of the Los Angeles CIO Council, which for a decade had enjoyed enormous influence and prestige within the liberal labor left. The CP also lost most of its influence in Hollywood. Contributing factors included the jurisdictional defeat of the Conference of Studio Unions by the International Association of Theatrical and Stage Employees (IATSE, AFL), the House Un-American Activities Committee's targeting of Communists, and the blacklisting of suspected Reds by studio executives. During this period the Catholic Church increased its role within the labor movement and the ethnic community by establishing the Catholic Labor Institute and endorsing the Mexican American–oriented Community Service Organization (CSO).[2]

Through CSO, the frequently victimized Latino community achieved unprecedented power, including the 1949 election of Edward R. Roybal to the Los Angeles city council. CSO represented the first efforts by Mexican Americans to organize themselves with the assistance of Saul Alinsky, the Chicago-based, independent radical, and head of the Industrial Areas Foundation (IAF). Alinsky hired Fred Ross as the CSO organizer. CSO fundamentally altered the political dynamic on the east side by registering 15,000 new voters and developing a membership of 1,000. It then leveraged this new power by forming multicultural alliances, particularly with liberal to radical Jews. Politically, CSO and Roybal created a new space between traditional Democratic Party liberalism and the Communist left, although it worked with elements of both; the CP and the CIO Council sought to gain influence among Latinos and endorsed Roybal's election in 1949. In becoming the first Mexican American elected to the city council in modern history, Roybal had mobilized Latinos while forming a broad multicultural coalition. The core of the progressive coalition consisted of Latinos and Jews, the Catholic Church, the CIO United Steelworkers, and the AFL International Ladies Garment Workers Union.[3]

By contrast, the AFL Central Labor Council and the Building Trades Council opposed Roybal, preferring to stay with the pro-labor incumbent, Parley P. Christensen. So, too, did the AFL Labor League of Hollywood Voters, a federation of twenty-odd Hollywood unions. It issued a statement that lauded Christensen and attacked Roybal for accepting support from the CIO Council and its leftist allies. "It is the position of the League of Hollywood Voters," the statement read, "that 'Stalinists' constitute the main menace to full democracy and complete civil rights at home and abroad, and any candidate who accepts their support is automatically an opponent of free labor and good citizens alike." Actors Guild president Ronald Reagan and IATSE head Roy Brewer, who was leading the attack on the Hollywood left, led the league.[4]

This represented a dramatic realignment on the liberal left, because Councilman Christensen was a leftist icon. In 1920 he served as the presidential candidate of the Farmer-Labor Party. That same year he visited Lenin in the Soviet Union and was very close to the CP and left-led Los Angeles CIO Council. When Roybal ran for the city council the first time in 1947, leftist voters stayed with the incumbent. "He had a long and vigorous record of support for the Left and it would have been ingratitude to reject him," said Dorothy Healey, head of the Los Angeles Communist Party.[5] But the CP's needs changed during the 1948 presidential campaign when it was seeking to build the Independent Progressive Party in California. This third party recruited two Latinos with CSO ties to run for public office, and for the first time the CIO Council and the CP supported a Latino against a pro-labor incumbent. This tactical development dovetailed with a new ideological construct. "The only way to combat racism" was "to support minority candidates," even against "more progressive" or "better prepared" white candidates, according to CP activist Leroy Parra.[6]

Standard Coil thrived as a secondary supplier in the booming civilian economy and the growing, federally subsidized, military industrial complex in Los Angeles. Its product line included both TV tuners and a part for the Sabre Jet. The company's workforce was young, 90 percent female, and 70 percent Mexican American. Memories vary as to conditions at the plant. Twenty-four-year-old Helen Almanza Hatch, who had completed only two years of high school and whose family had worked as farm and cannery workers, remembers the factory as providing good jobs.[7] In contrast, Marie Mundy, an Irish American whose husband was an active member of the AFL Plumbers Union, remembers it as "an awful place to work."[8] Records indicate that the company sought to increase profits by engaging in such old-fashioned techniques as speeding up the assembly line to finish a contract and then laying off workers until the next job was ready to start. The company reportedly tolerated sexual harassment, docked workers pay for taking too long to visit the company nurse, lacked maternity leave, showed favoritism in the assignment of jobs and layoffs, and paid women less than men for doing the same job.[9]

Local 1710 of the AFL IBEW represented the workers at Standard Coil. The 5,800-member local had grown out of the union's building trades local and represented more electrical workers in Los Angeles than either the independent UE or the IUE-CIO. Prior to the formation of Local 1710 in May 1951, Building Trades Local 11 represented Standard Coil workers. It is not clear why the members' loyalty to the union at Standard Coil was so tenuous. Possible causes include a weak and poorly enforced contract, constant membership turnover, a slowness to embrace ethnic community concerns, and a cultural and occupational gap between the male and non-Latino union building trades leadership and the largely female and Mexican American manufacturing workers. Another issue was that the union was not being democratically run; an IBEW representative with the power to appoint officers and shop stewards administered the new local. Management, moreover, did not cooperate with the union to implement modern employee relations practices, including the prompt handling of grievances.[10]

The IBEW, like the AFL Central Labor Council (CLC), had dutifully supported Christensen, an Anglo city council incumbent, instead of joining the social movement that swept Roybal into office in 1949. Shortly afterwards, however, IBEW Local 1710 embraced Roybal and engaged the Mexican American community by joining the CSO Labor Advisory Committee. The CLC worked to pass the Roybal-authored fair employment ordinance, and provided monetary and political help at key junctures, including Councilman Roybal's reelection in 1951. The CLC also pressured the city council in early 1952 to investigate the police beating of CSO President Tony Rios and the Bloody Christmas beatings, when drunken cops assaulted a group of young Latinos and Anglos in their custody.[11]

UE Local 1421 was a militant union with roughly 3,000 members that had contracts with Columbia Records, GE, RCA, Westinghouse, and other small shops and factories. The union had long supported Communist-guided Popular-Front organizations active among Mexican Americans, including the Spanish Speaking People's Congress, or "Congreso." The Congreso played a historic role in creating a broad-based Latino political presence, but the group shrank dramatically after it followed the shift in the Communist Party line after the signing of the Nazi-Soviet Non-Aggression Pact. The UE likewise played a leadership role in the Sleepy Lagoon Defense Committee. However, the UE, like the larger CP-led Los Angeles CIO Council, had not supported Latino city council or state legislative candidates, including Eduardo Quevedo, the first Congreso president. Not supporting Quevedo was "a toughie," according to former International Longshoremen's and Warehousemen's Union (ILWU) Warehouse Local 26 president Bert Corona. "We had to swallow our pride. We had to follow the CIO line because we needed labor."[12] This was also the case in 1947 when they joined the AFL in backing Councilman Christensen against Roybal and a Jewish candidate.

The UE decided in early 1951 to challenge the IBEW when its contract at Standard Coil expired in March 1952. In March 1951, as the IBEW's manufacturing workers were in the process of becoming a separate local, the UE began to identify dissatisfied employees and to organize them covertly within the plant. The UE also encouraged supporters to take jobs at the plant. The lead organizer was International Representative Henry Fiering, the UE's trouble-shooter on the West Coast and one of the union's top liaisons with the CP. He joined the CIO in 1936 and had worked for the Steelworkers and the United Auto Workers before moving to UE. "We acted like a union from the word go and we got our hands on the first group of people. Taught them how to solve grievances, how to fight grievances while they were building the union," stated Fiering proudly. "And we did it in such a way so that they protected themselves, they had an organization. . . . We carried on slowdowns, and the boss didn't know who was responsible, how it got started."[13]

Management at Standard Coil may not have been able to determine who initiated such job actions, but by August 1951 the IBEW (according to the International's summary of its own records), recognized that the union faced "organized resistance" and would "need cooperation from the employer." Management declined to help, apparently happy to see a divided workforce. The IBEW Local 1710 filed charges against the employer with the National Labor Relations Board (NLRB) "for aiding and assisting the U.E. to secure signatures for membership" and claimed in a worksite leaflet that the company was sponsoring "U.E. propaganda to stall contract negotiations." The IBEW later stated that the employer changed its attitude only when "the UE opened a campaign against Local 1710" in November 1951. The company's interest in the UE is unclear; either a dislike of the radical union or a patriotic request by the FBI, or both, could have motivated the company's new fight stance.[14]

The UE filed a petition for a representational election on 29 November 1951, when it had 433 signatures out of a thousand-member workforce. UE Organizer Louis Torre noted confidently in his internal report: "We have the initiative in the campaign so far and if we keep it moving, we will win."[15]

The UE rented a storefront office around the corner from the plant on Valley Boulevard, held regular small-group meetings with workers in different sections of the plant, conducted plant-wide meetings, and sponsored dances and other social events. Inside the plant, members of the Labor Youth League (the successor to the Young Communist League) formed the backbone of the sixteen-member organizing committee. The UE also sought to inoculate itself against future attacks on the issue of Communism by conducting "a very thorough educational job on the people," according to IUE National Organizer Lee Lundgren, who ominously wrote IUE President James Carey that Standard Coil "is going to be quite a project to undertake."[16]

Workers in the plant noticed subtle changes that they did not fully understand. Helen Almanza Hatch, who worked on the assembly line, recalls that "a bunch of people got hired about the same time and they seemed to know each other. They were very friendly and always talking. They threw big parties and invited all the girls. But they wore poor clothes. So I became suspicious. How did they afford to throw such big parties?"[17] Grace Almanza Carlos added, "The Communist-inspired union had sent in spies to wine and dine these girls who were very young and very impressionable."[18]

The IUE-CIO was alerted to the situation by an IBEW steward, who was confused by a UE-distributed flyer implying that it was part of the CIO. Soon thereafter the IUE filed the necessary authorization to appear on the ballot along with the UE and the IBEW. So did the AFL International Association of Machinists (IAM), which represented many auto mechanics and machinists in the airplane industry.[19]

The IUE's central purpose was to wrest control of the electrical industry from the UE through a series of union representational elections and thereby bring the electrical workforce back into the CIO. The IUE-CIO enjoyed the active support of the Catholic Church, President Truman, and numerous federal agencies. The liberal U.S. president shared the CIO's disdain toward the UE's policies—especially its defense of the Soviet Union's forceful annexation of Eastern Europe and the Baltics, its opposition to the Marshall Plan, and its efforts to torpedo Truman's 1948 election by supporting the candidacy of Henry Wallace. Federal government opposition to the UE came from both the liberal NLRB and the conservative FBI, which was preoccupied with fighting Communism.

While the IUE-CIO won key battles against the UE in other states, nationally it was facing tough financial times and it was a newcomer to the labor scene in Los Angeles. The CIO union had no contracts in LA, no budget, and only one staff member, who was working out of the office of CIO Southern California Regional Director Irwin DeShetler. The CIO's organizing staff was also stretched; the person Lundgren expected to help him at Standard Coil was assigned to the CIO Furniture Workers, which was competing against an independent leftist union and one sponsored by the AFL.[20]

Despite limited resources, Lundgren moved to establish himself and put together the necessary pieces for a successful campaign against the UE at Standard Coil. A welder in Chicago during World War II, Lundgren rose through the UE, first to chief shop steward, then secretary-treasurer, and finally to field representative for Local 1150. Following his election, the president of the union local recruited him into the Communist Party, where for the next five years he operated—by his own admission—as part of the Communist group that controlled the local union. Then in late 1950, Lundgren publicly broke with his former comrades and joined the staff of the new IUE. This conversion resulted in a fierce ideological commitment, a rare understanding of the UE's organizing tactics, and a firsthand knowledge that many of the UE leadership who had signed the legally required non-Communist affidavits were still active in the CP.[21]

Lundgren's strategy operated on at least four levels. First, he pressed the national IUE-CIO office to lobby the NLRB informally to delay the representational election at Standard Coil ("At the present time UE could win the election hands down," he told the IUE General Counsel).[22] Second, he distributed literature to the workers and identified possible supporters. Third, he used the good offices of the CIO to gain the support of labor leaders in Boyle Heights, particularly in the Steelworkers, Amalgamated Clothing Workers, and the International Ladies Garment Workers Union. Fourth, he went through the CIO and these local unions to gain support from key community groups such as the CSO and the Catholic Labor Institute. These groups were bound to the progressive anticommunist labor movement by personal ties, overlapping members, political alliances, and direct financial support.[23]

This network of heavily Latino unions assumed the role of a private IUE strategy team. To win the election, they advised Lundgren, the IUE needed to start an all-out campaign that included opening up an office near the plant, infiltrating a couple of loyal Mexican Americans into the plant, and hiring a Latino organizer from the Boyle Heights area.[24]

On 7 March, with the election date still not set, Lundgren wrote to National IUE President James Carey, reporting on the support for the CIO among Mexican Americans and emphasizing the importance of an IUE victory in LA:

> The Mexican people in the LA labor movement are particularly concerned [about the continued strength of the UE]. This is especially true of the Mexican organizers in both the CIO and AFL, who work very closely in the Community Service Organizations (CSO). This organization was set up primarily to fight for minority rights, and reduce the strength of the CP,

which was capitalizing on the discrimination against minority groups in LA. The CSO also did a very effective job in helping to elect councilman Roybal, the Mexican councilman in LA, who comes from the Boyle Heights area. As you can see, this organization carries quite a bit a weight in this community where the Standard Coil plant is located.

A victory for the UE in the Standard Coil plant would be a set back not only to IUE-CIO but also to this excellent group of anticommunists. We know with CSO support we can pressure Councilman Roybal to attack the UE as a Communist union. Roybal has tremendous influence among Mexicans in Boyle Heights and can materially help us.[25]

While Lundgren misstated that the CSO was designed to limit the CP influence, the Alinsky-affiliated organization nonetheless had that effect by empowering Mexican Americans to elect public officials and to influence public policy. The CP and its front group's appeal had been greatest when they spoke to unaddressed grievances.[26]

CIO Regional Director DeShetler, who had helped orchestrate the purge of the CIO Council and who had a reputation as a no-holds barred anticommunist, went on the offensive by publicly naming key UE organizers as Communists. He generated articles in the daily newspapers and the Catholic archdiocese paper, *The Tidings*, which served to alert the faithful about the impending representational election.[27]

Recognizing a heightened sense of frustration at the plant and threatened by the growing popularity of the UE, the IBEW and company management worked together to settle all grievances and conclude negotiations for a new contract. The company even flew in twenty women, covered by an IBEW contract with Standard Coil in Chicago, to champion the incumbent union. The UE responded to the worker wage-gains by saying: "We'll take all the raise and benefits we can get now and then go back for the rest after the election—WHEN UE NEGOTIATES A [NEW] CONTRACT."[28]

Organized labor was not the only organization interested in the unionization of immigrant workers and in fighting Communism. So too was the Catholic Church. The IUE gained an invaluable ally in the church when Archbishop James Francis McIntyre took a personal interest in the election. McIntyre's predecessor, Bishop John J. Cantwell, D.D., and his top aide in the field of social justice, the Right Reverend Monsignor Thomas O'Dwyer, had worked with individuals suspected of being Communists in a number of cases. This was particularly true in the case of Phillip "Slim" Connelly, a parochial school-trained, Mass-attending Communist who had headed the LA CIO Council from 1939 to 1949 (when the left lost control). The Catholic Interracial Council of Los Angeles, advised by the Reverend George Dunne, S.J., even awarded its Blessed Martin de Porres award to Connelly. Monsignor O'Dwyer, described as a "leftist" by James Mendez, a Trotskyist CSO leader, headed the CIO effort in 1946 to pass a California voter initiative to increase public housing. That same year, O'Dwyer, representing Bishop Cantwell, had tried to settle the Hollywood Studio Strike to the benefit of the leftist Conference of Studio Unions, which was led by Herb Sorrell, another Catholic who followed the CP line.[29]

Unlike the Interracial Council award to Connelly, whom the American Bishops identified as a Communist in their secret study "The Problem of American Communism in 1945," the actions of Cantwell and O'Dwyer fit comfortably within existing orthodoxy. According to the eyes-only report, ". . . no Catholic should join a strict front group. On the other hand, where Communists infiltrate an existing organization, such as a labor union, the situation is entirely different. Here is a legitimate organization, directed towards an essentially good purpose, and accidentally infected to some degree with Communism." The document added that Catholics should stay engaged in such groups and emphasized that "[t]he problem of Communism in the C.I.O. will be solved at the local, not the national level."[30]

In 1947 the church provided its imprimatur to the CSO in the form of a letter of support signed by Associate Bishop Joseph McGucken. CSO organizer Fred Ross effectively used the letter to provide assurance that the progressive Alinsky-affiliated organization had no ties with Communists. The church institutionalized its role in the CSO with the placement of Reverend William Barry on the CSO executive board. Even here, CSO, the church, and the Communists had a complex relationship. The CSO allowed Communists to join, while working to insure that they did not take control. Father Barry, for example, became reconciled to Communist participation in the CSO voter registration drive once Alinsky assured him that it was justified, provided it advanced CSO goals.[31]

The Archdiocese's toleration of Communists ended in 1948 when Pope Pius XII appointed McIntyre, a protégé of New York's Cardinal Francis Spellman, to head the church in Los Angeles. A product of Wall Street, McIntyre was by nature more conservative and more zealous in his anticommunist views than his predecessor. His personal convictions were reinforced by international developments. Unable to negotiate an understanding with Josef Stalin to stop the Communist slaughter of ordained religious leaders, particularly in Eastern Europe, the Pope declared in 1949 that a Communist could not be a Catholic, and he forbade Catholics from associating with Communists.[32] Then in 1952 the Vatican issued a "shocking catalogue" of 142 members of the Catholic hierarchy, most of them in Eastern Europe, who had been "either murdered, imprisoned, expelled or otherwise impeded in the exercise of their offices" by Communists. At the same time, the bishops also stressed the "plight of millions of Catholic laity" there.[33]

This evolution in dealing with Communists was also present among liberal and progressive Catholics, including labor priests, at a national level. Catholic leaders who had joined President Roosevelt and the CP in aiding the organization of the CIO during the thirties were becoming increasingly focused on removing the pro-Soviet left from the labor movement. In 1950, the Rev. Raymond A. McGowan, Director of Social Action for the National Catholic Welfare Conference, addressed the IUE's second annual convention. "You have broken loose from the old Communist-dominated union," he stated, adding, "Communist-controlled unions have lost all claim on the loyalty of their members. Communism helped the North Korean aggressors and threatens World War III."[34]

For Archbishop McIntyre, ambitious and strongly anticommunist, Standard Coil represented both an obligation and an opportunity. He used the issue of Communism to mold the Catholic faithful into a powerful political block, show his loyalty to Rome, and expand the church's influence with key economic and political groups in Los Angeles who shared a commitment to anticommunism. This included both the city's Protestant and conservative business leaders and also liberal labor leaders in the AFL and CIO. McIntyre also strengthened his relationship with organized labor by participating in the annual Labor Day Mass and decreeing that all new church construction would be union-built.[35]

The Archbishop's intervention set in motion a series of actions that reverberated throughout the east side and profoundly altered the pre-election dynamic at Standard Coil. Father John V. Coffield remembered getting the word from the archbishop: "The FBI contacted the archbishop and told him that at Standard Coil, these Communists were just about ready to have voting, take over from the IBEW, and transfer to the UE." Coffield continued, "So the archbishop got in touch with those of us who were interested, and said, 'Contact these gals and help them to understand what's at stake. These Communists are going to take over.'" For the east side priests, Americanism, Catholicism, and pastoral responsibility were now inseparable, and the Holy Mother Church had an opportunity to defeat godless Communism at Standard Coil.[36]

The east side clergy swung into action, using FBI-supplied lists of members working at Standard Coil. One of the clergy's most effective tactics was to meet with members of their congregation to explain the grave moral implications of supporting a union linked to the persecutors of Christians behind the Iron Curtain. The priests also skillfully involved the parents of young women workers to counterbalance UE influence. Reverend Coffield recalled how many of the young women were "real impressed" because the more worldly UE leaders sponsored parties with liquor. According to CSO President Anthony P. (Tony) Rios, "Father Coffield in El Monte called two meetings with [Standard Coil] workers and their families. Once he started, other churches followed suit."[37]

Priests like Coffield counseled parishioners such as Helen Almanza Hunt as part of these organized meetings and also served as spiritual advisors to workers in the plant such as Ramona Almanza Granados. Granados, age thirty-nine, had previously worked, along with her mother and daughter, in an El Monte walnut factory and as a farm worker in the Central Valley. She had become a dyed-in-the-wool New Deal Democrat and had two brothers serving in World War II. Now she was a "floor lady" to whom the younger women looked for advice. "Father Coffield used to be her mentor, teach her what was going on, because she didn't understand a lot of it," recalled her daughter.[38]

The warnings of the east side priests influenced the young workers because of the priests' popularity and their reputation as champions of both Mexican Americans and workers. Father Coffield, for example, was known as *Juanote* (or Big John). He was a student of Saul Alinsky and Dorothy Day and was known as a leftist within the church. After he learned that his Latino parishioners in the Hicks Camp barrio of El Monte were unwelcome in the larger English-speaking

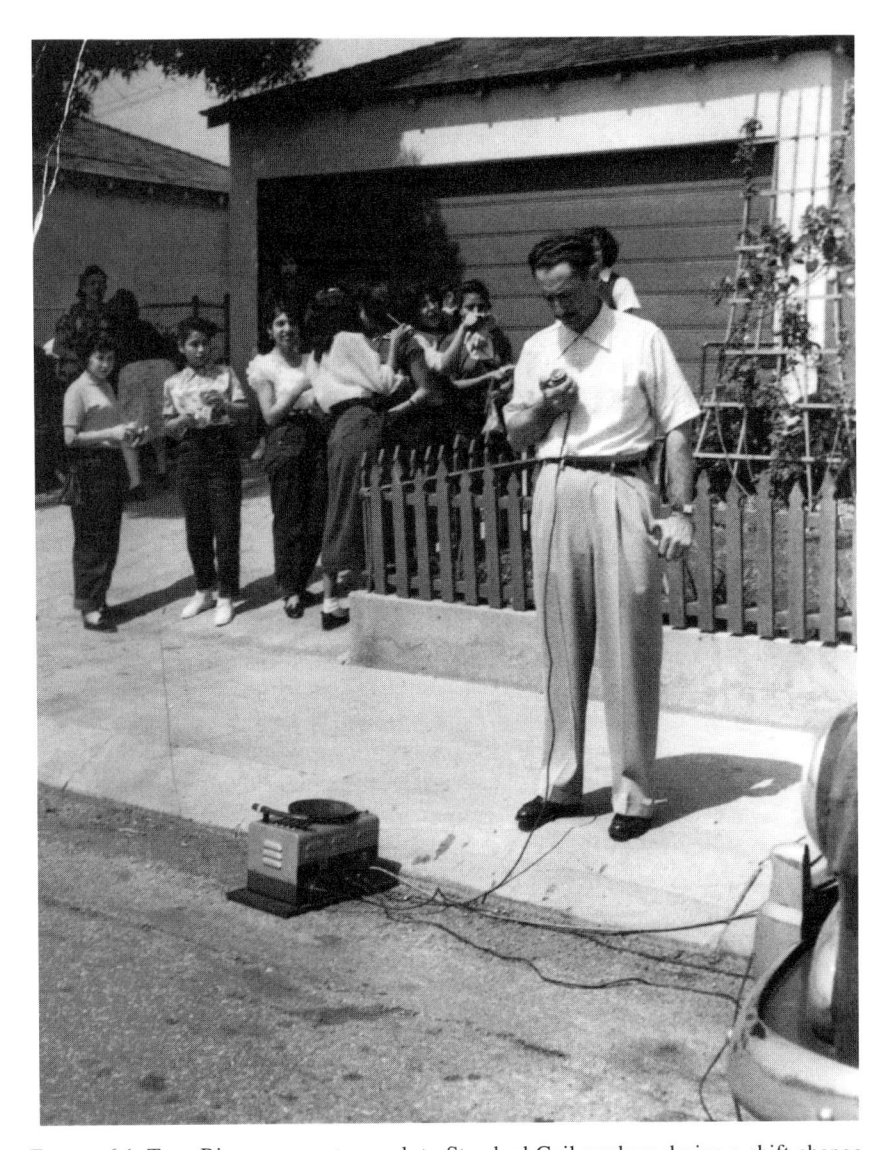

FIGURE 6.1 Tony Rios prepares to speak to Standard Coil workers during a shift change. The decision by the president of the Community Service Organization to become a full-time IUE organizer proved to be a critical turning point in the representation election. *Credit: Photo courtesy of Kenneth C. Burt.*

church, he formed a separate Spanish-speaking parish and built a sanctuary out of an old walnut factory. During World War II, the priest intervened with the military to keep rioting servicemen out of El Monte during the anti-Latino "Zoot Suit" riots. In the late forties he helped organize the Catholic Labor Institute's annual Labor Day Mass and helped found the Catholic Labor School at St. Mary's in Boyle Heights. Moreover, Reverend Coffield used the Young Catholic Student/Young

Catholic Worker program to teach the Social Gospel and to prepare the young adults for union leadership.[39]

With its own credibility now riding on the election, the church moved to insure that the IUE had the best possible Mexican American organizer, preferably one from the neighborhood. CSO President Tony Rios seemed the ideal candidate. A thirty-four-year-old steelworker, Rios was an officer in his union and a member of the Los Angeles County Democratic Central Committee. He was also an experienced labor and community organizer, with both deep roots in the east side and a broad political reach across Los Angeles. As a founder of the CSO, he had played a key role in registering 15,000 new voters, electing Councilman Roybal, establishing links to other civil rights groups, and generally establishing Latinos as a dynamic force within the community. Rios identified himself as a Catholic Worker or Christian Socialist, and he knew a large number of Communists. He also maintained relationships with people and groups within the growing anti-Stalinist left, which shared accumulated grievances against the CP and the Soviet Union, including Stalin's murder of Socialist labor leaders in Eastern Europe and the assassination of Leon Trotsky in Mexico.[40]

Perhaps most importantly, Rios had become an icon in Latino Los Angeles. He was the first Mexican American victim of police brutality to confront the Los Angeles Police Department (LAPD) and win. Rios was arrested in January 1952 for interfering with a police officer because he assisted a man being beaten outside a cafe by a drunken undercover cop. The police arrested Rios and then beat him at the police station. The beatings stopped only through the intervention of Roybal. Unintimidated by police threats to his life, Rios went public with charges of police brutality, and Fred Ross organized support for him within the Latino, labor, and liberal communities. Rios defeated the LAPD in court when an Anglo jury found him not guilty of "interfering with a police officer."[41]

Rios then attacked the systemic violence in the police department and encouraged the victims of another police beating to make their case public. He also arranged for Roybal, O'Dwyer, AFL and CIO leaders, and leaders in the Jewish, Japanese, and African American communities to join in demanding an investigation of police practices in minority communities. This provoked a citywide crisis of confidence in the police department that grew with a grand jury investigation into the LAPD's role in the "Bloody Christmas" beatings and resulted in a criminal trial and the first-ever imprisonment of police officers for abusing minorities.[42]

Lundgren could not convince Rios to work for the IUE. Rios was earning more at his foundry job and was steadfast in his commitment to the CSO, and he was reluctant to give up either. So Lundgren turned to the church for assistance. "Lee Lundgren and representatives of the eighteen priests who were pledged to fight the raid met with me to ask me to help them stop the UE," Rios vividly recalled. "They asked me to take a leave of absence from my job for ninety days, which I did."[43]

One of the first things Rios did was to attack the Communists for using his police beating to advance their own agenda. "We caught the UE raising money for my defense, but they never turned it in," Rios recalled. While emphasizing that the threat to American freedom and the problems of police brutality were real, Rios publicly attacked the Committee to Preserve American Freedoms as a "Communist front group" seeking to "exploit police abuses for their own totalitarian ends." He demanded that they cease using his name without authorization and urged "sincere community leaders who have been lured into unwittingly permitting their names to be used by this committee" to disassociate themselves from the group. Rios' attack served to highlight the Communist tactic of working through front organizations, thus reinforcing the IUE's claim that the UE was Communist-led.[44]

Rios' aggressive criticism of the Communists and his entry into the Standard Coil campaign as a CIO organizer served as a one-two punch to the UE. First, he dramatically undercut the legitimacy of the UE's civil rights work. Second, while the CSO as an organization did not take a position in the representational election, Rios symbolized the Roybal-church-labor-CSO coalition opposition to the UE. UE Organizer Fiering recalled "it became divisive with the CIO in there, particularly since we had made the great mistake in starting off by championing the cause of two people who had been victimized because they were Chicanos . . . one of whom was a CIO worker. And he comes out with a blast against us—Tony Rios." Rios benefited not only from his status as a victim of a police beating, but also from his links to the CIO, CSO, the Democratic Party, and the American Council of the Spanish-Speaking. So powerful was Rios' position in the community that Fiering described him as "really deputy . . . to Roybal."[45]

Roybal later acknowledged that he expressed his opposition to the UE raid while emphasizing that the CSO never took a position in the controversial election.[46] However, it seems that Roybal's role must have been largely behind-the-scenes. Only at one juncture does his name appear in any of the campaign leaflets or newspaper articles about the campaign, and it was to deny involvement. "Since Councilman Roybal's name was brought into the campaign by the opposition, the UE asked him for a statement on this matter," noted a small item at the bottom of a UE newsletter. "He authorized the UE to print the following: 'I am not a union organizer. I am a City Councilman and I am not taking any sides in the Standard Coil campaign.'"[47]

Roybal's influence was substantial. Not only was he the most prominent Mexican American in Los Angeles, but he was also the principal champion of labor, civil rights, and civil liberties on the city council. Roybal had even risked his political career to support the civil liberties of Communists by casting the lone vote against requiring Communists to register with the city—a principled position he developed with the assistance of the CSO's Fred Ross and Tony Rios.[48]

Now, under Rios' guidance, the IUE's underdog campaign began to hit its stride, although the UE continued to identify the incumbent IBEW as its principal adversary. The national IUE, convinced that they had a chance to win the election, opened its checkbook. It allowed the local union to mount an organizing campaign similar to that already deployed by UE and an increasingly aggressive IBEW, which sponsored a dance and a picnic in addition to negotiating for higher wages. The Standard Coil management, for its part, increased its scrutiny of UE activists inside the plant and fired workers who were a "security risk."[49]

One case of a UE activist firing involved Bette Hollcroft, who started at Standard Coil five years earlier after the UE lost their strike at her former employer, Sterling Electric. She then became the IBEW's Chief Steward for three years before returning to her UE roots when they opened their campaign at Standard Coil. After she was fired, she stated that the company had offered to make her a manager and to give her a shopping trip to New York if she would change sides. "Our eyes were opened up as to how red-baiting is used as a club over workers," wrote the UE in its newsletter. "This proves that red-baiting is the weapon of the bosses. The AFL and CIO gave [plant manager] Swanson the ammunition to use the phony charge of 'Communism' against workers who fight for better conditions."[50]

This was a time when support ran high for American troops fighting the Communists who had invaded non-Communist South Korea. The IUE-CIO reminded the workers that the UE refused to support their siblings, friends, and former classmates fighting in Korea. Standard Coil, they argued, was a defense plant. It made parts for the Sabre Jet, "the only plane," according to the official Air Force historian, "on the friendly side of the Iron Curtain that could consistently slug it out with the [Soviet built] MIG-15."[51]

The UE countered the attacks on its Communist ties by releasing rebuttals from workers such as Manuel Rodriquez, who wrote "I am a Standard Coil worker and of Mexican descent, Catholic, and a veteran of World War II. What is more I am a UE member and intend to stay one." The union also quoted the famous in its defense. A flyer, "UE Defends Democracy . . . and Religious Freedom," quoted a deceased Catholic cardinal who had criticized red-baiting during the Depression, when the Catholic Church and the CP were both supporting CIO organizing efforts. The UE also emphasized that many of its signatories had military contracts and there had never been any problems.[52]

The union likewise continued to emphasize workplace concerns, from poor pay, to the lack of seniority in layoffs, to the arbitrary nature of supervisors and the plant manager. Some of the most potent issues revolved around gender, which were being addressed nationally by UE staff member Betty Friedan.[53]

Organizationally, the UE responded to the increased competition from the IUE at Standard Coil by rushing in more of their best organizers along with UE activists from other area plants. The UE campaign now had five "nationally known" organizers (all non-Latino) and the Spanish-speaking Ignacio Hernandez, who took a leave from his job at Westinghouse to organize at Standard Coil. The union also received help from ILWU Warehouse Local 26 and Mine-Mill Local 700, both of which had large Mexican American memberships and were in internationals that were expelled from the CIO for following the Communist Party line. Ben Dobbs, labor secretary for the Los Angeles Communist Party, coordinated support for the UE. Finally, the UE promised that the workers at Standard Coil would have their own union local.[54]

The UE also sought to persuade and pressure the pro-labor clergy. One of the UE's targets was Father Coffield. "They were furious," recalled Coffield. "One of them came over to tell me what a betrayer of the working class I was." He then added: "But [the UE organizer] was most eager to find out what information the

FBI had on her. So I had to play dumb." He did not reveal that he had received copies of the FBI reports on "these Communist leaders."[55]

The UE also visited the Reverend Thaddeus Shubsda of San Antonio De Paula Parish in Boyle Heights. Shubsda was later the spiritual advisor for the Catholic Labor Institute before becoming Bishop of Ventura and Santa Barbara Counties. Father Shubsda received the UE-led delegation of sixteen workers, but the presence of William Elconin, as the UE union official leading the group, undermined their case because of his long association with the CP. Shubsda then turned the tables on the UE. He used their visit as an opportunity to issue an open letter to Socorro Serrano, the parishioner who most likely arranged the meeting, and the other workers. The letter addressed the close relationship between the UE and the Communist Party, and highlighted the opposition to the UE by political, labor and religious leaders.

> Socorro, it has been proved again and again that the Communist, whether he lives in Los Angeles, Korea, China or Moscow, Russia is part of the same worldwide conspiracy. He takes his orders from the men in the Kremlin who are causing so much misery in the world. They hate God and religion. They are responsible for the murder of thousands of bishops, priests, nuns and Catholic people. They would like to overthrow the United States Government and replace it with a Communist dictatorship, and they intend to use you and your fellow-workers to help them.
>
> In view of all this, it is hard to see how a good Christian, a good American, or any other honest and sensible person could join an organization which is under the thumb of this kind of leadership no matter what they promise you.

"Socorro, we know that there are a lot of things about the wages, benefits, and working conditions at Standard Coil that need plenty of improving," concluded Father Shubsda. "We believe that you need a good, strong, American union to defend your just rights."[56]

"We picked Father Shubsda [to sign the letter] because the Communists are confusing the girls by spreading the false rumor that he said that they are not Communists," Reverend Joseph Kearney wrote, on Catholic Labor Institute stationery, in a letter to east side pastors. He asked the priests to send a copy of the letter along with a "personal note" to their parishioners working at the plant.[57]

With the election scheduled for Tuesday, 20 May, emotions hit fever pitch. The UE sought to hold onto its support by reminding the workers about the unjust treatment by the employer and by contrasting their positive action to defend injured workers with the IUE's and IBEW's rhetoric. The UE charged that red-baiting was only a cover for discrimination against women. In a flyer, "Here's Why They Yell 'Communism,'" the UE reproduced part of a locally-negotiated IUE contract in Springfield, Mass., that stated that, in the event of a layoff, "it will first be applied among married women whose husbands are able to work." Another leaflet contrasted such discrimination to the treatment of women under UE contracts at Dutra Steel and Columbia Records in Los Angeles. There, women were allowed a year's maternity leave. "Her seniority is not only protected but the year she is off while having her baby is added to her seniority as if she had been working."[58]

UE's issue-oriented campaign was reportedly reinforced with threats of violence—what one internal IUE document referred to as "a female goon squad." IUE supporter Helen Almanza Hunt recalled that her older sister, "who worked in the other end of the plant, overheard some people saying that they were going to beat me up if I didn't support the other union. So she got up the courage to tell them that they were talking about her sister, and if they were going to beat me up, they had to go through her first."[59] Grace Almanza Carlos spoke of similar threats. "The girls were so confused, they were crying, going to [my] mother. They were threatening them that if they didn't vote with the other union they would beat them up," said Grace Almanza. "Of course my mother was very outspoken, and very confident, but she was afraid, and she told me she was very afraid. People would drive by [our house]. My mother told us never to go out in the front yard."[60]

The CIO's pro-IUE campaign was complemented by the church's anti-UE message. Rev. Coffield and a number of parish youths joined in leafleting before working at the plant. The banner headline on one flyer screamed: "THE CATHOLIC LABOR INSTITUTE SAYS: 'DON'T LET THE COMMIES FOOL YOU'!!!" The leaflet pushed the church's pro-labor, anticommunist message and stressed: "The Church knows that the Communist, whether he lives in Los Angeles or Moscow, is part of the same world-wide conspiracy." Priests as part of their Sunday sermon "probably" repeated this message, according to Reverend Kearney, the CLI spiritual advisor.[61]

On 20 May, 93 percent of the eligible workers went to the polls. The UE received 301 votes, IUE got 200, IBEW polled 137, and IAM placed last, with 58. Six workers voted for "no union" and 19 ballots were void or challenged. While the UE finished more than one hundred votes ahead of the IUE, it failed to secure a majority of the workers. This represented a major setback to the UE and quantifiably demonstrated the impact of the coordinated campaign that had been waged by the CIO and Catholic Church.[62]

"Immediately following the election we contacted the IBEW and IAM supporters," an elated Lundgren notified national IUE President Carey. "Most of the leaders of these two groups are now openly supporting us. On top of this we have won about ten or fifteen away from the UE. . . . If election could be held within next two weeks we would win."[63]

Now the UE adopted a delaying strategy. The UE filed charges with the NLRB that the company discharged or harassed its supporters while favoring the IUE-CIO. The UE received unwitting help from the IAM-AFL, which challenged the results of the May election based on violations by the UE and the company. Knowing that an expanded voter pool would increase its chance in the runoff, the UE demanded that roughly six hundred new employees be allowed to vote.[64]

The delay frustrated the IUE, which wanted a quick election and was once again facing a dire financial situation. Given that further delays seemed inevitable, however, Lundgren suggested to his national office in August that it should seek to have the election around 1 October to coincide with the House Un-American Activities Committee hearing planned for Los Angeles on 29 September.[65]

At this point, Standard Coil's New York headquarters formally weighed in, arguing to the NLRB that the election delay was interfering with its ability to provide "critical materials for the United States Armed Services." Soon thereafter, the NLRB set the election for 28 August. It also decided to follow precedent by maintaining the existing voter roll (which generally had the effect of making it more difficult for an employer to manipulate the election). The IUE and the UE publicly welcomed the decision to conduct the election in two weeks.[66]

Even with this new date, the IUE was benefiting from the actions of various government agencies investigating the UE's Communist connections.[67] In mid-July, the federal grand jury in Los Angeles had subpoenaed the UE organizer Carl Brant, and his subpoena and appearance before the grand jury made the newspapers. The grand jury directed Brant to come back for further questions on 27 August, the day before the vote at Standard Coil. On 26 August, two days before the election, the House Un-American Activities Committee subpoenaed three UE organizers, William Elconin, Henry Fiering, and Louis Torre, along with a number of rank-and-file members, directing them to testify at a special hearing in Los Angeles on 5 October. To dramatize the subpoena, a United States marshal delivered it to Fiering at the company gate. "Probe Slated on Reds in War Plant," ran the headline in the *Los Angeles Times*.[68]

On 27 August 1952, one day before the election, Brant again testified before the federal grand jury. Afterwards, in open court, the U.S. attorney read a verbatim transcript of Brant's grand jury testimony, complete with his repeated use of the Fifth Amendment, in response to questions about his Communist Party affiliations. This highly unusual legal move produced additional headlines during the final twenty-four hours before the representational election.[69]

Seeking to reduce the impact of these attacks, the UE issued a flyer, "Prominent Americans Expose the Un-American Activities Committee." The handbill quoted President Roosevelt, CIO President Philip Murray, AFL President William Green and Catholic and Protestant sources. The UE also continued to pound away at the unfairness of the IUE and Standard Coil's not supporting the right of all workers to vote.[70]

Finally, on 28 August, the workers at Standard Coil made their selection. The results: UE got 248 votes, IUE received 310, and 377 ballots were challenged. Most of the challenged votes came from newly-hired workers who had been ruled ineligible but wanted to cast a provisional ballot anyway. The UE continued to argue that recently-hired workers should have their ballots counted and claimed election violations by both the company and the IUE. The UE called for a "democratic election—an election which would include the new workers" and criticized the unfairness of the government's last minute efforts to smear the UE leaders. "This crude frame-up of the UE by the company, the IUE-CIO and the Un-American Committee was even admitted as such by an IUE-CIO leader," claimed the UE in its leaflet entitled, "Report of Standard Coil Election." "When [a] IUE-CIO stooge was asked, 'Why didn't you have the subpoenas served eight months ago?' the IUE-CIO leader replied, 'The CIO decided it was most convenient to have it served two days before the election at the plant gates so the people in the shop wouldn't have time to think it over.'" In the end, the NLRB certified that the IUE had won the representational election.[71]

With the vote certified by the NLRB, Rios, Lundgren, and a committee of workers negotiated a new contract at Standard Coil, the first for the IUE-CIO in Los Angeles. The contract provided for substantial wage increases, plant-wide seniority as the basis for promotions and layoffs, and five paid holidays. It also provided for a Christmas bonus, a paid summer vacation, health insurance (including pregnancy coverage), and accidental death and life insurance. The contract also eliminated extra pay for male workers, prohibited racial discrimination, guaranteed health and safety, and created a steward system and binding arbitration to handle grievances.[72]

Despite these major improvements, the factory remained a difficult place to work. The IUE-CIO faced the continuing presence of an organized UE faction within the plant, a company management driven by production schedules, and its own institutional weakness. The IUE held back on confronting the company over contract issues, as it needed to maintain labor peace at Standard Coil while it focused its limited resources on organizing workers at other, smaller plants and shops. (Between the time of the Standard Coil election and the completion of contract negotiations, for example, the IUE-CIO fought and beat the UE, the IAM, and the IBEW for the right to represent workers at RCA in West Los Angeles.) When the IUE decided not to be aggressive in enforcing the contract, Tony Rios resigned his position as IUE organizer "to protect my reputation."[73]

The battle for Standard Coil was the product of its time and place, a local event driven by individuals and organizations within a larger social, political, and economic environment. International, national, and local events all figured in the UE's failed raid, but local people and local relationships proved pivotal. The Catholic Labor Institute provided the most prominent opposition to the UE. But it worked as part of a broad anti-UE coalition, which ranged from the anticommunist left to the anticommunist right, with most participants coming from the liberal-left. Unlike the Association of Catholic Trade Unionists (ACTU) in the East and Midwest, anticommunism played a secondary role in the Los Angeles-based Catholic Labor Institute's overall mission.

The battle for Standard Coil may appear at first glance to be a carbon copy of other anti-UE campaigns. It contained many of the same components, including the intervention of federal agencies (particularly the FBI), the CIO, and the Catholic Church. In addition, evidence indicates that some of the Washington, D.C.-based elements within the anticommunist coalition, such as the House Un-American Activities Committee, did use almost a cookie-cutter approach to the election, following a pattern tested in other elections. The frontline combatants, including CSO president Tony Rios, labor priest John Coffield, and the organizers from the garment unions, were progressives or non-Communist leftists. The lead IUE organizer, Lee Lundgren, was a former CP operative within the UE. The National Labor Relations Board, the CIO, and the Catholic Church (with the exception of people like Archbishop McIntyre) stood on the "right" only where Communists were concerned. Within the larger political spectrum, they were progressive anticommunists. In fact, it was their positioning within the liberal left and their work in the Latino community that made their intervention so effective.

Just as the Standard Coil election was a battle within labor and the liberal left, local conditions and alliances determined the outcome. This helps explains that while the CSO never officially engaged in the conflict, many of those within the CSO milieu took the attack on the IBEW-AFL very seriously. The AFL was a key financial and political supporter of the CSO, and it had defended Tony Rios against his unfair arrest and protested his police beating. But it was the CIO and the Catholic Church to which CSO President Tony Rios was closest. The liberal priests who had helped in his trial defense aided union organizing efforts and played a critical role in the CSO's development. They played two important functions: aiding in parish-level mobilizing of the community, and in defending the CSO from unfair right-wing accusations that it was somehow Communistic. Once the CIO and the labor priests decided to act, people like Tony Rios felt an obligation to put aside other projects to help this effort.

Ultimately Tony Rios provides the key to understanding IUE's success, because his decision to organize for the IUE represents the convergence of political alliances and personal experiences. Rios seized the opportunity to strike a blow to a longtime adversary while at the same time working for the CIO, God, and country. The overlay of ethnicity, religion, ideology, and community reinforced Rios' strength. As a local, working class Latino hero who had defeated the LAPD in court, Rios personified the new east side (and, except for gender, the demographics of the workforce at Standard Coil). By contrast, Fiering, the principal UE organizer, was Jewish and from out of state. Rios was left of center in his politics, and his coalition colleagues included Catholic Workers, Socialists, Trotskyists, and independent radicals. Once Rios mobilized the full weight of this network, the CP lacked enough room on the left to put together a formidable coalition, thus increasing its reliance on CP cadres both inside and outside the Standard Coil plant.

The second most influential person was Father Coffield. Like Rios, he campaigned against the UE out of a sincere belief in the importance of building progressive, non-Communist unions. Forty-five years later he remained proud of his role in the Standard Coil election, listing it as a career highlight along with his successful efforts to keep rioting servicemen from attacking Mexican Americans in El Monte during the "Zoot Suit" riots. Nor was Coffield a mere lackey for Archbishop McIntyre. Coffield was a dedicated church radical whose advocacy on behalf of God's less fortunate often got him in trouble. Later, in the sixties, Cardinal McIntyre banished him from Los Angeles when he thought the priest had ignored a directive to remain silent on the 1964 Fair Housing proposition. Nonetheless, his fiftieth anniversary as a priest was celebrated by, among many others, one-time CSO organizer Cesar Chavez.[74]

Standard Coil and the other bitter battles over the role of Communists within the liberal left were thus largely settled before the national emergence of Senator Joseph McCarthy, whose brand of right-wing anticommunism would define the period in the popular imagination. Liberals and the anti-CP left had already routed the Communists from their perches of influence within liberal and labor groups;

McCarthy's right-wing anticommunism served largely as cover for business interests and their allies in the Republican Party. They were aided by the FBI, which, ironically, opened a file on Rios within months of the Standard Coil election. The FBI also continued a file on Fiering even after he left the UE, even though their own records showed that he quit the Communist Party in 1956—the year that the Soviet Union officially exposed the crimes against humanity committed by Stalin.[75]

Notes

1. University Library System, University of Pittsburgh (hereafter cited as UE Collection); the IUE Collection, Special Collections and Archives, Rutgers University Library, the State University of New Jersey (hereafter cited as IUE Collection); the Catholic Labor Institute Collection, Center for the Study of Los Angeles, Loyola Marymount University, Los Angeles; a chronology provided by the IBEW based on material housed in their office in Washington, D.C.; the Standard Coil file at the Southern California Library for Social Studies and Research, Los Angeles (hereafter cited as Standard Coil File); and the FBI files for Henry W. Fiering (released 31 May 2000), James F. McIntyre (released 16 May 2000), and Anthony P. Rios (released 18 May 2000), obtained by the author through the Freedom of Information Act. Oral histories from people with firsthand knowledge include: Monsignor John V. Coffield, interview by author, San Clemente, Calif. 10 February 1995; Helen Almanza Hunt, interview by author, telephone, 17 January 2000; Grace Almanza Carlos, interview by author, telephone, 17 January 2000; Tony Rios, interviews by author, Los Angeles, Calif., 1994–1998; Ben Dobbs, *Democracy and the American Communist Movement*, interview by Myrna C. Donahoe, 1990, University of California, Los Angeles (UCLA) Oral History; William B. Elconin, *The UE In Southern California*, interview by Myrna C. Donahoe, 1991, UCLA Oral History; Henry W. Fiering, *The UE, AFSCME, and Militant Trade Unionism*, interview by Myrna C. Donahoe, 1991, UCLA Oral History.

    These findings add a new dimension to what Schatz, Mantles and Higgins, and Filipelli and McColloch have uncovered in their work regarding other contested elections at other locations. See Ronald W. Schatz, *The Electrical Workers: A History of Labor at General Electric and Westinghouse, 1923–60* (Urbana: University of Illinois Press, 1983), especially chapter 8; Ronald L. Filippelli and Mark D. McColloch, *Cold War in the Working Class: The Rise and Decline of the United Electrical Workers* (Albany: State Univ. of NY, 1995); Grace Palladino, *Dreams of Dignity, Workers of Vision* (Washington, D.C.: IBEW, 1991); James J. Matles and James Higgins, *Them and Us: Struggles of a Rank-and-File Union* (Englewood, N.J.: Prentice-Hall, Inc., 1974); Robert H. Zieger, *The CIO, 1935–1950* (Chapel Hill: University of North Carolina, 1995).
2. Kenneth C. Burt, "Los Angeles Council, Congress of Industrial Organization," in Mari Jo Buhle, et. al., *Encyclopedia of the American Left*, 2d ed. (New York: Oxford University Press, 1998), 459–461; Kenneth C. Burt, "Latino Empowerment in Los Angeles: Postwar Dreams and Cold War Fears," *Labor's Heritage* 8 (Summer 1996):4–25.
3. Burt, "Latino Empowerment in Los Angeles."
4. "Christensen Endorsed By Labor League of Hollywood," *Eastside Sun*, 18 March 1947; "Hollywood Labor Group Backs Christensen," *Los Angeles Sentinel*, 19 May 1949, sec. A, p. 4; "Voter League OKs Candidates For April 5 Polls," *Los Angles Citizen*, 4 March 1949.
5. Dorothy Healey, letter to author, 10 March 1995.

6. Ismael Parra, interview by author, Whittier, Calif., 24 August 2001. Leroy Parra's son, Ismael, shared his father's passion for politics and involvement in the CP; the author considers his recollections of his father's thinking at the time to be as accurate.
7. Helen Almanza Hunt, interview, Grace Almanza Carlos, interview.
8. Daniel J. and Marie Mundy, interview by author, 13 December 1998.
9. IUE Collection; UE Collection.
10. Grace Palladino, *Dreams of Dignity, Workers of Vision*, 215–217; J. J. Barry, IBEW International President, letter to author, 16 September 1994, with attached, "Chronological List of Events Re: Standard Coil Co. and IBEW L.U. 1710"; Louis Torre, UE, to James Mantles, UE, 22 June 1951, Organizing Files of Lou Torre, Red Dot 90, UE Collection.
11. Rios, interview; CSO documents in author's possession; Minutes, Regular Meeting, Local 11, IBEW, 19 May 1949, 2, east L.A. Electrical Training Trust.
12. Bert Corona, interview by author, 9 August 2000.
13. "Henry Fiering," *The Federation News* (L.A. County Federation of Labor), 1987 March; Fiering UCLA interview; Fiering FBI File; IBEW Chronology, IBEW International; IUE Collection; UE Collection.
14. "Conspiracy Exposed," IBEW Local 1710, n.d., Standard Coil File, IBEW Chronology, IBEW International Union.
15. Louis Torre, Organizer's Report, 16–30 November 1951, Organizing Files of Lou Torre, 1986 Accession, Red Dot 90, UE Collection.
16. Lundgren to Carey, 26 November 1951, Lundgren Files, IUE Field Rep. for L.A., IUE Collection; Carlos, interview; Hatch, interview. Fiering, UCLA interview; Rios, interview; Louis Torre, Organizer's Report, November 1951–May 1952, Organizing Files of Lou Torre, 1986 Accession, Red Dot 90, UE Collection.
17. Hatch, interview.
18. Carlos, interview.
19. Lundgren to Carey, 26 November 1951, with attachments, including letter, Lucienne Miller to Dear Sir, 15 November 1951; Lundgren to Carey, 7 March 1952, IUE Collection.
20. Filippelli and McColloch, *Cold War in the Working Class*; Lundgren to Carey, 26 November 1951, Lundgren Files, IUE Field Rep. for L.A., IUE Collection.
21. IUE Records, President's Office, Box 2027, UE Research Files/Finnegan, Communist Party—Krane and Lundgren Quit UE and Party: Jan 1950, IUE Collection; Secretary-Treasurer's Office, Box 2080, Folder 6, Field Representatives Correspondence, Lee Lundgren, L.A., 1950–1952, Organizing Files of Lou Torre, 1986 Accession, Red Dot 90, UE Collection.
22. Lundgren to Ben Siegel, 9 April 1952, Office of General Council, Legal Department, NLRB Cases, Standard Coil Company, Case No. 21-RC-2288 and 2352, 1952, IUE Collection.
23. Cass Alvin, interviews by author, Downey, Calif. 27 June 1994 and Los Angeles, Calif. 6 May 1995; Coffield, interview; Abe F. Levy, interview by author, Los Angeles 1 May 1996; Rios, interview; IUE Collection.
24. Lundgren to Carey, 7 March 1952, Office of General Counsel, Legal Dept., NLRB-IUE Cases, Standard Coil Company, 21-RC-2288 and 2352, 1952, IUE Collection; Secretary-Treasurer's Office, Field Representative Correspondence Files, Lee Lundgren, Box 2080, Files 7–9, IUE Archives.
25. Letter, Lundgren to Carey, 7 March 1952, Office of General Counsel, Legal Dept., NLRB-IUE Cases, Standard Coil Company, 21-RC-2288 and 2352, 1952, IUE Collection; Secretary-Treasurer's Office, Field Representative Correspondence Files, Lee Lundgren, Box 2080, Files 7–9, IUE Collection.

26. Henry Nava, interview by author, 9 February 1995; Rios, interview; Edward R. Roybal, interview by author, Pasadena, Calif., 10 March 1995; Hope Mendoza Schechter, interviews by author, Sherman Oaks, Calif and by telephone, 1994–1998.
27. "UE Seeking Foothold on east side," *The Tidings*, 28 March 1952; Lundgren to Carey, 31 March 1952, Organizational Report, IUE Collection.
28. IBEW Chronology; Leaflet, "Why Doesn't Swanson Speak Up?" Standard Coil File, Lundgren to Carey, 7 March 1952, IUE Collection.
29. James L. Daugherty, interview by author, Lynwood, Calif. 11 February 1995; Rev. George H. Dunne, S.J., interview by author, Los Angeles, Calif., 7 March 1997; Rev. Michael Engh, S.J., interview by author, Los Angeles, Calif., 7 March 1997; "Presentation of the Blessed Martin De Porres Award For 1946 of the Catholic Interracial Council of Los Angeles to Philip M. Connelly, June 27, 1946," Philip Connelly Papers, Box 2, Folder 5, Special Collections, UCLA.
30. Rev. John F. Cronin, S.S., *The Problem of American Communism in 1945: Facts and Recommendations* (Washington, D.C.: National Catholic Welfare Conference, 1945), National Catholic Welfare Council, Box 24, Communism: Cronin, John F. Report, 1945, 23, 44a, 140, Catholic University of America.
31. Msgr. William J. Barry, interview by author, Newport Beach, Calif., November 2, 1994; Rios, interview; P. David Finks, *The Radical Vision of Saul Alinsky* (New York: Paulist Press, 1984), 40–41.
32. George Morris, *The Vatican Conspiracy in the Trade Union Movement* (New York: New Century Pubishers, 1950), reprinted from *Political Affairs* (Communist Party), June 1950; "Rome Will Excommunicate Communists," 13 July 1949, *Chronicle of the 20th Century* (New York: Prentice Hall, 1978), 665.
33. "Magnitude of War on Church Seen in Compilation of 142 Members of Hierarchy Victims of Reds: 'Modern Martyrology' Includes 2 Cardinals, 26 Archbishops; Names 15 Murdered by Communists," National Catholic Welfare Council, 2 February 1952, NCWC, Box 24, Communism: General, 1951–1952, Catholic University of America.
34. Rev. Raymond A. McGowan, address to Second Annual IUE Convention, National Catholic Welfare Department, Social Action, Labor Relations, 1950, Catholic University of America.
35. Patrick Henning, interviews by author, Sacramento, Calif. 1995 and 1996; Tim Cremmins, interviews by author, Sacramento, Calif., 1995 and 1996; Msgr. Francis J. Weber, *His Eminence of Los Angeles: James Francis Cardinal McIntyre* (Mission Hills: St. Francis Historical Society, 1997).
36. Coffield, interview; Monsignor John V. Coffield, *Memories of Juanote*, with introduction by Bishop William R. Johnson (self-published, 1999), 57. Interestingly, the oldest document in the FBI's file on Cardinal James Francis McIntyre, obtained by the author through the Freedom of Information Act, is dated 20 April 1956. However, it includes the statement that "Cardinal McIntyre has been extremely cooperative with this office in the past and is well known to me." Titular Bishop of California John Ward, in an interview with the author on 4 November 1994, indicated that McIntyre knew the FBI from his days in New York and had private dealings with law enforcement in Los Angeles.
37. Carlos, interview; Hatch, interview; Msgr. Joseph V. Kearney, interview by author, Carpinteria, Calif., January 23, 1995 interview; Rios, interview.
38. Carlos, interview; Hatch, interview.
39. Carlos, interview; Hunt, interview; Kearney, interview; Rios, interview; Rosie Vasquez, interview by author, Los Angeles, Calif., 1997–1999; "The Heyday and Decline of a

Lively Barrio," *Los Angeles Times*, 27 November 1995, sec. B p. 3; "Priest Holds Special 'Magic' With Poor to Be Celebrated," *Los Angeles Times*, 15 June 1991, sec. F, p. 17; Catholic Labor Institute, Archives Center, Archdiocese of Los Angeles.
40. Kenneth C. Burt, "Fighting for Fair Employment: Celebrating the 40th Anniversary of the FEPC," and "Anthony P. Rios, 1914–1999," Program, Jewish Labor Committee Annual Recognition Awards Brunch, Beverly Hills, 6 June 1999; Mendoza Schechter, interviews; Larry Margolin, interview; James Mendez, interview by author, Norwalk, Calif. 11 March 1995; Roybal, interview; Atara Mont, interviews by author, Los Angeles, Calif., 1995–1999; Zane Meckler, interviews by author, 1995–1999; Tony Rios, personal papers.
41. Kenneth C. Burt, "Tony Rios and Bloody Christmas: A Turning Point Between the Los Angeles Police Department and the Latino Community," Western *Legal History: The Journal of the Ninth Circuit Historical Society* 14 (Summer/Fall 2001):159–192.
42. Ibid.
43. Rios, interview.
44. "Hits at Reds Horning in on Cop Brutality," (Los Angeles) *Daily News*, 4 April 1952, Bloody Christmas, Southern California Library.
45. Petition, Standard Coil File; Fiering, UCLA interview, 252–253.
46. Roybal, interview.
47. "A Public Statement," Live Wire, UE-Standard Coil Organizing Committee, 1 April 1952, Standard Coil File.
48. Rios, interview; Roybal, interview; Councilman Edward Roybal, "Communist Control Ordinance," Ross Papers, Box 5, Folder 13, Stanford University; Dorothy Healey, letter to author, 10 March 1995.
49. Rios, interview; IUE Collection; UE Collection; Standard Coil File.
50. Lundgren to Carey, memo, Organizational Report, 31 March 1952, UE Collection; UE Live Wire, 4 April 1952, Standard Coil File.
51. IUE Collection; Richard Ward *North American F-86A-L Sabre in USAF & Foreign Service* (New York: ARCO Pub. Co. Inc., 1970); Robert Frank Futrell, USAF, *The United States Air Force in Korea, 1950–1953* (New York: Duell, Sloan and Pearce 1961), 233; Sergei N. Goncharov, et al., *Uncertain Partners: Stalin, Mao, and the Korean War* (Stanford: Stanford University Press, 1994).
52. Flyer, "'I Am For UE,' by Manuel Rodriquez," and "UE Defends Democracy . . . and Religious Freedom," Misc. Contracts, Red Dot 318, Standard Coil, UE Collection.
53. National Organizers Records, Red Dot 90, Torre files, UE Archives, University of Pittsburgh; Standard Coil File.
54. Lundgren to Hartnett, 14 July 1952, Office of General Counsel, Legal Department, NLRB Cases, Standard Coil Company, Case No. 21-RC-2288 and 2352, 1952, IUE Collection; Dobbs UCLA interview.
55. Coffield, interview, Kearney, interview; Catholic Labor Institute Collection, Loyola Marymount University.
56. Coffield interview; Elconin, UCLA interview; Lee Lundgren to Les Finnegan, 29 May 1952, with attached Open Letter from Father Shubsda, Finnegan files, IUE Collection.
57. Father Joe Kearney to Dear Father, n.d., Catholic Labor Institute Collection, Loyola Marymount University.
58. National Organizers Records, Red Dot 90, Torre files, UE Archives; Misc. Contracts, Red Dot 318, Standard Coil, UE Collection.
59. Hunt, interview; Lundgren to Carey, memo, Organizational Report, 31 March 1952, IUE Collection.

60. Carlos, interview.
61. Kearney, interview; Leaflet, "THE CATHOLIC LABOR INSTITUTE SAYS: 'DON'T LET THE COMMIES FOOL YOU'!!!", Catholic Labor Institute Collection, Loyola Marymount University; Files of Les Finnegan, IUE Collection.
62. Lundgren to Carey, memo, Organizational Report, 29 May 1952, Les Finnegan File, IUE Collection; Louis Torre, UE International Representative and Field Organizer's Report, April 16–May 15, Organizing Files of Lou Torre, 1986 Accession, Red Dot 90, UE Collection.
63. Lundgren to Carey, Organizational Report, 29 May 1952, IUE Collection.
64. E. M. Skagen, IAM, to Gentlemen, NLRB, 26 May 1952, Finnegan Files, IUE Collection; "UE Charges Against Standard Coil, filed 6/18/52," Office of General Council, Legal Department, NLRB Cases, Standard Coil Company, Case No. 21-RC-2288 and 2352, 1952, IUE Collection.
65. Lundgren to Hartnett, 14 July 1952, IUE Collection; Lundgren to Siegel, 13 August 1952, Office of General Council, Legal Department, NLRB Cases, Standard Coil Company, Case No. 21-RC-2288 and 2352, 1952, IUE Collection; Standard Coil, Red Dot 7 and 318, UE Collection.
66. Arthur Richenthal, Standard Coil, to George J. Bott, NLRB, 4 August 1952, Office of General Council, Legal Department, NLRB Cases, Standard Coil Company, Case No. 21-RC-2288 and 2352, 1952, IUE Collection.
67. "More problematical to discern is the extent of the Justice Department's hand in the affair. As you are well aware, the agencies of the federal government (FBI, Atomic Energy Commission, HUAC) were all at the disposal of the IUE in its struggle with the UE. In the case at hand I found no 'smoking gun.' However, the nature of the telegrams you now have in your hand seem odd to me. It seems that someone was providing Lee Lundgren with some copies of various UE telegrams—of course in some cases the UE forwarded copies to parties involved in the dispute. Some of this had to be obtained illegally. Throughout our collection (unfortunately not in this case) we have found dossiers and information relating to the movements and activities of various UE officials that was forwarded to IUE officials from outside unidentified persons and agencies. Obviously, the state apparatus was aiding and comforting the IUE." Dr. James P. Quigel, IUE archivist at Rutgers University, letter to author, 27 July 1994.
68. Standard Coil, Red Dot 318, UE Collection.
69. Standard Coil, Red Dot 318, UE Collection.
70. Standard Coil, Red Dot 318, UE Collection.
71. *Decisions and Orders of the National Labor Relations Board*, Vol. 1, Oct. 20–Dec. 31, 1952 (Washington, D.C.: Government Printing Office, 1953), 261–262; Office of General Counsel, Legal Dept., NLRB-IUE Cases, Standard Coil Company, 1952, IUE Collection; "Report of Standard Coil Election," and other items in Standard Coil, Red Dot 7 and 318, Standard Coil, UE Collection.
72. Agreement Between Standard Coil Products Co., Inc., and IUE Local 851 [1952], Research & Education Dept., Box 5, Folder 42, IUE Collection, Rutgers University; Leaflet, "IUE Certified," Standard Coil File; Standard Coil, Red Dot 318, UE Collection.
73. Lundgren to Carey, 25 November 1952, and Lundgren to Carey, 29 October 1953, IUE Collection; Rios, interview.
74. Coffield, interview; "O.C. Latinos Mourn Leader and Inspiration," *Los Angeles Times*, Orange County edition, 24 April 1993, sec. A, p. 1.
75. FBI records of Henry Fiering and Tony Rios.

Popular Anticommunism and the UE in Evansville, Indiana

Samuel W. White

Following World War II, Evansville, Indiana, proudly proclaimed itself the "refrigerator capital of the world." In 1946, International Harvester purchased the Republic Steel Plant and began producing refrigerators, supplementing the refrigerator production at Servel, Inc., and Seeger-Sunbeam. Refrigerators and automotive goods came to dominate the postwar economy of Evansville, which depended on the production of these consumer durables as never before. Evansville's workforce continued to climb after the war, from 64,000 in 1945 to 80,000 in 1950. Of the 80,000 workers employed in the city in 1950, 20,000 produced consumer durables, and more than 10,000 of these workers labored at one of the city's three refrigerator factories.[1]

By the end of 1946, Local 813 of the United Electrical, Radio, and Machine Workers of America (UE) had organized three of the city's leading employers: Seeger-Sunbeam, Faultless, and, finally, the Servel plant. Based largely on its reputation for getting higher wages and benefits for workers, Local 813 expanded from its base in the refrigerator factories to other plants such as George Koch & Sons, Bucyrus-Erie, and Hoosier Cardinal, quickly becoming the largest labor organization in the city, with over 7,000 members.[2]

UE's growth in Evansville was part of a general pattern of growth for the labor movement in the city during the previous decade. By 1949 the CIO alone would boast more than 15,000 members in Evansville, constituting nearly 50 percent of the workforce. While definite membership figures for the AFL are not available, it, too, grew during the 1930s and 1940s, with the building trades as its most organized and active jurisdiction. Even a conservative estimate of AFL membership in 1949 put the total organized Evansville workforce at well over 60 percent. The largest affiliates of the CIO remained the UE and the United Automobile Workers (UAW), the latter of which represented approximately 6,000 workers at the International Harvester, Briggs, and Chrysler plants in the city.[3]

In 1946, the labor movement in Evansville appeared to be in a position to consolidate the gains it had made during the previous decade. This changed quickly, however, as the Cold War, and what might be called "popular anticommunism," drove a wedge between the UE and the community, and, most importantly, between unions—effectively forestalling the opportunity to consolidate the labor movement that existed following the Second World War.

Of all the issues confronting the Evansville labor movement during the postwar period, anticommunism proved most divisive. While the local AFL unions and the Central Labor Union had long opposed Communism within the labor movement, the CIO became locked in a bitter struggle to reconcile the issue of Communism within its member unions. As the local CIO affiliates fought first to define and then resolve the issue, the AFL stood ready to raid the membership of those CIO affiliates weakened by internal strife. In July 1946, President Charles E. Wright of UE 813 predicted that

> The manufacturers in this community together with other forces will leave no stone unturned. They will use the old and much worn cry of red baiting. They will use racial prejudice to stir-up trouble and pit the workers against each other. They will attempt to pit the workers of each shop against one another. This union will become the target of these forces not only from without but also from . . . within our union.[4]

Wright's words proved prophetic as employers, government agencies, ordinary citizens of the community, and members of the labor movement itself moved to contain, and eventually to destroy, the UE in Evansville during the decade after the Second World War. Americans' Cold War fears and anxieties provided context for the struggle to roll back the UE in Evansville. While anticommunism had a long history in the city by 1946, politicians, working people, employers, the labor movement, and the general public found Communism to be an increasingly important issue in their lives during the postwar period. Both the major political parties and the labor movement joined employers in being "tough on Communism" during this period and, in doing so, created a more unified political culture in the city than had existed for more than a decade. The political consensus that emerged in late-1940s Evansville had its greatest impact on the labor movement as anticommunism within the ranks of labor altered the style and direction of labor in the city. In many ways, the interests of workers were lost in the storm of Cold War politics that emerged in Evansville during the postwar period. The multifaceted nature of anticommunism, extending from the shop floor to the state created a difficult set of challenges for left-led unions like the UE.[5]

In his 1983 autobiography, Arthur Kinoy, a one-time lawyer for the UE, observed "Evansville in September 1948 brought sharply into focus all the tensions that had been mounting in the labor movement since the end of the war."[6] For the labor movement in general, and especially local unions like UE 813, popular anticommunism severely weakened its position in the community. While few could attack the UE's trade union and shop floor success, the political positions of its leadership left locals like 813 open to attacks. As Ronald Filipelli and Mark McColloch discovered in their national study of the UE, in Evansville a combination of community concerns about Communism, external political pressure, and anticommunist factions within the union itself damaged Local 813's ability to function as an effective labor organization.[7]

During the years 1946 to 1949, several local CIO unions in Evansville began to stake out positions on the issue of Communism. Local 312 of the United Furniture Workers of America voted to uphold the elected officials of the union and branded the "red-baiting attempts" by an "opposition gang" as against the best interests of the membership. According to a Local 312 spokesman, "members here in Evansville will not fall for the propaganda that has been initiated by the renegades of the labor movement who espouse the program of the National Association of Manufacturers, the Evansville Cooperative League, and other anti-labor forces."[8]

UAW Local 265 chose to condemn "Communism and Fascism" in a resolution that also condemned the Taft-Hartley bill. Stating that Local 265 was "being made a battleground between the forces of capitalism on one side and Communism and Fascism on the other," the resolution concluded that neither conservative business organizations nor those organizations that seek to overthrow the government should be allowed to have control over their union.[9]

The Evansville Industrial Union Council, composed of CIO affiliates, moved to isolate known or alleged Communists within its ranks. In May 1947, IUC members voted a member of the United Packinghouse Workers, Dale Craig, into the office of council president, thereby removing from office Charles Wright, a member and president of UE Local 813. In doing so, IUC members responded to pressure from local CIO officials who believed the organization to be "UE-dominated" and who regarded Wright as personifying the "extreme left wing faction of the CIO." The press release covering the election results stated that the actions of the members would help to "restore confidence of the public in CIO unions" in Evansville. Following the withdrawal of the UE from the CIO in 1949, the IUC passed a resolution in November of the same year calling on workers at Servel and Faultless Caster to "throw-off the UE" and create a "strong, aggressive democratic union affiliated with the CIO." The Machinists, Automobile Workers, and the International Union of Electrical Workers (IUE) moved quickly to support the IUC's threat with action. Several years later, the IUC boldly proclaimed to all Evansville community agencies soliciting CIO support that they must choose between the CIO and UE Local 813. The resolution stated that "those who permit themselves to be used by the UE for propaganda purposes, and give all recognition and respectability to this organization, can look exclusively to the UE in the future for their aid and support." IUC president Hobert Butler commented further that the agencies that want CIO support will have to say "we don't want anything to do with the UE."[10]

By the early 1950s the IUE became the largest industrial labor organization in Evansville, primarily by raiding the membership of the UE in the city. The IUE became the vehicle the CIO used to rid itself of the UE and, as such, became the only CIO union chartered for the express purpose of raiding another union. In 1949 the IUE only represented workers at the Seeger refrigerator plant, but it maintained organizing activities in all UE plants, eventually filling the void left when the UE lost members to the rising tide of anticommunism in the city.[11]

A concerted employer offensive against the UE in Evansville began when the union organized the city's Bucyrus-Erie plant. Bucyrus had contracts with the United Steelworkers of America at other plants, but viewed the UE as a threat. The UE's demands at the Bucyrus plant differed from those of other unions encountered by Bucyrus-Erie management. After the NLRB election in 1946, UE insisted on partial control of the plant. Local 813 demanded the right to determine work schedules and overtime hours for all its members and the elimination of the standard "no-strike-no-lockout" and "management responsibility" clauses used in contracts between Bucyrus and the Steelworkers. Local 813 also demanded the resolution of a large number of grievances, top seniority for all stewards, and union security and maintenance of membership clauses.[12]

Politically, Local 813 members supported several progressive initiatives and candidates that provided employers and anticommunists with plenty of ammunition to attack the UE. The local's support of presidential candidate Henry Wallace in 1948 precipitated a community-wide reaction against all who supported the progressive candidate, and provided the context for a riot when Wallace spoke in Evansville during the campaign.

In the spring of 1948, Wallace faced strong protests from several prominent leaders in the community prior to his campaign stop in Evansville. Brigadier General Howard Maxwell, adjutant general in charge of the armory where Wallace was scheduled to speak, insisted that Paul Robeson not be allowed to appear with Wallace on threat of a ban to keep the candidate from speaking at all. Another performer substituted for Robeson, who did not accompany Wallace to Evansville. The Vanderburgh County Council of Veterans Organizations also hurled charges at Wallace, demanding to know why "he aspires to be President of these United States, at the same time accepting the support of groups dedicated to the overthrow of the very thing he seeks?" On the eve of the speech, a parade organized by the Spirit of Kilroy, a local organization comprising veterans employed in local industrial plants, protested Wallace's use of the Coliseum, which was the city's monument to service men. The parade barred "any persons who believe in Communist principles."[13]

On 7 April, Wallace found a city in opposition to his third-party candidacy. Those who came to hear him speak, estimated by the newspapers to be between 500 to 800 people, were met by a much larger crowd of protesters demonstrating against Wallace. The demonstrators paraded around the coliseum before forcefully entering the foyer to jeer Wallace and keep people from entering. Several skirmishes ensued, and a few Wallace supporters received injuries in what the *Courier* reported as a "riot." Following Wallace's visit, Evansville College dismissed Professor George Parker for acting as chairman of the local Wallace rally and for introducing the candidate at the coliseum. College officials stated that they fired Parker for "his political activity, both on and off campus."[14]

Other issues pitted the UE against rival unions in the city. UE Local 813's strong support for the continuation of the Fair Employment Practice Committee

(FEPC) met criticism by the UAW union and their counterparts in the city's shipyards, all of whom opposed the hiring and upgrading of African American workers during the war. Local 813 also opposed the Marshall Plan, which the rest of Evansville labor supported.[15]

Prior to the representation election at Bucyrus-Erie, H. R. Knox, president of the company, warned workers in the Evansville plant that, "the moment they [Bucyrus workers] get UE, Moscow will be ordering them to take a wage increase against their will and will supply specially trained dictators to do the ordering." Knox refused to deal with the UE after the Bucyrus election on the grounds that Communists dominated the union. Intending to cloud the economic issues with an anticommunist campaign, Knox refused all UE demands after the election and offered the standard contract that he gave to workers at other Bucyrus plants. Predictably, negotiations broke off in mid-1947 and did not resume until April 1948.[16]

As the UE struggled to win a contract at Bucyrus, an anticommunist faction within 813 began to consolidate. The anticommunist faction, referred to by members as the Committee for Democratic Action (CDA), profited from the anticommunist hysteria enveloping the community. The CDA, always a small group, precariously attempted to support the local's members and, at the same time, not discredit and damage the local's ability to fight employers, many of whom also accused 813 leaders of being Communists.[17]

By August 1948 the UE had no choice but to strike Bucyrus. The strike rocked the community of Evansville and received daily coverage in the local press. Several violent skirmishes occurred on the picket line when the CDA organized small groups of workers to cross the picket line and honor the company's back-to-work efforts. On 31 August, the Republican governor of Indiana, Ralph F. Gates, sent 140 state troopers to support a planned re-opening by the company. Following the worst day of violence in the strike, the state police managed only to escort about one-third of the plant's twelve hundred workers inside.[18]

On 7 September, Bucyrus secured a restraining order barring all picketing at the plant. The next day subpoenas were issued to Local 813 officers and selected members, calling on them to appear before a special subcommittee of the House Committee on Education and Labor, which was scheduled to conduct hearings in Evansville beginning 10 September. Republican Congressman Edward A. Mitchell, an Evansville native, chaired the hearings. Mitchell had for some time used his office in an attempt to identify Communists within the UE in his hometown.[19] The subpoenas, combined with the picket restraining orders, plunged Local 813's morale to a new low. The local called off the Bucyrus strike at midnight, 8 September, and prepared to meet the challenge of the congressional investigation.[20]

When the congressional hearings convened on 10 September, it became clear that they were geared to discredit and, thereby, weaken the leadership of Local 813. Without any legislative purpose, Representative Mitchell's line of inquiry turned on the two questions: "Are you a Communist?" and "Do you believe in God?" The press faithfully listed the names of those accused of being Communists. Spurred on by Mitchell's call, "I hope the press representatives will give them [the people of Evansville] a good job of exposing these people," the press

FIGURE 7.1 Indiana State Police stand guard at the Bucyrus-Erie plant during the strike by UE Local 813, 31 August 1948. *Credit: University of Southern Indiana, Archives and Special Collections, Labor History Collection.*

also listed as possible Communists those workers who refused to answer Mitchell's questions without their attorneys present. Mitchell incited vigilantes to action when he asked, in reference to those who asked for their counsel to be present, "would it be a violation of your constitutional rights if a group got together and hid behind the constitution and tarred and feathered you birds?" The sensationalism of the event, combined with the prestige of the members of congress who ran the hearings, damaged support for Local 813 in the community.[21]

On the second day of the hearings several workers from the UAW and UE testified. These workers were critical of the hearings and claimed that their organizations could solve their own problems without the committee's intervention. One worker criticized the Taft-Hartley Act on the grounds that the government used it "to hurt the common working people" of America. Another worker reiterated this sentiment, stating that the hearings and Taft-Hartley harm "workers who did not want the AFL again." Workers also attested to the link between the exploitative incentive-pay system used by Bucyrus and labor unrest. These workers frustrated Mitchell when they all stated that they had faith in God and were definitely not Communists. Obviously, the testimony of these workers refuted the stereotypical UE 813 member that Mitchell wished to expose. Mitchell then centered the remainder of the session on the sensational accusations of a single witness, Kathryn Bell, a member of the CDA. Bell proclaimed to have met most of UE 813's leaders at local meetings of the Communist Party, to which she admitted she had once belonged, and that many of the UE's militants were nothing more than plotting Communist conspirators. Bell's testimony received extended coverage in the press, while the issue of the situation at the Bucyrus plant and workers' grievances went unreported.[22]

After the subcommittee left town, anticommunist forces in Evansville took advantage of the hearings to carry out their own attacks against militant union members in the city.[23] On Monday, 14 September, gangs of CDA, Association of Catholic Trade Unionists (ACTU), and Ku Klux Klan members answered Mitchell's call to action when they surrounded, threatened, and escorted workers out of Seeger and Briggs Indiana Corporation. In all, fourteen men and women union members were driven out of five separate plants in Evansville by anticommunist vigilante groups, with the encouragement of plant managers. All fourteen workers had refused to testify during the subcommittee hearings. At Servel and Faultless, company foremen and supervisors led the workers out of the plants. Similar purges took place at the International Harvester plant. In all cases, plant managers took no steps to defend those workers led out of the shops. In short order the subcommittee accomplished its goals of breaking the Bucyrus strike and of dispersing rank-and-file member support for UE 813.[24]

In the end, the subcommittee found little evidence of Communist Party influence in the affairs of UE 813, but some of the information supplied by a few of the forty-six witnesses called during the hearings proved damaging to Local 813. The subcommittee appeared most concerned about three leaders of the UE in Evansville: William Sentner, who was UE District Eight President; James Payne, the Business Agent for Local 813; and Sadelle Berger, a staff member for the local.

William Sentner came to Evansville from St. Louis during the late 1930s to help organize the UE. He was one of the few CIO leaders to openly acknowledge his membership in the Communist Party. Due to his militant and aggressive unionism, Sentner gained popularity and respect from many rank-and-file workers involved in UE's struggle to organize workers in the Midwest. A talented organizer, Sentner fought for the UE at the factory gate and at the bargaining table. News of Sentner's organizing record and leadership abilities preceded his move to Evansville in the late 1930s. Local 813 leaders and members welcomed Sentner, quickly acknowledged his intelligence, and, most importantly, thought that Sentner knew what working people needed and how to get it for them. It was during this period that UE 813 members made Sentner an honorary member of their local. Before the Bucyrus-Erie strike of 1948, Sentner's politics mattered little to workers who saw in him the leadership qualities necessary to continue UE's fight to organize Evansville.[25]

James Payne, also from St. Louis, built a similar reputation and following among Evansville workers. Payne gained much of his reputation by serving as a gifted and inspirational public speaker. Bernard McAtee, a former UE shop steward at Servel, remembered Payne for his ability to "know exactly when and how to stir the members to action." McAtee went on to state, "Payne could incite a riot just as easily as he could put one down, just by giving a speech." Payne maintained a high degree of rank-and-file support and loyalty in Evansville until the UE disbanded its local there in 1955. While Payne did not openly acknowledge his political affiliations, he probably shared Sentner's Communist Party orientation. In 1956, after UE Local 813 voted to merge with the International Association of Machinists (IAM), the IAM put Payne on trial in St. Louis for allegations of ties to the Communist Party. Several former members of the UE in Evansville went to St. Louis to testify on Payne's behalf, demonstrating their loyalty to Payne and the UE.[26]

Sadelle Berger and her husband Sydney came to Evansville in 1946 from the Lower East Side of Manhattan. Sydney began practicing law in Evansville during the same year and eventually devoted considerable time to the legal challenges facing Local 813. Soon after their arrival in Evansville, the Jewish couple became friends of William Sentner. The close relationship between the Bergers and Sentner led to allegations that the Bergers were also members of the Communist Party, allegations that proved false. Sentner's eventual indictment under the Smith Act, and the attempted deportation of his wife Toni under the McCarran Act, became key aspects of Sadelle's daily "UE on the Air" radio program in Evansville and her ongoing efforts to counter the rising tide of anticommunism and reaction in postwar America.[27]

Given that the UE's international officers had not complied with the Taft-Hartley non-Communist affidavits, and, therefore, the UE enjoyed no rights under the act, employers in Evansville wasted little time in exercising their power in the workplace after the subcommittee left town. Emboldened by the congressional hearings, local employers reasserted themselves in ways that under normal conditions would constitute blatant violations of the NLRA, as amended by Taft-

Hartley. By doing so, employers sent a clear message to UE members: continued support for the UE would be costly. At Faultless, the company set up its own "Taft-Hartley affidavit room." Faultless personnel managers had prepared and notarized affidavits that asked workers to renounce Communism and asked for their religious affiliations as proof of their loyalty. Those workers who refused to sign the affidavits were fired. Faultless also prepared forms so workers could apply to the subcommittee for forgiveness. A company personnel manager told one worker, fired at Faultless for refusing to testify at the hearings, that he "would have to straighten himself out with [Representative] Mitchell. Mitchell is the only one who can get you out of this." Faultless took further advantage of the situation and stalled on all settlements of UE grievances.[28]

Other employers in Evansville used the hearings to crack down on working conditions in their plants. Seeger cut incentive rates in plant number two. Servel fired two union grievance committee members and laid off a steward without just cause. The Bucyrus Company, by this time, had fired a total of sixty-five workers, most of whom were never able to attain employment in the Evansville area again. The offensive launched by employers in the city made it difficult for UE 813 to recover from the sensational event of the hearings. Without these actions by employers, the damage done to Local 813 by the hearings probably could have been managed.[29]

By 1949 the internecine war within the labor movement in Evansville created a unified labor and political community aligned against the UE. While the more extreme elements of the Republican Party had been temporarily silenced, the Democratic Party, if not the political system as a whole, moved rightward and away from the New Deal of the late 1930s. Tolerance for unions like the UE waned as Evansville residents continued to support efforts to rid their community of the alleged Communist menace.

By 1950, in addition to unifying labor, anticommunism emerged stronger than ever as a means to combat the UE in Evansville. Shortly after the Bucyrus-Erie strike investigation by Congressmen Mitchell, an ad hoc local "anticommunist committee," chaired by Troy James, a Seeger employee and a leader of IUE Local 808, drafted a local "anti-Red ordinance" that Republican members of the city council worked to pass during the fall of 1950. The ordinance contained fifteen sections providing that any Communist, or anyone aiding and supporting Communists in any way, would be guilty of a misdemeanor and, on conviction, would be subject to a fine of not less than $499 and a jail sentence of not less than 179 days. An amendment drafted by local attorney Matthew Weinzapel, which was included in the measure, also made it unlawful for Communists to enter, live, or work in Evansville. The ordinance received endorsements from local posts of the American Legion, the local National Guard unit, the Knights of St. John, the Spirit of Kilroy, the local chapter of the Veterans of Foreign Wars, and the Indiana Parents Association. The city council voted in favor of the ordinance, but Mayor Diekmann vetoed the measure after receiving advice from city attorneys who found the violations included in the ordinance "too broad and too indefinite." When backers of the ordinance decided not to attempt to overturn Diekmann's veto, spokesmen for the anticommunist committee told the press that "Alger Hiss and Stalin tactics had been used to block the ordinance" and asked "what the boys in Korea would think of the council's action."[30]

Following an intense period of efforts designed to raid the membership of the UE in Evansville, the labor movement moved swiftly to finish off the independent union. By the mid-1950s, Local 813 could not count on the support of any other labor organizations in the Evansville area, a reality that hastened its efforts to consider merger with the IAM.

In early November 1954, Walter Reuther, then international president of the UAW, spoke in Evansville to a packed audience at the coliseum. Reuther devoted the first half of his speech, intended as part of a dedication ceremony for a new UAW local in the city, to making an appeal to Servel workers to throw off the "millstone" of the UE and rejoin the fold. Reuther concluded by stating that the labor movement was on record as saying "there is no place in American unionism for anyone who does not put the United States of America above all other nations."[31]

By 1955 the organizations and individuals set against the UE in Evansville succeeded in their decade-long struggle to eliminate the UE from the city. The defeat of the UE did not, however, end industrial conflict in the city as employers, politicians, and many of the city's residents had hoped. Rather, popular anticommunism during the postwar period merely submerged workers' issues and labor relations problems in Evansville, both of which resurfaced in the first half of the 1950s.

In his recent history of the CIO, Robert Zieger best summarizes both the impact that labor's internal war had on American society after the Second World War and the more recent decline of the labor movement. For Zieger, it was not the CIO's purging of progressive unions such as the UE during the postwar period that resulted in an irreversible setback for the labor movement. Rather, it was the subsequent failure to follow this period in history with a renewed effort to organize the unorganized and, thereby, increase the power and influence of labor in American society. Instead, labor's internal war drew heavily upon the resources of the labor movement, and the numerous raids that took place merely resulted in a reshuffled labor movement, not a measurably larger one. Zieger also argues that the CIO's "ardent embrace of economic growth, combined with the de-emphasis on redistributionist goals, helped pave the way for the contemporary assault on organized labor and the decline of union sentiment among workers."[32] Indeed, the continued embrace of economic growth by organized labor in Evansville coincided with a bitter war to silence those voices in the labor movement that articulated an alternative future. Perhaps this chapter in history, seen through the lens of Evansville, Indiana, best shows the limits of modern American liberalism as brought forth by the New Deal and the subsequent limits of democratic expression in American society following the Second World War. To paraphrase Gary Gerstle, at some point in the long historical period we refer to as postwar America, working class Americans and their organizations lost the ambition to re-create their world.[33]

Notes

1. Darrel E. Bigham, *An Evansville Album* (Bloomington: Indiana University Press, 1988), 70. See also, James E. Morlock, *The Evansville Story: A Cultural Interpretation* (Evansville: Creative Press, 1956), 205.
2. "William Sentner to Albert Fitzgerald," 22 March 1946, FF326, UE Archives, University of Pittsburgh, Pittsburgh, Pennsylvania (hereafter cited as UEAR); Esther Zieman, interview by Glenda Morrison, 6 and 12 August 1981, Special Collections, University of Southern Indiana; "Proceedings of First Annual Shop Delegates Conference," 21 July 1946, FF337, UEAR; Charles Berger, interview by author, Evansville, Ind., 9 May 1994; and Evansville *Courier*, 14 June 1946.
3. *Courier*, 30 October 1949.
4. "Local 813, United Electrical, Radio and Machine Workers of America-CIO, Proceedings of the First Annual Shop Delegate Conference" (Evansville, Ind.: 21 July 1946), 6–7, FF337, UEAR. Louis Ruthenburg was president of Servel, Inc., Evansville's largest employer.
5. For the most comprehensive treatment of anticommunism in postwar America, see Ellen Schrecker, *Many Are the Crimes: McCarthyism in America* (Boston: Little, Brown and Company, 1998).
6. Arthur Kinoy, *Rights on Trial: The Odyssey of a People's Lawyer* (Cambridge: Harvard University Press, 1983), 61.
7. See Filipelli and McColloch, *Cold War in the Working Class: The Rise of the United Electrical Workers* (Albany: State University of New York Press, 1995), especially Introduction, Chapters 4–6, and Conclusion. See also M. J. Heale, *American AntiCommunism: Combating the Enemy Within, 1830–1930* (Baltimore: John Hopkins University Press, 1990). Heale defines the 1948 to 1952 period as "The Republican Offensive," citing the important turning point of the 1948 presidential election after which the Republican Party asserted its own vehement anticommunist agenda, as the Democratic Party had done in response to the campaign of Henry Wallace.
8. *Courier*, 19 July 1947.
9. Ibid., 5 October 1947.
10. Ibid., 2 May 1946, 27 May 1947, 22 March, and 21 December 1948, 22 November 1949, and 22 February 1955. For the CIO's efforts to confront the issue of Communism within its ranks and the effects of the purges, see Steven Rosswurm, ed., *The CIO's Left-Led Unions* (New Brunswick, N.J.: Rutgers University Press, 1992); Irving Howe and B. J. Widick, *The UAW and Walter Reuther* (New York: Random House, 1949); Theodore Draper, *The Roots of American Communism* (New York: Viking Press, 1966) and *American Communism and Soviet Russia: The Formative Period* (New York: Viking Press, 1963); Irving Howe and Lewis Coser, *The American Communist Party: A Critical History, 1919–1957* (Boston: Beacon Press, 1957); David A. Shannon, *Decline of American Communism: A History of the Communist Party of the United States Since 1945* (New York: Harcourt, Brace, 1959); Bert Cochran, *Labor and Communism: The Conflict that Shaped American Unions* (Princeton: Princeton University Press, 1977); Harvey Klehr, *The Heyday of American Communism: The Depression Decade* (New York: Basic Books, 1984); Aileen S. Kraditor, *'Jimmy Higgins': The Mental World of the American Rank-and-File Communist, 1930–1958* (New York: Greenwood Press, 1988); Patricia Cayo Sexton, *The War on Labor and the Left: Understanding America's Unique Conservatism* (Boulder: Westview Press, 1991); for an overview of this literature, see Maurice Isserman, "Three Generations: Historians View American Communism," *Labor*

History 26 (Fall 1985): 518-23. For the effect of the purges on the UE, one of the CIO's largest affiliates, see Ronald L. Filipelli and Mark D. McColloch, *Cold War in the Working Class: The Rise and Decline of the United Electrical Workers* (Albany: State University of New York Press, 1995).

11. For the formation of the IUE, see Filipelli and McColloch, *Cold War in the Working Class*, chap. 6, and Robert H. Zieger, *The CIO, 1935-1955* (Chapel Hill: University of North Carolina Press, 1995), 284-290.

12. House Committee on Education and Labor, *Investigation of Communist Influence in the Bucyrus-Erie Strike, Hearings Before a Special Sub-Committee of the House Committee on Education and Labor*, 80th Cong., 2nd sess., 10, 11, and 18 September 1948, 3-4; and Kenneth H. Myers and Harold Williamson, *Designed for Digging: The First 75 Years of Bucyrus-Erie Company* (Evanston: Northwestern University Press, 1955), 283, 297.

13. *Courier*, 4, 5, and 6 April 1948.

14. Ibid., 7 April 1948; and Karl M. Schmidt, *Henry A. Wallace: Quixotic Crusade 1948* (Syracuse: Syracuse University Press, 1960), 86-87. The Spirit of Kilroy claimed about four hundred members at the time of Wallace's visit. Arthur Robinson, one of the group's leaders, was a well-known anticommunist who worked at the Briggs plant and who kept in touch with Congressman Mitchell about left-wing activities and individuals in the Evansville area. Robinson was later one of the star witnesses against UE Local 813 called by Mitchell during the congressional hearings in Evansville during the Bucyrus-Erie strike during the fall of 1948.

15. *Courier*, 26 September 1943; 4, 5, 6, 23, and 24 April and 1 November 1948; Max Pavin Cavnes, *The Hoosier Community at War* (Bloomington: Indiana University Press, 1961), 125-127, 153-160, and 419-422; "Resolution," 1947, FF291, UEAR; and Edward Mitchell Papers, "Resolution," 16 March 1947, Box 8, Folder 5, Indiana Division, Indiana State Library, Indianapolis, Ind.

16. See George Lipsitz, *Class and Culture in Cold War America: "A Rainbow at Midnight"* (New York: Praeger Publishers, 1981), 155-156; Myers and Williamson, *Designed for Digging*, 297; *UE News*, 7 June 1947; and Dale R. Sorenson, "The Anti-communist Consensus in Indiana 1945-1958" (Ph.D. diss., Indiana University, 1980), 69.

17. Evansville *Press*, 6 August 1948; *UE News*, 7 June 1947.

18. For information and analysis related to the strike, see Lipsitz, *Class and Culture*, 157-159 and my "Labor and Politics in Evansville, Indiana, 1919-1955" (Ph.D. diss., State University of New York at Binghamton, 1998), 225-232.

19. For background on Edward Mitchell, see the Edward A. Mitchell Papers, Indiana Division, Indiana State Library, Indianapolis, Ind. Mitchell's papers reveal an interesting trail of information concerning his role in "sponsoring" the congressional investigation of the Bucyrus-Erie strike. He maintained a close relationship with Louis Ruthenburg and other employers in Evansville and used his office to gather information about UE 813 leaders and members from a variety of informants working in the plants where the UE held contracts. See especially the correspondence in Boxes 8, 12, and 14. Many of those who provided Mitchell with information about the UE in 1947 and 1948 were called to testify against the union during the hearings.

20. See *Indianapolis Star*, 9 September 1948; *Courier*, 9 September 1948; Lipsitz, *Class and Culture*, 159; and Kinoy, *Rights on Trial*, 64.

21. See House Committee, *Investigation of Communist Influence in the Bucyrus-Erie Strike*, 62; *Press*, 10 September 1948; and *UE News*, 18 September 1948.

22. House Committee, *Investigation of Communist Influence in the Bucyrus-Erie Strike*,

70–85, 91–92, 128–130; *Indianapolis Star*, 12 September 1948; *Courier*, 12 September 1948; Lipsitz, *Class and Culture*, 159.
23. See House Committee, *Investigation of Communist Influence in the Bucyrus-Erie Strike*, 80–92, 128–130; *Press*, 11 September 1948; and *Indianapolis Star*, 12 September 1948.
24. See *UE News*, 25 September 1948; *Evansville Press*, 14 September 1948; *Indianapolis Star*, 15 September 1948; and Lipsitz, *Class and Culture*, 160.
25. Matles and Higgins, *Them and Us: Struggles of a Rank-and-File Union* (Boston: Beacon Press, 1975), 91; Sentner's appeal to 813 members is described in the Bernard McAtee interview. William Sentner's activities in St. Louis and Newton are discussed in James J. Matles and James Higgins, *Them and Us*, 74, 93–99. According to James Weinstein, Sentner was a section organizer for the Communist Party prior to being elected president of UE District 8, see Weinstein, "The Grand Illusion: A Review of 'Them and Us'," *Socialist Revolution* 24 (June 1975): 94–95; For a detailed summation of Sentner's activities in the St. Louis area, see Rosemary Feurer, "William Sentner, the UE, and Civic Unionism in St. Louis" in *The CIO's Left-Led Unions*, ed. Steve Rosswurm (New Brunswick: Rutgers University Press, 1992), 95–117. See also Len De Caux, *Labor Radical* (Boston: Beacon Press, 1970), 495.
26. McAtee, interview. UE Local 813 merged with the IAM in 1956, resulting in the final purge of the former leaders of the UE in Evansville such as James Payne.
27. For information about Sydney Berger, see *Evansville Press*, 1 August 1988; and *Evansville Courier*, 2 August 1988. For mention of Sydney Berger's role as a labor lawyer, see Arthur Kinoy, *Rights on Trial: The Odyssey of a People's Lawyer* (Cambridge: Harvard University Press, 1983), 67–69. For an overview of Sadelle Berger's life in Evansville, see "Death—Sadelle Berger—26 July 1984," Folder 54, Sadelle Berger Collection, Special Collections, University of Southern Indiana, Evansville, Ind.
28. *UE News*, 25 September 1948; and Ibid., 2 October 1948. The workers who were purged at Faultless were also former leaders of the militant UE 813 strike at the plant in 1946. This reinforces a certain continuity in employer attempts to break UE in the city. For the problems caused by the UE's refusal to conform with the Taft-Hartley affidavits, see Matles and Higgins, *Them and Us*, 167–170, 198–203; and Filipelli and McColloch, *Cold War in the Working Class*, 105–140. For a general discussion of the ways in which employers reasserted themselves against unions like the UE during the postwar period, see Howell John Harris, *The Right to Manage: Industrial Relations Policies of American Business in the 1940s* (Madison: University of Wisconsin Press, 1982), 129–158.
29. "Its You and Your Wages They're After," 14 September 1948, FF313, UEAR; House Committee, *Investigation of Communist Influence in the Bucyrus-Erie Strike*, 158; and Lipsitz, *Class and Culture*, 159.
30. "City Council Minutes," 18 September, 2 October, 6 November, and 4 December 1950, Willard Library, Evansville, Indiana; and *Courier*, 19 September, 6 and 7 November, and 5 December 1950.
31. *Courier*, 7 November 1954.
32. Zieger, *The CIO*, 372–377.
33. Gary Gerstle, *Working-Class Americanism: The Politics of Labor in a Textile City, 1914–1960* (New York: Cambridge University Press, 1991), 330.

"A Stern Struggle"
Catholic Activism and
San Francisco Labor, 1934–1958

WILLIAM ISSEL

On 24 November 1936, twenty-one-year-old Joseph L. Alioto delivered a prize-winning speech in San Francisco. A future mayor of San Francisco, Alioto would soon graduate from St. Mary's College and go on to earn a law degree at the Catholic University in Washington, D.C. In an address entitled "The Catholic Internationale," Alioto warned his audience at the St. Ignatius Council of the Young Men's Institute: "Communism has attained the position of a universal power [and] stands today as a cancer in the world's social organism." Given its international scope and its appeal as a "counterfeit religion," only a true religion "that is likewise international" would be able "to cut away this cancerous growth." "There is only one power in the world which answers that description: the Roman Catholic Church. The battle lines . . . are clearly marked: It is to be the Catholic Internationale arrayed against the Communist Internationale; Rome against Moscow; Christ against Anti-Christ."[1]

Alioto's speech was published in *The Moraga Quarterly*, a St. Mary's College publication that served as a forum for Catholic intellectual life in northern California. Three years later *The Moraga Quarterly* published another speech by a young San Franciscan, this one devoted to "the [necessary] preparation for entrance into the field of labor relations" and titled "The Catholic College Graduate and Labor." The author was John F. (Jack) Henning, a recent St. Mary's College graduate who later became the head of the California State Federation of Labor as well as Undersecretary of Labor in the Kennedy and Johnson administrations. Henning argued, "The army of the church is today engaged in a stern struggle" and "the need of the Catholic Church for an articulate laity in Labor is too gigantic to question." He stressed that Catholics in labor relations needed to fight both "American Way" individualism and the "painted panaceas" of "the land of Communism or the land of Fascism." Henning praised "those who act only as the voice of the membership, the voice of the rank and file, who administer their offices upon the direct rule of the majority of the membership." He also urged Catholics in the labor movement to avoid red-baiting: "question the motives of those leaders who

154

brand every militant surge of rank and file activity the result of 'red agitation.'"
Catholic workers should endorse genuinely democratic unionism and get involved
with the "Association of Catholic Trade Unionists, the Catholic Worker movement, and other similar enterprises which sponsor Catholic labor schools."[2]

During the 1930s, '40s, and '50s, Jack Henning and scores of militant Catholics in San Francisco mobilized on several fronts to build independent and democratic unions and to defeat both the labor left and the business right. Aided by diocesan priests under the leadership of Archbishops Edward J. Hanna and John J. Mitty and priests of the Jesuit order, unionists worked to shape the city's labor movement along the lines laid out in the labor encyclicals of Popes Leo XIII and Pius XI. Drawing upon the papal letters, San Francisco activists championed private property as well as the right of workers to dignity and a fair share of business profits. They condemned both *laissez-faire* capitalism and class conflict. They opposed Communism, to be sure, but anticommunism was not the sole or primary purpose of their work. San Francisco Catholic labor activism expressed first and foremost the conviction that Americans should build a moral economy jointly managed by labor unions, business organizations, and government, the latter representing the interests of the community at large.

This San Francisco story can best be understood as part of a larger national history with three overlapping themes: first, the growing power and influence of Catholics in American public life; second, the creation of a coast-to-coast network of Roman Catholic labor relations theorists and union organizers; and, third, the clash of ideologies and the struggle for power that pitted Catholics against Communists. This essay addresses four aspects of the San Francisco story: first, how Archbishops Hanna and Mitty developed political education programs based on the labor encyclicals promoting labor union legitimacy and encouraged cooperation between business and labor; then, how unionists organized a branch of the Association of Catholic Trade Unionists (ACTU) to facilitate their "stern struggle" against *laissez-faire* individualism and left-wing radicalism; third, how the Jesuits established a Catholic labor school, the University of San Francisco Labor Management School (LMS), which provided basic training in operating democratic unions and conducting collective bargaining; and, fourth, how the church and the labor movement cooperated during the late 1940s and 1950s to protect union rights against a robust revival of *laissez-faire* business activism.

San Francisco stood out among American cities in the extent to which Catholic social teachings influenced labor activism since the 1890s, when the notions of a moral economy in Pope Leo XIII's 1891 labor encyclical *Rerum Novarum* became an explicit part of the rationale for building the local labor movement.[3] In 1931, Pope Pius XI issued *Quadragesimo Anno*, reaffirming and extending the principles of the 1891 labor encyclical, and in 1937 he condemned Communism in *Divini Redemptoris*.

Catholics in San Francisco used the encyclicals in a communal effort to shape a labor movement with multiple dimensions. Labor organizers, officials, and negotiators pointed to the encyclicals as evidence that God was on their side as they fought to build and sustain their unions. Labor priests explained the encyclicals in their sermons and lectures demanding justice and dignity for workers. The archbishops cited the encyclicals as authority for their calls to resolve differences between labor and capital through compromise and arbitration, and they quoted the encyclicals as ammunition when they condemned right-wing businessmen and left-wing unionists.

The activism of the church during Archbishop Mitty's tenure was shaped by the events of the Pacific Coast maritime strike from May through July of 1934, as well as by Church teaching on social justice in general and the rights of labor in particular. On 9 June 1934, at the end of the first month of a coast-wide strike by longshoremen and sailors, the official Archdiocesan newspaper presented the Catholic Church's point of view in a front-page editorial on "The Maritime Strikes." "The rights of the ship-owners over their ships do not give them the right to impoverish the whole community; nor do the rights of the striking workers include the right to pursue their aims regardless of the consequences to the third party in the dispute, namely the people who are not directly involved, but whom [sic] depend upon cargoes for their livelihoods and sustenance."[4]

Sounding a theme that would prove continuous through the 1940s and 1950s, *The Monitor* urged "all Catholics, who are employers, or who are in any way directly connected [with management] to read and know the contents of the encyclicals . . . that treat of the problems of capital and labor . . . and to acquaint their associates and acquaintances with the contents of these encyclicals and to give them copies of them." Should Catholic San Franciscans fail in this duty, according to the editorialist, "then those Catholics will be held to answer."[5]

In addition to prescribing the moral responsibility of all San Franciscans to involve themselves personally in helping to settle labor conflicts according to Catholic principles, the editorial alerted Catholics to the particular danger posed by extremism. "Shipowners have a perfect right to refuse to deliver the management of their business to a Soviet. Longshoremen have a perfect right to organize in a union and to bargain collectively for wages and hours that will enable them to support their families in frugal comfort, to educate their children, and to lay something by for sickness and old age. But these rights are obscured because of the laissez faire extremists on the one hand and the Communist fanatics on the other. The public has had enough of both." "We regret that hate motivates both of these groups. The Communists hate injustice more than they love justice. The ruthless 'individualists' among employers do not consider justice at all, but hate all who check their lust for power and money."[6]

San Franciscans needed to organize a Catholic counterforce. "If Christian workers would stem the tide of Communism, they must bring to the workers' cause as devoted an energy and as strict a discipline as members of the Communist Party manifest. Communism is a religion—a materialistic religion [and] appeals to many workers because the apostles of Communism work with a zeal worthy of a better cause. They can be challenged and checked only by men, who for the love of God study the Catholic teaching as thoroughly as Communists study the Communist theory; who devote as much energy to the propagation of the principles contained in the encyclicals on labor as the Communists do in spreading the doctrine of Marx; who labor as industriously to apply Catholic principles as the Communists work to apply the principles of Lenin."[7]

During the worst violence of the waterfront strike, from 3 July to 5 July, Archbishop Hanna invited Sam Kagel, an economist who worked for the Pacific Coast Labor Bureau advising unions, and E. B. O'Grady, a union leader, to archdiocese headquarters and personally urged them to do what they could to stop the bloodshed.[8] Then on 13 July, with the city three days from a general strike, Hanna addressed San Franciscans in a speech broadcast over radio stations KGO, KPO, and KFRC. Returning to the themes enunciated in the 9 June editorial, the Archbishop explicitly endorsed both labor unions and collective bargaining, and condemned employer exploitation that ignored "the human character of the worker." Then, in a blunt rejection of the Communist Party slogan "class against class," Hanna criticized unionists who premised their activities on the necessity of "conflict between class and class," and warned leftist unionists, "rights must be religiously respected *wherever* they are found." Both sides in the waterfront strike, Hanna insisted, should move quickly to accept the results of arbitration, keeping in mind the "underlying principles, which have ever been the teaching of Christianity during 2000 years."[9]

Settlement of the waterfront strike came during the next two weeks, due in part to the intervention of John Francis Neylan, a prominent Catholic lawyer close to the Archbishop, and in part to the work of the National Longshoremen's Board on which Hanna served. The strike settlement realigned the relationship between organized labor and business in the direction called for by Catholic leaders. Business leaders agreed to arbitration. They expressed a public commitment to respect the rights of labor and to treat workers with dignity. They also pledged themselves, in the words of the chamber of commerce president, "to see that those isolated instances in which labor has been exploited shall be corrected."[10]

Moderates from business and labor and local government officials, many of them Catholic activists, constructed the settlement and brought the strike to an end. These leaders, and the city press, immediately set to work representing the settlement as a victory for business unionism, with its emphasis on putting pork chops on the table, and a defeat for radical unionism, with its call for proletarian revolution in the streets. The city's voters expressed their moderate character in many ways, perhaps none more dramatically than by reestablishing the right to peaceful picketing by unions, while at the same time consistently choosing for mayors and supervisors moderate businessmen over leftist reformers. Tension persisted in the city's public life. Business leaders' rhetorical affirmation of labor's rights clashed with their practical desire to limit union power, but the Catholic principles that had helped to shape the outcome of the Great Strike became increasingly a part of San Francisco's public culture in the decades to come.[11]

Archbishop John J. Mitty took office shortly after the settlement of the 1934 waterfront strike, in March 1935. Mitty was not new to the city, for he had served as auxiliary bishop and coadjutor of the archdiocese since 1932, but he did not serve on the kinds of high-profile mediation and arbitration boards that had made Hanna so well known. The new archbishop nonetheless worked effectively, typically relying upon trusted intermediaries recruited from both the clergy and the laity.[12]

Although Mitty tended to delegate authority in matters having to do with labor relations, he also used his office as a "bully pulpit" and he expressed himself in a forthright manner in private communications. Early in his administration, the new archbishop lectured one of the city's business leaders, shipping executive Hugh Gallagher, on the teachings of Leo XIII's labor encyclical. Mitty expressed his concern about the future, reminding Gallagher that "there is, then, grave danger of a duplication of the events of the summer of 1934—a general strike, violence, bloodshed and loss of life.[13]

> To avert this calamity, both groups should be willing to submit disputed points to an impartial board of arbitration. When conciliation and mediation have failed, this appears to be the only rational method of settling an industrial dispute on the basis of justice and equity, rather than on the basis of the economic power of the employers or the numerical strength and organization of the employees. San Francisco wants not a temporary truce but a permanent peace."

Throughout the first decade of Mitty's tenure, the Catholic Church rarely missed an opportunity to publicize the importance of conducting labor relations according to the principles expressed in the labor encyclicals. *The Monitor*, the official weekly newspaper of the archdiocese, routinely provided its readers with front-page coverage of local and national news of the labor movement. News of events that included speeches on labor issues by church leaders often ran as the lead story, with the text of the sermon or speech reprinted in full on the editorial page.

In the spring of 1937 the city's financial elite began pressing the chamber of commerce to formulate a cooperative, institutionalized working relationship with citywide central bodies of the American Federation of Labor (AFL) and the Congress of Industrial Organizations (CIO). This process continued during and after World War II.[14] *The Monitor* frequently added its voice to the discussion, and in 1947 the paper devoted an entire special edition promoting the need for such cooperation as a necessary precondition for the future economic prosperity of the bay area.[15] Throughout the 1930s and 1940s, only those of Communism and World War II rivaled issues involving labor and capital for frequency of coverage in *The Monitor's* editorial columns. While focusing on specific incidents and events, these editorials consistently invoked the labor encyclicals, alternately emphasizing the rights of workers, the need for labor and capital to cooperate, and the responsibilities of the state.[16]

The church also took advantage of a variety of opportunities to promote the labor encyclicals. Many of these opportunities arose in connection with events that were directly related to either the working class in general or organized labor in particular. The celebration of Labor Day provided one such opportunity. Designated in 1910 by Archbishop Riordan as an occasion for special ceremonies dedicated to working men and women, the Labor Day Mass had become a city tra-

Figure 8.1 "This Is the May Day Celebration We Want." The official newspaper of the Archdiocese of San Francisco printed this illustration on the front page of the 4 May 1935 edition. The Catholic labor agenda of cooperation and mutual obligation, with its stress on the (white) man as the breadwinner, is explicitly linked to future prosperity. *Credit:* The Monitor, *4 May 1935.*

dition by 1935. Archbishop Mitty used the Mass both as a forum in which to preach at length on labor issues and as an opportunity for the church hierarchy to appear in public with labor leaders in a dramatic gesture of support for unions.[17] The emphases of the sermons changed over time. One typical of the mid-1930s stressed the rights of labor, while another delivered in 1943 emphasized the need for unity typical of World War II. However, they were all based almost exclusively on the teachings set forth in the labor encyclicals and frequently included quotations from the documents.[18]

In addition to the Labor Day Mass, other events that were more directly connected to organized labor provided similar opportunities. At the funeral services for Michael J. Casey in May 1937, the archbishop eulogized the longtime president of the San Francisco Teamster's Union. Mitty praised Casey for his solidarity with members of his union who had voted their support for the general strike, even though Casey had opposed it. Casey had "put into practice the teachings of both Leo XIII and Pius XI," had been "fair and just in the demands that he made upon industry and he was likewise insistent that labor give its full meed of justice to industry." A staunch opponent of Communism, Casey's conservative, Catholic unionism provided a model for the future, according to Mitty: "Here we have a fair solution of the problems that confront our city and country today."[19] Labor leaders also regularly sought church representation at a variety of union functions. Although these events did not always provide a platform from which to speak on the labor encyclicals, church participation in them was nonetheless important as a public display of solidarity with organized labor.[20]

Other more neutral events and occasions, both secular and religious, also afforded opportunities for the church to publicize the labor encyclicals. In 1940, for instance, the Rev. Hugh A. Donohoe represented the archbishop at the State Conference of Social Workers. Donohoe delivered an address on "The church and Labor Unions," in which he called for a "united front of organized employees led by men who think in terms of the general welfare."[21] The archbishop himself often invoked the labor encyclicals and consistently called for the application of Christian principles to everyday life when speaking at meetings of various Catholic lay organizations. Mitty liked to point out that a "religion is worthless unless it has a message for human beings in every phase of human life." He repeatedly exhorted the members of lay organizations, such as parish Holy Name societies, the San Francisco Academy of Catholic Men, and the local chapter of the National Council of Catholic Women, to heed the call of Pius XI and bring Christian principles "into industrial and economic matters, into legislative problems, and into political questions."[22]

The labor encyclicals themselves often gave rise to events that publicized their message. The anniversaries of their publication were invariably marked by public lectures and occasionally by radio broadcasts, as well as by luncheons and discussion groups hosted by lay organizations and featuring addresses by local authorities on the labor encyclicals. These events always received extensive coverage in *The Monitor* and often attracted the attention of the major daily papers as well. In 1936 and 1941—years that marked major jubilees of *Rerum Novarum* and

Quadragesimo Anno—the church sponsored elaborate events that not only served to publicize the principles of the encyclicals but also brought leaders of business, labor, and government together to discuss labor relations policy questions.[23]

Archbishop Mitty worked to put the principles of the labor encyclicals into practice by involving the church in activities that fostered cooperation among business, labor, and government. Between 1935 and America's entry into World War II, the formative years of the evolving, albeit tension-filled, business, labor and government relationship in San Francisco, the church sponsored three major programs designed to bring together leaders of business, labor, and government. Two of those programs were specifically designed to provide a forum for the discussion that would lead to the creation of a cooperative, even corporatist, system of local labor relations.[24] In subsequent years, the church participated in or lent its support to government-sponsored programs that were characterized by extensive cooperation between labor and capital and thus served to strengthen the partnership between the two.[25]

In the summer of 1937 the archdiocese sponsored the Social Action School for Priests. The purpose of this intensive summer program was to provide priests with training that would enable them to better aid their parishioners in contending with social and economic problems. Part of a national program, the San Francisco event fit nicely with the archbishop's overall strategy in connection with Pius XI's promotion of "Catholic Action," as well as his concern with local conflicts between labor and capital. The church-sponsored program aimed to influence future industrial relations activities involving leaders of organized labor and business, as well as representatives of government, academia, and the clergy.[26]

The character of the program itself indicates the level of importance the church placed on labor relations and expressed the papal doctrine that the resolution of such problems required the cooperation of all affected parties. Although a "social action school" might address a wide variety of issues, the city's program was devoted almost exclusively to labor issues. Indeed, one local newspaper described it as "a unique labor school."[27] Five broad courses were offered: The Principles of Social and Distributive Justice, Catholic Social Philosophy, The Labor Problem, The Agricultural Problem, and The History of the American Labor Movement. The latter course focused primarily on the growth of the CIO. Although all but one of the regular faculty were members of the clergy, no less than sixteen outside experts were drawn from organized labor, business, government, and academia. Among the guest lecturers were professors of economics and history from Dominican College and Stanford University; Burton Edises, regional attorney of the National Labor Relations Board; Almon Roth, president of the San Francisco Waterfront Employers Association; and John Brophy, national director of the Congress of Industrial Organizations.[28]

The church also sponsored programs that were explicitly designed to foster cooperation between various elements of society, especially organized labor and business. In 1936 and again in 1941 (the years marking jubilees of the labor encyclicals), San Francisco hosted regional Catholic conferences on industrial problems. Cosponsored by the archdiocese and the National Catholic Welfare

Conference, these conferences were not merely another way for the church to publicize the principles of the encyclicals. They also represented a deliberate attempt to make Catholic unionism the model for the practice of labor relations in San Francisco. Representatives of various interest groups were brought together to "examine economic maladjustments which are obstacles to a social order based on Christian principles."[29] The two-day conferences were open to the public and featured a dozen different sessions focusing on specific issues related to labor and industry. Speakers were drawn from government, academia, the church, business, and organized labor, and speakers emphasized the validity of each of their different perspectives. Frederick J. Koster made one of the keynote addresses at the 1936 conference, but labor leaders and church officials constituted the majority of speakers and their contributions received the most extensive coverage in *The Monitor*. In his opening address, Archbishop Mitty explained, "This is a conference to discuss, to learn. We have the highest respect for the principles of other people. We feel that they are holding them in good faith and that they have a right to present their point of view. We do not deal with personalities. We are merely dealing with issues and with principles."[30]

Differences in the tone and makeup of the two conferences are suggestive of the progress made toward greater cooperation between labor and capital between 1936 and 1941. In his remarks to the 1936 conference, Archbishop Mitty not only reminded the participants of the need to respect each other's viewpoints but also forcefully asserted the rights of the working class and defended the church's intervention in labor relations. An excerpt from Mitty's opening address is illustrative.[31]

> We teach that man has certain God-given rights that no government and no group of individuals, no corporations can take away. If industry tends to take them away, or if the social order tends to do it, then it is trespassing on God-given rights. If in industry people are not given a living wage, if they have to live under conditions that destroy morality, then they are touching upon moral principles. It is the duty of [the] Church to speak up in defense of the individual because of her duty as the teacher of mankind.

In 1941, the archbishop's remarks were more evenhanded, emphasizing that both labor and capital bore responsibility for achieving a social order along the lines of that outlined in the labor encyclicals. Moreover, while representatives of the church and organized labor dominated the 1936 conference, the 1941 conference provided a much greater opportunity for participation by business leaders and government officials. Mayor Angelo Rossi delivered the opening address, and Almon E. Roth, now president of the San Francisco Employers Council, spoke on the status of employer-employee relations in the city. Frank P. Foisie, Roth's successor as president of the Waterfront Employers Association, led a discussion of the role of the individual within a mass economy.[32]

Although American involvement in the Second World War understandably diverted church interests, energies, and resources away from elaborate labor-related events and programs, Archbishop Mitty continued to involve the church in activities designed to promote cooperation between labor and business. He gave active and outspoken support to a number of war-related programs. The Salvage for Victory and the War Chest campaigns attracted his patronage. Both campaigns were premised upon cooperation between business and labor, and the AFL and CIO county councils regarded the programs as a means to promote union respectability. From the church's perspective, these patriotic service activities could both dramatize Catholic loyalty to the American nation and further the construction of a local Catholic Christian commonwealth.[33] Mitty also lent support to the War Labor Board and to the voluntary labor-management committees encouraged by the War Production Board. Because these organizations included equal representation of both labor and capital, the church viewed them not only as necessary for the war effort but also as excellent examples of the kind of cooperative associations that Pius XI had endorsed in *Quadragesimo Anno*. Union leaders received reminders of the importance of defining their roles in a broad fashion that would encompass the needs of the community as well as the demands of their constituents. They were also encouraged to participate in labor-management committees and to honor the decisions of the War Labor Board.[34]

Church efforts to promote the practice of Catholic unionism during World War II also benefited from the appointment of the Reverend Hugh A. Donohoe in November 1942 to succeed Gordon O'Neill as editor of *The Monitor*. Donohoe was a close confidant of the archbishop and a rising star within the local church hierarchy. A product of the city's heavily Irish, Catholic, working-class Mission District, Donohoe was a classmate of John F. Shelley at St. Paul's school. Shelley became president and secretary-treasurer of the AFL county council, president of the state labor federation, state senator, congressman, and mayor, and the two men remained close friends. Ordained in 1930, the priest had earned the confidence of the labor movement by his support for the longshoremen and the sailors during the 1934 waterfront strike.

Like his Baltimore counterpart, Father John Francis Cronin, Donohoe completed his doctoral work at Catholic University under the supervision of Monsignor John A. Ryan. Ryan's books, articles, graduate courses, and personal inspiration had shaped the Catholic social justice movement for three decades. Donohoe's dissertation analyzed "Collective Bargaining Under the NIRA," and he became the Bay Area's leading expert on the labor encyclicals.[35] Donohoe was San Francisco's most prominent "labor priest," and he actively involved himself in the entire range of archdiocesan activities related to labor relations as early as October 1936, when he drafted the letter that Mitty sent to Hugh Gallagher. Besides editing the official newspaper from 1942 though 1947, during which time he increased the paper's pro-labor slant, Donohoe was also regularly drafted to deliver Labor Day sermons and public lectures on the labor encyclicals, as well as to represent the archbishop at various union functions. A professor of social science at the archdiocese's St. Patrick's Seminary in Menlo Park, Donohoe taught classes in industrial ethics. He not only taught one of the courses offered at the Social Action School for Priests, but he also organized and administered the entire program.[36]

Reverend Donohoe also played a key role in Archbishop Mitty's efforts to support moderate alternatives to radical unionism. Given the influence of Catholic social teaching on labor activism in the city, San Francisco Catholics had long regarded principled anticommunism and militant trade unionism as fitting together as comfortably as the two halves of a walnut. The papal teachings did not conflict with the interests and the hopes for the future of the predominantly Catholic working class in San Francisco. On the contrary, the new encyclical of 1931 reaffirmed both the uncompromising demands for dignity and justice associated with the firebrand Father Peter Yorke and the patient willingness to cooperate and compromise that had been characteristic of Archbishop Hanna.[37]

At the same time, where issues of labor were concerned, the large numbers of Catholic lay activists who owned and operated business firms found the church's positions on labor relations and Communism compatible with their own points of view. Even before *Divini Redemptoris*, the Catholic Church displayed a consistent opposition to Communism, a doctrine that many business leaders in San Francisco (Catholic and otherwise) perceived to be the cause of labor radicalism.

Archbishop Mitty supported the struggle by anticommunist unions for greater influence in the city's public life while he simultaneously waged a campaign against Communism. The evidence from San Francisco supports historian David J. O'Brien's generalization that "Since the middle of the nineteenth century Communism was regarded as the great enemy of Catholicism, the ultimate expression of modern man's revolt against God, the church, and civilization."[38] However, to his credit, the archbishop refused to encourage the personal vilification and character assassination practiced by red-baiting super-patriots.[39] Catholic labor activists followed suit. Various anticommunists condemned left-wing influence in waterfront labor unions in San Francisco and claimed that Harry Bridges of the International Longshoremen and Warehousemen's Union (ILWU) was a tool of the Communist Party. Jack Henning and other activists refused, however, to support the campaigns to deport Bridges, and he and other Catholic labor leaders maintained cordial relations with Bridges.[40] Also, in the late 1940s and early 1950s, during the frenzied fear-mongering that accompanied the revelations of Soviet espionage, Jack Shelley outspokenly defended individuals targeted as subversives and victimized by guilt-by-association tactics.[41]

The church in San Francisco used the same forums through which it promoted mainstream unionism to combat left-wing unionism: *The Monitor*, Labor Day sermons, public lectures, special events and programs, and union functions. It was not uncommon for the church to engage in public defense of management against those who were viewed as radical unionists.[42] During the intra-union strife between Communists and anticommunists that accompanied the onset of the Cold War, Archbishop Mitty lent his full support to the latter group. In one instance in 1946, he issued explicit instructions to individual priests to "advise [cannery workers] to vote to remain in the AFL" rather than to affiliate with the CIO in a union election supervised by the National Labor Relations Board. This was to be done "diplomatically, without using the name of the Archbishop or this office" because the CIO outfit "is a Communistic organization."[43]

In addition to his own work in combating Communist influence in the union movement, the archbishop also endorsed Catholic lay activists who established a

San Francisco branch of the Association of Catholic Trade Unionists (ACTU). The ACTU was founded in New York in March 1937 by several former members of the Catholic Worker Movement who had grown dissatisfied with what they saw as the utopian character of that organization. Their new group proposed to promote unionization and to increase the practice of Catholic principles within the labor movement. The organization conducted labor schools, sponsored public lectures, published pamphlets and newspapers, supported strikes, provided legal assistance for the rank and file, and solicited church support for union activities. By 1940 Catholic unionists had established eight regional chapters in cities across the nation. While modeled after the New York organization, each chapter emerged under various local conditions and remained essentially autonomous.[44]

San Francisco unionists organized a chapter in 1938, during a retail clerk's strike, in response to an incident in which three nuns crossed a picket line. Angered and frustrated by the nuns' insensitivity to the strike effort, not to mention their apparent ignorance of Catholic teachings, several Catholic unionists formed an ad hoc committee to inform the public of the church's position on labor issues. This committee quickly evolved into a local chapter of the ACTU, the formation of which was announced in a press release dated 18 September 1938.[45] The new organization, its membership restricted to Catholics, ratified a constitution that declared as its purpose "To foster and spread . . . sound trade unionism built on Christian principles" along the lines of the ACTU program, which drew upon Catholic labor teachings and stressed both the rights and the duties of workers.[46] The rights included job security, an income high enough to allow a family to live a decent life, collective bargaining through independent, democratic unions, a decent share in employer profits, the right to strike and picket for a just cause, a just price, and decent hours and working conditions. Duties included performing an honest day's work, joining a union, striking only for a just cause, refraining from violence, respecting property rights, living up to agreements freely made, enforcing honesty and democracy in the union, and cooperating with employers in establishing industry councils and producer cooperatives. In San Francisco and elsewhere, the ACTU sponsored educational programs designed to increase the number and influence of Catholic unionists as organizers, officers, and negotiators. In 1948 the local chapter amended the constitution to add clauses requiring "strict honesty within the union and a square deal for everybody regardless of race, color, or creed" and prohibiting membership to anyone "who is a member of any subversive organization."[47]

Archbishop Mitty gave the ACTU his "wholehearted approval," and he gave his blessing to Hugh A. Donohoe's request to serve as its chaplain, the only ACTU office that was not an elective position. Initially, the archbishop instructed Donohoe to steer the ACTU away from "political activities and from possible difficulties between various labor organizations."[48] However, as Mitty became convinced of the ACTU's commitment to the spread of unionism based on Christian principles, he quickly recognized the organization's potential to counter the influence of Communism within the local labor movement, and he gave it his unreserved full support. The ACTU received public praise as an excellent example of the type of

Catholic worker societies called for by Pius XI in *Quadragesimo Anno*. Business leaders received assurance that the new organization had the endorsement of the archdiocese. Catholic workers received encouragement to join the group.[49]

John F. Maguire served as president of the ACTU during its active years from 1939 to the mid-1950s. Like Donohoe and John Shelley, Maguire was a graduate of St. Paul's grammar school in the heavily Catholic Mission District. By 1944, ACTU membership within the archdiocese had swelled to the point where a second chapter was established in Oakland. The Oakland chaplain was Father Bernard Cronin, a graduate of the Social Action School for Priests.[50] During twenty-five years of operation, some 750 applications were distributed and 600 union members joined and paid dues, though monthly meetings and communion breakfasts typically attracted fewer than two-dozen activists. By the time Laura Smith, a Retail Clerk's Union member who had been a founding member, closed the checking account in 1963, the group had been largely inactive for five years.[51]

During its first fifteen years, San Francisco ACTU members worked to make a difference in the San Francisco labor movement, particularly on the waterfront. The most dramatic evidence of the ACTU's work occurred in Local 10 of the ILWU, where ACTU members made a concerted effort to compete with left-wing candidates for local offices. Harry Bridges was international president of the ILWU, and he scoffed at charges that he operated a Communist dictatorship and boasted of his union's democratic procedures.[52] Bridges had a point. In 1943, James Stanley Kearney, who joined the ACTU in early 1940, ran against Communist Party member Archie Brown in the election for Local vice-president in 1943. Kearney won the election. Then, during the subsequent twenty-seven years, Kearney won elections for nine one-year terms as the president of Local 10. Kearney was serving as president when he died suddenly in 1970, and the entire waterfront shut down to honor his memory. It is not surprising that Paul Pinsky, the director of the Research Department of the ILWU, sent to ACTU meetings an informant who took notes on the proceedings. Kearney's electoral success, and that of George Bradley, another Local 10 officer and ACTU activist, has been relatively ignored in previous accounts of the ILWU. When Catholic activists have been acknowledged, they have been described using the pejorative phrase "rightwing faction."[53] They have been mistakenly characterized solely as anticommunists, and their religious principles and motives have been ignored.[54]

Along with the ACTU, the University of San Francisco (USF) Labor Management School also promoted alternatives to radical unionism. The idea for the establishment of the labor management school emerged in a series of discussions in 1946 between Father Hugh A. Donohoe and Jesuit Father Andrew C. Boss of USF. Boss was a graduate of Gonzaga College with a graduate degree in labor economics and industrial relations from Georgetown University. Like Donohoe, Alioto, Henning, McGuire, and Shelley, Boss was a San Francisco native, one of six sons of a Mission District barber. Like Donohoe, Boss saw the establishment of a local branch of the national network of Jesuit labor schools as a way to enhance the status and power of the mainstream labor movement as well as to more effectively compete against the Communist Party in San Francisco. Donohoe and

Boss regarded the new school as one element of a two-part strategy. The ACTU, which was nearly a decade old at the time, would continue its work within the local labor movement, and the Jesuits at USF would operate an educational program that could effectively compete with the Communist-supported California Labor School. Father Boss recalled in a 1972 interview:[55]

> It was a bad time for labor, with the depression still a sharp memory and the Postwar turmoil creating fertile ground for the commies. They had a Communist labor school in San Francisco, and it was touch and go as to the influence they were beginning to have on the labor movement. We needed something to shift the spotlight onto the sound teachings of the church about the dignity of the workingman and his rights.

The USF Labor-Management School opened its doors in the spring of 1948 and received the enthusiastic support of both Archbishop Mitty and his new Auxiliary Bishop, Hugh A. Donohoe. Father Boss became the director in 1950 and served in that position until his retirement in 1975. In 1978 the institution ceased to operate independently, and its courses were absorbed into the USF Business School curriculum. As was the case with the ACTU, the school received considerable publicity in the official newspaper of the archdiocese, *The Monitor*, and Catholic unionists were encouraged to attend. Unlike the ACTU educational programs, one did not have to be Catholic or a union member to attend. The USF school was open to union members and to management personnel who were directly involved in negotiations with unions. This more inclusive admission policy, coupled with greater resources that allowed for a wider variety of courses, made the USF program a much more viable alternative to the California Labor School than were the ACTU-sponsored programs.[56]

The school offered two ten-week sessions each year to mixed classes of union members and officials, management personnel, and lawyers involved in labor-management negotiations. Jesuits from the USF faculty, union officials, and management executives taught the non-credit evening courses. Topics included practical offerings such as parliamentary procedure, public speaking, and how to take a case to the NLRB, as well as broader offerings such as "Election Year—1948," "Philosophy of Communism," and "Soviet Expansion."[57]

During Archbishop Mitty's tenure, attendance at the fall and spring sessions averaged 120. The largest enrollment (230) came in the spring of 1949, during the adjustment period after the passage of the Taft-Hartley Act. The second-largest enrollment (199) occurred in the spring of 1958 during the McClellan hearings leading to the passage of the Landrum-Griffin Act in the following year. From 1948 through 1950, the first three years of its existence, the school attracted over 500 students to its programs. By the beginning of the fall 1958 session, 1,500 Bay Area union and management people had graduated from the school. By 1969 graduates numbered over 5,000 and included representatives of approximately five hundred different labor unions and two hundred businesses.[58]

Besides running the two sessions each year, with four to six evening classes each session, the Labor Management School also published a monthly magazine,

The USF Labor Management School Panel, and sponsored conferences and symposia devoted to particular issues. Prior to the AFL-CIO merger, the county labor council presidents of each organization actively participated in courses and conferences, as did business agents, presidents, vice presidents, and research directors of individual local unions from AFL and CIO unions. Jack Henning regularly taught courses and spoke at conferences. During the 1950s the Labor Management School cooperated with the San Francisco Urban League and the Council for Civic Unity on behalf of liberal racial reform measures, and in 1957 Mayor George Christopher appointed Henning to the city's new Commission on Equal Employment Opportunity.[59]

By the end of the 1940s organized labor had established itself as a legitimate, even welcome, partner alongside business and government in the liberal growth coalition that shaped San Francisco's urban development into the 1970s. Archbishop Mitty continued to put the influence of the church on the side of the labor movement at a time when business sought to roll back some of the gains unions had made since the New Deal. This position often placed him at odds with the more conservative business leaders of the city. In 1947, Mitty joined Republican Party leaders Governor Earl Warren and Mayor Roger Lapham at the opening ceremonies of the American Federation of Labor's 1947 convention in the city.[60] Lapham, who had come a long way from his call in 1934 for violent repression of the waterfront strike, had accepted the legal right of unions to represent their members and to participate in collective bargaining with employers. However, Lapham continued to endorse measures such as the Taft-Hartley Act of 1947 and the unsuccessful "Right to Work" state ballot initiative in 1958, both aimed at limiting the powers available to labor unions.[61] The archbishop, on the other hand, put the church on record as being strongly opposed to Taft-Hartley, and *The Monitor* provided considerable space to national and local union leaders who condemned the measure during Congressional debates and deplored its passage when it was passed over President Truman's veto.[62]

In the case of the so-called "Right to Work" initiative of 1958, Proposition 18, which California voters rejected by a substantial margin, Mitty's initial strategy was cautious. In July he consulted with his counterparts Joseph T. McGucken in Sacramento and J. Francis Cardinal McIntyre in Los Angeles, and then announced that the church's official position would be to stay neutral. Roger Lapham was anything but neutral. The former mayor served as the Northern California chairman for the Proposition 18 campaign. In October Lapham debated the measure on public television with Harry Bridges of the ILWU and before a San Francisco State College audience with Jack Henning—then research director for the California Federation of Labor.[63]

Then attorney Gregory A. Harrison made a move that changed the dynamics of the campaign entirely. Harrison was the brother of Maurice E. Harrison, one of the founding members of the city's St. Thomas More Society and a staunch supporter of the archbishop's Catholic Action initiative of the late 1930s.[64] Both brothers were partners in the law firm of Brobeck, Phleger, and Harrison, the firm that had represented the shipowners from the early thirties to the late forties. In 1948, however, the shipowners' organization had taken their business to a rival firm, one that was critical of the older tradition of employer intransigence and supportive of the "New Look" in labor relations that had been developing since the settlement of the 1934 strike.[65] Now, just days before the November election, Harrison bought a large ad in all the major newspapers headlined "Popes, Prelates and Priests Urge Voluntary Unionism." Pictures of Popes Pius XI, Pius XII, Leo XIII, and Cardinal Francis Spellman were placed alongside carefully selected quotations that implied that the Catholic Church urged a "yes" vote on "Right to Work."[66] Mitty responded by issuing another almost full-page newspaper ad that appeared the day before the election. The archbishop's statement rejected the claim "that so-called 'voluntary unionism' is the official teaching of the Catholic Church" and condemned Gregory Harrison's "gross misrepresentation of the facts." Mitty's recommendation that voters "vote as they see fit on any issue in accordance with their conscience" appeared again. The ad also contained explicit criticisms of Proposition 18 by Monsignor Matthew Connelly, the chaplain of the San Francisco Port, and Father Boss, dean of the USF Labor Management School.[67] When the election was over and the votes had been counted, California voters rejected the measure by a substantial margin, and the president of the state labor federation sent a warm "thank you" letter to archdiocesan headquarters.[68]

Throughout the period from 1932 to 1958, Catholic activism represented a communal enterprise of a positive character in San Francisco. During the New Deal years and beyond, Catholic activists played a progressive role in the city's labor movement. They acted out of a genuine commitment to a distinctive religious program of economic and social justice for workers and a democratic union movement. The archbishops drew upon the labor encyclicals to promote a Catholic doctrine of labor relations. Labor leaders, rank-and-file union members, and labor priests inspired by Monsignor John A. Ryan's pro-labor Catholic social teachings cooperated to build a labor movement shaped by Catholic principles. The San Francisco case challenges the conventional wisdom about Catholics in the labor movement during the Cold War, because the city's Catholic activists competed against left-wing activists without stooping to red-baiting and super-patriotic demagoguery, and they defended unions against right-wing business politicians during the revival of free enterprise ideology after World War II.

The institutional relationships developed by the Catholic Church and union activists in San Francisco during the quarter-century after the tumultuous year of 1934 played a significant role in the establishment of the city's post-World War II liberal political culture. It would be an exaggeration to assert that Catholic activism, premised upon principles derived from church teachings, constituted the sole, or even the most important, cause of the success of the corporatist system of labor relations that operated in the city by 1958. However, it would be equally erroneous to conclude that San Francisco Catholics and church officials constituted a hegemonic anti-progressive ideological entity that produced negative consequences for the San Francisco labor movement. The evidence is clear that the archbishop assiduously involved diocesan priests in labor relations, but it is also clear that union leaders actively sought out Church support, and that both leaders and rank-and-file union members participated actively in labor-related programs sponsored by the archdiocese. By the beginning of the 1950s the city's postwar political culture was established. Moderate labor unions, with Roman Catholic unionists occupying many of the key local and statewide positions, and nearly all of those in the local and state AFL, made common cause with a reformed business community that had rejected the pre-1934 old-guard *laissez-faire* philosophy. This political culture has been represented in previous accounts as a pragmatic reformulation of older booster principles generated by the structural and functional dynamics of postwar political economy and the politics of national political parties.[69]

Such a deterministic interpretation of the city's "growth machine" political culture represents a substantial oversimplification. Material interests played an important causal role in the creation of the postwar politics of growth.[70] At the same time, ideas also mattered, particularly the belief that anti-radical unions organized along the lines of Catholic labor philosophy promised to be the most authentic representatives of the working class.

This study of San Francisco brings evidence of a distinctive West Coast Catholic progressivism into a historiography that has typically utilized limited East Coast and Midwestern evidence to draw conclusions about Catholics in the labor movement nationally and has too often adopted anachronistic criteria for what constituted progressivism in the period. Nearly twenty years ago historian Ronald Schatz described the difficulty of assessing the impact of Catholic principles and activities in the labor movement. Schatz concluded, "the influence of the Catholic Church in 20th-century American labor history is . . . at once ubiquitous and elusive."[71] Research during the past decade has added considerable substance to that assessment and undercuts arguments that an equivalency existed between an undifferentiated Catholic conservative anticommunism and Catholic labor activism.[72] In 1991, Dennis Deslippe described a variety of successful positive initiatives undertaken by the ACTU in Detroit, and Joseph McShane documented the effectiveness of the Jesuit labor schools on the East Coast.[73] In 1993, Monsignor George C. Higgins, a well-known labor activist during his thirty-six years with the National Catholic Welfare Conference, published his *Reflections of a "Labor Priest."* Higgins pointed out the grassroots origins and the positive character of Catholic labor activism from the thirties to the sixties. He also revealed how the Detroit ACTU and Archbishop Edward Mooney worked together to reduce the influence of the demagogic Father Charles Coughlin. More recently, Kenneth J. Heineman provided detailed evidence of the existence of *A Catholic New Deal* in Pittsburgh, James T. Fisher has explored the activities of Father John M. Corridan on the New York Waterfront, and Steve Rosswurm has analyzed the work of labor priests in CIO unions.[74] The new evidence from New York, Detroit, Pittsburgh, Chicago, and, as demonstrated in this essay, San Francisco, calls into question "the thesis of a 'conservative' church that joined the labor struggle merely to oppose Communism or . . . to serve narrow, institutional interests." The new evidence instead supports the claim of Monsignor Higgins that "action for the genuine progress of labor was the rule rather than the exception in the Catholic social action movement."[75]

Notes

The author would like to thank Jeffrey Burns, Archivist at the Chancery Archives of the Archdiocese of San Francisco; Michael Kotlanger, S.J., Archivist at the University of San Francisco; Susan Parker Sherwood, Acting Director, and Catherine Powell and Carol Cuenod, Outreach Archivists, at the Northern California Labor Archives and Research Center; Susan Goldstein, Director, and Pat Akre, Photographic Collections Director, at the San Francisco History Center, San Francisco Main Public Library; Eugene Vrana, Archivist at the Anne Rand Library of the International Longshoremen's and Warehousemen's Union. Robert W. Cherny and Kerry Taylor asked thought-provoking questions and suggested useful revisions. Special thanks are due to James Collins, who agreed to pursue this subject as a paper in the author's "Politics and Society from 1930 to 1960" graduate research seminar in the History Department at San Francisco State University, and who then co-authored an earlier version of this essay, which appeared as "The Catholic Church and Organized Labor in San Francisco, 1932–1958" in *Records of the American Catholic Historical Society of Philadelphia*, 109 (spring/summer 1999): 81–112.

1. Joseph L. Alioto, "The Catholic Internationale," *The Moraga Quarterly* 7 (winter 1936): 68–72. Thirty years later, Communist competition in the United States long since vanquished, Mayor Alioto put a symbolic flourish to his side's victory when he appointed veteran old Reds to several San Francisco city commissions.
2. Jack Henning, "The Catholic College Graduate and Labor," *The Moraga Quarterly* 9, no. 3 (spring 1939): 165–70.
3. See William Issel, "Business Power and Political Culture in San Francisco, 1900–1940," *Journal of Urban History* 16 (November 1989): 52–77 for a description of the influence of Catholic social thought in the city's public life.
4. *The Monitor*, 9 June 1934.
5. Ibid.
6. Ibid.
7. Ibid.
8. Sam Kagel, interview by author, 15 June 1998. Hanna, having been involved in a variety of labor arbitration roles during the 1920s (at a time when many leftist unionists spelled arbitration "arbetraytion"), was then serving on President Franklin Roosevelt's National Longshoremen's Board. Kagel and O'Grady served on the Joint Maritime Strike Committee. See David F. Selvin, *A Terrible Anger: The 1934 Waterfront and General Strikes in San Francisco* (Detroit: Wayne State University Press, 1996), 100, 159.
9. *San Franciso News*, 14 July 1934. The San Francisco Academy of Catholic Men, an organization of businessmen and professionals, also mobilized in favor of a settlement. Catholic arguments on behalf of cooperation between labor and business earned particular scorn from Communist activists. The author of a 1950 article in a Communist Party publication, critical of "clerical fascism," argued that the Catholic rejection of "the line of militant struggle" led directly to "the company-union, class-collaborationist nature of the papal and A.C.T.U. program." See George Morris, *The Vatican Conspiracy in the Trade Union Movement* (New York: New Century Publishers, 1950), reprinted from *Political Affairs* [Communist Party] (June 1950): 13–14.
10. John W. Mailliard, quoted in *San Francisco News*, 23 July 1934.
11. For a detailed analysis of these developments see William Issel, "New Deal and World War II Origins of San Francisco's Postwar Political Culture," in *The Way We Really Were: The Golden State in the Second Great War*, ed. Roger W. Lotchin (Urbana:

University of Illinois Press, 2000), and William Issel, "Liberalism and Urban Policy in San Francisco from the 1930s to the 1960s," in *Western Historical Quarterly* 22 (November 1991): 431–450.

12. Jeffrey M. Burns, "Mitty, John Joseph," in *The Encyclopedia of American Catholic History*, ed. Michael Glazier and Thomas J. Shelley (Collegeville, Minn.: The Liturgical Press, 1997), 967–68; "Life Summary of Archbishop Mitty," *The Monitor*, 31 August 1935.
13. John J. Mitty to Hugh Gallagher, 6 October 1936, in Labor File, 1934–1939, Chancery Archives of the Archdiocese of San Francisco, St. Patrick's Seminary, Menlo Park, California (hereafter cited as CAASF).
14. See Issel, "Business Power and Political Culture," 72–73, and "New Deal and World War II Origins."
15. *The Monitor*, Bay Area Development Edition, 1 May 1937. *The Monitor*, sec. 2, 17 May 1947.
16. For representative articles and editorials, see *The Monitor*, 8 June 1935; 17 April 1937; 23 March 1940; 21 October 1944; 29 August 1947; 10 October 1947.
17. Issel, "Business Power and Political Culture," 66.
18. *The Monitor*, 7 September 1935; *The Monitor*, 11 September 1943.
19. *The Monitor*, 8 May 1937. Labor arbitrator Sam Kagel, a close friend of Michael Casey, recalls the teamster president as a regular attendant at Sunday Mass, and remembers having to wait until after church services to drive to a union meeting in San Jose. Kagel, interview, 15 June 1998.
20. W. R. Otto to Mitty, 1 March 1938, Labor File, 1934–1939; Edward D. Vandeleur to Mitty, 3 January 1941, Labor File, 1939–1943; John A. O'Connell to Mitty, 13 May 1946, Labor File/Miscellaneous, 1946–1974, all in CAASF.
21. *The Monitor*, 20 April 1940.
22. Mitty, "Address to Regional Conference on Industrial Problems," 8 June 1936, in Archbishop Mitty's Sermons, Dedications and Talks (*Sermons*), January–June 1936 folder; Mitty, "Address to Archdiocese Council of the National Conference of Catholic Women," 29 May 1937, *Sermons*, January–June 1937 folder; Mitty, "Address on Catholic Action," 29 October 1938, *Sermons* July–December 1938 folder, CAASF.
23. *San Francisco Examiner*, 16 May 1936; *The Monitor*, 23 May 1936; *The Monitor*, 17 May 1941.
24. On the corporatist character of business, labor, and government cooperation in San Francisco, see Issel, "New Deal and World War II Origins." On Catholic discourse regarding corporatism, albeit at the level of the national, rather than the local or state, see David J. O'Brien, *American Catholics and Social Reform: The New Deal Years* (New York: Oxford University Press, 1968), 25–26. For an important New England study, see Gary Gerstle, "Catholic Corporatism, French Canadian Workers, and Industrial Unionism in Rhode Island, 1938–1956," in *Labor Divided: Race and Ethnicity in United States Labor Struggles, 1835–1960*, ed. Robert Asher and Charles Stephenson (Albany: State University of New York, 1990), 209–225. See also Larry G. Gerber, "Corporatism and State Theory: A Review Essay for Historians," in *Social Science History* 19 (fall 1995): 313–332.
25. Edward J. Kennedy (Assistant Chancellor) to Hurford Sharon, 11 June 1937, Labor File, 1934–1939, CAASF.
26. *The Monitor*, 17 April 1937; 26 June 1937.
27. *San Francisco Chronicle*, 18 June 1937, emphasis added.

28. "Summary Report on the Social Action School for Priests," 25 June 1937, Social Action School file, 1937–1939, CAASF.
29. Mitty's address to the 1941 Regional Catholic Conference on Industrial Problems, quoted in *The Monitor*, 4 October 1941.
30. *The Monitor*, 13 June 1936.
31. Ibid.
32. Ibid.
33. *The Monitor*, 5 February 1942; 10 October 1942. See also Issel, "Liberalism and Urban Policy," 436.
34. Rev. Hugh Donohoe, "Labor Day Sermon," delivered in St. Mary's Cathedral, *The Monitor*, 2 September 1942. Rev. Vincent Breen, "Address to San Francisco Association of Catholic Trade Unionists," 6 June 1943, *The Monitor*, 12 June 1943. Rev. Joseph Munier, "Labor Day Sermon," delivered in St. Mary's Cathedral, 5 September 1943, *The Monitor*, 11 September 1943. Rev. Joseph Munier, "Labor Unions After the War," *The Monitor*, United Nations Security Conference Supplement, 5 May 1945.
35. Biography file, Hugh A. Donohoe, CAASF. Kagel, interview. "S.F. Labor Honors Bishop Donohoe," in *The Monitor*, 24 October 1947. See Joshua B. Freeman and Steve Rosswurm, "The Education of an Anti-Communist: Father John F. Cronin and the Baltimore Labor Movement," *Labor History* 33 (spring 1992): 217–247.
36. Donohoe continued to play an active role in labor activities for at least seven years after his consecration on 7 October 1947. Charles J. Foehn to Donohoe, 31 December 1954, Labor file 1946–1974, CAASF.
37. For a detailed discussion of the imprint of Catholic teachings in San Francisco political culture during this period see Issel, "Business Power and Political Culture," 52–77. See also David J. O'Brien, *Public Catholicism*, 2d ed. (Maryknoll, N.Y.: Orbis Books, 1996), 144, and Ronald W. Schatz, "American Labor and the Catholic Church," in *International Labor and Working Class History* 20 (fall 1981): 49–50.
38. O'Brien, *American Catholics and Social Reform*, 81–82.
39. For the contrasting case of Pittsburgh, see the exchange of letters in 1948 between Harry Bridges and Rev. Charles Owen Rice of Pittsburgh as reprinted in Charles J. McCollester, *Fighter With a Heart: Writings of Charles Owen Rice, Pittsburgh Labor Priest* (Pittsburgh: University of Pittsburgh Press, 1996), 68–70. See also Steve Rosswurm, "Symposium on Fighter with a Heart—Writings of Monsignor Charles Owen Rice," *Labor History* 40 (1999): 53–68.
40. Jack Henning, interview by author, San Francisco, 7 October 1998. Robert W. Cherny, "Harry Bridges and the Communist Party: New Evidence, Old Questions; Old Evidence, New Questions," a paper delivered at the annual meeting of the Organization of American Historians, 4 April 1998, copy in author's possession. See also Harvey Klehr, John Earl Haynes, & Fridrikh Igorevich Firsov, *The Secret World of American Communism* (New Haven: Yale University Press, 1995), 127.
41. Shelley's refusal to engage in red-baiting and his courageous defense of victims of McCarthyism during the red scare is described in Sierra Gehrke, "John Francis Shelley" (Honors Thesis, Department of History, San Francisco State University, 26 May 1998). The importance of distinguishing between "responsible" anticommunism and "extremist" red-baiting is a theme of Richard Gid Powers, *Not Without Honor: The History of American Anticommunism* (New York: Free Press, 1995).
42. *The Monitor*, 12 September 1936; 13 February 1937; 1 May 1937; 11 September 1937; 10 September 1938; 20 April 1940; 7 September 1940; 12 April 1941.

43. Rev. Harold Collins, Secretary to the Archbishop, to Rev. Hammond, 20 August 1946; Rev. Collins to Msgr. McGough, 20 August 1946, Labor/Miscellaneous file, 1946, CAASF.
44. Msgr. George G. Higgins with William Bole, *Organized Labor and the church: Reflections of a "Labor Priest"* (New York: Paulist Press, 1993), 58–62; Dennis A. Deslippe, "'A Revolution of Its Own': The Social Doctrine of the Association of Catholic Trade Unionists in Detroit, 1939–50," in *Records* of the American Catholic Historical Society of Philadelphia 102 (winter 1991): 19–36. John C. Cort, "ACTU and the Auto Workers," *US Catholic Historian* 9 (fall 1990): 335–351. See also O'Brien, *American Catholics and Social Reform*, 115–116 and Neil Betten, *Catholic Activism and the Industrial Worker* (Gainesville, Fla.: University Presses of Florida, 1976), 124–125.
45. Laura Smith to Msgr. Connolly, enclosing a copy of a mimeographed pamphlet, "It's Our City Too," 26 September 1938, Labor file, 1934–1939. Gus Gaynor, Brotherhood of Railway Clerks, press release dated 18 October 1938, Labor file, 1934–1939, CAASF.
46. Constitution of the ACTU of San Francisco, reprinted in *The Monitor*, 28 January 1939.
47. "ACTU Preamble, Constitution, Pledge," and "Proposed Changes . . . San Francisco Chapter 6," mimeo, 8 July 1948, in the Labor Management School Records/ACTU Archives of the University of San Francisco (hereafter cited as ACTU Records).
48. Mitty to Hugh Donohoe, 14 January 1939. Donohoe Papers, Assorted Correspondence, folder 8, CAASF.
49. *The Monitor*, 9 September 1939; 10 May 1941; 28 August 1943; 18 November 1944; 26 April 1947; 5 March 1948. Mitty to Hugh Gallagher of Matson Navigation Co., 20 March 1941, Labor file, 1939–1943, CAASF.
50. *The Monitor*, 15 January 1944.
51. Data on the ACTU is from the organization's membership and dues ledgers, checking account statements, attendance lists from meetings, and correspondence in the ACTU Records. At the point of its greatest activity, the organization had 599 dues-paying members. I have been able to identify the union membership of all but 64. The waterfront unions dominated the organization, with the 274 members from the ILWU divided as follows: 191 from Local 10, and 16 from Local 6. Another 67 belonged to Warehouse Union Local 34. Fifty teamsters from Local 85 belonged to the ACTU, as did 40 retail clerks from Local 1100. Membership in the ACTU appears to have been concentrated in the San Francisco unions in which ACTU leaders perceived a CP influence that would pose a threat to Catholic labor principles. The building trades, for instance, were poorly represented.
52. Robert W. Cherny, "Harry Bridges and the Communist Party: New Evidence, Old Questions; Old Evidence, New Questions," a paper delivered at the annual meeting of the Organization of American Historians, 4 April 1998, copy in author's possession.
53. Data on Kearney's and Bradley's electoral successes in Local 10 is from the subject card files and from various issues of the union's newspaper *The Dispatcher* in the ILWU's Anne Rand Library. See Howard Kimeldorf, *Reds or Rackets? The Making of Radical and Conservative Unions on the Waterfront* Berkeley: University of California Press, 1988), 138, 150, for a typical treatment of the opposition to the leftist officers and members. Kearney's Catholicism is ignored by Kimmeldorf, as are the dozens of ILWU members who paid dues to the ACTU as well as to the ILWU. Kearney merits a mention as a popular officer of Local 10 and one of many Catholic officers in various CIO unions in Vincent Silverman's recent book. Silverman, however, does not take the religious character of the ACTU seriously, characterizing it wholly negatively as an an-

ticommunist outfit. He appears to have ignored the ACTU records altogether and mistakenly dismisses the importance of Kearney's Catholicism and the ACTU work in San Francisco on the basis of oral history testimony by a single informant. To his credit, Silverman is forthright about his point of view: "I grew up almost instinctively hating such nefarious figures as Walter Reuther, James Carey, and Joe Curran." See Vincent Silverman, *Imagining Internationalism in American and British Labor, 1939–49* (Urbana: University of Illinois Press, 2000), xi, 130, 242.

54. Handwritten notes taken at ACTU meetings are in the Paul Pinsky Collection, Northern California Labor Archives and Research Center. That the leftist officers of the ILWU's International organization took the ACTU considerably more seriously than have subsequent historians is evident from the research director's careful monitoring of its activities during the late 1940s.

55. Quoted in James W. Kelly, Jr., "USF Labor-Management School, 1972," *Western Jesuit* (autumn 1972): 22. On the labor schools, see William J. Smith, *The Catholic Labor School: Common Sense in Action* (New York: Paulist Press, 1941), and Peter McDonough, *Men Astutely Trained: A History of the Jesuits in the American Century* (New York: Free Press, 1992), 309–16.

56. The role of the Communist Party in the California Labor School is described by one of its founders, David Jenkins, in his oral history. See "The Union Movement, the California Labor School, and San Francisco Politics," an oral history interview conducted in 1987 and 1988 by Lisa Rubens, Regional Oral History Office, Bancroft Library, University of California, Berkeley (1993). See also Joseph M. McShane, S.J., "A Survey of the History of the Jesuit Labor Schools in New York: An American Social Gospel in Action," in *Records of the American Catholic Historical Society of Philadelphia* 102 (winter 1991): 37–64.

57. USF-Labor Management School Course Schedules, various years, Labor Management School Collection, Archives of the University of San Francisco.

58. Ibid. Summary Enrollment Statistics, Records Department, University of San Francisco.

59. *San Francisco Chronicle*, 13 October 1957. See also "Discrimination in Employment," in *Labor Management Panel* 4, no. 5 (January 1954):1–4; "The Employment Problems of the Negro Worker in San Francisco," Ibid., 7, no. 1 (January 1956): 1, 4.

60. *The Monitor*, 10 October 1947.

61. Issel, "New Deal and World War II Origins." *San Francisco Chronicle*, 28, 30 October 1958.

62. *The Monitor*, 17 May 1947; 27 June 1947.

63. Right Reverend Leo T. Maher, Chancellor-Secretary, to J. Francis Cardinal McIntyre, 11 July 1958; Joseph T. McGucken to Rt. Rev. Msgr. Leo T. Maher, 14 July 1958, Labor/Miscellaneous file, 1946–1974, CAASF. *The Monitor*, 26 April 1947. *San Francisco Chronicle*, 24, 30 October 1958, 12 May 1970.

64. Maurice E. Harrison, "The College Man in the New World," *The Moraga Quarterly* 7 (summer 1937): 192–197; Maurice E. Harrison, "St. Thomas More," *The Moraga Quarterly* 12 (autumn 1941): 26–33, College Archives, St. Albert Hall Library, St. Mary's College of California, Moraga, Calif.; Maurice Harrison to My Dear Archbishop Mitty, 2 November 1942, Correspondence 1942, folder HA-HD, CAASF.

65. Norman Leonard, "Life of a Leftist Labor Leader," an interview conducted by Estolv E. Ward in 1985, Regional Oral History Office, Bancroft Library, University of California at Berkeley (1986). Clark Kerr and Lloyd Fisher, "Conflict on the Waterfront," *Atlantic Monthly* 184 (September 1949): 17–23.

66. *San Francisco Chronicle*, 31 October 1958.

67. *San Francisco Chronicle*, 3 November 1958.
68. Thomas L. Pitts, President, California State Federation of Labor, to The Most Rev. John J. Mitty, 26 November 1958; Most Rev. Hugh A. Donohoe to Rev. F.C. Falque, 28 November 1958, Labor/Miscellaneous file, 1946–1974, CAASF.
69. Chester Hartman with Sarah Carnochan, *City for Sale: The Transformation of San Francisco*, rev. ed. (Berkeley: University of California Press, 2002); John Mollenkopf, *The Contested City* (Princeton: Princeton University Press, 1983).
70. Chris Carlsson, "The Progress Club: 1934 and Class Memory," in *Reclaiming San Francisco: History, Politics, Culture*, ed. James Brook, Chris Carlsson, and Nancy J. Peters (San Francisco: City Lights Books, 1998), 67–87.
71. Ronald W. Schatz, "American Labor and the Catholic Church," 51. See also Ronald W. Schatz, "Connecticut's Working Class in the 1950s: A Catholic Perspective," *Labor History* 25 (winter 1984): 199–224.
72. See Kathleen Neils Conzen, "The Place of Religion in Urban and Community Studies," in *Religion and American Culture* 6 (summer 1996): 108–114; Ken Fones-Wolf, "Religious Inspiration in the CIO: Catholics, Protestants and the New Deal Industrial Relations System," a paper presented at the session, "Religion, Labor, and Poverty During the Great Depression," 2003 OAH Convention, Memphis, Tennessee, 5 April 2003, copy in author's possession; Joseph A. McCartin, "Industrial Unionism as Liberator or Leash? The Limits of 'Rank-and-Filism' in American Labor Historiography," in *Journal of Social History* 31 (spring 1998): 701–710; Michael Kazin, "A People Not a Class: Rethinking the Political language of the Modern U.S. Labor Movement," in *Reshaping the U. S. Left: Popular Struggles in the 1980s*, ed. Mike Davis and Michael Sprinker (London: Verso, 1988), 257–286.
73. Deslippe, "A Revolution of its Own"; McShane, "Jesuit Labor Schools."
74. Higgins and Bole, *Organized Labor and the church*, 62; Kenneth J. Heineman, "A Catholic New Deal: Religion and Labor in 1930s Pittsburgh," *The Pennsylvania Magazine of History and Biography* 118 (October 1994): 363–94, and *A Catholic New Deal: Religion and Reform in Depression Pittsburgh* (University Park, Pa.: Pennsylvania State University Press, 1999; James T. Fisher, "John M. Corridan, S.J., and the Battle for the Soul of the Waterfront," *US Catholic Historian* 16 (fall 1998): 71–87; Steve Rosswurm, "Heeding the Papal Cry 'Go to the Workers': The Social Action Department and the Labor Priests," a paper delivered at the conference on Catholicism in Twentieth-Century America, The Cushwa Center for the Study of American Catholicism, University of Notre Dame, 9–11 March 2000, copy in author's possession.
75. Higgins and Bole, *Organized Labor and the church*, 62. Higgins's positive assessment fifty years after the fact, particularly his affirmation of the progressive character of the Catholic labor agenda, stands in some contrast to the reminiscences of his contemporary, Reverend Charles Owen Rice. See Rice's comments in the conclusion of Don Watson's essay, chapter 3 of this book, and additional material in Charles McCollester, ed., *Fighter with a Heart: Writings of Charles Owen Rice, Pittsburgh Labor Priest* (Pittsburgh: University of Pittsburgh Press, 1996), especially 96–98.

Memories of the Red Decade

HUAC Investigations in Maryland

☼

Vernon L. Pedersen

The fall of the Soviet Union and the collapse of international Communism have prompted historians to reevaluate many aspects of Cold War America. Some of the recently published works, such as the Yale University Press series The Annals of Communism, or Allen Weinstein's *The Haunted Wood*, are based upon newly released documents and focus on resolving old controversies. Weinstein's book deals with Soviet spies in the United States and offers convincing evidence of the guilt of both Alger Hiss and Julius Rosenberg. John Haynes and Harvey Klehr have published two volumes of documents, *The Secret World of American Communism* and *The Soviet World of American Communism*, drawn from the files of the Russian State Archive of Social and Political History (RGASPI). The two collections detail the close relationship of the American party with the Soviet Union, reveal the organization of the party's underground apparatus and establish the party membership of such controversial figures as the West Coast longshoremen's union leader, Harry Bridges. Other authors, however, have reconsidered the domestic aspects of the Cold War by looking at previously available sources with an eye informed by the recent revelations.

Two of the most important efforts are Richard Gid Powers' 1994 book, *Not Without Honor: The History of American Anticommunism*, and Ellen Schrecker's *Many are the Crimes: McCarthyism in America*. Both books agree that, although opposition to Communism was often unjustifiably extreme, most of the individuals and organizations targeted by anticommunists were, in fact, tied to the Communist Party USA (CPUSA). Powers, as his title implies, finds some anticommunism to have been legitimate and responsible. Schrecker, however, concludes that, even acknowledging the many shortcomings of the Communist Party, and despite the new proof of a solid basis for American fears of subversion, McCarthyism was a "disgrace."[1]

If Schrecker refers only to the antics of the junior senator from Wisconsin and the group of extremists and opportunists that surrounded him, then there is little to argue about. However, anticommunism cannot be exclusively identified with

Joseph McCarthy. Indeed the best aspect of Powers' book is that it portrays anticommunism as a complex, pluralistic movement with elements ranging from responsible, principled anticommunists to conspiracy-obsessed extremists. Schrecker is less interested in the make-up of anticommunism than in exploring the wider impact of McCarthyism, which she concludes resulted in setbacks for labor, restriction of debate on social issues, and severe personal consequences for many individuals identified with leftist causes.

Powers looks at anticommunism over a seventy-year span and locates the beginning of the movement in the nation's reaction to the Bolshevik Revolution. Schrecker focuses most of her study on the height of anticommunism in the 1950s and roots the movement in domestic opposition to the New Deal, rather than reaction to events abroad. Powers draws on sources written from the anticommunist perspective, while Schrecker takes her information primarily from sources hostile to anticommunism. This essay combines the two perspectives and seeks to evaluate both the consequences of anticommunism and the mix of responsible and extremist elements within the movement by examining the investigations of the House Committee on Un-American Activities (HUAC) into the Communist Party of Maryland.

HUAC specifically targeted the Maryland party on five occasions, in 1940, 1944, 1951, 1954 and 1957. The 1940 hearings established a pattern followed, to varying degrees, by all the rest. Although ostensibly concerned with the general issue of un-American propaganda, the hearings in fact exclusively targeted the Communist Party and took place within a year of an international event, the Nazi-Soviet pact, which highlighted fears of the Soviet Union as a potential threat to American security. Most importantly, they were followed by a combination of official and informal reprisals against the Communist Party. The 1944 and 1954 hearings depart from this pattern in several ways but conform to a fourth aspect that all the hearings share: the close involvement of organizations and individuals with long histories of firmly held anticommunist beliefs.

In 1940 J.B. Matthews, whom Powers describes as the archetype of a 1920s-era fellow traveler, ably filled this role. Matthews began his career as a pacifist Methodist missionary in Burma. Upon his return to the United States he became involved in the 1924 La Follette presidential campaign. Convinced that the Communist Party was the only organization capable of uniting the various left-wing groups in America, Matthews joined a dizzying variety of party fronts and worked hard for the Communist cause. He traveled to the Soviet Union every year between the years 1927 and 1932, and served as chair of the United States Congress Against War, later known as the League Against War and Fascism. Matthews's exposure to the inner world of international Communism eventually disillusioned him, prompting him to resign from the League Against War and Fascism in 1934 and to break completely with Communism in 1935. In August 1938, Matthews accepted a job as the chief investigator for Martin Dies' newly formed congressional committee, and began a life-long career as an anticommunist.[2]

In the wake of the Nazi-Soviet pact and the partition of Poland, Matthews prepared a series of hearings involving both national and regional Communist

Party leaders that were designed to expose the subversive nature of the organization. Matthews' hearings were not the first federal investigation of Communists in Maryland. In 1919 the Bureau of Investigation, predecessor of the FBI, placed the Maryland Communist Party under surveillance and arrested dozens of its members in Baltimore during the Palmer raids. In 1930, Hamilton Fish, concerned about the rise in Communist activity since the onset of the Depression, formed a special congressional committee to investigate radicals. Interested in the Baltimore situation, Fish first invited police inspector George Henry to come to Washington to testify. When Henry refused, on the grounds that there was "no Communist problem in Baltimore," Fish hastily substituted Mrs. Ruben Ross Holloway, who was active in a number of patriotic organizations. She testified that the city had become "a little center of red activity."[3]

Despite the Palmer raids, Fish committee hearings, and regular surveillance by the FBI and military intelligence, there was surprisingly little concrete information available on the Maryland party, prompting Matthews to send HUAC agents armed with subpoenas to the party's Baltimore headquarters. There, agents Charles Randal and I.H. O'Hanion seized membership records, the minutes of district meetings, and served Dorothy Rose Blumberg, wife of district secretary Albert Blumberg, with a summons requiring her to give testimony before the committee in Washington.[4]

The hearings began the day after the raid on the morning of March 29, 1940. Matthews conducted much of the questioning himself, showing particular interest in documents indicating that several individuals had joined the party under false names. Blumberg turned aside Matthews' questions with protestations of ignorance, which, although false, defeated all attempts to pry information out of her. Albert Blumberg, served with a summons while attending his wife's session, was not so fortunate. After a failed attempt to invoke the First Amendment, he refused to discuss anyone but himself, resulting in a contempt-of-Congress charge. Both informal, community reactions and formal, legal repercussions immediately followed the hearings. The Ku Klux Klan burned a cross on the Blumbergs' lawn, and Johns Hopkins University, where Albert had taught philosophy, barred him from speaking on campus. Thomas D'Alesandro, congressman from Maryland, demanded further investigations into "red" activities, and the legislature passed a law restricting third-party access to the state ballot.[5]

Dorothy Rose Blumberg, who directed the petition drive that secured Communist candidates a place on the ballot for the 1940 elections, suffered the worst backlash from the hearings. In June, Dies committee investigators acquired copies of the party's election petitions and sent letters to all 2,200 signers. The letters advised them that the Dies Committee possessed evidence of fraud relating to the petition and implied, in selective quotes from the petition's fine print, that signing the document was tantamount to admitting party membership. The committee received 302 replies from intimidated signers, in which they either claimed they had been misled or denied having signed the petition at all. Maryland State Attorney J. Bernard Wells then initiated perjury charges against Dorothy Rose Blumberg and five other signature collectors. All six were convicted, and three individuals, including Blumberg, were forced to pay fines of up to one thousand dollars to avoid jail sentences.[6]

Although initially damaging, the Dies committee backlash had no long-term effect on the Maryland party, because America's entrance into the Second World War as allies of the Soviet Union severely blunted anticommunist arguments. By 1944 the party had more than 2,000 members and possibly as many as 10,000 supporters. Its members led locals of the International Union of Marine and Shipbuilding Workers of America (IUMSWA), the National Maritime Union (NMU), the Cumberland branch of the International Textile Workers union, and enjoyed a strong position on the Baltimore Industrial Union council. Although operating openly and regularly sponsoring radio broadcasts that, by 1944, had become completely supportive of the Roosevelt administration's policies, the party continued to maintain some front groups. The two most successful of these were the Total War Employment Committee (TWEC), which sought the hiring of blacks into jobs formerly reserved for whites, and the Sweethearts of Servicemen (SOS), which conducted activities similar to the United Service Organization (USO).[7]

The party's wartime endeavors attracted the attention of numerous opponents. The most important adversary was the FBI, which resumed active surveillance and planted several spies and informers within the Maryland party. The party's most visible adversary, however, was John Francis Cronin, a Baltimore priest. A former student of Father John Ryan at Catholic University, whose course on distributive justice inspired many of the church's "labor priests," Cronin is an excellent example of the responsible anticommunists described by Powers. Cronin came to Baltimore determined to use the 1931 encyclical, *Quadragesimo Anno* (literally "In the Fortieth Year," but generally known as the encyclical on social justice), issued by Pope Pius XI as a lever to expand Catholic influence in union circles. Besides establishing a labor school at the Catholic community house on Broadway, Cronin was active in the organization of a number of CIO locals in Baltimore, in particular those attached to the IUMSWA. Although Cronin took an interest in the problem of Communist influence in labor unions, he initially discounted such tales as the fantasies of frustrated politicians.[8]

In 1942, however, workers at the Fairfield shipyard and FBI agents approached Cronin separately and asked him to help prevent a Communist Party takeover of IUMSWA Local 43. Cronin obliged and conducted a bruising two-year fight against the Communists at the yards. He ultimately lost the struggle because of the cohesion and discipline of Maryland party secretary Al Lannon's cadres and Cronin's willingness, which he later came to regret, to ally himself with opportunists and racists on the grounds of Catholicism and shared anticommunism. Cronin's defeat earned him the sympathy of Martin Dies and J.B. Matthews, who devoted a portion of their 1944 hearings on Communist influence in the CIO to Local 43. The committee called as witnesses several shipyard employees with intimate knowledge of party activities, who accurately described the extent of party control over the union. However, the general public ignored the hearings and the party seems to have suffered no adverse consequences.[9]

In the fall of 1944 the Communist Party reached the height of its influence in Maryland. Bernard "Whitey" Goodfriend, a party organizer at the Fairfield shipyards, habitually carried around a four-inch stack of membership cards and openly signed up new recruits. Party members in the armed forces wore their uniforms to party meetings, and prominent state officials spoke at thinly disguised Communist rallies organized in support of the war. On 3 November 1944, the Communists capped their campaign for a fourth term for Franklin Roosevelt with a mass rally at the Fifth Regiment Armory. Officially sponsored by the CIO's Political Action Committee (which, in Baltimore, was entirely controlled by the party), the rally drew over 8,000 people. The official Democratic Party rally, held a few days later, drew only 3,500.[10]

The Maryland party's triumph proved fleeting. The very next year the national leadership of the IUMSWA took decisive action against the Communists at the Fairfield yards by suspending the autonomy of Local 43. Ross D. Blood, the IUMSWA national secretary, personally went to Baltimore to reorganize the local and offered the Communists an equal role with the anticommunists on the local's interim board. However, the Communists rejected Blood's overtures, launched a smear campaign against John Green, the IUMSWA president, and adopted a policy of disruption of union meetings. The tactics proved to be a serious miscalculation that cost the Communists all their hard-won influence. Setbacks also took place within the one-time Communist stronghold of the National Maritime Union. The problems began when Harry Connor, the NMU port agent, became convinced that the union's secretary, Florence Schwartz, a Communist Party member, was conspiring against him. Connor fired Schwartz, beginning a chain of events which, combined with national president Joe Curran's turn against the party, resulted in an almost complete loss of party influence by 1947. The collapse on the waterfront inspired party leaders to attempt to expand the Steel Club at Bethlehem Steel's Sparrows Point plant, but an aggressive transfer of cadres resulted in only a small, and largely ineffective, organization.[11]

The Catholic Church, emboldened by the party's weakness, launched an energetic campaign that excoriated the party in the press and led to the firing of a Baltimore schoolteacher, Regina Frankfeld, wife of Philip Frankfeld, the general secretary of the Maryland Party. The spread of anticommunist sentiment, fueled by the Cold War, the arrest of eleven national party leaders under the Smith Act, and mounting spy scandals resulting from the testimony of Elizabeth Bently and Whittaker Chambers spurred the Maryland legislature to action. In 1947, William McGrath, delegate from Prince George's county, proposed an amendment to the Maryland constitution barring from public office anyone who advocated the overthrow of the United States government by force or violence. The amendment passed by a wide margin in 1948 but lacked any means of enforcement. Accordingly, the legislature requested that the governor form a commission to draft a comprehensive counter-subversive measure. The commission, headed by Frank B. Ober, an anticommunist attorney and prominent Catholic layman, presented its results late in the year and the measure, dubbed the Ober Law, passed the Maryland assembly with a single dissenting vote in 1949.[12]

The Ober Law required detailed loyalty oaths of all public employees, demanded rigorous efforts from schools to stamp out subversive influences, and mandated the creation of public records on all disloyal persons and organizations. Fearing that the law damaged personal liberty far more than it protected the state against subversion, a coalition of individuals and groups joined the Communist Party in a campaign to have the act declared unconstitutional. Organized as the Citizen's Committee Against the Ober Law, the group included the Maryland branch of Henry Wallace's Progressive Party, the Marine Cooks and Stewards union, the Maryland chapter of the American Association of Social Workers, and several black attorneys who feared the Ober Law might be used to roll back civil rights advances. The coalition enjoyed early success and forced a referendum vote on the Ober Law as part of the 1950 general election.

In February, however, Senator Joseph McCarthy burst on the scene with his allegations of Communist spies in the State Department, in June the Korean War began, and in July Julius and Ethel Rosenberg were arrested on charges of betraying the secret of the atom bomb to the Soviets. The combination of aggression by a Communist country and fears of internal subversion ensured approval of the Ober Law, which received 259,000 votes in favor and only 79,000 votes against. Although aimed at Communists, the only individuals ever prosecuted under the Ober Law were several pacifists and Quakers, whose religion forbade oath taking.[13]

In the summer of 1951, bolstered by public insecurity, HUAC focused its full attention on the Maryland party. In a direct appeal to the public's sense of insecurity, HUAC declared that it was investigating Communist activities in the Baltimore defense area. The hearings singled out party activities in labor unions and the majority of the witnesses called were union, as well as party, members. None of the first twenty-four witnesses could be coaxed to admit anything, with the exception of William Spegal, who related that he had rented his apartment to Whittaker Chambers and his partner in espionage, David Carpenter, during the late 1930s. At the time of the hearings, Chambers, famous for his branding of Alger Hiss as a Soviet spy, was embroiled in controversy over accusations—later dismissed as unfounded—that State department official O. Edmund Clubb had been a Soviet courier. Spegal's testimony appears to have been included by HUAC investigators to provide support for Chambers and to link the party with espionage in the public mind.[14]

The hearings bogged down and had begun attracting ridicule from the Baltimore press until the committee brought Mary Stalcup Markward to the stand. Markward, a former beautician, had spent seven years inside the Maryland party as an informant for the FBI until ill health forced her to resign. When HUAC subpoenaed Markward as a Communist, the FBI agreed to let her come in from the cold and testify. Markward's testimony covered a wide range of topics, from the extent of Communist influence over Henry Wallace's Progressive Party, to the increasingly tight, almost paranoid, security arrangements adopted by Philip Frankfeld. Markward also tried to explain the subtleties of Communist ideology, but the committee wasted much of her time reading long lists of names to her and requesting that she identify the individuals as Party members. Many of the people named were no longer in the Baltimore area, and at least one was dead.[15]

One month after the completion of the 1951 hearings, Federal agents arrested six people as part of the "second string" Smith Act trials. Three of them, George Meyers (head of the CP in Baltimore), Leroy Wood (head of the CP in Washington, D.C.), and Maurice Braverman, a lawyer, were active in the regional Party. Two others, Philip Frankfeld (former head of the state CP organization) and his wife Regina, had transferred out of Maryland only a few months previously. One of the arrested individuals, however, had had little recent contact with the party in Maryland, but a long relationship with HUAC: Dorothy Rose Blumberg. Federal authorities also issued subpoenas authorizing the arrest of her husband Albert, but he had gone underground as one of the party's "unavailables."

The "Red Round-up," as the press dubbed the Smith Act arrests, made good copy. The Baltimore papers regularly ran stories detailing the legal battles between the opposing camps of lawyers and following the activities of the defendants after their release from jail. On 17 September 1951, the *Baltimore Sun* printed a full-page article with accompanying photos describing the intense surveillance that the FBI placed on Dorothy Rose Blumberg and the two Frankfelds. One photo shows the trio of Communists walking through Druid Hill Park followed closely by two agents, in another they are sitting on a park bench while an agent peers at them from behind a tree. As many as four carloads of agents shadowed the former party leaders everywhere they went, agents accompanied them into movie theaters and, on one occasion, even flagged a taxi for them after a shopping trip. An air of amusement over the Bureau's obsessive behavior, and sympathy for the accused reds, clearly comes through the sober journalistic prose. However, the *Sun* also ran a series of articles by Herbert Philbrick based on his book *I lead Three Lives*, which recounted his years as an FBI informant in the Communist Party. Defense lawyers attempted to block publication of the series, arguing that they created a "prejudicial atmosphere," but the petition was dismissed.[16]

The Baltimore Smith Act trial began on 11 March 1952, and followed virtually the same pattern as the HUAC hearings that preceded it; but there was one noteworthy difference. The first three people called to testify—Paul Crouch, John Lautner, and William Odell Nowell—were ex-Communists who had no connection with the Maryland party except for a passing acquaintance with Philip Frankfeld. Lautner had known Frankfeld as one of many regional organizers. Crouch had worked with him in the New York Young Communist League, where they drew up plans for the infiltration of Communists into the U.S. Army. Nowell testified that he had met Frankfeld in 1931 when they both attended the Lenin School in Moscow. There, Nowell recalled, they had studied ideology and security techniques and received paramilitary training. Frankfeld had worked for years as an open Communist, so there was no need for the three men to identify him as a party member. The real purpose of their testimony was to present Communist ideology and tactics and to establish that, no matter how innocuous the activities of a particular defendant might seem, they were all linked to a ruthless, international, revolutionary organization.[17]

All six defendants were convicted under the membership clause of the Smith Act, fined one thousand dollars each, and sentenced to prison terms of two to five years. Two years later FBI agents in New York City arrested Albert Blumberg on Smith Act charges. Quickly extradited to Philadelphia, Blumberg was indicted in October, beginning a lengthy legal process which brought his case to trial in February of 1956. Although his trial lacked the intensity of the earlier proceedings, he too was convicted and sentenced to jail.[18]

The publicity and pressure brought against the Maryland Communist Party during the HUAC hearings and the Smith Act trial stripped the party of all but its most dedicated members and subjected those remaining to extreme levels of stress. Although not fired from their jobs, the witnesses employed at Sparrows Point endured a long period of ostracism during which their fellow employees refused to speak to them or acknowledge their presence, outside the immediate demands of their jobs. Despite this, the party's Steel Club continued to function, and the party worked through a variety of front groups for such causes as civil rights and the defense of the Rosenbergs. Although FBI agents remained within the Maryland party, tightened security seriously limited their effectiveness. As a result, when HUAC targeted Maryland in 1954, it looked not to recent activities, but to the heady days of the Popular Front.[19]

On 15 March 1954, HUAC investigators opened a series of meetings featuring the testimony of former Baltimore clergymen John Hutchinson and Joseph Nowak. The hearings followed by a year the publication of J. B. Matthews' conspiracy-ridden book, *Reds and our Churches*, but none of the witnesses called had been active in the party in Maryland since the 1940s. Joseph Nowak, who had left the ministry and gone to work for the YMCA in Chicago, sadly confessed to his former membership in the party. John Hutchinson denied having any contact with the CPUSA. However, two former Maryland party leaders, Earl Reno and Leonard Patterson, both of whom had left the party in the late 1940s, identified both ministers as close fellow-travelers. Reno and Patterson presented an interesting contrast on the stand. Reno related the details of his work, organizing the steel industry and spreading Communist influence in western Maryland, with an odd mixture of pride and regret. Patterson, a black waterfront organizer, had nothing but criticism for the party and played to the Committee by praising the state of race relations in the United States. The hearings had no discernable impact on the Maryland party. A month later, the televised Army-McCarthy hearings destroyed Senator Joseph McCarthy's reputation, leading to his eventual humiliation and censure by the U.S. Senate.[20]

Two years later, when George Meyers returned from prison and resumed leadership of the Maryland district, the party showed some signs of recovery. In addition, much of the community reaction rising from the events of 1951 and 1952 had become diluted with the end of the Korean War and the fall of Senator McCarthy. Then, in February 1956, Nikita Khrushchev stunned the world with revelations of Stalin's crimes. The speech precipitated a split in the CPUSA between those who remained committed to the hard line and those, led loosely by *Daily Worker* editor John Gates, who advocated dramatic reform. Nine months later the Soviet Union suppressed the Hungarian revolt, which the CPUSA publicly supported, to its detriment.

The internal debate over the Khrushchev speech severely weakened the Communist Party, while defense of Soviet actions in Hungary raised the specter of Soviet aggression in the minds of the public and emboldened the party's enemies. On 1 May 1957 spokesmen for HUAC and the Maryland Subversive Activities Unit (a state agency that had been created to monitor radicals and enforce the Ober Law) announced joint hearings on Communist influence in local industry. The substance of the planned hearings differed little from the 1951 HUAC investigations and included a number of the same witnesses. The style, however, proved to be very different. The 1951 hearings had lost much of their intended effect by being held in Washington and stretched out over three weeks. The new hearings lasted only three days, were held in Baltimore, broadcast live on television, and attended by a handpicked audience drawn from "patriotic and civic" organizations that could be depended upon to boo and hiss at all the right times.[21]

The hearings featured prominently the testimony of Clifford Miller, a West Virginian who had briefly joined the party in the late 1940s and then, rather enthusiastically, became an informant for the FBI and later the Ober Law Commission. Miller told a dark tale of secret meetings, code names, and misguided idealism, his intensity and candor contrasting starkly with the behavior of subpoenaed party members on the stand. Irving Kandel, who led the party during Meyer's imprisonment, constantly rocked back and forth in his chair and only reluctantly yielded such small pieces of information as his address and educational background. Others angrily denounced the committee as unconstitutional and defended the party as an advocate of civil rights. Wearing a stylish dress with matching hat and gloves, Sirkka Tuomi Lee, a former actress and Rosenberg activist, played to the cameras. Lee tried to use the witness stand as a podium to speak out on social issues and to urge Marylanders to actively participate in civic organizations, but she also took the Fifth Amendment sixteen times, depriving her testimony of much of its strength.[22]

The 1957 hearings devastated the party, completing the process begun by the Khrushchev speech. The day after the hearings ended, Bethlehem Steel fired all of their employees who had appeared before the committee. Within a week five more witnesses lost their jobs, while others were publicly threatened or had their homes vandalized. Party leaders assumed that the FBI was unlikely to have given up all of its informants, and began an obsessive hunt for the remaining spies. Supporters of John Gates were subject to particular suspicion, and by 1960 all but the hard liners had abandoned the party, reducing it to seventy members divided between Baltimore and Washington. Subjected to almost unbearable social pressure, riven internally by factionalism and consumed by paranoia, the Maryland Communist Party, in the words of party member William Wood, "tore at itself in frustration" and nearly perished.[23]

HUAC never conducted another investigation of the Maryland party, even though several FBI informants continued to monitor its activities; it had no need to. The 1957 hearings, coming at a moment when the organization was critically weakened, destroyed the party as an effective influence in Maryland. A fragment of the party survived and even revived a bit in the late 1960s and early 1970s, but HUAC itself was gone by then, a victim of its own excesses.

Although the HUAC investigations, aided by extensive regional support, and combined with the party's internal crises eventually crushed the Maryland Communist Party, they had little negative effect beyond their intended targets. Schrecker holds anticommunism responsible for serious setbacks to labor, however this was not the case in Maryland. HUAC twice claimed to be investigating the labor situation and subpoenaed numerous union members, but in fact labor was never the issue. Union strength in Baltimore did not decline in the wake of any of the hearings and remained robust as long as heavy industry thrived. However, the tone of unionism changed.

IUMSWA Local 43 at the Fairfield shipyards had once been a hotbed of social reform, with union members, often under party leadership, passing frequent resolutions on racial and social equality. After 1945 and the expulsion of the Communists, the union became quiet, its minutes concerned with dues collection and financial matters rather than broader social and political issues. The steel union at Sparrows Point underwent a similar change. In the 1930s and 1940s, shop stewards had been militant representatives of their union members, but by the late 1950s they were primarily concerned with organizing union picnics and other morale-building exercises. It is difficult, however, to measure how much of this change in mood was due to anticommunism and how much to postwar prosperity.[24]

The greatest social damage caused by anticommunism came not from HUAC, but from the locally enacted Ober Law. Several individuals lost their jobs and suffered harm because of the law's stipulation that public employees take a loyalty oath. Worse, none of the individuals prosecuted under the Ober Law were Communists. Here is definite evidence of the kind of collateral damage that Ellen Schrecker describes at length. However, bad as it was, it cannot be considered widespread or catastrophic.[25]

The Maryland situation upholds the broader outlines of Richard Gid Power's work. Powers described HUAC as torn between responsible and extremist varieties of anticommunism, as exemplified by the contrast between HUAC's relatively moderate publications and its tendency to stage spectacular hearings featuring a cast of conspiracy theorists. In the same way, the HUAC investigators who laid the groundwork for the Maryland hearings may be said to have behaved responsibly, in that no "innocents" were targeted. All of the individuals subpoenaed by HUAC in the state were in fact members of the Communist Party. But the Maryland hearings themselves, while beginning as relatively low-key affairs, ended with the 1957 televised hearings that can only be described as public spectacle.

The transformation of HUAC's efforts in Maryland seems to have been driven by a sense of frustration that increased over time as a result of the party's ability to resist and recover from the committee's repeated investigations. The anticommunists' frustration, and perhaps their anxiety, was no doubt elevated because the party was always semi-concealed, making it difficult to determine how badly it had been hurt. As a result, the hearings increased in intensity as time went on, and HUAC, at least in Maryland, showed a tendency to return to past targets again and again. This explains Dorothy Rose Blumberg's Smith Act arrest, the cast of characters from the Popular Front at the 1954 sessions, the presence of seven 1951 witnesses (plus the wives of two others) at the 1957 hearing, and the obsession with naming names.

The determined effort on the part of anticommunists to reveal the party as subversive, conspiratorial, and dangerous also accounts for the prominent place given to the three ex-Communists at the Smith act trial. Although the organizers and supporters of HUAC had a very clear vision of Communism as a conspiratorial, subversive, foreign-controlled movement, most individual Communists did not conform to that image. The testimony of the ex-Communists allowed the investigators to break through what they saw as the party's façade—the face presented by the Maryland party leaders—to the reality that the anticommunists were convinced lay just below the surface. J. B. Matthews became so frustrated by party members' abilities to hide successfully behind other organizations that he became a compulsive conspiracy theorist. Father Cronin, on the other hand, resisted the temptation and retained a balanced view. By the early 1960s he fell under attack by right-wing extremists for his claims that Communist subversion was *not* a danger to the United States.

The Maryland HUAC hearings reveal a number of interesting patterns, but perhaps the most significant is that HUAC's most effective assaults against the Maryland Communist Party were all tied to international events that heightened public fears about the Soviet Union. The tense public mood contributed to the assaults against the party that followed the hearings. By contrast, the hearings in 1944—while the United States was a Soviet ally—and 1954, after the end of the Korean War, triggered little or no public reaction. Anticommunism enjoyed widespread endorsement only in times of threats (real or perceived) to national security and, at least in the mid-Atlantic, was not a form of "witch hunting" but the manifestation of a genuine contest between ideologies.

Notes

1. Harvey Klehr, John Earl Haynes, and Fridrikh Firsov, *The Secret World of American Communism* (New Haven: Yale University Press, 1995); Harvey Klehr, John Earl Haynes, and Kyrill M. Anderson, *The Soviet World of American Communism* (New Haven: Yale University Press, 1998); Allen Weinstein, *The Haunted Wood* (New York: Random House, 1998); Richard Gid Powers, *Not Without Honor: The History of American Anticommunism* (New York: The Free Press, 1994); Ellen Schrecker, *Many are the Crimes: McCarthyism in America* (Boston: Little Brown and Company, 1998), xviii.
2. Powers, *Not Without Honor*, 104, 126.
3. Mrs. Holloway became interested in Communism after the onset of the Russian Revolution convinced her that Communist principles were an intolerable danger to American values. When not confronting radicals she divided her time between campaigning for the adoption of "The Star Spangled Banner" as the national anthem and membership on a variety of conservative committees which included the Children of the American Revolution, the Daughters of the American Revolution's "Correct Use of the Flag

Committee," and the Daughters of the Confederacy. "23 Reds Taken in Baltimore Round-up," *Baltimore News*, 3 January 1920, "Baltimore Woman at Radical Probe," *Baltimore Sun*, 26 November 1930.
4. "Two Persons Ordered to Appear in Capital Today For Questioning," *Baltimore Sun*, 29 March 1930.
5. "Dies and K.K.K. Acts Linked in Probe Demand," 12 April 1940, "Maryland W.P.A. to Oust Nazis, Reds, by July," 23 June 1940, "Affidavits Show No Reds in State WPA," 6 July 1940, *Baltimore Sun*; "Hopkins Bars Blumberg; He Talks in Park," 11 April 1940, "Asks Another Probe of City's Communists," 19 June 1940, *Evening Sun*.
6. The individuals charged, besides Dorothy Rose Blumberg, were Sophie Kaplan, Minnie Stambler, Paul Jarvis, Benjamin Davis, and Richard Bourne. Although over fifteen members of the Communist Party had assisted in collecting signatures, these six were singled out because they had collected at least part of the contested signatures. "Fraud Evidence Found By Dies Group Against Baltimore Communists," 29 August 1940, "Red Petition Signers To Be Questioned," 31 August 1940, "Grand Jury Presents Six In Red Probe," 19 September 1940, *Baltimore Sun*.
7. Full details of the Communist Party's wartime activities can be found in a series of unexpurgated FBI files housed in the Maryland Room of the McKeldin Library at the University of Maryland. The files are entitled, *Federal Bureau of Investigations, Investigation of Communist Activity in Maryland*, Maryland Manuscripts 4008.
8. Father John Francis Cronin, interview by Reverend Thomas E. Blantz, CSC, Baltimore, Md., 17 March 1978, University of Notre Dame Archives, South Bend, Indiana, 2, 16; Cronin to Chancellor Joseph Nelligan, 20 October 1939, Chancery Records, Nelligan Collection, General Correspondence, Archives of the Archdiocese, Baltimore, Maryland.
9. House Subcommittee of the Special Committee to Investigate Un-American Activities, *Investigation of Un-American Propaganda Activities in the United States*, 78th Cong., 2d sess., 28 September 1944, relevant testimony pp. 10351–10387; Cronin to John Green, 28 January 1943, Box 91, IUMSWA records, Maryland Room, McKeldin Library University of Maryland, College Park.
10. Statements of Joseph Poe, J.L. Stallings, and Philip Bowman, 20 November 1942, IUMSWA records, Box 91, Series V, Maryland Room, McKeldin Library, University of Maryland, College Park, Maryland; General Intelligence Reports, Re Communist Activities, Baltimore, Maryland, 4 December, 1944, Maryland Manuscripts 4008, University of Maryland, College Park, Maryland.
11. General Intelligence Surveys for April and May 1945, Maryland Manuscripts; Letter of John Green to Charles Mesko, suspending local's autonomy, 12 April 1945, "National Fiddles While Local 43 Burns," IUMSWA, Box 92; General Intelligence Survey for March and May 1945, Maryland Manuscripts.
12. George H. Callcott, *Maryland and America, 1940–1980* (Baltimore: Johns Hopkins University Press, 1985), 121–123.
13. "Fiery Hearing Held On Law to Ban Reds," 11 February 1949, "Modification Urged in Md. Subversive Bill," 4 March 1949, *The Washington Post*; Testimony of Mary Stalcup Markward, House Committee on Un-American Activities, *Hearings Related to Communist Activities in the Defense Area of Baltimore*, 82d Cong. 1st sess., 19 June–13 July 1951, 784; "Dr. Brailey Must Go Now Office Rules," "Two Teachers Out, Refused Loyalty Oath," press clippings, Box 148, File 4, J.B. Matthews Papers, Special Collections Department, Perkins Library, Duke University, Durham, North Carolina (hereafter cited as Matthews Papers).

14. "Steelworker Keeps Silent at Probe," Price Day, "Witnesses Balk at Probe on Reds," "Six Witnesses Balk at Probe," "3 More Balk at Probe on Red Activity," Price Day, "Probers Uncover 'Black Box' Clue," "Defense Area Probe For Red Cells Delayed Until July 9," Box 184 File 3, Matthews Papers.
15. Price Day, "City's Industrial Firms Called Communist Goals," *Baltimore Sun*, 12 July 1951; Markward, *Defense Area*, 748–777.
16. "Red Round-Up," 8 August 1951, "FBI Keeps 24-Hour Watch on Communists," 17 September 1951, "Defendants Decry Articles on Reds," 9 February 1952, Baltimore Sun, Box 148, File 5, Matthews Papers.
17. "Instructed At Moscow With Frankfeld Witness Says," "Frankfeld Took War Lessons Court Told," "U.S. Jury Hears Ex-Red at Plot Trial Here," "Widespread Plot Charged to Reds," "Frankfeld Red Leader Plot Jury Told," "Says Reds Plan Revolt In Crisis," Box 148, File 5, Matthews Papers.
18. "Instructed At Moscow With Frankfeld Witness Says," "Frankfeld Took War Lessons Court Told," Box 148, File 5, Matthews Papers; George J. Hiltner, "Blumberg Trial Hears Data On Secret Meetings of Reds," 21 February 1956, "Dr. Blumberg is Convicted on Smith Act," 7 March 1956, Baltimore Sun.
19. Sirrka Lee Holm, interview by author, Francistown, New Hampshire, 15 November 1989; Martha Richards, interview by author, Baltimore, Maryland, 10 January 1990; William Wood, interview by author, Baltimore, Maryland, 23 May 1990.
20. House Committee on Un-American Activities, Investigation of Communist Activities in the Baltimore Area, Parts 1–3 83rd Cong., 2d sess., 1954.
21. "4 More Called in Baltimore Probe," "Red Probe Here to Be Telecast," Box 148, File 3, Matthews Papers.
22. Richard K. Tucker and William F. Pyne, "Miller's Break with Reds Was Intellectual Decision," Evening Sun, 17 May 1957; Charles G. Whiteford, "Three Called Red Leaders in Local Area," 9 May 1957, "Unfriendly Witnesses Total 22 as House Unit Ends Its Hearings Here," 10 May 1957, Baltimore Sun.
23. "Bethlehem to Fire Six," "Brick Thrown Into Home of One," 10 May 1957, "Legal Group Plans Another Action on Buchman," 11 May 1957, Box 148, File 3, Matthews Papers.
24. Robert H. Zieger, The CIO, 1935–1955 (Chapel Hill: University of North Carolina Press, 1995), 325–326; Mark Reutter, Sparrows Point: Making Steel, The Rise and Ruin of Industrial Might (New York: Summit Books, 1988), 358–359; Box 93, IUMSWA.
25. Schrecker, Many Are the Crimes, 67–70.

Negotiating Cold War Politics

The Washington Pension Union and the Labor Left in the 1940s and 1950s

☼

MARGARET MILLER

Though it was often vilified in the mainstream press for its Communist leadership, the Washington Pension Union (WPU)—a state-level welfare rights lobby—remains scarcely known, even in histories of the American left. The pension union's predecessor, the Washington Commonwealth Federation, has been hailed as "one of the most active and broad-based left-wing movements in U.S. history."[1] However, the WPU, formed by the Commonwealth Federation in 1937, quickly eclipsed its precursor in both membership and clout and became a major player in state political debates over social welfare provision, labor organization, and civil rights. It built a vibrant and nationally recognized social movement, noted for its adaptability and resilience. The story of the WPU's success in creating a more equitable welfare state and in building a movement that fused labor and welfare rights advocacy reveals significant continuities in left politics from the 1930s to the early Cold War era.

In 1949, *Time* alarmingly characterized the WPU as an eager participant in the Pacific Coast "holy wars," led by "power-hungry Communists, vote-hungry politicos, sharp-eyed promoters, and croupy and lugubrious old bucks" to raid state treasuries. The *Time* journalist claimed that WPU president William Pennock was a "crafty smooth-talking party-liner" who deceptively "herded" the aged.[2] Conventional accounts similarly dismiss the pension union as a Communist front with a pernicious plan: first, to bankrupt state finances through generous public assistance payments, then to provoke popular discontent and weaken the state, and ultimately to hasten the spread of Communism.[3] Curiously, in an otherwise thoughtful and persuasive study of Popular Front politics in Washington, the author described the pension union in freakish terms; he likened it to "Frankenstein's monster . . . loom[ing] larger than its creator."[4]

The formation of a pension union did seem odd, and a strange digression, even to sympathetic observers in 1937. When Morris Rappaport, the district organizer for the Communist Party's District 12 (the Northwest, centered in Seattle), first heard of the idea, he was reportedly struck speechless. In the late 1930s, the left had set its sights on labor and the Democratic Party, not on senior citizens.[5] Nevertheless, this strategy to revive labor-left politics by organizing Old Age Assistance recipients was a prescient one. Activists appropriated a popular cause and used it, in part, to promote a more ambitious reform agenda, eventually conjoining welfare, labor, and civil rights. The broader social movement that ensued—its successes and failures—must be understood as part of larger transformations and relationships rooted in the political economy of Washington State and not simply the result of a Communist conspiracy.

A telling anecdote reveals the extent to which antipathy toward alleged Communists in the WPU clouded perceptions of the union. In the fall of 1950 Washington's governor, Arthur Langlie, received a letter from WPU president William Pennock. It was like many Pennock would write during his activist career; it revealed a detailed and keen understanding of state legal obligations and urged that more ameliorative measures be put in place to extend public assistance provision. To the governor's office, however, Pennock's appeal seemed of minor concern, and the letter was stamped simply, "No reply." And yet, a prominently positioned silhouette in the pension union letterhead puzzled someone in the governor's office. Penned in the margins next to the silhouette was a telling query; "Who is this?" the writer wondered, "-Pennock?" With a quick glance, one would easily recognize the silhouette as that of the nation's first president, George Washington. But in this popular cultural symbol, the governor's office could see only its Communist adversary, William Pennock.[6]

There is no question that members of the Communist Party were heavily involved in the pension union's leadership, and that WPU ballot initiative campaigns and related causes reflected Popular Front political sensibilities. Opponents, however, feared that the WPU was a false front for Soviet-inspired subversion. Critical observers found particular activities troubling, such as the union's petition in 1941 to free Earl Browder, the imprisoned Communist Party secretary. Although the WPU leadership publicly steered clear of sectarian political stances, such as the CP's staunch opposition to the United States' entry into the war during the Nazi-Soviet Pact period, its careful avoidance of public controversy did little to calm concerns about Communist infiltration. Such fears appeared to be justified when three WPU leaders admitted Communist Party membership during Seattle's Smith Act trials in 1953. Eventually, the pension union reluctantly acquiesced to the Subversive Activities Control Board's demand that it register as a Communist front in 1959.[7]

Undoubtedly, CP politics gave some shape to the WPU's reform agenda. From civil rights advocacy to peace campaigns, Communists and others on the left creatively used pension politics as a platform for a wide array of causes. However, the pension union—with its diverse mass base and autonomous locals—never simply functioned as a Communist front organization. In fact, its tenacity is best explained by examining the organization's distinctly regional political, economic, and social origins. Why and how could Old Age Assistance advocacy sustain the state's flagging labor-left coalition and earn widespread public support in an increasingly hostile era? First, so-called "pension" advocacy was a rich vein to mine. The popularity of public assistance for the aged was already well-proven by the depression-era Townsend movement, with its call for a two hundred dollar-a-month pension for all elderly citizens. Although the fiscal imprudence of the plan rendered it impractical, the Townsend movement forced politicians to deal with the pension issue, as "many of them were running scared at the signs of supporters-loads of petitions, letters, and telegrams arriving daily."[8] "Pensions," moreover, were popular, especially with "articulate" white-collar and educated Americans as well as with adult children of elderly parents who looked to the state for relief.[9] Politicians knew that the Townsend Plan and the more theatrical Ham and Eggers' call for "Thirty Dollars Every Thursday" for the aged in California were unsound schemes. However, they could not avoid the weighty influence of the aged and their advocates. As a writer in *The Nation's Business* noted, pension pressure groups could "elect, or defeat, men running for office. They can, will, and do, devote their full time to the job."[10]

Important changes in New Deal policy also provided activists at the local level with resources and opportunities necessary to build a movement based upon welfare rights advocacy. The Social Security Act (1935) legitimated the practice of assistance to the elderly by establishing an Old Age Assistance (OAA) program, in which states held wide discretionary control and through which activists could wield influence. Moreover, elements of the Old Age Assistance program and its practical administration reflected efforts to distance OAA provision from more stigmatized forms of relief. The act allowed applicants who were denied benefits the opportunity to appeal decisions through a fair hearing process and barred federal provision of any "in-kind" payments, such as food and clothing, associated with conventional relief or charity. In addition, Old Age Assistance offices were usually separate from those administering "relief," and applications for OAA could be readily found in "post offices, banks, and newspaper offices."[11]

Old Age Assistance proved so compelling that some states submitted bold proposals to provide all elderly residents, regardless of need, with a "pension." In Washington, Governor Clarence Martin and conservative Democrats envisioned a more modest program and proposed mostly voluntarist solutions, such as self-help and cooperation, to the human and economic crises of the Great Depression. The Martin administration's insistence that the needy seek support from relatives stirred widespread opposition and galvanized support for liberalized public assistance. In July 1937 at Seattle's Moose Hall, over one thousand people attended a "mass meeting" to discuss the formation of a pension union. By 1940, thirty thousand people had joined the Washington Pension Union through 163 locals across the state.[12]

The WPU emerged, in part, to revive the faltering Washington Commonwealth Federation. However, demographic, socio-economic, and political developments in the state turned this organizational innovation into a burgeoning social movement. From 1920 to 1930, Washington had the fastest growing proportion of elderly residents in the nation, reflecting in part the in-migration of retirees during that period.[13] In addition, many ethnic fraternal organizations and the Washington State Federation of Scandinavian-American Democratic Clubs supported the WPU, because their own members had previous experience with pension provision in their native countries and viewed statist policies favorably.[14] Of critical importance too were the state's predominantly extractive economy and its highly seasonal and unstable employment patterns. As the WPU demonstrated, a political program that linked welfare and labor rights could gain strong support from the state's working-class communities dependent upon, for example, the timber and maritime industries.

Finally, the state's political structure encouraged grassroots organizing. The open or "blanket" primary, established in 1935, permitted voters to cross party lines and build issue-oriented movements around political candidacies, as was well proven by the Washington Commonwealth Federation and by public power proponents. The ballot initiative process was another valuable tool for coalition building. It provided activists with the means to organize politically, to educate voters, and to exert direct influence on the legislative process. WPU canvassers routinely collected two to three times the number of signatures required to get an initiative on the ballot. They were motivated not only by incentives or awards, such as a ham or an electric frying pan presented by a WPU officer, but also by their desire to educate and inform the electorate. Furthermore, as journalist and activist Terry Pettus explained, the pension union wanted more than the signature; it "wanted that vote" for WPU measures and candidates.[15]

Social welfare advocacy proved strong enough to carry left politics into the post-World War II era and profoundly transformed the left in Washington. Activists from the Depression-era Unemployed Councils, the Workers' Alliance, the Washington Commonwealth Federation, American Federation of Labor (AFL) and Congresss of Industrial Organizations (CIO) locals joined pension union members to place social welfare provision at the center of public debate. For over fifteen years, the WPU pressured state government to increase social welfare benefits for the aged, the blind, Aid to Dependent Children recipients, and the unemployed though passage of its incessant state ballot initiatives and through legislative lobbying. Supporters elected WPU stalwarts to the state legislature through the Democratic Party and built resourceful alliances with a broad array of labor organizations, the Grange, Townsend Clubs, and the public power movement. And, in the mid-to-late 1940s, the pension union introduced a movement ideology that explicitly linked social welfare, labor, and civil rights, and their overlapping constituencies.

The WPU's ties to organized labor and its explicit appeal to working people were central to its success and longevity. An early observer noted that the WPU leadership included socialists, Communists, wobblies, and "strong union members." It was no accident that the organization, named a "union," not a club or an association, appropriated the familiar forms of labor organizations with locals, county councils, a state board, and an executive committee.[16] This model also included local grievance committees that directed assistance recipients' complaints through the pension union to the state. Essentially, the WPU acted as a bargaining agent. Leaders lobbied the state legislature for liberalized assistance and provided counsel and representation for recipients in fair hearings with state officials. Within its first three years, the pension union had taken up fourteen hundred cases through fair hearings, 140 of which had made their way to court.[17]

Members were drawn to the pension union for a variety of reasons and found it sufficiently flexible to accommodate diverse levels of commitment and interest. For the aging "old left," Old Age Assistance advocacy resonated with their concerns about making ends meet during the Depression; the aged, after all, were over-represented among the unemployed and faced great difficulties securing relief and employment. Older women in need were particularly vulnerable. Relief work and Old Age Insurance ("social security") narrowly targeted the predominantly male industrial workforce. Furthermore, despite the boom in industrial production during World War II, civil and private defense manufacturers routinely barred women over age thirty-five from employment. The Boeing Company deliberately limited the number of older women hired, yet it received sixteen thousand job applications from women over age fifty-five during the first year of the war alone.[18] For many, Old Age Assistance became a critical resource and, as a result, a highly charged political issue.

Pension politics and the WPU's broader vision for the state also neatly dovetailed with the past political experiences of "native radicals," including Debsian socialists, Populists, and Farmer-Labor Party advocates. Etta Tripp, for example, who eventually became WPU vice-president and also Master of the Curley Creek Grange in the late 1940s, chose to become a pension-movement leader in her later years, after a lifetime devoted to progressive causes in Washington State. In 1910 she supported female suffrage campaigns and joined the Socialist Party. During the 1920s she worked on the Farmer-Labor Party's campaigns and in the 1930s and 1940s she became a Democratic Party precinct committeewoman, a member of a county executive committee, and delegate to the state Democratic Convention. She also taught in the Workers Education Division of the Works Progress Administration (WPA) during the Depression, organized WPA workers in the Workers' Alliance and helped found the Washington Pension Union in 1937.[19]

Leaders like Tripp could deliver on their promises. They brought an end to lien laws affecting assistance recipients' estates, helped abolish the practice of "relative responsibility" (a state requirement that able family members financially support aged relatives in need), and advocated for individual recipients with grievances against county or state welfare offices. By establishing a grievance committee in every WPU local, the union not only involved those interested in advocacy, but established a readily accessible channel to the state's fair hearing process, where individuals—members or not—could be represented by skilled activists.

The pension union also launched political careers. Politically ambitious leaders such as William Pennock, Tom Rabbitt, Lenus Westman, Nathan Atkinson, John Caughlin, Emma Taylor Harmon, and Edward Pettus served terms in the state legislature during the late 1930s and the 1940s. In addition, WPU officers cultivated close political relationships with members of the state congressional delegation, such as John Coffee (Democrat), and with Jerry O'Connell, chair of the

CIO's Political Action Committee (CIO-PAC). Local members garnered political experience and influence through the union as well. Evelyn Gardner, a WPU member in Yakima, for example, won the 14th District race in primary elections for state senate in 1942.[20] Pension union members also eagerly sought positions on Democratic Party precinct committees. For young activists from the Workers' Alliance, the Democratic Party, and the Communist Party, membership in the pension union offered effective training in precinct canvassing and grassroots community organizing. It also provided precocious political aspirants with an established network and mass base essential to their successful candidacies in state legislative races. According to WPU supporter Terry Pettus, "there were great opportunities" for young organizers "funneled through" the pension union, so great that people frequently joked that "in Washington state, the youth movement was in the . . . Pension Union."[21]

Members also turned to the pension union to build a rewarding social life. Although some more doctrinaire members occasionally lamented that local meetings were "just social hours" and not politically "effective," social activities were both highly valued and essential to maintaining involvement in the union. The famed hootenannies, indigenous to the Washington left and held by the WPU, together with labor unions and the Washington Commonwealth Federation, served as fundraisers for the left and gave WPU members an opportunity to mingle with progressives from a variety of backgrounds and causes. Hootenannies not only raised political consciousness, but spirits as well. If the music, beer, and bratwurst of Washington's Hootenannies did not appeal, pension union members could attend an informative mass meeting every Sunday at Seattle's Shipscalers' Hall. At these weekly meetings, they discussed WPU business and, importantly, viewed comedies by Abbott & Costello, documentaries, and plays, or listened to readings of Abraham Lincoln's speeches and Mark Twain's satire. In members' recollections of the WPU, social and cultural events were as vivid as the union's political work. Many had high praise for Louise Pennock, a former Seattle Repertory Playhouse instructor and actor who entertained members across the state with her accordion music and who was fondly known as the WPU's "portable orchestra." For members in rural communities far from the pension union's Puget Sound strongholds, such visits coupled with the WPU's widely-broadcast daily radio programs to keep members in touch with state-level leadership. WPU social events also stirred grassroots civil rights campaigns by bringing together the membership with civil rights leaders and African American intellectuals such as Paul Robeson, Eslanda Robeson, and W.E.B. Du Bois.[22]

Old Age Assistance advocacy thus proved to be an important strategy to build the political careers of left activists, particularly Communists, and to sustain an ambitious reform agenda. As Etta Tripp intimated in 1941, welfare activists could "capitalize on our grievance work—in other words, politicize it."[23] WPU leaders encouraged rank-and-file members to vote Democratic, to participate in precinct-level party organizing, and to view the fight for liberalized public assistance as part of a broader vision connecting a variety of political communities. In 1944, for example, the pension union pulled together an array of representatives from local labor unions, the AFL, central labor councils, CIO industrial union councils, the Washington Federation of Labor and the state CIO, the Democratic Party, the CIO-PAC, and the Social Workers Council to back an ambitious initiative measure. As Robert Zieger argues, from the perspective of many CIO stalwarts, "the flux of the reconversion period offered a unique opportunity to rewrite the rules governing the management of the American economy and the political and social order that it undergirded." While a return to pre–New Deal liberalism seemed unfathomable, he argues that it remained unclear what "new rules" would govern postwar America.[24] The Washington Pension Union and its labor allies had some clear proposals. Their "social security" program in 1944 supported federal full employment measures and called for higher Old Age Assistance grants. The measure also sought to raise unemployment compensation, with coverage extended to agricultural workers, and to establish maternity grants for working women.[25]

Although this particular ballot initiative lost in the general election, the movement itself flourished, particularly among workers in the state's unstable core industries where the confluence of labor and welfare rights made sense to working people who had occasion to turn to public assistance. Electoral support for the WPU's initiatives remained strong in working-class communities in the Puget Sound region and in the timber and fishing industry communities on the coast. Its importance as a source of potential political capital in working-class communities was clear from the beginning. After the WPU's first successful initiative campaign in 1940, for example, membership increased 400 percent in Aberdeen, a mill town and a CIO stronghold.[26] Throughout the 1940s the pension union's reform program earned endorsements from the state CIO, the Washington Federation of Labor, and a diverse array of local labor unions. Most consistently supportive were left-leaning locals from the Building Service Employees Union, the International Longshoremen's and Warehousemen's Union, the International Woodworkers of America, and the Marine Cooks and Stewards Union.

Eventually, working-class women and African Americans pointed the WPU in new directions. Both groups were only marginally incorporated into the region's booming war industries during the early 1940s and frequently looked beyond conventional advocacy groups for support. The Washington Pension Union's early ballot initiative success in 1941 drew the attention of other public assistance recipients. In that year, families dissatisfied with the government's notoriously meager Aid to Dependent Children (ADC) grants formed the ADC Union, modeled on the pension union. The organizations worked in tandem and paid careful attention to a variety of issues such as rent control, affordable housing development, affordable childcare, pay equity, equity in public assistance provision, and anti-discrimination campaigns. The broadening of the WPU's mission to include issues of gender and race reflected the pressing concerns of the state's increasingly diverse polity, the wartime strains on old-timers and newcomers alike, and the responsiveness of the union's leadership to these developments.[27]

Long before the formation of the National Welfare Rights Organization (NWRO) in the 1960s, parents of poor children in Washington built a movement in Washington State through the ADC Union. Its membership, comprised mostly of women, surpassed that of the better-known NWRO, and its assertive tactics, including a two-day occupation of the secretary of state's office in the capitol in 1952, rivaled later civil and welfare rights protest activities. Photographs of ADC Union actions and other related sources strongly suggest that the WPU did not practice the left's "sentimental maternalism," with its propensity to view women primarily as nurturers of people and peace or as "auxiliaries" in labor's struggles.[28] Old Age Assistance and ADC recipients included a larger percentage of women, who subsequently made a place for themselves as leaders in the state organization and at the local level. Importantly, WPU and ADC Union activists deliberately chose inclusive language. They argued that equitable welfare rights were due "citizens," "pioneers," and "workers," and, with a few exceptions, largely avoided gendered constructions and maternalist rhetoric.

The WPU's enlightened sexual politics were matched by its involvement in postwar anti-discrimination campaigns. Racial justice had been far from the center of labor-left pursuits in the late 1930s and early 1940s. In fact, pension union leaders purposefully avoided involvement in controversial issues such as anti-alien land laws and Japanese internment, though they did lead opposition in the state legislature to restrictive residential covenants, to discrimination and segregation in public facilities, and to a ban on interracial marriage. During and after World War II, African Americans and others in the WPU and the ADC Union fought hard against discrimination in the workplace, in the housing market, and in welfare provision. The WPU's "Negro-White Unity" campaigns addressed such issues and reflected, in part, its egalitarian politics. Interestingly, the remarkable vitality of the Communist-led Civil Rights Congress (CRC) in the state during the late 1940s was due, in large part, to the support of WPU members with prior experiences in local anti-discrimination campaigns. CRC chapters in Seattle and Anacortes were among the few consistently reliable ones in the nation and received high praise for their timely payment of dues and myriad fundraising activities.[29] It was through the WPU's local meetings and publications, however, that CRC causes gained wider attention throughout the state. Tellingly, in correspondence from rank-and-file WPU members to President Truman, support for CRC causes figured prominently.[30]

Despite the WPU's ability to refashion a Popular-Front politics for the postwar era, the defining experiences of this labor-welfare-rights movement in the late 1940s and 1950s appear to be political repression from external opponents and isolation that was often self-imposed. In 1946 the state Democratic Party leadership began a purge of alleged Communists and eliminated state party offices held by those believed to be a liability.[31] Republicans had effectively used anticommunism in the 1946 elections to win a two-thirds majority in the House and they attracted the support of enough Democrats on key issues to control the Senate. While the state Democratic hierarchy hoped to reassert its influence by crippling the party's left wing, its actions had unexpected implications. Many alleged Communists in the Democratic Party not only lost their legislative races in the 1946 elections, but also found what they saw as good reason to leave the Democratic fold and to explore third-party possibilities just two years later.

In 1948, WPU leaders broke from the Democratic Party, endorsed the Progressive Party's full national slate, and campaigned as Progressives for state offices. It proved to be a disastrous move. Terry Pettus recalled that "there were hundreds of [p]rogressive Democratic precinct committeemen [who followed the CP's lead to Henry Wallace's campaign]. And they were individually served with a demand to resign and they resigned by the score and we tore down an organization that we had worked so hard over the years to build up." He conceded, "we burned our bridges."[32]

While the pension union leadership further alienated itself from mainstream politics with its hopeful turn to the Progressive Party, powerful forces in state politics and core industries worked doubly hard to destroy the WPU. In 1948 the pension union came under investigation by the state legislature's Joint Fact-Finding Committee on Un-American Activities, known also as the Canwell Committee.[33] In 1950, following on the heels of the Canwell Committee, the Citizens' Public Assistance Committee (CPAC) introduced a ballot initiative to curb welfare benefits and to expose the WPU as a false front. According to pension union sources, CPAC was "[Governor] Langlie's committee . . . of insurance companies, the timber and allied companies, [and] the big businesses of Washington."[34] Its visible leadership appeared less conspiratorial. The CPAC's sponsoring committee for the initiative consisted of state businessmen in agriculture and publishing, while rank-and-file support came from groups like the American Legion.[35] These opponents claimed that the WPU's program was "squarely in line with the SOVIET policy of compelling us to spend ourselves to destruction" and "serve[d] the designs of the Supreme Soviet at Moscow."[36] As an added dramatic maneuver in this ideologically charged fight, CPAC delivered its initiative signature petitions to the state capitol in a heavily guarded armored car.[37]

Conditions worsened for welfare activists. The state required public assistance recipients to take loyalty oaths, which further stigmatized assistance provision and implied that welfare rights advocates harbored subversives. Authorities sought to harass individual activists. The state police broke up a WPU event in a state park in the summer of 1950 and various pension union members faced arrest while advocating for individual recipients at local welfare offices.[38] In the fall of 1952, the arrests of WPU president William Pennock, WPU organizer Paul Bowen, and journalist Terry Pettus, along with four other alleged Communists, threw the movement into disarray. During the trial of Seattle's Smith Act defendants, charged with conspiring to teach and to advocate the overthrow of the United States government, Pension Union president William Pennock admitted belonging to the CP. According to Terry Pettus it was a disastrous move, as his "declaration created havoc."[39]

These were harsh times for the labor left and the pension union leadership, yet also a period of surprising achievements. In 1948 alone, the political fallout from Progressive Party endorsements, the Canwell Committee investigations, and purges within the labor movement and the Democratic Party were potentially devastating. Communists themselves were divided over how to respond, and the party leadership compounded these problems by sending a significant part of its leader-

FIGURE 10.1 Leaders and members of the Washington Pension Union delivered signatures for the innovative ballot initiative 172 to the state capitol in 1948. Pictured in the second row center (sixth and seventh from left) are Vice-President Nora McCoy and President William J. Pennock. Etta Tripp is seated in the first row, far left. Credit: MSCUA, University of Washington Libraries, UW22281.

ship cadres underground. Nevertheless, the movement survived and experienced measurable successes because it was, at base, driven by citizens' pragmatic and tangible concerns. For workers in the state's primary industries, the pension union remained an effective proponent of what was essentially a New Deal vision linking labor and welfare rights. In 1948, a politically tumultuous year, voters passed a groundbreaking pension union ballot initiative by a wide margin. Initiative 172, "an act relating to Citizens' Security," provided a minimum monthly grant of sixty dollars to the aged in need, and more significantly, mandated uniformity of treatment for all categories of assistance recipients, including those who received Aid to Dependent Children and General Assistance. This was a significant achievement. The initiative established parity among all categories of assistance, bridged the historic divide between the "deserving" and "undeserving" poor, and made assistance a "right" due citizens. It also made national news. A writer in *Newsweek* claimed that the measure "would . . . make Washington the nation's first welfare state."[40]

The initiative campaign in 1948 also drew support from the labor left and from working-class communities, which together reflected a strong desire to craft a better and newer deal in postwar Washington. Various locals from the Building Service Employees Union, the International Woodworkers of America, and the International Longshoremen and Warehousemen's Union, for example, joined central bodies such as the Bellingham Industrial Union Council to offer financial contributions. The measure passed by its widest margins in counties where the timber, fishing, or canning industries were prevalent, in many places earning over 70 percent of the vote.[41]

At the same time, the popular basis for progressive reform contracted after 1948. No longer could the allegedly Communist-dominated WPU attract the broad-based support from labor as it did during earlier initiative campaigns. It remained an effective advocate, however, because it was responsive to new emerging constituencies. Unemployment, especially among workers in the state's timber and wood-products industries, had provoked heated contest between labor and the state over social welfare provision in 1949 and 1950.[42] In 1949, WPU leaders worked with sixty representatives from AFL and CIO unions to establish the Union Counseling Committee to address workers' unemployment compensation grievances, to press for increased benefits, and to lobby for a prevailing-wage federal public works program.

Organizing the unemployed was not a marginal endeavor, and the stakes were high. The state director of Public Assistance, for example, was a former timber-industry executive employed by the Weyerhaeuser Company and a prominent public relations consultant for corporate clients. As expected, he swiftly removed 50,000 able-bodied men from the General Assistance rolls, forcing them into an already flooded labor market in 1950. Such tangible connections between social welfare and labor rights continued to provide dynamism to the movement. Throughout the early 1950s the WPU supported the state CIO's related campaign to increase unemployment compensation and successfully fought against state right-to-work initiatives in 1956 and 1958.[43]

It was widely recognized in the mainstream press at the time, and in later observations, that social welfare was a hot state issue and that it dominated state politics from 1940 through the 1950s.[44] Yet despite such heated polemics, including attempts by state legislators to portray recipients as "chiselers" and activists as subversives, public assistance had become a matter of convention and of "community responsibility." Moreover, many elements of the WPU's once-controversial program were put into practice, and Democratic Governor Albert Rosellini eagerly met with Pension Union leaders at the state capitol in 1957.

By the late 1950s, however, little remained of a movement. Anticommunist repression surely took its toll, while other factors contributed to the union's decline. William Pennock, a Smith Act defendant, died tragically from a Nembutal overdose during the trial in August 1953. At his defense Pennock admitted proudly that he belonged to the CP and earnestly detailed his political philosophies and the pragmatic and legitimate endeavors they inspired. Those who knew him well, however, feared that he would not hold up to the prosecution's "foul methods at cross-examination."[45] Paul Bowen and Terry Pettus, prominent activists involved in the WPU, were also among those convicted of conspiring to advocate the overthrow of the United States government. In 1948 the WPU demonstrated its uncanny ability to beat the political odds. The trial in 1953, however, put the WPU's resilience to its ultimate test. It not only broke William Pennock's spirit but also severely weakened the movement. Meanwhile, elderly activists and local supporters passed away. Some members, alienated by the sectarian politics of leaders, bolted from the union. Organized labor traded its stake in public welfare for private benefits won through the collective bargaining process. In addition, Old Age Insurance, or "social security," began to cover more of the state's aged, thus making public assistance a less pivotal issue.

Recent scholarship makes some compelling assertions about Cold War society that counter the more familiar themes of the era, such as suburban complacency and consumerism, political repression, and the valorization of female domesticity. In the 1950s, for example, women entered new sectors of employment in increasing numbers and built political communities through the Community Service Organization and the National Association for the Advancement of Colored People. A civil rights movement rooted itself firmly in the contested terrain of the era, while an old left searched for ways to cultivate a new left. As some historians argue, the postwar era now appears "less dark and static" than presumed and, in many ways, "bridged" New Deal era activism with that of the 1960s.[46] The Washington Pension Union's story could end with its remarkable electoral successes in 1948, its repression in 1953, its attempts to revive a welfare rights movement in 1960, its formal dissolution in 1961, or perhaps with portraits of activists who endured to build new political communities in the 1960s. Terry Pettus, through his community organizing work in Seattle, and Paul Bowen, in his voter registration project in Seattle's African American communities in the 1960s, moved from the activism of the 1930s to that of the 1960s. Viewed collectively, all of these possible endings to the WPU's story underscore the essential tension between resilience and repression, and between continuity and disjuncture, which characterize the history of the left during this politically dynamic era.

Antistatist politics also made critical headway during the fifties. In Washington state, the far right garnered valuable political capital out of its antiwelfare campaigns and its anticommunist sparring with the WPU. The right's calls for local control over welfare, for a reversion to the meager system of assistance prior to 1935, and for the dismantling of "socialist" legislation were all measures to build popular support, increasingly concentrated in central and eastern Washington's agricultural communities. While the Cold War right sought to control and curtail welfare provision in the fifties, liberal reform groups and some surviving elements of the New Deal era left did manage to pique public concern for long-neglected constituencies, such as migrant and seasonal farm workers. As one keen observer of Washington politics noted in 1950, social welfare was "one of those things which becomes the standard for crusades in all directions."[47]

It is tempting, also, to think of new beginnings, of "bridges." Just three years after the Washington Pension Union's formal dissolution in 1961, a new labor-based social welfare rights movement, fueled by President Lyndon Johnson's declaration of a War on Poverty, gained momentum in the state's agricultural heartland. This later movement was comprised of a loose coalition of community-based organizations (churches, community action agencies, and farm labor advocacy organizations) and eventually headed by emergent Mexican American community organizers and farm labor activists. The pension union's work and the political legacy left by earlier welfare and labor rights' advocates helped pave the way for this later movement. In the 1940s and 1950s, for example, the WPU sought to end restrictive residency requirements barring ready access to assistance for those in need, such as migrant farm workers. After her husband's death in 1953, Louise Pennock and the ADC Union were among the first in the state to publicize the poor working and living conditions of migrant farm workers and their families. In the mid-to-late 1950s, this same campaign became the primary focus of both state and national advocates for migrant and seasonal farm laborers.

Ironically, Cold War anticommunists' swashbuckling attacks on the WPU in the 1950s may have played a crucial part in reform renewal. The welfare backlash, so vital to the right's political project, kept social welfare issues at center stage in state politics. The far right eventually dulled welfare politics' radical edge, making advocacy appear less dangerous and consequently more appealing to moderate reform elements (the Council of Churches, liberal professionals) that stepped in to fill the void. New coalitions with surviving elements of the Old Left's institutional base, and with an alleged Communist or two, emerged in the 1950s and 1960s and laid the groundwork for movement renewal in the mid 1960s. As a writer in the last edition of the WPU's *Pension Builder* presciently observed in 1961, "[a]n organization that served the people at the grassroots in their distress and need cannot be buried even though legally it may cease to exist."[48]

Notes

1. John de Graaf, "Washington Commonwealth Federation," in *Encyclopedia of the American Left,* ed. Mari Jo Buhle, Paul Buhle and Dan Georgakas (Urbana: University of Illinois Press, 1992), 820. The Washington Commonwealth Federation evolved from a "production for use" proponent to encompass a broad and tenuous coalition that sought to build a powerful left wing in the state Democratic Party. See Albert Acena, "The Washington Commonwealth Federation: Reform Politics and the Popular Front" (Ph.D. diss., University of Washington, 1975).
2. "Nothing's Too Good for Grandpa," *Time,* 5 September 1949, 16–17.
3. See, for example, Timothy Frederick, *Albert F. Canwell: An Oral History* (Olympia: Washington State Oral History Program, 1997), 176, 296.
4. Acena, "The Washington Commonwealth Federation," 380.
5. Ibid., 192.
6. Letter, William Pennock to Arthur Langlie, 9 October 1950, Box 31, File 16: Communistic Material II, Arthur Langlie Papers, University of Washington Libraries.
7. "WPU State Board Minutes," 6 September 1941, Box 3, File 18: Minutes 1941, Washington Pension Union Papers, University of Washington Libraries (hereafter cited as WPU Papers). Jane Sanders, *Cold War on the Campus: Academic Freedom at the University of Washington, 1946–64* (Seattle: University of Washington Press, 1979), 30. *Pension Builder,* April 1959, Box 7, File 28: Pension Builder 1959, WPU Papers.

8. Blanche D. Coll, *Safety Net: Welfare and Social Security, 1929–1979* (New Brunswick, N.J.: Rutgers University Press, 1995), 50–51.
9. Michael B. Katz, *In the Shadow of the Poorhouse: A Social History of Welfare in America* (New York: Basic Books, 1986), 202–204. The latter point is much more difficult to document, as James Patterson concedes. See James T. Patterson, *America's Struggle Against Poverty, 1900–1985* (Cambridge: Harvard University Press, 1986), 74. WPU officer Arthur Lindsay made a similar observation that adult children on WPA relief were responsible for assisting their parents and therefore doubly affected by the Depression. Lindsay seems to suggest that support for pensions arose from overly-burdened offspring. See Arthur Lindsay, "The Washington Old Age Pension Union: A Political Pressure Group" (master's thesis, University of Washington, 1940), 23.
10. Coll, *Safety Net*, 50–51. J. Gilbert Hill, "They're All Afraid of the Old Folks," *Nation's Business* 29 (October 1941): 64. For discussion of the pension movement in California, see Kevin Starr, *Endangered Dreams: The Great Depression in California* (New York: Oxford University Press, 1996), 205–207, 209–211.
11. Coll, *Safety Net*, 53. 82–83.
12. Lindsay, "The Washington Old Age Pension Union," 27, 73.
13. Mildred E. Buck, *Public Welfare in Washington: A State-Wide Study of Problems of Public Welfare Administration* (Olympia: Washington State Planning Council, 1934), 29. In Washington State in 1930, 6.4 percent of the population was over sixty-five, while the national average was 5.5 percent.
14. Victor P. Lysell to James M. Hay, 6 February 1939, Box 8, File 174-2: Old Age Pensions-Correspondence, Robert E. Burke Collection, University of Washington Libraries.
15. "Terry Pettus Interview," 16, Box 2, File 2: Terry Pettus Interview #2, Terry Pettus Papers, University of Washington Libraries.
16. Lindsay, "The Washington Old Age Pension Union," 11.
17. "WPU State Board Minutes," 6 September 1941.
18. Karen Anderson, *Wartime Women: Sex Roles, Family Relations and the Status of Women During World War II* (Westport, Conn.: Greenwood Press, 1981), 42. Richard C. Berner, *Seattle, 1921–1940: From Boom to Bust* (Seattle: Charles Press, 1992), 303. Virginia Shapiro, "The Gender Basis of American Social Policy," in *Women, the State, and Welfare*, ed. Linda Gordon (Madison: University of Wisconsin Press, 1990), 43, and Gwendolyn Mink, "The Lady and the Tramp: Gender, Race, and the Origins of the American Welfare State," in ibid., 111.
19. "Terry Pettus Interview," 24; *Pension Builder*, October 1951, Box 7, File 21: Pension Builder 1951–1952, WPU Papers.
20. Lindsay, "The Washington Old Age Pension Union," 84, 96; "Five Pension Union Officers Nominated," *Washington New Dealer*, 18 September 1942.
21. "Terry Pettus Interview," 5.
22. "By Members of the WPU As Told To Fair Taylor," n.d., Box 10, File 13: Wm. Pennock Biographical Materials, WPU Papers.
23. "WPU State Board Minutes," 3 May 1941, Box 3, File 18: Minutes 1941. WPU Papers.
24. Robert Zieger, *The CIO, 1935–1955* (Chapel Hill: University of North Carolina Press, 1995), 219.
25. Secretary of State (Belle Reeves), "Initiative Measure No. 157" in *A Pamphlet* (Olympia: State Printing Plant, 1944), 4–12. Unions represented included the Shipscalers', BSEU, ILWU, IWA, IAM, Aeromechanics, Tailors, Carpenters, and Fishermen's unions.

26. "State Board Minutes," 3 May 1941, Box 3, File 18: Minutes 1941, WPU Papers.
27. Karen Anderson, *Wartime Women*, 65, 77–78, 87, 124–125. Quintard Taylor, *The Forging of a Black Community: Seattle's Central District from 1870 Through the Civil Rights Era* (Seattle: University of Washington Press, 1994), 172–173, 178.
28. See Michael Denning's critique of Popular Front sexual politics and his assessment of Paula Rabinowitz's analysis, in Michael Denning, *The Cultural Front* (New York: Verso, 1997), 32, 136–138. Robert Zieger, *Age of the CIO*, 349.
29. Gerald Horne, *Communist Front: The Civil Rights Congress, 1946–1956* (Cranbury, N.J.: Associated University Presses, 1988), 48, 70, 91, 349.
30. "WPU Documents from the Truman Library," University of Washington Libraries.
31. Vern Countryman, *Un-American Activities in the State of Washington: The Work of the Canwell Committee* (Ithaca: Cornell University Press, 1951), 11, 19.
32. "Terry Pettus Interview," 32.
33. See, for example, "Un-American Probes Get Green Light in Northwest," *Christian Science Monitor*, 26 March 1948, in Frederick, *Albert F. Canwell: An Oral History*.
34. Flyer [1950], Box 7, File 5: Legislative Initiatives 1950 (176, 178), WPU Papers.
35. Newman H. Clark to State Committee and Local Chairmen, 9 June 1950, Box 11, File 46: Citizens' Public Assistance Committee, Arthur Langlie Papers.
36. "Argument Against Initiative Measure No. 176" in Earl Coe, *Official Voters Pamphlet* (Olympia: State Printing Office, 1950), 15.
37. *Pension Builder*, August 1950, Box 7, File 20: Pension Builder 1950–1951, WPU Papers.
38. Etta Tripp to John R. Vanderzischt, 8 August 1950, Box 31, File 15: Communistic Material I, Arthur B. Langlie Papers; *Pension Builder*, March–April 1951, May 1951, June–July 1951, October 1951, Box 7, File 21: *Pension Builder*, 1951–1952, WPU Papers.
39. "Terry Pettus Interview," 43.
40. "The Welfare State: Everyone's Feeling Much Better," *Newsweek*, 15 August 1949, 24–25.
41. Washington (State), Secretary of State, *Abstract of Votes* (Olympia: State Printing Office, 1948).
42. *Pension Builder*, February 1949, Box 7, File 18: Pension Builder: 1949. Radio Broadcast transcript, KRKL 30 October 1949, Box 6, File 3: Radio Broadcasts, 1946–1947. *Washington Labor Pension Builder*, October 1949, Box 7, File 19: Pension Builder 1950. Radio Broadcast Transcript, 5 March 1950, Box 6, File 4: Radio Broadcasts, 1950, WPU Papers.
43. *Pension Builder*, June 1954, July 1954, Box 7, File 23: *Pension Builder*, 1953–1954. "Initiative 196," Box 7, File 8: Legislative Materials Initiative 1954 (196). Flyer, "United Labor Advisory Committee Against Initiative 198." Flyer, "Myth Exploded: Non-Union Workers Do Pay Dues," Box 7, File 9: Legislative Material 1956 (200, 198). *Pension Builder*, February 1956, April 1956, June 1956, November 1956, WPU Papers.
44. Terry Pettus Interview, 46; Herbert Sydney Duncombe, "Decision-Making in Public Assistance: A Study of Influences on Decision-Making in the Washington Department of Public Assistance" (Ph.D. diss., University of Washington, 1963), 33–34.
45. Ed. M. Fitzroy, "Subversive Activities Control Board Hearings," 130, University of Washington Libraries.
46. Maurice Isserman, *If I Had a Hammer . . . The Death of the Old Left and the Birth of the New Left* (New York: Basic Books, 1987), xiii. Joanne Meyerowitz, *Not June Cleaver: Women and Gender in Postwar America* (Philadelphia: Temple University Press, 1994).
47. Editorial, "The True Meaning," *Yakima Morning Herald*, 30 July 1950, 4.
48. *Pension Builder*, August 1961, Box 7, File 30: Pension Builder 1961, WPU Papers.

The Lost World of United States Labor Education

Curricula at East and West Coast Communist Schools, 1944–1957

☼

MARVIN GETTLEMAN

As the tide of battle in World War II swung decisively against the Axis in 1943–1944, the United States Communist Party transformed and upgraded its main East and West Coast labor schools—the Jefferson School of Social Science in New York City, and the California Labor School in San Francisco/Oakland. These changes were responses to the tremendous increase in war production in both cities, and the opportunity, indeed the necessity, to train workers (many of whom, especially in California, had recently migrated from the rural South) in trade union principles and in anti-racism, so as to protect the home front war effort. Under Earl Browder's wartime leadership, the Communist Party at this time took a super-patriotic ideological turn, adopting a wartime no-strike pledge, advancing the new slogan "Communism is Twentieth Century Americanism," and naming its Eastern and Midwestern adult schools after more or less mainstream American heroes—the Samuel Adams School in Boston, Tom Paine in Philadelphia, George Washington Carver in Harlem, Abraham Lincoln in Chicago, and Jefferson in New York. On the West Coast, simple geographical names—the Pacific Northwest Labor School (in Seattle), and the California Labor School—sufficed.

Since the early 1920s the party had sponsored open, adult educational centers (often under the name Workers Schools), but the wartime schools were conducted on a vastly expanded scale.[1] Not only were there many more students than had attended the earlier schools—thousands each term, at each of the dozen or so new schools—but the curriculum was also greatly expanded. Hundreds of courses were offered at the schools' main centers and in outlying extension annexes.[2] During wartime the schools' primary (but, not only) aim was to forge in their classrooms and lecture halls "mass weapons, as sharp and decisive as bullets in the struggle against fascism."[3]

In the immediate postwar period the slogan "Education for Jobs and Peace,"[4] (and corresponding curricular changes) prevailed. By 1946, with Roosevelt dead and Browder ousted from party leadership, Browder's signature strategy—that the Communists should aim at being respected and welcome allies of the New Deal—was rapidly fraying. The Jefferson School catalog warned in 1946 that "Fascism is not dead. . . . Oppression of the Negro people and anti-Semitism are increasing. . . . Resurgent imperialism, especially American imperialism, menaces the American people and the forward-marching peoples of all countries." As the threatening Cold War clouds gathered, the Jefferson School (along with its counterparts on the West Coast, and elsewhere) attempted "to provide the scientific understanding necessary to solve these vital problems through individual and collective action."[5] How these educational institutions tried to do so is the subject of this essay.

One way was to open the schools to "the whole mass of the people,"[6] as the Jefferson School at first put it—later adding the qualification ". . . except known enemies of the working class."[7] The same inclusive sentiment, phrased differently, appeared in the California Labor School's catalog description of entrance requirements, which was stated simply: "There are none."[8] The rare obstreperous anti-communists who were identifiable by their classroom behavior could be easily dealt with, but neither of the two major party schools (the only ones formally prosecuted by the U.S. government's Subversive Activities Control Board [SACB]) were unable to weed out secretly unfriendly students—especially those planted by the FBI. The very openness of these schools refuted (and was clearly intended to refute) the widespread view that Communists operated mainly by secretive and stealthy means. As hostility to Communism rose in the late 1940's and 1950s, the Jefferson School announced that attendance would no longer be taken in class so that Communist students (who had good reason to believe they would face harassment if their party membership were known), and non-Communists too, would be protected by a "veil of anonymity."[9] But this precaution did little to deter the FBI. Hoover's Bureau, which always took the dimmest view possible of Communism and Communists,[10] recruited (and paid) informers to attend the party schools in order to collect data for the suppression that eventually came when the SACB forced both the Jefferson School and the California Labor School to close their doors in the mid-1950s.[11]

When these doors had opened a dozen years earlier, students flocked through them and found a rich treat of curricular and extra-curricular choices offered by a group of talented intellectuals in and near the Communist Party. Two years after its establishment, the Jefferson School offered at its Sixteenth Street "main campus"[12] no less than four hundred courses in a dozen different fields![13] History and contemporary affairs comprised the largest category. Twin brothers Jack and Philip Foner, who in 1946 offered Monday and Tuesday evening sections of an introductory American history course, had been fired in 1941 from their teaching jobs at the municipal colleges of New York City, as had the Jefferson School's director, the philosopher Howard Selsam, his assistant David Goldway, and several other teachers and administrators. These firings were the main (and clearly intended) results of New York State's own rehearsal for McCarthyism—the "Rapp-Coudert" investigation and purge of the colleges.[14]

The California Labor School boasted at least as distinguished a faculty, even if its first director, Dave Jenkins, had only an eighth-grade formal education. The school's education director, Holland Roberts, who earlier had been a Stanford University professor of education, succeeded Jenkins in 1948.[15] Most of the teachers of economic and political subjects were Communist Party officials, like Oleta Yates, Jules Carson and Celeste Strack, or trade union officials (mainly from the ILWU and West Coast public workers unions). Whatever else it did, the California Labor School was also a kind of beaux-arts academy,[16] and many of its finest teachers were in the arts, dance and theater departments. For example, the renowned muralist Anton Refregier, who attracted many students to his art classes at the school, offered when he was in California to do the Rincon Postal Annex murals. The experienced and dedicated drama director Dave Sarvis helped produce and direct many of the California Labor School's elaborate theatrical presentations, among them the powerful labor drama *Stevedore*, set on the waterfront, and a political spoof on the musical *South Pacific*, entitled (soon after the establishment of the anticommunist alliance, NATO) *North Atlantic*.[17] There was also a vigorous literary movement (and journal, *The San Francisco Writers Workshop*) that flourished at the West Coast school, in which the future *New York Times* writer Anthony Boucher and the novelist and later historian Alexander Saxton were involved.[18] West Coast psychiatrists and public health people taught some of the most popular courses at the California Labor School. A bitter behind-the-scenes battle flourished over these unorthodox offerings, and sometimes Jefferson School personnel were brought in from the East Coast to lay down the "correct" anti-Freudian line, but soon eclectic psychological doctrines would, at least while Dave Jenkins was director, creep back into the curriculum.[19] One of the latter moments may have been the appearance of the young non-Communist Erik Erikson delivering a lecture in a California Labor School course called "Mental Hygiene Today."[20]

Aside from the very different East and West Coast approaches to psychology, there was much cooperation and intellectual cross-fertilization between the two schools—mainly taking the form of using writings by such faculty at the New York school as Philip S. Foner, Howard Selsam, Herbert Aptheker and Herbert Morais in West Coast courses.[21] An important history course taught under a variety of titles at both the Jefferson School and the California Labor School and at every earlier and later party school was in the fall of 1946 called "History and Problems of the Negro in America." At the West Coast school the director Dave Jenkins (who later admitted he had been woefully under-prepared) usually taught the Negro history and related courses—until a group of African American trade unionists from the school's Oakland campus took over.[22] The Jefferson School instructor in this course was the immeasurably better-prepared Doxey A. Wilkerson, who had earlier taught at Howard University and had served on the staff of Gunnar Myrdal's Carnegie Corporation-funded project that eventually produced the immensely influential study of race, *An American Dilemma* (1944). Wilkerson, whose wife Yolanda also taught at the Jefferson School, later became faculty and curriculum director and served on the Communist Party's defense team in the main Smith Act case, *Dennis v. U.S.* In 1956, disillusioned with the party and its intellectual rigidity, Doxey Wilkerson was given the thankless but highly responsible task of closing up and selling off the Jefferson School—after which he resigned his long-time Communist Party membership.[23]

Another veteran and victim of New York's Rapp-Coudert purges, George Squier, headed the Jefferson School's Trade Union Division, seeing to it that a comprehensive array of courses on collective bargaining, labor journalism and history, parliamentary procedure, public speaking, strike strategy, etc., were available. This division offered many of these courses at union halls and at Jefferson School annexes around New York City, as well as at the main campus. In addition, on request, the school dispatched its teachers to shops and factories for lunch-hour talks, which left-wing bosses and foremen sometimes attended along with the workers.[24] Not only did the Jefferson School serve those unions in the clothing and light-industrial shops in the New York area that were willing to accept them (this, of course, excluded any shop where David Dubinsky's profoundly anticommunist International Ladies' Garment Workers Union—with its own internal educational programs—held sway), it was a union shop, itself. Permanent Jefferson School employees, all members of State, County and Municipal Workers of America Local 555, were entitled to one-week paid vacation, sick leave, and an employee-friendly severance procedure. Women working there were entitled to maternity leave, with assured return to their jobs. Salary levels varied from $65 per week for the director down to switchboard operators at $35.[25]

Although faculty and staff appear not to have been themselves unionized on the West Coast, the course offerings in labor studies were far richer at the California Labor School—double the number at the Jefferson School in 1946. Some covered the same ground: organizing strategies, contact negotiations, and duties of union officers and stewards.[26] California Trade Union director Irwin Elber (a former organizer for the United Federal Workers union) administered a broad range of labor educational services, which at first won begrudging support from Pacific Coast AFL unions whose leaders were famously hostile to Communism, but who had no comparable educational programs. Some of the older non-Communist rank-and-file members in these unions fondly remembered the ultra-radical Industrial Workers of the World (IWW), and had a measure of sympathy, or at least respect—perhaps derived from the legendary 1934 waterfront strikes in which Communists played an heroic role—for Communism.[27] In San Francisco/Oakland, seventy-five AFL and CIO unions (plus the American Veterans Committee and the NAACP) initially sponsored and helped finance the California Labor School, but the single union that gave the most continuous and generous support was the International Longshoremen's and Warehousemen's Union (ILWU), whose fiery leader Harry Bridges personally believed that all the education a worker needed took "place on the shop floor or the docks." Despite this, Bridges saw to it that substantial financial aid went regularly to the California Labor School.[28] Like the Jefferson School, but in a much different labor context, the California Labor School also offered its services—preparing union pamphlets and newspapers, even offering to conduct dance concerts and theatrical shows at local meetings. Such unions as the ILWU, the Marine Cooks and Stewards, and many others eagerly accepted these programs.[29] The school's active drama department sometimes

FIGURE 11.1 The California Labor School curriculum provided opportunities for local unionists and other students to hear from both local and national figures. From right to left: founding director David Jenkins, singer and actor Paul Robeson, playwright and screenwriter John Howard Lawson, and San Francisco longshoremen's union activist Revels Cayton. Credit: *Labor Archives and Research Center, San Francisco State University.*

sent theatrical troupes into dangerous strike situations in California's Central Valley to entertain and encourage agricultural workers who faced growers determined to beat back all attempts at unionization in the fields. Often the actors had to bring burly longshoremen along for defense against company goons.[30]

At these Communist schools the teaching of Marxism was deemed no less a necessity than labor studies. In that "lost world" of pre-McCarthy radicalism, Marxism was considered "the theory," and other subjects in the curriculum the praxis that would test, and possibly validate, the theory. The Jefferson School staff offered most of its basic instruction in Marxist tenets in a course significantly titled "The Science of Society." Inscribed in this course title was the conviction that Marxism was the science of society, and little else (besides anthropology and psychology) need be done to supplement it in the social studies curriculum, a view that seemed to be more prevalent at the party school in New York than the one in San Francisco/Oakland.

At the Jefferson School in 1946 no fewer than ten sections of Science of Society (a pre-requisite for advanced courses) were offered, including a Saturday morning section for students on the night shift during the week. Sometimes a

Spanish-language section (*Principios de Marxismo*) was added.[31] The announced educational aim was "the scientific study of social life and development." The enumerated topics dealt with in The Science of Society were fairly comprehensive: The Origin and Nature of Capitalist Society; Imperialism: The Highest Stage of Capitalism; The Meaning of Fascism; What is a Nation?; Capitalist Democracy and Socialist Revolution; The Theory and Practice of Socialism; Just and Unjust Wars; The Problem of World Security; The Role of the Working Class and Its Organizations; The Tactics of the Class Struggle; The Materialist Conception of History.[32]

Probably no other course in the Jefferson School curriculum varied so much as The Science of Society, changing each term as society itself changed, and as the party line also shifted. In 1949, when party schools everywhere in the U.S. were coming under government attack, several of the courses were altered. The concept of class struggle was elevated from a subject whose tactics were explored, to "the history of social development," itself. "The Negro Question" was added, along with the concept of "socialist democracy."[33] These changes reflected a waning of enthusiasm for Truman-era liberalism in party circles (more than reciprocated in the post-FDR White House), and a perceived need to defend the "peoples' democracies" in Soviet-dominated eastern Europe—in short, the key issues in the rapidly oncoming Cold War era.

The Cold War and the domestic repression that accompanied it destroyed the Communist schools in the United States and much else of the Communist movement. This destruction, and the later collapse of Communism in the Soviet Union and Eastern Europe constitutes such a fundamental historical break that only a strenuous exercise of historical imagination can recapture the lost world of Communist education. This is especially true of what might be called the traditional cultural elements of the party school curricula. Some anticommunists, noting courses like "Modern Art: Cézanne to the Present," Beethoven's chamber music, Shakespeare's plays, "The Novel and the People," mural painting (taught at the California Labor School by the eminent muralist Anton Refregier), and "The Mystery Story" (taught at the Jefferson School by Dashiell Hammett),[34] dismissed them as mere "come-ons" to draw people into the subversive Communist conspiracy.[35]

From a less ideological, post-Cold War perspective, these cultural aspects of the party schools' curricula can be seen to have several other pedagogical functions not dreamed of in the rarefied world of anticommunist polemics. One of these might have been a "hidden curriculum" at the Communist schools—a hunger among the students for literary culture and self improvement (not antithetical to the announced aims of these schools, but also not quite what they hoped to foster).

Another set of courses offered at East and West Coast schools, which could not claim the status of high culture, seemed to be directed at the improvement of employment and lifestyle. For example, a 1944 Jefferson School "Beauty and Fashion Clinic: Making the Most of your Appearance," bears some resemblance to later dress-and-groom-for-success exhortations aimed at individual advancement, but clearly had another audience, and another aim, in mind.

This course will show the busy working woman how she can make herself more attractive with the least expenditure of time and money. She will develop not only a technique to meet her individual problems of appearance, but an understanding of the factors involved in beauty and fashion. The student will be taught how to put on make-up correctly, the best colors and types, ingredients of cosmetics and their effect on various skin types; protection of hands and skin for the woman industrial worker; how to balance a diet for health and beauty; how to control weight; exercises for posture and figure improvement, how to sit, stand and walk; how to choose the most becoming coiffures, how to care for the hair; clothes to flatter the figure, good and bad taste in fashion, how to dress for type, figure and job.[36]

Such offerings were directed at women factory and office workers who might be union shop stewards or members of contract-negotiation committees and who had learned that to be taken seriously by bosses, male union comrades, and even men in the party, a certain level of dress and grooming had to be attained. But many of the women were from immigrant families, with mothers and aunts who were unable to advise them on American concepts of acceptable beauty and fashion care. The Communist Party stepped in to remedy the situation.[37]

Whatever else the party schools did, they had to address problems of student literacy, especially since difficult Marxist texts had to be taught in educational institutions tethered to such a theory-driven organization. The issues of teaching skills, student motivation, and literacy training were not easily handled by the Communist pedagogues at these schools. But such concerns came to their attention in a variety of ways:[38] many students lacked prior schooling, and teachers (many of whom were autodidacts, or learned scholars unused to working-class students) sometimes neglected coherence and clarity in classroom communication. What set off alarm bells were classes where few or none of the initial students returned for the second session. Teachers would have to be taken in hand, given advice and coaching by Doxey Wilkerson, or Assistant Director David Goldway. This was far more serious a matter than statistical attrition or forfeited tuition fees. Students who lost interest in classes were in danger of being lost to the movement—and building a movement was what Communism was all about.

By the time attention became focused on students with learning problems and undeveloped study habits, the party schools were already under government threat. Belated though they may have been, these concerns prompted at the Jefferson School (and less formally at the California Labor School) creative but stillborn pedagogical initiatives. The main point was to sever teaching from all connection with the idea of student failure. The absence of grades in both CLS and the Jefferson School facilitated acceptance of this policy, which received its most extensive West Coast elaboration in an unpublished text by CLS Education Director Holland Roberts.[39] The Jefferson School produced a pedagogical pamphlet in the final bruising years of governmental assault and doomed fight-back. This five-cent, sixteen-page, pocket-sized *How to Study* (1954),[40] almost totally unknown, deserves the status of a minor educational classic. It sought to motivate students by stressing that the "capitalist rulers" of the United States, out of fear of Marxism, attempted to spread the false belief that sophisticated theories such as Marxism were "only for the select few," and not for working people. Therefore people who did study Marxism on their own, or in such places as the Jefferson School, besides gaining the satisfaction that came from mastery of a difficult subject, had the added incentive of waging just and wholesome class struggle, and confounding the capitalist oppressors, when they did their homework.[41] Encapsulating the now widely-accepted pedagogical notion that a student's confidence in *the ability to learn* should properly precede and sustain learning itself, *How to Study*, and parallel ideas that developed at the California Labor School, emerged organically from the lost world of Communist labor education. Such ideas could conceivably help to address the present-day global crisis in education.

The Marxist provenance of their educational concepts and curricula is perhaps what most clearly indicates that these schools represent a "lost world" of pedagogical innovation. Many now dispatch Marxism to the dustbin of quaint antiquated beliefs, and attempts to understand the era of Marxist legitimacy demand a considerable exercise of historical imagination. One must grasp the efforts of dedicated pedagogues directly inspired by Marx's celebrated "eleventh thesis" on Feuerbach—the necessity not only of interpreting the world, but also changing it. I call this conviction of education as action to change the world "engaged pedagogy." It describes an epoch in the recent past during which teaching and learning were conceived of as active, not passive, processes, which included such collective action as students marching alongside teachers and school staff in May Day parades, or transmuting the mere study of "Negro history" into demonstrations and letter-writing campaigns against segregation, lynching, and the poll tax. After World War II the ideal of transmuting theory into action found application in militant trade union activity. This essay has attempted to show that, at least in the United States,[42] a curriculum of liberation-oriented labor education once animated the pedagogy of Communist Party educators. These activities deserve attention because, despite their flaws, Communists took the responsibility of teaching Marxism—both theory and praxis—seriously, and thus infused their educational projects with the rare quality of passionate commitment.

Notes

1. This essay is drawn from a book in-progress to be titled, *"Training for the Class Struggle": Communist Education in the U.S., 1923–1957*. The author acknowledges the help of Lisa Rubens, Robert Cherny, William Issel, Annette T. Rubinstein, David Goldway (1907–1990), Alan Wald, Alexander Saxton, and Ellen Schrecker. On the first of the Communist Party schools, see Marvin E. Gettleman, "The New York Workers School, 1923–1944: Communist Education in American Society," in *New Studies in the Politics and Culture of U.S. Communism*, ed. Michael Brown, et al. (New York: Monthly Review Press, 1993), 261–280. The author is also indebted to Professor Clyde Barrow of the University of Massachusetts/Dartmouth for sharing his unpublished manuscript on the Workers School.

2. The Jefferson School had extension branches in the Bronx, Brooklyn, and New Jersey. The artist and writer Gwendolyn Bennett headed the Jefferson School's Harlem sub-branch, named the George Washington Carver School. A small collection of materials on the Carver School may be found in the New York Public Library's Schomburg Center for Research in Black Culture (New York City). The California Labor School (hereafter cited as CLS), based in San Francisco, established extension centers in Santa Rosa, Sacramento, Stockton, Fresno, and other Northern California locales, and a sub-branch in Oakland directed by Gordon Williams. See brochure, *California Labor School Expands* [n.d. (1946)], in the Library of the California State University, Northridge. In 1947 the CLS opened another branch in Los Angeles, directed by David Hedley (superseding the earlier party school there, the People's Educational Center). When Hedley died in 1948 the CLS branch in Los Angeles limped along a few more years, but closed in the early '50s. Records of the Los Angeles CLS and the People's Educational Center are found at California State University, Northridge, and at the Southern California Library for Social Science and Research, Los Angeles.
3. Course Listings, Jefferson School of Social Science (winter 1944), Reference Center for Marxist Studies, New York City (hereafter cited as RCMS).
4. These are the slogans that appeared on CLS brochures in the 1945–47 period. These brochures have been preserved in the Labor Archives and Research Center, San Francisco State University (hereafter cited as LARC/SFSU), in the Library of California State University (Northridge), and in the Southern California Library for Social Science and Research (Los Angeles).
5. Course Listings, Jefferson School of Social Science (fall 1946), RCMS.
6. Course Listings, Jefferson School of Social Science (winter 1944), epigraph (a quotation from Thomas Jefferson's letter to James Madison, 20 December 1787), RCMS. The *New York Times,* 29 April 1944, carried a news story announcing the Jefferson School's opening, while the *San Francisco News,* 16 May 1944 carried an announcement of the CLS spring and summer plans.
7. Course Listings, Jefferson School of Social Science (fall 1949), 3, RCMS.
8. Course Listings, CLS (fall 1946), 8, LARC/SFSU.
9. *New York Times*, 3 October 1950.
10. On Hoover and the FBI, and the anticommunist animus that obsessed both, see Ellen Schrecker, *Many Are the Crimes: McCarthyism in America* (Princeton, N.J.: Princeton University Press, 1998), chap. 6.
11. On how FBI witnesses' hostile testimony fit into the U.S. government's argument that Communist schools were "agents of a foreign power" see reels 29 (Jefferson School) and 51 (CLS) of the microfilm edition of *Records of the Subversive Activities Control Board, 1950–1972* (Frederick, Md.: University Publications of America, 1989).
12. See Marvin E. Gettleman, "'No Varsity Teams,' New York's Jefferson School of Social Science, 1943–1956," *Science & Society* 66 (fall 2002): 336–359.
13. The data here is drawn from the ninety-page Course Listings, Jefferson School of Social Science (fall 1946), RCMS. This paper describes only the adult curricula at the Jefferson School and CLS. Both schools had a small number of classes for children and teenagers.
14. On the Rapp-Coudert rehearsal for McCarthyism, see Ellen Schrecker, *No Ivory Tower: McCarthyism & the Universities* (New York: Oxford University Press, 1986), chap. 3, and Stephen Leberstein, "Purging the Profs: The Rapp-Coudert Committee in New York," in *New Studies in the Politics and Culture of American Communism*, ed. Brown, et al., 91–122.

15. Roberts' autobiographical memoir of the CLS, "The Dangerous School," is in the Holland Roberts Papers, LARC/SFSU, but must be supplemented by the acerbic critical comments in Dave Jenkins, "The Union Movement, the California Labor School and San Francisco Politics, 1926–1988," 150, 174, oral history by Lisa Rubens in the Bancroft Library, University of California, Berkeley (hereafter cited as Bancroft).
16. This point is vividly made in Jenkins, "The Union Movement, the CLS and San Francisco Politics, 1926–1988," 156–159, Bancroft, and in Jenkins, interview by author, San Francisco, 9 June 1990.
17. The author gratefully acknowledges Professor Ben Harris of the University of Wisconsin, for calling his attention to the mimeographed lyrics of *North Atlantic* in the CLS papers, State Historical Society of Wisconsin, Madison. Cf. Dave Sarvis, interview by author, San Anselmo and Mill Valley, Calif., 10 June 1990.
18. Alexander Saxton, interview by author, Santa Rosa Calif., 1 October 1999.
19. One of the CLS psychology faculty, Cavendish Moxon, set forth the rationale for an eclectic psychotherapy in "Psychotherapy for Progressives," *Science & Society* 21 (spring 1948): 197–217. Cf. Ben Harris, "'Don't Be Unconscious; Join Our Ranks:' Psychology, Politics and Communist Education," *Rethinking Marxism* 6 (spring 1993): 1–32.
20. Course listings, CLS (fall 1945), 15, LARC/SFSU.
21. Syllabii of CLS courses in LARC/SFSU and in the Southern California Library for Social Studies and Research, Los Angeles, record dozens of instances in which books and articles by such Jefferson School teachers as Howard Selsam, Philip Foner, and Herbert Aptheker were used in CLS courses. All three also delivered lectures at CLS.
22. Dave Jenkins, interview.
23. Doxey and Yolanda Wilkerson, interview by author, South Norwalk, Conn., 18 July 1990; the *New York Times* obituary, 18 June 1993. For Wilkerson's admission of dogmatism at the Jefferson School, see his letter (co-authored with Howard Selsam and David Goldway) in *Daily Worker*, 6 May 1956.
24. George Squier, interview by author, Ocean Bay Park, New York, 13 October 1974; Course Listings, Jefferson School of Social Sciences (fall 1946), 10–11, 27–30, RCMS, and other Jefferson School bulletins at RCMS, the Tamiment Library (New York University), and the Jefferson School Papers (State Historical Society of Wisconsin).
25. Memorandum on Personnel Practice (1944?), Jefferson School Papers (microfilm edition, frame 134), State Historical Society of Wisconsin.
26. See for example Course Listings, CLS (spring 1946), 9–12, LARC/SFSU. One of the labor courses, dealing with welfare benefits available to unionists and World War II veterans in San Francisco, was taught by the writer Tillie Olsen, then director of the CIO Community Services in California.
27. Bill Clifford, interview by author, Atlanta, Ga., 4 November 1900. Clifford had been a student at CLS, and a West Coast trade unionist.
28. Dave Jenkins, interview; Jenkins, "Union Movement, the CLS and San Francisco Politics, 1926–1988," 151, Bancroft.
29. Course Listings, CLS (spring 1946), 6–7, LARC/SFSU.
30. David Sarvis (formerly of CLS Drama Department), interview by author, San Anselmo and Mill Valley, Calif., 9 June 1990.
31. Course listings, Jefferson School of Social Science (winter 1955), 8, Tamiment Library, New York University.
32. Course Listings, Jefferson School of Social Science (fall 1946), 14–15, RCMS.
33. Course Outline, The Science of Society: An Introduction to Marxism (1949), Jefferson School Papers, Tamiment Library, New York University.

34. Course Listings, Jefferson School of Social Science (fall 1946), 39–48, RCMS.
35. Frank S. Meyer, Jefferson School of Social Science SACB testimony, reel 29, 117; CLS, SACB testimony, reel 51, 23–25, 32. Meyer, who directed the Chicago Workers School before the Second World War, and taught at the Jefferson School after the war, became a fanatical anticommunist and professional anticommunist witness at several trials.
36. Course Listings, Jefferson School of Social Science (winter 1944), 46, RCMS.
37. Belle Bailynson Meyers, interview by author, New York City, 28 February 1988. A former Jefferson School student, and former worker at an electrical manufacturing shop whose workforce was organized into the left-led United Electrical Workers (UE), Bell Meyers made clear to this author what social reality underlay this course on beauty and fashion.
38. Interviews with administrators at both the CLS and Jefferson School clarified the ways in which pedagogical concerns arose there. Especially useful were the author's previously-cited David Jenkins and Doxey Wilkerson interviews, and an interview with David Goldway, former Assistant Director of the Jefferson School, in New York City, 4 February 1988.
39. See the handwritten draft by Holland Roberts, CLS Educational Director, of a memoir, "The War Years at Stanford and the CLS," n.d., LARC/SFSU, where the idea of schools without even the possibility of failure was advanced—an unknown precursor of some of the best contemporary pedagogical thinking (e.g., William Glasser, *Schools Without Failure* [New York: Harper & Row, 1969].)
40. *How to Study: A Guide for Students* (New York: The Jefferson School of Social Science, n.d. [dated 1954, by internal evidence]). Attributed to left-wing New York psychoanalyst Harry K. Wells by Doxey Wilkerson (interview by author, 18 July 1990), this pamphlet is among the Jefferson School papers in the Tamiment Library, New York University. It has recently been re-edited and adapted (dropping adulatory references to Joseph Stalin and Harry Haywood) for present-day college students by Henry Foner and is in use at the City College of New York Center for Worker Education in New York City.
41. In Jefferson School courses on Marxism this homework often included such knotty texts as Marx's "Wage Labor and Capital," an embryonic statement of the future argument in *Capital*, prepared in 1847 for a group of workers in Brussels, Belgium.
42. Marxist and especially Communist education cannot be fully understood solely within national borders; it was an international phenomenon. To understand this broader dimension, the author has founded the Project on the Comparative International History of Left Education. For an indication of the kind of cross-cultural scholarship fostered by this project, see the issue of *Paedagogica Historica* 35 (1999) [Ghent, Belgium], guest-edited by the author, and devoted to selected topics in the history of left education in nineteenth and twentieth century Europe.

Operation Dixie, the Red Scare, and the Defeat of Southern Labor Organizing
☼

Michael K. Honey

Historic possibilities for changing the South seemed to exist at the end of World War II, based on new hopes for organizing southern workers. Just as the war galvanized the American economy, pulling it out of the Depression of the 1930s, it also accelerated industrialization and urbanization in the South. The number of industrial workers in the region jumped from 1.6 million before the war to 2.4 million by August 1945. Growing manufacturing and commercial centers increasingly overshadowed the traditional economy of cotton and agricultural goods production. During the war, one-quarter of the South's farm population left the land for northern or southern employment in cities and factories. The manufacturing economy began to displace cotton as "king" and transform the face of the region.[1]

Many labor activists, civil rights leaders, and New Deal liberals hoped that the corollary to economic growth would be the creation of movements to transform southern society that would produce rapid advances in living standards, education, economic security, political rights, and union organization for southern workers. A core of activists had struggled for years to change the South from a reactionary bastion of local ruling elites who used anti-unionism, racism, and anti-communism interchangeably to stay in power. By the end of the war, these activists became very optimistic that the South would move away from farm tenancy and poverty and toward greater democracy, racial justice, and economic advance. Former first lady Eleanor Roosevelt, among others, felt that "the era of the low standard of living and low labor costs is probably rapidly drawing to an end."[2]

Like most New Dealers and Progressives of the time, Mrs. Roosevelt based her hopes on the expansion of unions. The war had to some degree thwarted anti-union campaigns by southern employers, who had in the past flagrantly violated federal labor laws and crushed organizing through the use of racism, red-baiting,

216

and brute force. When faced with the potential loss of federal contracts, however, many politicians and some employers tempered their rhetoric and behavior. The War Labor Board and other federal agencies, though timidly and reluctantly, established a floor of minimum wages, and imposed union security and minimal job rights in southern factories with federal war contracts. This, far more than the Wagner Act during the New Deal 1930s, gave unions new room to organize.[3]

Organizers had good reason to believe that they could defeat the anti-unionism of the South's ruling class of planters, merchants, bankers and industrialists, for unions had reached a new level of strength at the end of the war. Aided by the War Labor Board, the Congress of Industrial Organizations (CIO) expanded its southern membership from a pre-war high of 150,000 to 225,000 members. In addition, 100,000 belonged to the United Mine Workers, which became independent of the CIO in 1942. Southern membership in the American Federation of Labor (AFL), which claimed 1.8 million in the region, grew even faster. Nationally, unions had reached a new high point, with some 10 million AFL and 4.5 million CIO members comprising about 35 percent of the civilian work force. From this position of strength, tackling the anti-union South seemed very feasible.[4]

Many also believed that the rapid spread of unions in the South would be the beginning of the end of the South's system of racial segregation. Lucy Randolph Mason, a publicist and civil rights trouble-shooter for the CIO, thought many southern white workers had come to accept blacks into their unions as equal partners during the war. She seemed to ignore the fact that race riots in the Mississippi shipyards and violent attacks by whites against African American soldiers during the war pointed in quite a different direction.[5] Yet the expansion of unions during the war among both white and black workers gave southern liberals and civil rights leaders reason to hope that white workers could accept blacks as union members and ultimately accept them as citizens, as well. Roosevelt, W.E.B. Du Bois, and many others saw the CIO as the most promising vehicle for making this happen. No other interracial organization of such size existed in either the South or the rest of the country. And even though many whites in its member unions practiced racism and discrimination on a daily basis, the CIO as an institution had fully committed itself to integration. Based on its record of organizing and its policies of interracialism, Mason believed, by the war's end the CIO had already brought "more hope for progress to Negroes than any other social institution in the South."[6]

Progressives hoped that, in time, unionization and a continuing federal presence might overwhelm white opposition to black rights. They were not just engaging in wishful thinking, for they had already seen some changes in the racial system ushered in by the union movement. Under the auspices of the CIO, southern workers throughout the 1930s and during the war had come together in support of common economic demands, usually within and sometimes outside the normal confines of segregation. The elimination of opposition to biracial unionization among white workers already seemed well under way. African Americans, who worked in most of the region's industries, had already become the CIO's strongest supporters. Many in the CIO and the black community saw the cause of civil rights for black people and the right of workers to organize as inseparably bound in the

South, for both strategic and moral reasons. Without black support, unionization could not succeed in many industries. And, after millions had died fighting a war against fascism, the ultimate expression of racism, the necessity of fighting for the human rights for all people seemed obvious.[7]

A powerful force for interracial organizing also existed within the left-wing unions of the CIO. The trade union left had been crucial to organizing African Americans and the South. The Communist Party had organized campaigns to save victims of racism such as the Scottsboro defendants and made opposition to racism central to its goal of transforming American social and economic institutions. Left-wing unions such as the United Packinghouse Workers of America (UPWA), the Food, Tobacco, Agricultural, and Allied Workers Union of America (FTA), the International Longshoremen's and Warehousemen's Union (ILWU), the United Electrical, Radio and Machine Workers (UE) and others made equal rights a core part of their educational programs and organizing agenda. Indeed, the packinghouse union would never have succeeded in the 1930s or survived during the 1940s without a strong anti-racist and pro-civil rights program.[8] Left-led unions had long taken the position that fighting racism and racial division was crucial to any effort to organize workers in the South.

Indeed, there is no exaggeration in Robert Zieger's assessment that "in regard to race and gender the Communist-influenced CIO affiliates stood in the vanguard" in moving the whole CIO toward an equal rights philosophy. In the formative years of industrial unionism, leftist unions played key roles in forging an anti-racist consensus, which became part of what Communists called the "left-center" coalition within the CIO. The United Mine Workers of America (UMW), the United Auto Workers (UAW), the United Steelworkers of America (USWA), and other major CIO unions not only accepted Communists and other leftist organizers into their ranks but also came to see interracial organizing as one of the keys to CIO success. Although they disagreed on how far to move on issues of racial equality, both the small and large unions and the "center" and "left" leadership within the CIO at least rhetorically accepted the need for anti-discrimination policies and for interracial organizing. Most AFL unions, by contrast, excluded or segregated African American and other minority workers, even when paying lip service to anti-discrimination principles.[9]

During the war, however, the Communist Party downplayed racial militancy and supported the CIO's no-strike pledge in support of maximum war production. For their zealousness in support of the no-strike pledge and all-out efforts to maximize production, Communists lost some strength and credibility in the UAW and other unions. Yet at the shop-floor level, unionists throughout the CIO often sidestepped the no-strike position, as workers themselves enforced their demands through quick wildcat strikes and other job actions. Rank-and-file discontent with speed up, long hours of work, and a wage freeze eventually led to the biggest strike wave in United States history. Neither Communists nor any other union leaders could control worker militancy, and some did not try. Black workers too became increasingly impatient on all fronts. In the South, leftists hoped that this unrest among both black and white workers could be used to forge a greater degree of unity in action and help to break down, rather than build up, racial divisions. They based their optimism also on continued existence of a "center-left" bloc in CIO unions.[10]

The rise of a center-left bloc in the unions had its corollary in the rise of a people's movement in the South before and during the war. It too revolved to a significant degree around the issue of equal rights for all, including African Americans and women. Before the war, liberals, civil-rights advocates and unionists had joined forces in the Southern Conference for Human Welfare (SCHW). During the war, the "popular front" of labor and liberal organizations and activists spread, and it continued to grow in the immediate postwar period. The National Association for the Advancement of Colored People (NAACP) expanded dramatically all over the South and among black workers in northern factory towns like Detroit. Even in a citadel of white supremacy such as South Carolina, NAACP membership jumped from 800 in 1939 to over 14,000 by 1948. The NAACP became a central partner to the CIO in all its campaigns for equal rights after the war.[11]

The interracial and liberal Southern Conference also remained an important partner in efforts to organize workers and to implement dreams of human equality. The SCHW had its most rapid expansion in 1945–1946, growing to 10,000 members, and with a budget of $200,000. Its program mirrored the CIO's. In coalition with the CIO's Political Action Committee, the SCHW mapped a postwar strategy to bring organized workers, the African American community, and liberals into a majority coalition. This coalition, it hoped, would eliminate the poll tax and otherwise enfranchise blacks and poor whites. Through an alliance of working-class, farming, and middle-class voters, the SCHW hoped to remove elected Southern reactionaries who held back developments in the South and blocked progressive legislation in Congress. The SCHW further anticipated that these changes would open the way to reconstruct the educational, political, and economic systems that had been imposed on the South by an oligarchy of elites since the era of Reconstruction. The election of more liberal elements in 1944 and the South's underground traditions of Populism and agrarian socialism provided some tangible signs of hope for a people's movement to transform the region[12]

The success of Highlander Folk School in Tennessee also suggested growing possibilities for an alliance of white and black, both as workers and as citizens. Highlander had experienced a doubling of the number of workers in its courses in the last year of the war and had trained thousands of CIO members in trade-union philosophy and action. After the war, Highlander held its programs on an interracial basis and continued to expand as a labor school. The Southern Conference, Highlander, the NAACP, and the CIO enjoyed a solid partnership in 1946. These organizations moved toward ever more open resistance to segregation at the end of the war. Allan S. Haywood, director of organization for the CIO, indicated as much at the closing session of Highlander's CIO summer school in 1945, declaring, "we must stamp out all forms of discrimination," for "only with a unified movement based on equal rights" could labor's attempt to organize the South succeed.[13]

An important aspect of the coalition and the CIO's developing unity around equal rights issues at the end of the war had to do with a muting of anticommunism. The CIO and its partner organizations mostly followed a "don't ask, don't tell" policy and allowed Communists and Socialists to function freely. The CIO repeatedly defended Highlander and the Southern Conference from continual attacks in the media and by elected officials who called them "Communist" because of their support for labor rights and interracialism. Wartime unity between the United States and the Soviet Union had diluted the "Communist" charge. As one white worker from Georgia at Highlander's 1945 session commented, "we used to fall for this red baiting stuff, but now we know what it's used for." Many unionists had come to see anticommunism as not just an attack on members of the Communist Party, but as a device to attack all liberals and radicals and divide the labor movement.[14]

A significant coalition of union supporters envisioned a movement to overturn the old order in the South, and they had built the institutions and the unity that could make it happen. Their hopes seemed to match the realities of southern working-class consciousness to a significant degree. Returning enlisted men expected better wages and working conditions and improved standards of living. In Athens, Tennessee, the GI Non-Partisan League ran a slate of candidates in the fall of 1946 to oust a corrupt city machine that was allied with political boss Edward H. Crump in Memphis. After a six-hour gun battle over impoundment of the city's election ballots by the authorities, white GI's nearly lynched the sheriff and his men for shooting a black supporter of the GI ticket in the back. Black veterans also expressed heightened expectations for change, and often fought back militantly against Jim Crow. In Columbia, Tennessee, they armed themselves to resist an onslaught of violence by police, state troopers and white vigilantes in February 1946.[15]

Activist white and black veterans both figured heavily in the CIO's plans to organize the South. More than whites, however, black workers were primed for change. In factories, black war veterans like Matthew Davis in Memphis carried themselves with pride and refused to shuffle or grin at the indignities of segregation. A basic shift in rights consciousness had occurred not only among black war veterans, but also among people who had spent the war years struggling for better conditions in factories and other work places throughout the South. Aided by the War Labor Board and other federal agencies, African American workers became highly conscious of the opportunities that existed to organize at the work place and to confront the many indignities that Jim Crow heaped upon them outside of work. Leftist unions and civil rights advocates within the CIO particularly understood this dynamic and tried to use it to spread union organization wherever possible.[16]

Despite signs of change, however, major obstacles confronted southern unionists. The CIO had already organized many of the southern facilities of major national corporations that were under union contract in the North, but organizing the next tier of industries promised to be very tough. The largest percentage of the industries yet to be organized were locally-owned enterprises in competition with each other. These low-wage industries included textiles and woodworking, plus producers of food and agricultural goods. Employers in such low-wage bastions could be expected to go all out to defeat unionization. Since the days of slavery, southern businessmen had believed that low labor costs provided their main advantage, compared to the North. Southern unionists knew that such employers would fight viciously when they faced unionization.[17]

Maintaining the South's elaborate racial system had everything to do with keeping wages low. Many southern employers relied heavily on black labor. The racial caste system had deprived black workers of basic civil and political rights, making it difficult for them to demand improvements. It also separated white and black workers into superior and subordinate in nearly every aspect of their lives and work. Racial divide-and-rule by southern legislatures, courts, the police, the news media, and the churches kept unions and working-class political activity weak. Southern congressmen during the New Deal had excluded agricultural employees and domestic workers, the vast majority of them black southerners, from Wagner Act coverage. Employers excluded blacks from textile production jobs but threatened to introduce them, should white workers ever demand too much or go on strike. Even though World War II created a higher-wage industrial sector that some chambers of commerce appreciated, most business people still thought keeping wages low and blacks subordinate and unorganized remained the keys to getting industries to move to the South. In the postwar years most employers did everything possible to enforce the color line and to keep unions out.[18]

At the war's end, a stone wall of opposition to unions made it very difficult for the CIO to reach beyond the core of southern work places they had already organized. Exceptional dedication and innovative long-term strategies at the work place and in the community were required for any further organizing to succeed. But many CIO leaders had a different model in mind. "Flying squadrons," dramatic confrontations, and quick victories during the sit-down strikes and organizing drives of the 1930s misled many CIO leaders into thinking they could move quickly in the South. According to historian Barbara Griffith, "the idea of targeting the most powerful corporations," defeating them, and then getting other companies to fall in line "became a cornerstone of CIO belief." Such a strategy required a sympathetic government and labor law and an aroused and liberal electorate. Such a strategy would not work in the South. As Highlander's Myles Horton later pointed out, organizing indigenous southern industries required long campaigns, worker education, grass-roots activities in the trenches of company towns and urban centers, and infinite patience.[19]

It also required a deep commitment to struggling for black civil rights. Blacks predominated or held a large share of jobs in most of the unorganized sectors, except for textiles. To organize them would require breaking down the racism of white workers and resisting the paternalistic ideology and racism of owners. It would require labor educational campaigns to change the southern white workers' self image in order to open up the possibility of joining with an interracial CIO. Successful organizing would require fighting for the rights of African Americans to function as citizens, with the right to speak, associate, and organize together and with whites. It also meant changing the whole of southern society, as the Southern

Conference envisioned. To get political power out of the hands of the southern oligarchy of business people and landed elites meant campaigns to defeat antidemocratic measures such as the poll tax and literacy laws, and gaining voting rights for blacks as well as poor whites.[20] Although CIO organizers spoke optimistically of organizing the South, most of them were not prepared actually to do it.

In early 1946 the CIO announced Operation Dixie, a million-dollar campaign to hire two hundred people to organize the region. It was the single-largest labor organizing drive ever undertaken in the South. In its postwar optimism, the CIO hoped that the drive would bring civil rights as well as labor rights to the South, that white workers as well as blacks would join the drive, that the CIO itself would be united and maintain a strong united front with progressive organizations, and that the federal government and labor laws would provide a sympathetic and supportive framework for southern organizing. All these assumptions were very quickly dashed on the hard rocks of the red scare, segregationist upsurge, and the Cold War.[21]

The CIO's first reports on the drive seemed to show great success. In the summer of 1946, the CIO reported ten new locals affiliating per week, and twenty affiliating per week by September; it reported enrolling 280,000 new members at the end of the first year of the campaign, and 400,000 new members by the end of the first year and a half. Tennessee led the way, with 70,000 to 85,000 new members by February 1947. Some 22,000 new members were reported in North Carolina, 15,000 in Alabama, 14,500 in Texas, and 7,000 in Virginia. Some of these figures were inflated, and by late 1947 the overall estimate of new members leveled out at 280,000. The CIO also made important breakthroughs in Arkansas, where membership doubled. In Mississippi the CIO took the important Masonite plant away from the AFL because of strong support from black workers.[22]

One definite area of advance emerged from the organizing of the left-wing Food, Tobacco and Agricultural (FTA) workers' union. The FTA expanded the CIO's organizing among the poorest and most neglected Southern workers, namely the tobacco and cotton-press workers of the Carolinas, west Tennessee, and Arkansas. In the second year of Operation Dixie the FTA won 111 elections covering 15,000 workers in the South, second only to the International Woodworkers of America (IWA) in the number of organizing victories in the early months of the Southern campaign. Both unions mainly organized black workers, who continued to demonstrate much stronger support for the CIO than whites. In addition to such organizational advances, CIO voters contributed to the election of southern liberals to statewide offices, including Estes Kefauver in Tennessee, Jim Folsom in Alabama, and Frank Porter Graham in North Carolina.[23]

Although the organizing drive had impressive beginnings, union statistics were sometimes misleading. Many workers who signed cards for a union, or even voted for one, never enjoyed the benefits of unionization due to obstructionist actions taken by their employers. Some union estimates were gross exaggerations. In some cases, the number of workers organized still represented a pittance. Only about 4 percent of textile workers belonged to unions, compared to hundreds of thousands of still-unorganized workers, for example. In fact, more textile workers voted against unions than for them during Operation Dixie.[24]

Yet the CIO's initiative proved credible enough to spur the AFL to undertake its own southern drive. As it had done all along, the AFL reacted to industrial organizing by attacking fellow unionists in the CIO. The AFL stressed cooperation between employers and unions as an alternative to supposed CIO policies of confrontation. It also appealed to workers and employers as a safe alternative to the "Communist"-dominated CIO. At its conference opening the organizing drive, AFL southern director George Googe told delegates the CIO consisted of "political manipulators, who wish to undermine our present American form of government as well as life." AFL secretary-treasurer George Meany called Operation Dixie the "CIO-Communist drive in the South."[25]

Interestingly, the AFL itself focused heavily on organizing African Americans. Some 450,000 of the AFL's 650,000 black members in 1946 were southerners, many of them in longshore work and in laboring occupations within the building trades. The AFL unions in the South actually had more black members (450,000) than did the CIO (200,000). But the CIO, as an organization primarily focusing on non-craft workers, threatened to take many of these workers away. Its victory at Masonite in Laurel spurred the AFL to hire black organizers and to appeal openly to black workers.[26] The AFL attacked CIO unions with high-ranking blacks as being Communist-led, but red-baiting by the AFL and by employers did not seem to frighten many blacks away from CIO unions. Indeed, Leroy Boyd in Memphis felt he and other blacks were more likely to believe a union might stand up for them when whites attacked it as being led by Communists. "Among Negroes, they didn't pay any attention" to Communist baiting, Boyd recalled, "because they knew how white men felt about another white man speaking up for the Negro. He was just branded a Communist." For the same reason, however, red-baiting did cause many Southern white workers to turn away; for them, as for blacks, "Communist" usually meant integrationist. Such white workers often favored the AFL, if they favored a union at all, because they saw it as a white supremacist organization.[27]

Despite the AFL's appeals for inter-class collaboration, employers frequently attacked AFL as well as CIO organizers with anti-union propaganda, arrests, and vigilante violence. The AFL claimed a half-million new members in the South, yet it seems that the AFL gained far fewer new members than hoped for or claimed. The AFL scuttled its southern campaign after little more than a year and increasingly resorted to raids on existing CIO unions to gain new members. But since the AFL still had a significant number of black members and a range of racial practices, the CIO still had to prove itself as an effective organization, to blacks as well as whites.[28]

Not surprisingly, the CIO ran into even more opposition than the AFL. Indeed, the external forces against unionization proved overwhelming. Although the Operation Dixie drive began when labor organizations and a revived postwar New Deal coalition seemed to be at their height, within months the Cold War had begun in earnest and it soon wrecked whatever chances had existed for changing the South. The Democratic Party dumped labor-supporter Henry Wallace in favor of the more conservative Harry Truman as vice-president in 1944. More significantly,

Republicans took over both the House and the Senate in the nation's Congress during the 1946 election. The turn to the right in American politics virtually destroyed federal support for southern labor organizing. Indeed, this was one of the major objectives of business and political leaders in the Republican Party. The news media, the Republican party, the Chamber of Commerce and the National Association of Manufacturers barraged the public with anti-unionism and anticommunism in response to a national strike wave in 1946, leading to the Republican victories in the fall elections. As Robert Zieger points out, the CIO had gained much of its success due to a supportive or at least sympathetic president and Congress during the New Deal and World War II, but conditions now changed dramatically.[29]

As Republicans and, increasingly, Democrats began to shift the politics of the nation to the right, supporters of the old order in the South emphasized not simply their support for racial segregation, but the threat to the nation of "Communist" labor and civil rights organizing. In the aftermath of Nazism, pounding on the racial issue by itself would not necessarily gain Southern leaders allies at the national level, but it quickly became apparent that pounding on the "Communist" issue might. Southern Democrats had joined with Republicans in Congress to establish a permanent House Un-American Activities Committee in 1945, and HUAC and employer organizations unleashed an aggressive propaganda barrage to convince public opinion that the CIO, Highlander, and the Southern Conference were all subversive.[30]

Both on a national level and in the South, the intensifying red-baiting aimed at dividing the labor movement internally and isolating the CIO from both its allies and the general public. Journalist Stetson Kennedy documented in great detail the collaboration of employers, various elements of the right wing, and segregationists in circulating racist and anti-union propaganda in the South. The Southern States Industrial Council distributed its *Militant Truth* newspaper in a special "labor edition" of 100,000 copies. This publication not only harped on the subversion question, but also raised the specter of "black domination" in the South, with one of its leaflets attacking fair employment proceedings under the heading "Shall We Be Ruled By Whites or Blacks?" Harding College in Arkansas planned in 1946 to spend $450,000 to spread anti-labor literature, and over the years it developed a National Education Program taught anticommunist propaganda at military bases across the South. Texas lumber and oil barons funded Christian America, probably the most well-endowed anti-union organization in the South, which helped to launch anticommunist crusaders like Billy James Hargis, Robert Welch of the John Birch Society, and former general Edwin A. Walker.[31]

Throughout the region, labor organizing touched off a mean and ugly war, as Southern businessmen, landed elites, and politicians mobilized to save the "southern way of life" of segregation and low wages. Labor's use of the picket line, marches, boycotts, and the joining of white and black workers as allies all seemed akin to revolution to many white southern leaders. The CIO's plans to end the poll tax and remove reactionary Southern political leaders in order to pass national health care and other social legislation seemed equally revolutionary. With racist and anti-union propaganda circulating in the millions and filtering through the

Southern news media, state legislatures and city councils passed a raft of anti-union ordinances, requiring organizers to have a "license," outlawing picketing, or implementing "right to work" laws that banned the union shop.[32]

The effects of the anti-union barrage could be brutal. In Arkansas, when an anti-union militant killed a black member of the FTA who was on picket duty, the state exonerated the attackers but sentenced the other picketers to the penitentiary for violating the state's "anti-violence" law. The re-emergence of the Ku Klux Klan galvanized the anti-union campaign. In 1946, KKK members beat and murdered black workers in Georgia, openly burned crosses in Chattanooga and South Carolina, and ran a candidate for Congress in Birmingham.[33] Thugs beat up white organizer John Riffe in Columbia, South Carolina. A non-union employee shot to death Lowell Simmons, a textile union organizer, in Bemis, Tennessee.[34] In Tifton, Georgia, twenty-nine workers found themselves fired from their jobs and blacklisted everywhere in town for their organizing activities.[35] This war against the right to organize forced workers to soberly calculate their chances for survival before joining a union. And racial apartheid impeded every step of the organizing process in many workplaces, from shaking hands to leafleting plant gates.

The labor movement, particularly in the South, had always confronted repression, racism, and red-baiting. However, as the Cold War accelerated in 1947 and 1948, the CIO confronted the most hostile opposition it had faced since the bloody 1930s. Well-funded attacks on the right of labor to organize and terrorism against blacks and unionists escalated even further after passage of the Taft-Hartley law in the summer of 1947. The new law allowed states to ban the union shop, made secondary boycotts and picketing illegal, required union leaders to sign an anticommunist oath, allowed greater government intervention against strikes, and limited union political contributions. Within a year of Taft-Hartley's passage, seven of the thirteen Southern states had passed "right to work" laws.

As they lost federal support for the right to organize, unionists experienced defeat after defeat. A five-month campaign to bring the east Tennessee textile industry into the CIO stalled because the CIO's textile union had not filed anticommunist affidavits with the National Labor Relations Board, which therefore would not place it on the ballot in elections to determine whether it could represent the workers. Here, in the most heavily industrial portion of the state, as in many other instances, the Taft-Hartley's new provisions virtually destroyed CIO organizing. In Nashville the CIO's steelworkers union likewise lost a plant because the union had not filed anticommunist affidavits with the NLRB, and similar cases appeared across the South. The CIO as a whole at first resisted this provision of the law, but when unions finally did comply, they faced other bureaucratic barriers erected by the law's reorganization of NLRB procedures. By 1949 the NLRB had such a massive backlog of cases that the certification process took a year or more, ruining numerous organizing efforts. Organizers began to give way to lawyers, for only they could follow the intricacies of the new law.[36]

Taft-Hartley encouraged state anti-labor legislation, hamstrung the union election procedure, and emasculated federal protections for organizing. It also undercut much of the CIO's relationship with friends in the federal government. Its allies in the Democratic Party began moving to the right, as demagogic anticommunists began to take control of Congress and the media. In the South, the accelerating anticommunist rhetoric had the effect of cloaking segregationist and anti-union appeals with a new degree of patriotic respectability. Backed by the accusations of HUAC, Southern Congressmen, and the news media, segregationists could argue more convincingly than ever before that groups organizing for labor and civil rights were subversive and that persecuting them furthered American interests in the Cold War with the Soviet Union. Anticommunism and Cold War patriotism in effect gave segregation a new lease on life.[37]

The CIO had always faced fierce repression and combined attacks of racism and anticommunism in the South, but the CIO unions had maintained a semblance of internal unity. Now external pressures coincided with a demoralizing internal battle to sap the energies of unionists. Because of the actions of many CIO unionists themselves, Operation Dixie left an embarrassing record of failure and an ugly legacy of internal persecution that AFL-CIO leaders later tried to forget. As historian Numan Bartley summarized its results, "the organizing drive that some hoped would rally southern reformers resulted instead in the disaggregation and ultimate decimation of liberalism in the region."[38] If anything, Operation Dixie taught a potent lesson in how not to organize, showing how internal divisions within the labor movement could undermine all efforts to confront its more powerful foes in American corporations.

The Operation Dixie organizing campaign reflected political and racial divisions from its inception. Van Bittner, the Southern Organizing Committee (SOC) director, was an adamant anticommunist who virtually excluded left-wing and African American activists from Operation Dixie. In so doing, he removed from the campaign the people most committed to the principle of black-white unity and most willing to put their lives on the line in organizing situations. Bittner believed that hiring conservative white male organizers from the South could belie the image of the CIO as a radical outsider. He regularly issued directives that organizers should not broach broader issues of politics and fair employment practices, the very issues that animated the postwar Progressive coalition and that could attract African American support. Bittner told SOC organizers to cut all ties to the CIO's own Political Action Committees, in which Communists played a strong role, in order to avoid political issues and appeal to workers on strictly economic grounds—wages, hours, working conditions. "We are not mentioning the color of people," he said, and even stated there was "no Negro problem in the South." Hence, when organizers in the FTA, the Mine-Mill, and other leftists tried to advance civil rights issues, the SOC charged them with subverting the campaign. In Memphis, for example, CIO leaders pushed leftists out of SOC activities for supporting the work of the National Negro Congress.[39]

In an effort to remove the taint of association with interracialism and radicalism, the CIO also practically severed its links to its left-liberal supporters in the South. In line with the trend established at the CIO Convention in 1946, which passed a resolution strongly censuring the Communist Party, Bittner openly attacked the Southern Conference, which he claimed was "living off the CIO." Due primarily to the red scare, the CIO Executive Board removed the conference from its list of approved organizations. With CIO funding and political support gone, the conference quickly went into decline. The CIO still supported the NAACP, but that organization also began censuring and expelling its own leftists. Under the pressure of segregation's counter-offensive and burgeoning red-baiting, the SOC detached the CIO from what few allies it had, namely those people who belonged to the Progressive movement in the South. In so doing, it alienated and marginalized potential African American recruits, as well as cut off much-needed support by labor radicals and southern Progressives.[40]

Bittner hoped that portraying the CIO as a non-racial, non-liberal organization would lessen attacks against it and win over white workers. Racial issues could not be avoided, however, as civil rights supporters in the larger society fought to enact fair employment laws at the state and federal levels, to desegregate the armed forces, colleges, and schools, and to attain voting rights for blacks in the postwar period. Defenders of the status quo such as Strom Thurmond and the State's Rights (Dixiecrat) Party, the KKK, and later the White Citizens Councils would all fan the flames of white worker reaction against civil rights advances. Under these circumstances, neither the CIO nor anyone else could prevent intensified racial conflict, and no simple strategy for organizing black and white workers, together or apart, could be relied upon. But clearly some method had to be found for bringing both blacks and whites into the unions on a working basis, and Bittner and the SOC did not seem to have one.[41]

Lacking a clear strategy and perspective on how to deal with the problem of racism, Operation Dixie leaders did not prepare for the long-term and difficult process required to organize in southern communities. They thought they would crack the non-union South primarily by organizing the massive textile industry. The largest number of southerners worked in textiles, and CIO leaders sought to do as the CIO in the North had in the 1930s, when the Steel Workers and the Auto Workers unions won campaigns at some of the largest companies and thereby caused smaller employers (sometimes after much resistance, to be certain) to fall into line eventually. But this strategy did not work in southern textiles, for a number of reasons.

Whites overwhelmingly dominated textiles, with only a few blacks employed as janitors and in other non-operative positions. They proved especially resistant to organizing in the postwar period, though not because "lint heads" had no class-consciousness, as employers said. In fact, southern textile workers had led one of the most militant industry-wide strikes in American history in 1934. Employers and the state together blacklisted, jailed, and even killed them in the streets, and as a result of their defeat, those textile workers who still had jobs sought desperately to hold onto their precarious niche. Many of them left as soon as better jobs opened during World War II. According to historian Timothy Minchin, most of the white workers who remained during the postwar period felt they had improved their lot and at this point were not willing to risk their jobs by joining a union. Furthermore, in this bastion of white industrial employment, few white workers could envision themselves as part of the interracial labor movement of the CIO. Employers played heavily upon white workers' fears that they might lose their jobs to blacks, and the SOC organizing drives at major mills were complete disasters. For example, twenty Cannon plants employing 24,000 workers around Kannapolis, North Carolina, provided juicy targets for organizing; but most white workers would not join, and some even threatened organizers and chased them away.[42]

By focusing on textiles at the onset of Operation Dixie, the SOC put its resources into a losing battle. They might instead have focused more resources on organizing in woodworking, furniture factories, food processing, and other industries where blacks made up a significant portion of the work force. These industries required hard, long-term, and expensive organizing in a variety of shops whose numbers, in most cases, paled by comparison to the massive numbers of workers that could be found in some of the largest textile plants. Nonetheless, CIO interracialism attracted black workers, who became the strongest supporters of unionization. And, as leftist FTA organizers Ed McCrea in Memphis and Karl Korstad in Winston-Salem, North Carolina, observed, even in a majority-black work force sometimes unions could attract enough whites to build effective multiracial unions with a significant degree of power on the shop floor.[43]

The left-led FTA's organizing campaigns in the Memphis food industry and in North Carolina's tobacco industry did just that; FTA organized a nucleus of shops during the war and created the most dynamic postwar movement in the CIO. In Memphis, FTA Local 19 had a black president and an energetic shop steward system that led the expansion of the city's CIO membership; the FTA also doubled its membership in Mississippi Delta food and cotton processing plants between 1944 and the fall of 1946. In eastern North Carolina, the FTA signed up workers in sixty-six tobacco-leaf houses and gained 8,000 members, based on civil rights unionism and strong black leadership. These activities were not all tied to Operation Dixie, but the FTA demonstrated that strong black participation and the acquiescence or participation of a smaller number of whites could bring success in low-wage industries. In the furniture industry, black organizer Leroy Clark recalled, exciting organizing occurred during Operation Dixie precisely because the United Furniture Workers Union (UFWA) had dared to organize black and white workers together. This entailed risks to organizers, who sometimes had to meet with workers at night in the fields, but UFWA organizing produced results. Indeed, based largely on initiatives by labor's left, at the end of 1946 the CIO claimed to have lost only 54 of 288 labor elections across the South, and the FTA claimed 15,000 new workers and 111 election wins in Operation Dixie's first two years.[44]

Women, not coincidentally, made up 50 percent of the new union members during Operation Dixie. Women in large numbers had moved into industry during the war, and many of them—especially black women—continued to work after the war, even if forced into lower-paying employment when soldiers returned home. As Robert Korstad documents, both during and after the war black women provided a potent organizing force in low-wage industries. The FTA's Moranda Smith became the first black woman to hold a regional leadership post within the CIO, and black women played a key role in creating the FTA's dynamic Local 22. Not

FIGURE 12.1 During the war, CIO unions organized the black workers at Nickey Brothers hardwood flooring company and in many other low wage shops. "Red" William Davis of the National Maritime Union, the Communist Party district organizer, set up picket lines of white NMU members to support blacks during a 1946 strike at Nickey Brothers, but soon the CIO expelled Davis and others leading interracial activities. *Credit: Photo courtesy of Ed McCrea.*

only in the tobacco industry, but also in woodworking, textile, and various service industries, women workers potentially provided a new base, if unions applied a suitable strategy of community and rights-based organizing.[45]

And, as historian William Jones shows, success in organizing black workers was not just limited to left-led unions. With few known leftists among them, black workers in the IWA fueled a series of successful organizing drives among woodworkers in eastern North Carolina, in a period when most CIO unions had begun to flounder. They picked up strong support in the black community and among rank-and-file workers. Typically, employers refused to bargain even after the workers voted for the IWA, forcing its members in Elizabethtown to strike one of the major employers in the region. Despite arrests, beatings, evictions from company housing, and anti-union propaganda in the local media, workers persisted in their strike and forced the employer to bargain. Black workers, Jones notes, also forced the CIO's Operation Dixie leaders in that state to realize that civil rights unionism could be far more effective than the SOC's "race neutral" approach to organizing, which spoke only about wages and conditions and avoided the very issues of dignity and social welfare that most concerned black workers.[46]

These examples suggested alternatives to the Southern Organizing Committee's centralized structure, its focus on white workers, and its emphasis on economic gains only, instead of a larger vision relating unionization to broader black community demands for equal treatment and dignity. But anticommunism and racism, and perhaps a bureaucratic mind-set, cut short consideration of such experiments in the South. "The privileging of textiles, the marginalization of the left, and the relegation of blacks to a subsidiary role shaped every aspect of the campaign," as Zieger summarized the CIO's southern strategy.[47] Faced with an incredible external climate of reaction built up by the Republican Party, the media and corporate leaders in the late 1940s, the CIO's internal climate of conservatism also crippled organizing. Moreover, after passage of the Taft-Hartley Act in 1947, the CIO moved into an even more depressing chapter of its history in which it destroyed many of the organizers and the unions that fought hardest for black civil rights and interracial unionism. This Cold War within the CIO defeated the creation of a labor movement culture of organizing for years to come.

Operation Dixie simply codified what numerous CIO regional directors in the South (all of them white males) had long sought to do: to marginalize leftists and interracial activities in the industrial unions. For example, although he was a liberal, CIO regional director Paul Christopher purposefully gave control of the Memphis Industrial Union Council and the CIO's Operation Dixie activities to the racially conservative W.A. "Red" Copeland in order to marginalize the left. Copeland and his friends from the American Newspaper Guild sought to put an indelible stamp of anticommunism and racial conservatism on the Memphis CIO. Pete Swim of the Guild became Operation Dixie's public relations director, and later went to work in Southeast Asia to support the U.S. State Department's anticommunist program in Vietnam and elsewhere. Copeland, Swim, people like Earl Crowder of the Steel Workers, and other CIO union appointees mobilized the local CIO against "Communist" policies of civil rights, interracialism, and United States detente with the Soviet Union associated with the FTA and other left-led unions. Copeland, typical of a number of the CIO's Operation Dixie leaders, did not associate with blacks and refused to allow blacks or women prominent roles either as organizers or workers in CIO offices. According to Myles Horton at Highlander, SOC leaders thought union organizing consisted mainly of getting workers to sign union cards, pay dues, and support collective bargaining. They did not particularly support rank-and-file participation and control, a strong shop steward system, or contestation over social issues, the very things that leftists such as Horton thought made unions worth having.[48]

In 1948 conflict between local and national CIO leaders and CIO leftists at all levels came to a head during the presidential elections. The CIO had at first opposed the illiberal (in comparison to Franklin Roosevelt or his former Vice-President Henry Wallace) Harry Truman in his bid for re-election, but it eventually swung to his support. Under pressure from the Democratic Party left, Truman ultimately adopted a civil rights plank and defied a backlash from Strom Thurmond, Boss Crump, and other southern Democrats who walked out of the Democratic convention to form the Dixiecrat party. Remnants of the Southern Conference, along with activists from the Mine-Mill, the FTA, and some of the other Communist and left-led unions, however, did not accept Truman, who had already initiated an aggressive Cold War foreign policy. Instead, they endorsed Henry Wallace as a third-party candidate calling for a renewed New Deal and detente with the Soviet Union. Against the wishes of the national CIO, the heads of various left unions endorsed Wallace and urged people to work for his election. In the South, New Deal liberals and leftist unionists organized a Southern speaking tour for Wallace's Progressive Party ticket. They also ran black candidates for Congress and other elected offices. Wallace had an interracial entourage, including singer-actor Paul Robeson, and refused to abide by segregated seating or other conventions of white supremacy. Some of the most daring interracial and civil rights organizing of the era occurred during this campaign, despite terrifying mob attacks against Wallace and his entourage in North Carolina, Alabama, and elsewhere in the South.[49]

After the Wallace campaign the CIO severed its remaining connections with progressive interracial allies in the South, who now organized into the Southern Conference Educational Fund (SCEF). White Southern CIO representatives ignored SCEF and increasingly pressed for Highlander to adopt an exclusionary anticommunist policy. Its director, Myles Horton, resented this political intrusion, which went against the basic purpose of the school to serve unionists and community activists of all persuasions. He believed that this demand actually reflected growing anger by some white CIO leaders at the increasing use of Highlander's facilities by black workers and its policy of holding meetings on an integrated basis.[50] The national CIO likewise pressured Highlander to establish a policy of political orthodoxy, asking it to specifically exclude the Mine-Mill. That union had long been a participant at Highlander and brought the most integrated delegations to the school. The CIO also asked Highlander to place an anticommunist provision in its statement of principles. Horton refused to do either thing. In July 1949, the CIO told Highlander that no Southern school would be held that year, and, as segregationist accusations of "Communism" against Highlander accelerated, the school's formal relations with the CIO came virtually to a halt. As Highlander went on to help build the foundations for the civil rights movement without AFL or CIO support, the State of Tennessee repeatedly tried, unsuccessfully, to destroy it.[51]

With the active involvement of Operation Dixie director Van Bittner, the CIO now began to destroy its own member unions. The 1948 and 1949 CIO conventions proscribed the unions whose programs were supposedly directed toward achievement of the Communist Party program. CIO President Philip Murray in 1948 scourged Communist union leaders as "degraded thinkers, dry rot leaders, afflictions on mankind," and by 1949 labeled them "sulking cowards, apostles of hate." In places like Memphis, conservative white males in the CIO leadership especially appreciated this attack on the left, which had been all too insistent on racial equality. Communist labor organizers Ed McCrea in the FTA and Red Davis in the National Maritime Union (NMU) had built the CIO from the ground up in Memphis, bringing poor whites and blacks together on the waterfront and in the cotton processing mills. Now the Memphis Labor Council expelled them after they insisted on desegregating the CIO hall, claiming that their fight for desegregation was merely a Communist ploy. At the local level throughout the South, the right wing of the labor movement took over by pandering to anticommunism, and often to racism as well. Frightened centrists, people such as Richard Routon of the Rubber Workers union in Memphis, who had gone to Highlander and had long worked with Communists in the CIO, went silent, rather than make themselves targets for red-baiting.[52]

Historian Philip Foner accurately concluded that the CIO leadership ultimately "devoted more attention after 1948 to destroying unions than to organizing the South." The CIO expelled eleven of its unions with close to one million members, including the Mine-Mill and the FTA, both mainstays of interracial southern organizing since the 1930s. Both of these pioneer unions were destroyed, and so were others. Some left-led unions with strong anti-racist programs managed to stay in the CIO, most notably the United Packinghouse Workers Union, which used its model anti-racist programs as moral pressure to stop CIO leaders from purging them, and the Furniture Workers Union and the NMU, both of which eliminated Communist leaders and organizers. The CIO now deemed pioneers who had built the CIO "unfit to associate with decent men and women in free democratic trade unions," if they were Communists or thought to be Communists, and discarded a number of the unions they had helped to create.[53]

In pursuing the purge, the CIO completely ignored due process rights and First Amendment guarantees of freedom of thought and freedom of speech. They ignored rights of member unions to make their own decisions, elect their own leaders, and follow their own policies. Union autonomy was a treasured craft union principle that would continue to be invoked after the AFL-CIO merger as an excuse for the continued existence of union segregation, but it was ignored during the CIO's red scare. The CIO's hearings were, in fact, little more than kangaroo courts, in which the prosecution and judge were one and the same, and which resulted, not surprisingly, in the CIO "convicting" left-led unions of ideological crimes. The "evidence" consisted primarily of the similarity of statements and resolutions passed by Communist union leaders to positions taken by the Communist Party or the Soviet Union. As in the trials of the Haymarket martyrs of 1886, or the Industrial Workers of the World and Socialist Party leaders during the red scare of the World War I era, the CIO convicted its own members largely for what they thought.[54] Ultimately, such leaders as Copeland went even further toward supporting what became known as "McCarthyism" by working with the Federal Bureau of Investigation, HUAC and its twin, the Senate Internal Security Subcommittee (SISS), and local and state "red hunters" to completely banish leftists from the labor movement.[55]

The CIO claimed the left-led unions did not adequately represent their members, but more balanced appraisals by scholars, including Robert Zieger, indicate that they represented their members as well or better than most unions, had more union democracy, and fought more aggressively against racial and gender discrimination. And, as Harvey Levenstein's even-handed study long ago documented, Communist-led unions proved perfectly willing to share power and even behave obsequiously within the CIO. "There is little evidence of pattern or grand design in the mosaic of Communist unions," much less the conspiracy to undermine the unions on behalf of Moscow of which they stood accused. On the other hand, the purge enforced a new conformity within CIO unions such as the UAW that, as Martin Halpern shows, undermined union democracy and rank-and-file initiatives.[56]

From the beginning, the CIO's Southern Organizing Committee had pursued a strategy of appealing to southern whites and accommodating the right-wing climate in the region. Once the red scare within the CIO took off, it eased the way for resurgence of segregated locals and discriminatory practices, as segregationists across the South intensified their efforts to make the labor movement a bastion of white supremacy. CIO top leaders claimed they were only concerned about "hard core" Communists, but in the South, especially, the anticommunist dragnet included anyone who stood up against segregation or the U.S. government's escalating atomic testing and its military intervention in Korea, Vietnam, and throughout the world. CIO attacks on member unions in the South that passed civil rights or peace resolutions now gave credence to segregationist charges that union organizers, especially those who insisted on black-white equality, were actually trying to stir up sedition and bring about Communist revolution.

Employers and segregationists in the Birmingham area leveled this charge against the Bessemer local of the Mine-Mill, in which black workers had played a leading role since the 1930s. In 1949 the local suffered heavy attacks by a movement of white racists who wanted to take union affairs into their own hands. At the same time, vigilantes and police subjected blacks in the "Bombingham" area to an increasingly virulent campaign of bombings, beatings, and murders, creating a climate of terror that continued into the 1950s and 1960s. Following a number of confrontations and assaults on Mine-Mill members, white Steelworkers took over the Bessemer local by a narrow margin, in a vote that proceeded strictly along racial lines. Yet both the Steelworkers' president David McDonald and the CIO Executive Board later blamed the Mine-Mill for using the "Communist weapon of fear" and "racial hatred" to split white and black workers. The CIO continued to support the USWA local even as it became the preserve of lily-white leaders. Despite subsequent efforts by Alabama's AFL-CIO leader Barney Weeks to moderate the actions of some white union segregationists, much damage had already been done to union interracialism.[57]

In Winston-Salem, North Carolina, Local 22 of the FTA became one of the most tragic victims of the red scare. The CIO's attack on "Communist" unions aided efforts by the R.J. Reynolds Tobacco Company, the local segregationist establishment, and HUAC to destroy FTA's Local 22, which represented some 7,000 tobacco workers as early as 1941 and had obtained widespread support from the CIO and Southern liberals in its 1947 strike. Local 22's successes, the result of its strong support from black tobacco workers, many of them women, and its strong ties to the black community as a whole, made it a base for civil rights and labor organizing in the state and led to the election of the first African American alderman in Winston-Salem since Reconstruction. HUAC's "investigation," a red-baiting campaign in the press, and challenges in 1949 NLRB elections by the CIO's black-led but right-wing United Transport Service Workers union ultimately destroyed Local 22. This left the huge Reynolds tobacco plant unorganized—as it has been ever since. As in Birmingham, in the name of fighting Communism the CIO lent its support in North Carolina to the destruction of a militant, black-led union actively involved in the fight for black civil rights. As historian Robert Korstad demonstrated in agonizing detail, the destruction of the local undermined a generation of black working-class activists and largely severed the emerging civil rights movement from working-class leadership.[58]

These two incidents "constitute some of the most unsavory episodes in CIO history," according to Zieger, but there were many others. Black Furniture Union organizer Leroy Clark recalled how he was maneuvered into destroying a black leader of his union in Memphis as a "Communist" simply because he was too militant on civil rights. He also remembered how white CIO leaders during and after the red scare consolidated their power in order to keep the leadership white and create peace with employers. CIO director "Red" Copeland led the way in "naming" Communists within the local labor movement, in CIO meetings, before the press and with FBI agents, and finally as a star witness at the SISS hearings on Communism in the labor movement held in Memphis in 1952. Segregationist leader and United States Senator James Eastland and CIO leaders, the Urban League, and the news media ganged up on FTA Local 19 to destroy its leadership and decimate a union that had a strong interracial presence and leadership in low-wage food processing and cotton compressing industries. The purges not only robbed the unions of strong black leaders, but of black union leaders' strongest white supporters.[59]

At this point, more of the CIO's energy in Memphis went to promoting groups like the "Crusade for Freedom," aimed at "fighting Communism," than to organizing workers. It is not too much to say that some unionists turned anticommunism into a substitute for class-consciousness. Indeed, John Riffe, who became the last director of Operation Dixie after the death of Van Bittner in 1949, through anticommunism began a "comradeship beyond class" with some of the richest men in America in a group called Moral Re-Armament. The purges helped to create an ideological wasteland and to reinforce the most bureaucratic local leaders.

In his book on the CIO, Zieger justifies the expulsion of the left unions as necessary to save the CIO's political soul from Communists and to secure its practical relationships to the Democratic Party. Yet his own research shows how disastrous the purge and the Cold War proved to be for the CIO. As he acknowledges, it decimated the unions that had done the most to organize African Americans, other workers of color, and women; it created an atmosphere of conformity within the CIO that made all civil rights and peace movements suspect; and it strengthened the hand of the CIO's right wing. In the South, white men like Copeland in Memphis sought to impose segregation and an ideological pro-capitalist straight jacket on all trade unionists. CIO national leaders still hoped that Operation Dixie would provide "living proof" that the CIO could organize without its left wing. With such leaders as Copeland, however, they soon found that Operation Dixie proved just the opposite. Right-wing leaders with racist attitudes toward black workers proved incapable and unwilling to organize the unorganized.[60]

The failure of Operation Dixie paved the way for a new period in which organizing came to almost a complete standstill. From 1946 to 1953 the AFL's percentage of membership in the South increased slightly, while the CIO's overall percentage of southern union members slightly declined. For years, the two federations raided each other's members in the South. According to Ray Marshall, the CIO won 44,000 members away from AFL unions and the AFL won 40,000 members away from CIO unions, a net exchange of 4,000 members. CIO unions also heavily raided the unions of expelled left-led unions, wrecking or absorbing most of them. Following the abolition of the Southern Organizing Committee in 1953 and the AFL and CIO merger in 1955, organizing practically halted in an era of "right-center" unity. Textile union educator Lawrence Rogin, himself a supporter of purging Communists, remembered many years later how ludicrous the red scare had become, as one of the CIO's textile union leaders blamed Communists for the union's failure to organize white workers, in a union which had no Communists to speak of.[61]

Most unions ceased to be agents of social change. Black workers like Leroy Clark, George Holloway, Leroy Boyd, and others in Memphis remembered the 1950s as a time in which the unions turned away from their increasing demands for equal rights. In already-organized mass-production industries such as steel, auto, electrical, and rubber, lethargic AFL-CIO union leaders failed to challenge departmental seniority, segregated jobs, and the marginalization of racial minorities and women as union leaders. Nor did they move decisively into organizing minority and women workers in service industries, or even into organizing the growing ranks of white-collar workers. The AFL-CIO's increasingly white, male, bureaucratic leadership weakened union links to the growing civil rights movement. Although the national AFL-CIO did much to lobby for the civil rights legislation of the 1960s, it did not endorse the March on Washington of 1963 or the Poor People's Campaign of 1968, nor did it decisively challenge discrimination within its ranks. Black workers and the black community generally turned increasingly away from supposed allies in labor to create all-black labor organizations and union caucuses and to build the civil rights movement.[62]

However, the defeat of the CIO in the South cannot be chalked up solely to the overwhelming power of ruling elites dead set against unionization, or to the self-defeating politics of anticommunism within the CIO. Increasingly virulent racism among southern white workers, fanned by the segregationist movement, HUAC, the Dixiecrats, and Cold War hysteria made it more and more difficult for the CIO to do anything about organizing the South. It might even be tempting to conclude that dreams of creating an egalitarian labor movement could never have succeeded in the postwar South. Industrial unionists had long sought to convince white workers that they had more to gain by joining together with black workers than by trying to keep them down, yet egalitarian organizing efforts had been repeatedly defeated by employer appeals to whites to place their supposed racial interests above their class interests. Many white workers did believe they had a stake in segregation, for this system placed black workers at their disposal as "helpers," reserved the best-paid jobs for whites, and generally placed whites in a position of social superiority over blacks. Racism among white workers has always clearly been an obstacle to change in the South.[63]

CIO organizers had long argued that the racial division of labor, far from enriching the white worker, undermined unions and thereby pulled down wages for everyone, and helped to keep Southern workers among the poorest in the United States. CIO Communists like Ed McCrea, Red Davis, and Karl Korstad believed that reactionary racism among white workers had been in decline after World War II, and that the red scare's purpose was in part to close this potential opening toward class realignment in the South. They blamed the Cold War and the CIO's red scare for derailing the possibility of change, and they certainly did.[64] Yet white supremacy's wide and deep roots in the working class made the union movement vulnerable to an escalating campaign of racism after the war. Not only in the South, but also in places like Detroit, racism within the working class helped to bury the postwar dream of equality and mass unionization.[65] For example, in the wake of the Supreme Court's 1954 *Brown* school desegregation decision, many white workers in Memphis joined racist organizations and fought to maintain segregated job assignments, seniority lists, and union halls at the International Harvester plant. The pattern of working-class as well as middle- and upper-class white support for job and housing discrimination existed almost everywhere. Historian Bruce Nelson documents in great detail that racism remained the Achilles' heel of the American labor movement.[66]

Indeed, Allan Draper suggests that hopes for interracial labor organizing in the South after World War II were badly misplaced. He argues for a practical accounting of interracial unionism in the South; it worked when blacks were a majority, or exercised control over key aspects of the production process, but when whites had clear control they almost always used unions to keep blacks out of leadership and in the worst jobs. African Americans recognized these grim realities and had realistic expectations of what the union could and could not do for them under the circumstances. Draper contends that "the new southern labor history," some of which has focused on the daring efforts to cross the color line by Communist and leftist organizers in the FTA, Mine-Mill, Highlander and elsewhere, "may be blinded by romanticism." The left's idea that that racism could be overcome by "a racially principled, committed, visionary leadership," he says, fails "to appreciate the paralyzing dilemma that confronted organizers and labor leaders who recognized the costs of segregation but were constrained by a membership and region that were determined to defend it."[67]

The fact that deep racism among white workers created a huge obstacle does not prove, however, that no opening existed for organizing the South at the end of World War II. The CIO's "opportunities lost" after the war did indeed exist. CIO organizers had overcome racism among whites in the worst places and at the worst times, both in the North and the South, and the postwar era also provided numerous examples that organizing blacks and whites together could work.[68] By the period documented by Draper from the middle 1950s forward, however, the damage had been done, and organizing proved far more difficult. The left had been nearly destroyed, and segregationist and red scare propaganda had fanned flames of hatred and fear into a raging fire. Barbara Griffith's study of Operation Dixie shows that many factors account for the ultimate inability of the CIO to overcome the obstacles it faced in the South. But how tragic, that the CIO itself joined in the hysteria that made possibilities for interracial and civil rights unionism so dim.

Zieger believes that, as unsavory as its actions were, the CIO had no choice but to purge unions led by Communists who seemed blind to the bureaucracy and terror of the Soviet Union. "How long could a CIO tainted with the practical and moral incubus of Communist association have remained an effective force?" he asks. Looked at another way, however, the labor movement could not afford to lose its leftist pariahs. Even from the perspective of the AFL-CIO leadership, one might question whether the alliance or the ideological purity imposed by the Cold War was worth the price.[69] The expulsion of much of the left diverted attention from labor's real problems and it did not stop its factional fighting. Faction fighting within the CIO's textile union and between the AFL and CIO unions weakened the already disastrous position of unions within the southern textile industry, for example. Although Operation Dixie leaders had seen textiles as key to organizing the South, by 1952 only 15 percent of Southern textile workers belonged to unions, as compared to 20 percent prior to Operation Dixie. By the mid-1960s, this dwindled to 8 percent, one measure of the ultimate failure of southern organizing. In 1953 only 17 percent of the South's nonagricultural work force belonged to unions, roughly the same proportion as at the start of Operation Dixie.[70]

During the 1950s, with textile unionism in decline, black-led unions smashed, and the bulk of Southern-based industries still untouched by labor organization, the stage had been set for decades of decline. Unions in the South became increasingly moribund placeholders for a shrinking proportion of mostly white and male workers. Unable to organize a significant interracial base in the South, the union movement as a whole could not stop the hemorrhaging of organized industries out of the North to the South, nor from the South to unorganized areas of the Third World. And it could not revive its own status as a leader of social reform. At a national level, the loss of radical organizers and the ideological reorientation of the AFL-CIO led it to support American efforts to roll back peasant and worker movements in Latin America, Southeast Asia, and the very areas of the world that desperately needed organizing. As Nelson Lichtenstein argues, strategic failures by the unions led to their alienation from social movements of the 1960s and 1970s and their increasing marginalization by the end of the century.[71]

If the Cold War undermined the labor movement, it also undercut a more wide-ranging civil rights struggle. Only when civil rights laws in the 1960s opened up textile employment to African Americans did workers in that industry start to join unions again.[72] But by then it was almost too late, as industries began to move beyond United States borders. Splitting labor radicalism from organized labor and from the civil rights movement also helped produce a leadership of Cold War liberals in the Democratic party who, unlike those in the earlier Southern

Conference, Highlander, and CIO alliance, "identified national and international corporate expansion with the growth of democratic values" and "came to view corporate business development as an engine of southern progress," in the words of historian Newman Bartley.[73] Failure to address the economic issues tied to segregation and racism gave ample opening to demagogues like George Wallace, Richard Nixon, and later Ronald Reagan to mobilize white workers against their own class interests. Instead of the broadened coalition for equality that people like Martin Luther King, Jr., sought in the aftermath of the civil rights revolution, a new generation of Republican conservatives kept defensive, resurgent racism alive while brazenly representing the interests of capital.[74]

It would be absurd to argue that if only Communists and alleged Communists had not been purged, or if only Operation Dixie had been conducted differently, our entire labor history would be different. The forces against change were indeed powerful. Yet there is an important difference between fighting the good fight and losing, and fighting a bad fight and losing. Unionists often draw on the lessons of defeat and the remnants of previous movements to prevail in new circumstances. Some workers, particularly blacks, did bring knowledge and resources aquired from both successes and defeats in the labor movement into subsequent struggles for civil rights.[75] Although it has acknowledged the damage done, however, the AFL-CIO and member unions remain mostly reluctant to fully discuss the internal red scare and its effects. And the failure to organize the postwar South, at a time when the American labor movement had reached its strongest point, weighs heavily on the state of the unions to the present day.

Perhaps the persistence of a popular front program that linked the fates of poor people and workers across color lines might have provided more of a platform for continuing equal rights struggles; perhaps a more radical presence in the unions might have kept the urge to organize alive. We don't know what might have been. But we do know that the Cold War attacks on economic radicalism, on the right to organize, and on interracialism, together with the split within the labor movement, helped to open the way to an onslaught of an aggressive capitalism determined to whittle away the power of organized labor. Under this onslaught, the percentage of workers belonging to unions in the United States as a whole ultimately dropped far below the 17 percent who belonged to unions in the South in 1953. By the end of the twentieth century, most of the United States looked like the 1950s non-union South.[76]

In the 1980s and 1990s, factories closed, capital moved overseas, corporations broke unions, and labor laws typically became more of a hindrance than a help to organizers. With a weak labor movement, racial antagonisms often flared and African Americans, other workers of color, and especially women still occupied a disproportionate share of bad jobs, or held no jobs. Economic and racial inequalities widened, and neither political party seemed willing to deeply challenge these inequities. In the South, the labor movement remained at its lowest ebb. North Carolina, one of the most industrialized states in the region, still had the lowest rate of unionization (2.5 percent, as of 1997), while many other southern states followed closely behind.[77]

Many factors account for these conditions, and they are certainly not limited to what happened to unions, or even to the American South, during the Cold War. But it is important that we understand just how deeply the defeat of southern organizing in the postwar era cut into the history of American labor. It is a defeat from which the United States labor movement has yet to recover, in an era of global capitalism that has made organizing more difficult than ever.

Notes

1. Parts of this article were previously published as Michael K. Honey, "Operation Dixie: Labor and Civil Rights in the Postwar South," in *The Mississippi Quarterly* 45 (fall 1992): 439–452, used by permission. F. Ray Marshall, *Labor in the South* (Cambridge: Harvard University Press, 1967), 225–227; Numan V. Bartley, *The New South, 1945–1980* (Baton Rouge: Louisiana State University Press, 1995), 11.
2. Bartley, *The New South*, 23–33. Eleanor Roosevelt, "The South in Postwar America," *Southern Patriot*, June 1944.
3. See Nelson Lichtenstein, *Labor's War at Home: The CIO in World War II* (Cambridge: Harvard University Press, 1982), for a description of how union participation in the War Labor Board and other war planning agencies legitimized union organization through partnership with the federal government.
4. Robert H. Zieger, *The CIO, 1935–1955* (Chapel Hill: University of North Carolina Press, 1995), 229, on southern CIO figures; Robert H. Zieger, *American Workers, American Unions,* 2d ed. (Baltimore: Johns Hopkins University Press, 1994), 100–101, on CIO and AFL statistics; F. Ray Marshall, *Labor in the South* (Cambridge: Harvard University Press, 1967), 225–227; and Bartley, *The New South*, 48, on AFL southern membership.
5. See Bruce Nelson, "Organized Labor and the Struggle for Black Equality in Mobile During World War II," *Journal of American History* 80 (December 1993): 952–988.
6. Lucy Randolph Mason, "The CIO in the South," *The South and World Affairs* (April 1944); and Mason, *To Win These Rights: A Personal Story of the CIO in the South* (New York: Harper and Row, 1952), 30. See also John A. Salmond, *Miss Lucy of the CIO: The Life and Times of Lucy Randolph Mason* (Athens: University of Georgia Press, 1988).
7. See accounts of the role of black workers in Michael K. Honey, *Southern Labor and Black Civil Rights: Organizing Memphis Workers* (Urbana: University of Illinois Press, 1993); Horace R. Cayton and George S. Mitchell, *Black Workers and the New Unions* (Chapel Hill: University of North Carolina Press, 1939); Robin D. G. Kelley, *Hammer and Hoe: Alabama Communists During the Great Depression* (Chapel Hill: University of North Carolina Press, 1990).
8. See Steve Rosswurm, ed., *The CIO's Left-Led Unions* (New Brunswick: Rutgers University Press, 1992); Rick Halpern, *Down on the Killing Floor: Black and White Workers in Chicago's Packinghouses, 1904–54* (Urbana: University of Illinois Press, 1997); Roger Horowitz, *"Negro and White, Unite and Fight!" A Social History of Industrial Unionism in Meatpacking, 1930–90* (Urbana: University of Illinois Press, 1997); Roger Keeran, *The Communist Party and the Auto Workers' Unions* (New York: International Publishers, 1980).
9. See Philip S. Foner, *Organized Labor and the Black Worker, 1619–1981*, 2d ed. (New York: International Publishers, 1981). Zieger, *The CIO*, 255.

10. It is easy to criticize CP support for the no-strike pledge, but its position was the same as that of the CIO as a whole, and organizers often ignored it. Interviews by author: Karl Korstad, Greensboro, North Carolina, 20 May 1981; Ed McCrea, Nashville, Tennessee, 6 March and 17 October 1983, 29 October 1984, 25 May 1988; W.E. Davis, St. Louis, Missouri, 26–28 January 1983 (personal interviews are in author's possession). See Honey, *Southern Labor and Black Civil Rights*, 198–202; Lichtenstein, *Labor's War at Home*, passim, Keeran, *The Communist Party and the Auto Workers' Unions*, chap. 10, and Levenstein, *Communism, Anticommunism, and the CIO* (Westport: Greenwood Press, 1981), chaps. 8–10.

11. South Carolina figures in Bartley, *The New South*, 29. Robert Korstad and Nelson Lichtenstein, "Opportunities Found and Lost: Labor, Radicals, and the Early Civil Rights Movement," *Journal of American History* 75 (1988): 786–811.

12. On the coalition strategy, see "CIO" (1945), a pamphlet of the Department of Education and Research, Congress of Industrial Organizations, in the CIO Secretary-Treasurer Files, Part 2, George Weaver files, box 212, Archives of Labor and Urban Affairs, Walter P. Reuther Library, Wayne State University, Detroit. On the Southern Conference, see *Southern Patriot*, 1945–1946; Thomas A. Krueger, *And Promises to Keep: The Southern Conference for Human Welfare, 1938–1948* (Nashville: Vanderbilt University Press, 1967); Frank T. Adams, *James A. Dombrowski, An American Heretic, 1897–1983* (Knoxville: University of Tennessee Press, 1992), chaps. 8–10; Bartley, *The New South*, 36.

13. Quoted in the union newspaper *UAW*, 15 July 1942, and Federated Press news release, 10 August 1945, Highlander clippings on microfilm, and the *Southern Patriot*, 1944–46, also on microfilm, Wisconsin Historical Society (hereafter cited as WHS), Madison. On Highlander, see John M. Glen, *Highlander, No Ordinary School, 1932–1962* (Lexington: University Press of Kentucky, 1988).

14. Quoted in *International Oil Worker*, July 1945, microfilm, Highlander Clippings File, WHS.

15. On the Athens and Columbia riots, see *Southern Patriot*, March and August 1946; the Tennessee edition of the *CIO News*, 1946; the Columbia race riot files, in Region 8 files of Paul Christopher Papers, Southern Labor Archives, Georgia State University; and Gail Williams O'Brien, *The Color of the Law: Race, Violence, and Justice in the Post–World War II South* (Chapel Hill: University of North Carolina Press, 1999).

16. See Robert Rogers Korstad, *Civil Rights Unionism: Tobacco Workers and the Struggle for Democracy in the Mid-Twentieth-Century South* (Chapel Hill: University of North Carolina Press, 2003); and Michael K. Honey, *Southern Labor and Black Civil Rights*, and *BlackWorkers Remember: An Oral History of Segregation, Unionism, and the Freedom Struggle* (Berkeley: University of California Press, 1999).

17. Zieger, *The CIO*, 228–230; James C. Cobb, *The Selling of the South: The Southern Crusade for Industrial Development, 1936–1980* (Baton Rouge: Louisiana State University Press, 1982), and *Industrialization and Southern Society, 1877–1984* (Lexington: University of Kentucky Press, 1984); Gavin Wright, *Old South, New South: Revolutions in the Southern Economy Since the Civil War* (New York: Basic Books, 1986); Bartley, *The New South*, 40. McCrea, interview, and Korstad, interview.

18. To see how the racial system kept wages down, see Honey, *Southern Labor and Black Civil Rights*, chap. 1.

19. Barbara W. Griffith, *The Crisis of American Labor: Operation Dixie and the Defeat of the CIO* (Philadelphia: Temple University Press, 1988), 10. Myles Horton, interview by author, New Market, Tennessee, 1, 2 June, 1981.

20. For a close account of how class power hinged on the racial system, see Honey, *Southern Labor and Black Civil Rights*, and, in another context, see Michael K. Honey, "Class, Race, and Power in the South: Racial Violence and the Delusions of White Supremacy," in *Democracy Betrayed: The Wilmington Race Riot of 1898 and Its Legacy*, ed. David S. Cecelski and Timothy B. Tyson (Chapel Hill: University of North Carolina Press, 1998).
21. See Griffith, *The Crisis of American Labor*, passim.
22. Statistics in Joseph Yates Garrison, "Paul Revere Christopher: Southern Labor Leader, 1910–1974," (Ph.D. diss., Georgia State University, 1976), 161; Marshall, *Labor in the South*, 264–266; different statistics are found in Bartley, *The New South*, 48, and Zieger, *The CIO*, 238.
23. FTA statistics in Allan S. Haywood to C. W. Fowler, Press and Publicity Director, Food Tobacco and Agricultural Workers Union, 28 March 1947; and Donald Henderson to Allan S. Haywood, 18 August 1947, both in Philip Murray papers, box 25, Catholic University, Washington, D.C. On elections, see Bartley, *The New South*, 70, and Steven F. Lawson, *Black Politics: Voting Rights in the South, 1944–1969* (New York: Columbia University Press, 1976), 127–128. As Lawson notes, however, unionized whites proved, at best, to be uncertain allies of blacks in electoral politics.
24. Zieger, *The CIO*, 238–239.
25. Bartley, *The New South*, 46–47.
26. The AFL had twelve blacks and two women organizers and more black members than the CIO in the South, according to Marshall, *Labor in the South*, 248, 249. The FTA and other left unions had black leaders and organizers, but, according to its records, the CIO's Operation Dixie Southern Organizing Committee did not seem to have employed any African American organizers. Operation Dixie Papers, Special Collections Department, Perkins Library, Duke University, Durham, North Carolina.
27. F. Ray Marshall, *The Negro and Organized Labor* (New York: John Wiley and Sons, 1965), 42–43, and *Labor in the South*, 247. Boyd quoted in Honey, *Black Workers Remember*, 202.
28. Marshall, *Labor in the South*, 269; Bartley, *The New South*, 48; Marshall, *The Negro and Organized Labor*, passim.
29. Zieger, *The CIO*, passim.
30. Wayne Addison Clark, "An Analysis of the Relationship Between Anti-Communism and Segregationist Thought in the Deep South, 1948–1965," (Ph.D. diss., University of North Carolina at Chapel Hill, 1976), 183–184. *Southern Patriot*, January 1945–December 1946.
31. *Southern Patriot*, June 1946; Stetson Kennedy, *Southern Exposure* (Garden City, N.Y.: Doubleday and Company, 1946); Lori L. Bogle, "The U.S. Military, the Radical Rights, and Harding College's National Education Program: Propaganda Partners of the Cold War, 1958–1962," a paper given at the Organization of American Historians conference, Chicago, Illinois, 28–31 March 1996.
32. *Southern Patriot*, May 1946 through 1953.
33. *Southern Patriot*, May 1946, July 1946. See also Robert C. Corley, "The Quest for Racial Harmony: Race Relations in Birmingham, Alabama, 1947–63," (Ph.D. diss., University of Virginia, 1979).
34. Mason, *To Win These Rights*, 103, 114–115; *The Packinghouse Worker* (January 1952): 10, on the Bemis incident.
35. J. C. Bradshaw to Lewis J. Clark, 19 September 1948, and Grover Hathaway to Ralph Helstein, 10 August 1948, United Packinghouse Workers Files, Office of the President, box 49, WHS MS 118; and Mason, *To Win These Rights*, 114–117.

36. The preceding two paragraphs are drawn from the correspondence of W. A. Copeland, August 1947, in the Operation Dixie files, Tennessee Organizing Committee, Perkins Library Manuscripts Collection, Duke University; Garrison, "Paul Revere Christopher," 166; and Honey, *Southern, Labor and Black Civil Rights*, chap. 8.
37. See Ellen Schrecker's *Many Are the Crimes: McCarthyism in America* (New York: Little, Brown, 1998) and see Clark, "Anticommunism and Segregationist Thought." The *Southern Patriot* in the postwar years provides many examples of the virulent conjunction of anticommunism, anti-unionism and racism. See also Honey, *Southern Labor and Black Civil Rights*, chaps. 8 and 9, and Honey, "Labor, the Left, and Civil Rights in the South: Memphis During the CIO Era, 1937–1955," and Judith Joel and Gerald M. Erickson, eds., *Anticommunism: The Politics of Manipulation* (Minneapolis: MEP Publications, 1987).
38. Bartley, *The New South*, 42.
39. Bittner, quote from Zieger, *The CIO*, 233–234. Honey, *Southern Labor and Black Civil Rights*, 232–233.
40. Zieger, *The CIO*, 233; Bartley, *The New South*, 45–48; Krueger, *And Promises to Keep*, 140, 142.
41. Barbara Griffith explains Bittner's approach sympathetically, but also suggests that only a few unions, led by leftists, had a strategy for interracial organizing: Griffith, *The Crisis of American Labor*, 62–87.
42. Timothy J. Minchin, *What Do We Need a Union For? The TWUA in the South, 1945–1955* (Chapel Hill: University of North Carolina Press, 1977); Griffith, *The Crisis of American Labor*, 46–61; Zieger, *The CIO*, 235–238.
43. Korstad, interview, and McCrea, interview.
44. Honey, *Southern Labor and Black Civil Rights*, 233–34, 227; Robert Rogers Korstad, *Civil Rights Unionism*, passim; Leroy Clark in Honey, *Black Workers Remember*, 185.
45. Korstadt, *Civil Rights Unionism*.
46. William P. Jones, "Black Workers and the CIO's Turn Toward Racial Liberalism: Operation Dixie and the North Carolina Lumber Industry, 1946–1953," *Labor History* 41 (2000): 279–306.
47. Zieger, *The CIO*, 234.
48. Horton, interview, and Honey, *Southern Labor and Black Civil Rights*, 228–229.
49. Patricia Sullivan, *Days of Hope: Race and Democracy in the New Deal Era* (Chapel Hill: University of North Carolina Press, 1996), 259–70; Curtis MacDougall, *Gideon's Army*, 3 vols. (New York: Marzani, 1965); Honey, *Southern Labor and Black Civil Rights*, 249–252.
50. Horton, interview, and "CIO Controversy" file, Highlander Research and Education Center Archives, New Market, Tennessee.
51. "Interracial Education Comes to Dixie," *The Carolinian*, 28 December 1946, and *St. Louis Post Dispatch*, 10 June 1949. On the controversy with the CIO, see notes on the meeting of Tennessee State Industrial Union council representatives with the Highlander staff, n.d.; Stanley Ruttenberg to Myles Horton, 5 July 1949; and Horton to J. Lewis Henderson, 25 February 1950, "CIO Controversy" file, Highlander Center files. See Frank Adams, *Unearthing Seeds of Fire: The Idea of Highlander* (Winston-Salem, N.C.: John F. Blair, 1975), 86–87, and Glen, *No Ordinary School*.
52. Murray quoted in Griffith, *The Crisis of American Labor*, 160. See Honey, *Southern Labor and Black Civil Rights*, chap. 9. Richard Routon, interview by author, Memphis, 18 February 1983.
53. Foner, *Organized Labor and the Black Worker*, 281. "Official Reports on the Expulsion

of Communist Dominated Organizations from the CIO," September 1954, 32, Publicity Department, Congress of Industrial Organizations, in CIO Secretary-Treasurer's files, box 109, Walter Reuther Archives, Wayne State University, Detroit; "CIO Rules Governing Councils Issued by the CIO Executive Board," 5 November 1949, 118, UPWA Office of the President, box 53, WHS.
54. "Official Reports on the Expulsion of Communist Dominated Organizations from the CIO," cited above.
55. Honey, *Southern Labor and Black Civil Rights*, chap. 9, and Honey, "Labor, the Left, and Civil Rights in the South."
56. Zieger, *The CIO*, 255–256; Harvey Levenstein, *Communism, Anti-Communism, and the CIO* (Westport: Greenwood Press, 1981), 70, 71; Martin Halpern, *UAW Politics in the Cold War Era* (Albany: SUNY Press, 1988).
57. *Southern Patriot*, October 1946; Marshall, *Labor in the South*, 259–263, 276; Horace Huntley, "Iron Ore Miners and Mine Mill in Alabama: 1933–1952," (Ph.D. diss., University of Pittsburgh, 1977). For a contrasting view, see Judith Stein, *Running Steel, Running America: Race, Economic Policy and the Decline of Liberalism* (Chapel Hill: University of North Carolina Press, 1998). Alan Draper, *Conflict of Interests: Organized Labor and the Civil Rights Movement in the South, 1954–1968* (Ithaca: ILR Press, 1994), 22–23.
58. Foner, *Organized Labor and the Black Worker*, 282; Akosua Barthwell, "Trade Unionism in North Carolina: The Strike Against Reynolds Tobacco, 1947," AIMS occasional paper No. 21 (New York: American Institute for Marxist Studies, 1977); and Robert Rogers Korstad, *Civil Rights Unionism*.
59. Zieger, *The CIO*, 375; Honey, *Southern Labor and Black Civil Rights*, chap. 9, *Black Workers Remember*, 186–192, 264–269, and "Labor, the Left, and Civil Rights in the South."
60. Zieger, *The CIO*, 376; Honey, *Southern Labor and Black Civil Rights*, 275–277.
61. Statistics from Marshall, *Labor in the South*, 269. Lawrence Rogin, personal interview, Washington, D.C., 11 June 1981.
62. These observations are hardly news to labor historians. See Bruce Nelson, "Working-Class Agency and Racial Inequality," *International Review of Social History* 41 (1996): 407–420; Herbert Hill, "The AFL-CIO and the Black Worker: Twenty-Five Years After the Merger," *The Journal of Intergroup Relations* 10 (spring 1982): 5–61; Foner, *Organized Labor and the Black Worker*, chaps. 19–21. See also the narratives of Holloway, Clark, and Leroy Boyd in Honey, *Black Workers Remember*.
63. Among other accounts previously cited, see also Michael K. Honey, "Anti-Racism, Black Workers, and Southern Labor Organizing: Historical Notes on a Continuing Struggle," *Labor Studies Journal* 25 (spring 2000): 10–26.
64. Davis, McCrea, and Korstad, interviews by author, and see Korstad, "Black and White Together: Organizing in the South with the Food, Tobacco, Agricultural and Allied Workers Union (FTA-CIO), 1946–1952," in Steve Rosswurm, ed., *The CIO's Left-LedUnions*, 69–94.
65. See Thomas J. Sugrue, *The Origins of the Urban Crisis: Race and Inequality in Postwar Detroit* (Princeton: Princeton University Press, 1996), and Kevin Boyle, "'There Are No Union Sorrows That the Union Can't Heal': The Struggle for Racial Equality in the United Automobile Workers, 1940–1960," in *Labor History* 36 (winter 1995): 5–23, and Boyle, "The Kiss: Racial and Gender Conflict in a 1950s Detroit Auto Factory," in *The Journal of American History* 84 (September 1997): 496–523.
66. Bruce Nelson shows that white workers in northern and southern steel plants used

union contracts to make it more, rather than less, difficult for black workers to obtain skilled jobs, in "'CIO Meant One Thing for the Whites and Another Thing for Us': Steelworkers and Civil Rights, 1936–1974," in *Southern Labor in Transition, 1940–1975*, ed. Robert H. Zieger (Knoxville: University of Tennessee Press, 1997), 113–145. And see his monumental study, *Divided We Stand: American Workers and the Struggle for Black Equality* (Princeton and Oxford: Princeton University Press, 2001).
67. Alan Draper, *Conflict of Interests: Organized Labor and the Civil Rights Movement in the South, 1954–1968* (Ithaca: Cornell University Press, 1994), 10–13, and see Honey, *Black Workers Remember*.
68. Halpern, *Down on the Killing Floor*, Horowitz, '*Negro and White, Unite and Fight*', Honey, *Southern Labor and Black Civil Rights*, and Foner, *Organized Labor and the Black Worker* all provide examples of unions successfully organizing in the CIO era despite white worker racism. Michael Goldfield in various studies has argued that the CIO had great opportunities but squandered them. See "Race and the CIO: The Possibilities for Racial Egalitarianism During the 1930s and 1940s," *International Labor and Working-Class History* 44 (fall 1993): 1–32, and see responses, 33–63.
69. Zieger, *The CIO*, 376.
70. *Southern Patriot*, October 1946; Marshall, *Labor in the South*, 259–263, 276.
71. Nelson Lichtenstein, in *What's Next for Organized Labor? The Report of the Century Foundation Task Force on the Future of Unions*, (New York: Century Foundation Press, 1999), 59–108.
72. Timothy J. Minchin, "Black Activism, the 1964 Civil Rights Act, and the Racial Integration of the Southern Textile Industry," *The Journal of Southern History* 65 (November 1999): 809–844, and Minchin, *Hiring the Black Worker: The Racial Integration of the Southern Textile Industry, 1960–1980* (Chapel Hill: University of North Carolina Press, 1999).
73. Bartley, *The New South*, 69, 73.
74. Dan T. Carter, *The Politics of Rage: George Wallace, The Origins of the New Conservatism, and the Transformation of American Politics* (Baton Rouge: Louisiana State University Press, 1995).
75. See the testimonies in Honey, *Black Workers Remember*, and Jones, "Black Workers and the CIO's Turn Toward Racial Liberalism," 305–306.
76. Lichtenstein, *What's Next for Organized Labor?*
77. The statistic on North Carolina's low rate of unionization is in the Raleigh *News and Observer*, 31 August 1997, cited in Jones, "Black Workers and the CIO's Liberalism," 280.

"A Dangerous Demagogue"

Containing the Influence of the Mexican Labor-Left and Its United States Allies

☼

GIGI PETERSON

Through the last decade of the twentieth century, coalitions of Mexican and U.S. activists worked to address the tangled issues of workers' rights, inter- and intra-American inequities, and racial and ethnic discrimination. Their work echoes that of a previous generation of Mexican and U.S. activists, whose efforts marked the beginning, rather than the end, of the Cold War period. From the mid-thirties through the immediate postwar years, a Mexican labor-left and its allies across the border evoked the U.S. government's Good Neighbor Policy as justification for anti-imperialist, anti-discrimination, and pro-labor struggles. These activists may be termed "grassroots Good Neighbors," for they challenged U.S. policies that fostered hegemony over other American countries, U.S. corporate actions that encouraged Latin Americans' economic dependency, and Anglo American claims of superiority over other American peoples. Their challenges helped shape U.S. officials' "containment" of progressive forces in the Americas.

In both Mexico and the United States, the ranks of the grassroots Good Neighbors included the overlapping categories of union organizers, Communist Party members and sympathizers, community and civil rights activists, and Marxist intellectuals. The Mexican labor-left discussed here coalesced around the dynamic figure of Vicente Lombardo Toledano, a Marxist lawyer-turned-labor leader who helped found the Confederación de Trabajadores de México (Confederation of Mexican Workers, or CTM) in early 1936. Soon after, Lombardo and his circle also inaugurated the Universidad Obrera de México (UOM, or Workers University of Mexico), which by that summer had developed an English-language newsletter and summer school to foster cross-border solidarity.[1] Inspiration for the newsletter sprang from the contacts established by Lombardo and other CTM leaders in the spring of 1936 when, soon after the founding of their own labor confederation, they toured the United States to meet with leaders of the newly-formed CIO and with other U.S. organizations, including communist groups and schools.[2]

Working from the late 1930s through the mid-1940s, the *lombardistas* and their U.S. allies helped shape a unique period of relative symmetry between Mexican and U.S. organized labor. The grassroots Good Neighbors found encouragement and useful rhetoric in the much-publicized "Good Neighbor Policy" of Franklin Delano Roosevelt's administration. Numerous factors shaped this policy, including earlier administrations' shift away from military occupations that came to be seen as ineffective or counterproductive. As articulated in 1933, the policy promised to end U.S. military intervention in Latin America and to give Latin Americans "a fair share" of their nations' earnings.[3] Policymakers in the Roosevelt administration also hoped that an improved U.S. image would enhance trade relations with Latin American countries. Initially, this dimension of the Good Neighbor Policy also included support for modest Latin American development programs, aimed at increasing the potential consumer market for U.S. goods.

Elements of the U.S. policy fit well with the Mexican labor-left's work to build an anti-imperialist lobby in the United States, particularly during the mid- to-late 1930s. These marked the final years both of Lázaro Cárdenas's presidential term and of the last major reformist phase of the Mexican Revolution. *Cardenismo*, the policies swirling around the charismatic figure of President Cárdenas, included land and labor reform, economic nationalism, and attempts to institute socialist education. Cardenistas comprised a heterogenous set of supporters, the lombardistas among them. Recognizing that cardenista reforms sometimes threatened foreign properties and ignited anti-Mexican campaigns in U.S. investors' circles, the lombardistas defended cardenismo as a "Mexican New Deal."

Paralleling New Deal plans for economic recovery from the Great Depression, by the late 1930s the Good Neighbor Policy shifted from redistribution and industrialization to emphasis on wartime production. By the end of the decade, the policy had evolved to stress hemispheric solidarity against the Axis powers.[4] At the same time, influential U.S. policymakers came to view Latin American nationalism and statism as threats to their economic plans for the postwar world.

Likewise, by late 1941 the lombardistas' cross-border campaigns had moved from emphasizing that neighbors keep their "hands off" the Mexican Revolution to promoting inter-American cooperation with the Allied war effort. Nevertheless, they consistently linked labor and civil rights struggles to the international struggle against fascism, and by the war's end reinvigorated their criticism of foreign capital's penetration of Latin American economies.

Lombardo, especially, began to address domestic issues in the United States, comparing racist and nativist currents in the Americas to fascist ideologies in Europe. He also emerged as a strong and visible Latin American critic of the U.S. government's postwar visions for the Americas. As described in one internal U.S. State Department report, "the long-range economic policy of the United States" was to develop in Mexico "a balanced and exporting economy . . . [that would be] an economic and strategic bulwark to ours, and a growing market for American goods and services."[5] The lombardistas' objections were part of a wider Latin American leftist prescription for development that countered the U.S. approach by calling for a strong state role in the economy and curbs on foreign capital and imports.

Universidad Obrera publications reveal that the lombardistas hewed to the Soviet line about participation in the Allied war effort; for the duration of the Molotov-Ribentropp Pact, for example, the lombardistas criticized the "imperialistic" warmongering of the Allies. To dismiss Lombardo Toledano as a simple tool of the Soviets would be facile, however, for he adapted tenets of international communism to fit the unique relations between Mexico and the United States. He was also an outspoken and consistent critic of fascism and anti-Semitism.

Lombardo was one of Latin America's most prominent leftists in the 1930s, and his rise intersected with that of Lázaro Cárdenas, president of Mexico from 1934 to 1940. Lombardo's political star had begun to ascend in Mexico in the middle of the decade, by which time the young attorney had converted to Marxism.[6] Though never a member of Mexico's Communist Party, during the mid-1930s to early 1940s Lombardo was perhaps Mexico's most important collaborator with the Soviet Union and the U.S. Communist Party (CPUSA).[7] After visiting the U.S.S.R. in 1935 he promoted both its foreign policy and its domestic programs, co-editing in 1935 a book with a title that summarized his positive assessment: *Un Viaje al Mundo del Porvenir* (A Trip to the World of the Future).[8]

Lombardo's early career in educational and government posts typified that of many well-educated Mexican leftists, and in the late 1920s through early 1930s he also held important posts in Mexico's major labor confederation, the Confederación Regional Obrera Mexicana (CROM).[9] Among his projects for the CROM was conducting "worker education" programs that "planted the seeds of humanistic culture" in workers. Under scrutiny for various forms of misconduct, CROM leaders welcomed what they viewed as a "diversion" of worker attention.[10] Dissatisfied with the growing ineptitude and corruption of the CROM, in 1933 Lombardo and fellow leftists engineered a diversion of another sort: they founded a breakaway union movement that eventually became the nucleus of the CTM.

Even before these left-wing unionists reorganized themselves in the CTM in early 1936, they proved an important pillar of support for President Cárdenas. From the early days of his administration, Cárdenas faced significant opposition to land and labor reforms, and attempts to institute "socialist education" (that is, secular and materialist educational approaches).[11] Organized in a "National Committee in Defense of the Proletariat" (Comité Nacional en Defensa Proletaria, or CNDP), the Mexican labor-left supported cardenismo against enemies such as former president Plutarco Calles, a CROM ally whose dictatorial ambitions eventually earned him exile in Los Angeles. The CNDP, comprised of overlapping categories of Mexican Communists, lombardistas, and other left-leaning unionists, served as the basis for the CTM, which held its founding congress in February

1936.[12] In return for their support for cardenismo, the lombardistas and the CTM enjoyed significant, though not unqualified, support from Cárdenas.[13]

While circulating through prominent positions in the CTM, Lombardo and his circle also drew on their backgrounds as educators by operating the Universidad Obrera de México and publishing periodicals and pamphlets. Dedicated in 1936, the UOM offered "class-conscious education" to Mexican workers and developed an English language summer school that brought its first class to Mexico City in July 1936. The roots of the Universidad Obrera de México lay in a preparatory school created to serve disadvantaged students, the Preparatoria Gabino Barreda, founded by Lombardo and other educational reformers in 1933. Reorganized as the Universidad Gabino Barreda, its faculty included Lombardo and others who had been expelled from the National University of Mexico for their Marxist ideas.[14]

The same year the summer school began, the UOM began to publish *The Mexican Labor News*. The editors aimed to publish weekly, though during some spells the publication came out less often; it ran three-to-four mimeographed pages in length. This English-language paper reported on Mexican labor and politics from the point of view of the lombardistas. Mailed to "labor and liberal circles" that ranged from unions to university libraries, the *Mexican Labor News* emphasized Mexican parallels to and solidarity with the CIO and other "progressive" forces in the United States.[15] Another Universidad Obrera publication with transnational reach was the monthly magazine *Futuro*. Directed toward Spanish-reading leftists, this publication presented content that was decidedly more radical. Published from 1933 to 1945, *Futuro* covered international issues from a perspective that reflected Soviet interpretations as well as the influence of Spanish Republicans, many of whom became exiles in Mexico—with some contributing writings and artwork to *Futuro* and other UOM publications.[16] The magazine also devoted considerable attention to U.S. politics and often featured articles in translation by prominent U.S. leftists. Coverage of U.S. developments also marked another of the lombardistas' regular publications, the CTM organ *El Popular*, which was directed at a general Mexican readership. The content of this CTM daily reflected the lombardistas' steady exchange of information with labor and left-wing sources in the United States, as evidenced by laudatory articles on the CIO, on Earl Browder and other U.S. Communists, and by reprinted articles and photographs.[17]

Sources vary in their discussion of the degree of official state support for the Universidad Obrera during the Cárdenas presidency. Some make the reasonable assertion that the Universidad received government funds. Lombardo's daughter, Adriana Lombardo, insisted that the Universidad functioned on a portion of unions' dues, and that while he was president, Cárdenas offered no financial help but provided assistance with matters such as visas and passports for traveling lombardistas.[18] What is clear is that Lombardo traveled for many years on a diplomatic passport, and Cárdenas gave the Universidad Obrera his blessing, providing donations and serving on its consulting council after he left the presidency.[19] In addition, the CTM enjoyed a symbiotic if not entirely conflict-free relationship with the Mexican state and, especially in its initial years, benefited from many favorable rulings by federal labor arbitrators.[20] The *Mexican Labor News* serves as one window through which to trace these rulings and the CTM leadership's responses.

The Universidad Obrera's publishing activities helped maintain Lombardo's visibility throughout the Americas, even though his domestic influence declined after 1940—when he stepped down as general secretary of the CTM and Cárdenas left office. Mexican national politics moved rightward under President Manuel Avila Camacho, who worked to dilute the power of former cardenistas, including the left wing of the CTM. Cognizant of a rightward shift generally in Mexican politics, both Lombardo and Cárdenas accepted and supported Avila Camacho's candidacy and presidency.[21]

While the CTM's new general secretary, Fidel Velázquez, continued to cement ties between the CTM and the state, Lombardo increasingly turned his energies to international activities. He maintained a steady stream of visits and other contacts with labor and left-wing activists in the United States. His travels and speeches also extended to other parts of the Americas as he promoted the Confederation of Latin American Workers (CTAL) that he had founded in 1938 to unite Latin American labor in an organization that would be independent of U.S. influence.[22] The CTAL differed from previous and later inter-American labor organizations in uniting only Latin American confederations. This marked a self-conscious attempt to avoid the U.S. domination of other eras, as in the Pan-American Federation of Labor, which the AFL attempted to resurrect in 1939 in order to undercut the CTAL. Because of these transnational efforts, especially, many key U.S. State Department officials viewed Lombardo as an influential and potentially dangerous Latin American figure.

In sum, even after his influence in the CTM began to decline, the highly visible Lombardo engaged in international activities that alarmed U.S. officials on several major counts: he maintained friendly ties with CPUSA and left-wing CIO leaders; he gradually became involved in the issue of domestic discrimination in the United States; and he offered left-wing leadership to a pan-Latin American labor organization, the CTAL, which in its heyday boasted three-quarters of Latin America's organized workers as members.[23] As World War II drew to a close, a fourth concern emerged as Lombardo advocated Latin American development strategies characterized by economic nationalism and state planning. These views collided with U.S. policy shapers' visions of private capital and free trade ruling the hemisphere's economies.

Over the years, many of Lombardo's critics focused on his close ties to the Comintern, and then the Soviet and U.S. Communist Parties, but the more astute minds among them recognized that the real danger lay in his inter-American influence in the four areas mentioned above. A sophisticated thinker as well as a prodigious writer and public speaker, Lombardo infused Marxist critiques of inequality and imperialism with the rhetoric and imagery of the Good Neighbor, the New Deal, and the struggle against fascism. The consensus among many U.S. policymakers seemed to support the assessment of U.S. Ambassador to Mexico George Messersmith, an accomplished State Department veteran sent to Mexico in February 1942 to ensure wartime collaboration.[24] Replacing the elderly Josephus Daniels, whose sympathies lay with many of the redistributive aspects of cardenismo, Messermith expressed sensibilities that fit within the rightward shifts in both the Mexican and U.S. administrations. Lombardo, Messersmith observed in 1942, was "a dangerous demagogue and may be one of the forces with which we have to reckon in the postwar world."[25]

The *Mexican Labor News* and *Futuro* reported frequently on Lombardo's travels, and U.S. State Department records supplement this record of his itineraries. Lombardo's frequent U.S. visits covered a wide range of venues and audiences, including Fourth of July and Labor Day rallies in Texas, California State CIO Conventions, and a fellow Mexican intellectual's class at George Washington University.[26] Though Lombardo was perhaps the most well-known and well-traveled of the Mexican labor-left's "ambassadors" to the United States, he was part of a much broader stream of individuals and information that flowed between the CTM and CIO. From 1936 through the early 1940s, CTM and CIO leaders exchanged friendly correspondence and sent delegates to each other's conventions, both for national and regional confederations and for unions in particular industries. Illustrating the range of such exchanges were the CTM representatives who journeyed north for the 1936 American Federation of Teachers convention, and the U.S. oilworkers who served as fraternal delegates to the Third Congress of the CTAL.[27] With much fanfare, John L. Lewis himself had addressed the founding convention of the CTAL in 1938. Like the lombardistas, Lewis also linked union struggles to international concerns. His speech to the CTAL convention echoed themes the lombardistas often emphasized in their overtures to U.S. labor, including the idea that the CIO would join with "the workers of the Western Hemisphere and workers everywhere to fight our common foe and to a common end."[28]

Lewis's appearance in Mexico City paralleled Lombardo's many visits to the United States. As diplomatic historian Samuel Flagg Bemis, a contemporary, noted, "Mexican and American labor leaders fraternized conspicuously in the capitals of both countries. Labor had now become a factor to be reckoned with in inter-American diplomacy."[29] Engaging in some diplomacy of its own, the CIO established a Committee on Latin American Affairs in 1939. Its members included Mine Mill and Smelter Worker (Mine-Mill) President Reid Robinson, and Kathryn Lewis, daughter and personal secretary of the CIO's John L. Lewis.[30] Ms. Lewis's travels to Latin America included traveling to the 1939 Eighth Pan American Conference in Lima as a U.S. delegate appointed by President Roosevelt.[31] The following year she followed in her father's footsteps by attending the CTAL convention in Mexico City as a CIO delegate.[32]

Especially while Lombardo and Lewis headed their respective labor confederations, a steady stream of telegrams and other messages of solidarity passed between the CTM and CIO. The *Mexican Labor News*, especially, touted these communiqués, often quoting them to illustrate the "brotherly relations" between the national confederations and their leaders.[33] One measure of the efficacy of these alternative diplomatic channels became apparent in 1938, when President Cárdenas nationalized the properties of petroleum companies that had defied Mexico's labor law and its Supreme Court. Through the years of wrangling over compensation, calls for U.S. intervention, and oil companies' boycott of Mexican petroleum, the cooperation among grassroots Good Neighbors helped shape the CIO's response to the nationalization. The U.S. organization swung solidly in support of Cárdenas and the CTM. Reporting on one manifestation of this solidarity, U.S. Ambassador to Mexico Josephus Daniels informed the Secretary of State that "all the [Mexico City] morning papers give considerable prominence to the exchange of telegrams between Licenciado Lombardo Toledano . . . and Mr. John L. Lewis." Even the conservative paper *Excelsior*, he noted, published a copy of Lewis's telegram of support, "under the headlines: 'C.I.O. backs Oil Workers.' "[34]

Back in the United States, certain West Coast CIO locals, including some with significant Latino membership, sent letters to the State Department and urged a settlement that would respect Mexican sovereignty.[35] The ILWU stood among the Pacific Coast unions supporting Cárdenas's nationalization, and the San Francisco CIO Industrial Union Council as a whole also supported the Mexican position.[36] John L. Lewis even helped circumvent the boycott by arranging contacts with a middleman who channeled Mexican oil to other markets, including Axis powers.[37] All of these factors helped prompt Roosevelt Administration officials to engineer a face-saving resolution for all sides.[38]

In addition to these demonstrations of solidarity and links among top leaders, CTM and CIO locals engaged in collaboration of a more practical nature, aiding each other's strikes and organizing Mexican-descent workers in the western and southwestern United States.[39] In 1936, for example, Mexican dockworkers refused to handle ships loaded by strikebreakers in the United States. By 1938, the West Coast International Longshoremen's and Warehousemen's Union (ILWU) refused to handle "hot cargoes" from Mexico, as defined by Mexican waterfront unions.[40] The ILWU's internationalism stemmed from many members of its rank and file, and from the radical leadership of Harry Bridges, whose affinity for Mexican labor developed in the early 1920s, when he was "thrilled" to learn of organized labor's gains there. Meanwhile, laudatory coverage of Bridges graced Mexican left-wing publications. Lombardo's attendance at California CIO conventions also demonstrated the ties between the Mexican labor-left and the ILWU, which included not only dockworkers but warehouse and pharmaceutical workers, many of them Latinos.[41]

In other industries, cross-border solidarity and reciprocal aid also shaped union activities, especially in the border regions. The Mine Mill workers were especially adept in using transnational collaboration to build their locals.[42] With deep historical roots in the radical movements of Western miners, Mine-Mill's internationalism was shaped by leftist leaders, significant numbers of Latino mineral workers, and the fact that labor on both sides of the U.S.–Mexican border had long battled common enemies like the American Smelting and Refining Company (ASARCO)—a point frequently emphasized in the *Mexican Labor News*.[43] Exemplifying the U.S. unionists' desire for collaboration was a 1937 letter that the Denver Mine Mill branch sent to a CTM local, pledging moral, and if necessary, financial support to their Mexican counterparts who were battling ASARCO.[44]

In other locations, solidarity extended to union organizing itself. Mine-Mill organizing drives in Laredo, El Paso, and other parts of Texas were assisted by the CTM and by sympathetic Mexican consuls. For a 1939 organizing campaign in El Paso, the CTM lent Mine-Mill one of its organizers, and set about organizing Mexican smelter workers (who would cross the border to work in the United States) in their home city of Ciudad Juárez. The unionists also received support from a cardenista Mexican consul stationed in El Paso.[45] Noting this collaboration and reports of reciprocal aid during strikes, the U.S. Consul General in Ciudad Juárez communicated his alarm to Secretary of State Cordell Hull.

This transnational union activity, worried Consul William Blocker, "might possibly be indicative of an important change in the relations between worker and employer in the entire hemisphere."[46] Deep suspicion of the Mexican labor-left colored many of Blocker's communications to the State Department. From a previous post at the U.S. Consulate in Monterrey, in 1938 he had warned that the "intelligent class of Mexicans" feared that the boycott of Mexican oil might press the Mexican government so severely that "close advisors of the President, namely Toledano [sic], [Francisco] Múgica, and [Luis] Rodríguez, will forc[e] upon President Cárdenas an openly communistic program." With the support of workers who "believe[d] in Cárdenas," they would seize all industry and instigate a coup.[47] Though the feared coup never transpired, Blocker moved to another key post in the border region, the Ciudad Juárez Consulate. In 1941 he was entrusted with a "strictly confidential" survey of another important issue in U.S.–Mexican relations: discrimination against Mexican ethnics in the Southwestern United States.[48] The "Texas-reared" Blocker based much of his report on frank conversations with political officials in his home state, from Governor Coke Stevenson to local mayors and sheriffs,[49] and even old friends and a "kinsman" within the Texas state bureaucracy.[50] The final report downplayed reports of discrimination and sharply criticized the influences that had seeped northward across the Mexican-U.S. border.

Blocker linked the Mexican labor-left not only to labor struggles in the southwestern United States, but to anti-discrimination activism that exposed the less-than-neighborly treatment of ethnic Mexicans.[51] In his 1942 report to the State Department on the issue of discrimination, Blocker warned of a dangerous combination of Mexican influences. The CTM had "whipped into line" politicians and business sectors, he argued, and encouraged by the reformist government of President Lázaro Cárdenas, new attitudes of "social freedom . . . spread like wildfire," including into the United States. These dangerous attitudes "inspire[d] Mexicans to demand a better status wherever they may be found."[52]

In the United States, Blocker argued, this "wildfire" of spreading radicalism threatened longtime social and economic practices, encouraging Latino organizations and Mexican consuls to make "mountains out of molehills" of incidents of alleged discrimination.[53] These activists and consuls used the Good Neighbor Policy "to force special recognition of social privileges" and championed even the "lower strata" of ethnic Mexicans, who had formerly been "willing and hard workers" content with their lot.[54] Though Blocker's report illustrates an unsympathetic view of these influences, he observed what both contemporaries and later scholars have pointed out, that popular memories of the Mexican Revolution *did* influence political culture—and many social movements—among Mexican immigrants and Mexican Americans in the United States. Just as the lombardistas evoked the imagery of the Mexican Revolution to portray, to their U.S. allies, a progressive Mexico in which CTM unionists were on the march, so ethnic Mexicans could evoke their Mexico's revolutionary traditions—reworked and re-imagined—to justify struggles for justice on U.S. soil.[55]

Blocker's report reflected the biases of those fellow Texans—Anglos, all of them—whom he had interviewed. Blocker cast anti-Mexican discrimination in his home state as an issue of class. Defending local norms, he concluded that with a few rare exceptions, "white collar class" Mexicans were treated with courtesy, and that when discrimination occurred, it was based on hygiene and "social status derived from the position in the community rather than from racial classification." Blocker argued that "Lulacs" [chapters of the League of United Latin-American Citizens (LULAC), a middle-class, assimilationist-oriented organization] and consuls "have been reaching too far down into the lower strata of their people for equal social recognition."[56] The Latin psyche also played a role, he argued, for in "the battle of temperament between the Indian blood mixed with the Moor and the Castilian," emotionalism and hyper-sensitivity resulted.[57]

Blocker's report reveals many blind spots in its denial of discrimination, which had become a sore point in U.S.–Mexican relations by the early 1940s.[58] Allegations of discrimination against U.S. workers of Mexican descent hampered negotiations over Mexico's sending guest workers, or braceros, to the United States to alleviate wartime labor shortages, primarily in agriculture. In its initial agreement with the U.S. government, the Mexican government even refused to send braceros to Texas, the state with the most abuses.

Blocker's views bore some similarities to those of another border area official who sent the State Department frequent warnings about Mexican radicalism. Chris Fox, sheriff of El Paso County, Texas, saw a grand Communist conspiracy in the collaboration among the CTM, CIO, and U.S. groups such as LULAC and El Congreso del Pueblo de Habla Española (the Spanish-Speaking People's Congress).

Sheriff Fox harassed and arrested unionists and other activists in his jurisdiction, from Mine-Mill members to El Paso's Mexican Consul Manuel Esparza, who assisted labor and civil rights activists and ended up being reassigned because of U.S. pressure.[59] As vice president and general manager of the El Paso Chamber of Commerce, Fox also expressed resentment of outsiders' attempts to raise the issue of discrimination in Texas. In one letter to Blocker, he railed against holding Fair Employment Practices Committee (FEPC) hearings in Texas, arguing that "another one of the President's Committee[s] [would be] stirring up strife, trouble, fear, and suspicion," just when Anglo Texans "sponsored many celebrations" and went to great effort and expense to "iron out difficulties."[60] Seconding Fox's arguments against using this wartime commission to probe the issue of discrimination, Blocker advised the State Department against holding public hearings, asserting that they would "antagonize employers and cast doubt in the mind of Latin employees as to the friendly attitude of Anglo employers."[61] State Department officials were not of one mind regarding the hearings, and for many, their positions changed over time. Blocker's input appears to have been influential. U.S. Ambassador to Mexico George Messersmith weighed in as well, and in the end State Department officials opposed FEPC hearings in the Southwest.[62]

Though Blocker's and Fox's concerns about the swirl of radicalism in the border region reflect their own attitudes about challenges to economic and social relations, the two officials were correct about the fact of collaboration among the CTM, Mexican consuls, and U.S. organizations, including El Congreso del Pueblo de Habla Española. Established in 1938 as an umbrella organization for labor and civil rights groups, the Congreso del Pueblo had many members who were CIO and CPUSA activists (or both).[63] The CTM sent Adolfo Orive Alba, of its Mexicali branch, as its representative to the founding convention of the Congreso del Pueblo.[64] An important left-winger in the CTM, Orive maintained contact with the U.S. organization's leaders, requesting information about California legislation that would halt relief for Mexican families and offering CTM support for the Congreso's campaign against such measures.[65] In another instance of cross-border solidarity, Congreso Secretary Josefina Fierro asked Vicente Lombardo Toledano to send a CTAL delegate to a Congreso rally in Los Angeles. The U.S. censor intercepting this letter noted that previously Lombardo had sent Fierro a packet of Universidad Obrera publications.[66]

Contacts with U.S. activists influenced the ways the Mexican labor-left addressed various domestic developments in the United States. The issue of anti-Mexican discrimination in wartime Los Angeles serves as a prominent illustration of this exchange. The connections between grassroots Good Neighbors lent a transnational dimension to one important issue in U.S.–Mexican relations: discrimination against Mexican American youth, many of them characterized as "*pachucos*" or "zoot suiters" who sported a counter-cultural style in dress and manners.[67] In Mexican slang, a "pachuco" was a young Mexican American man (or in the case of a "pachuca," young woman) who had become "Americanized" in speech and manners and who had adopted clothing styles and habits that affected a "rebel" status. While some pachucos smoked marijuana and engaged in fisticuffs with "clubs" from other neighborhoods, many others simply wore the loose-fitting pants and other styles popular among wartime youth.[68]

Characterized by baggy pants, pegged at the ankle, and a long and broad-shouldered jacket, versions of the zoot suit emerged among various urban minority populations in the 1920s and 1930s. Better-known wearers included some of the African American entertainment giants who emerged during the Harlem Renaissance, and urban youth of African American, Filipino, and Latino descent. In parallels to other epochs, the garb that began as a mark of urban counter-culture came to be part of an over-the-counter culture, as elements of the "zoot suit" style were adopted by young men in the U.S. mainstream. As one Los Angeles-area activist recalled, "kids all over the country were wearing drapes" (the loose-fitting, pleated pants that were part of a zoot suit).[69] But in Los Angeles in the early 1940s, the press equated pachucos and zoot suiters with outlaws and wartime saboteurs.[70] After clashes between groups of Mexican American youth in August 1942, the *Los*

Angeles Times reported that "Boy 'Wars'" and "Juvenile Terrorism" left a "grisly toll."[71] Headlines continued to emphasize this "warfare" and a "reign of terror" by gangs.[72] Like other area papers, the *Times* frequently quoted public officials who raged about the "terrorists" who posed a wartime threat. In one article, for example, Chief Probation Officer Karl Holton argued that "kid gangsters" whose behavior diverted scarce wartime resources were "all saboteurs."[73] A perusal of *Los Angeles Times* articles shortly before the Sleepy Lagoon case reveals the regular emphasis on the "un-American" and "traitorous" activities of labor and community activists, often emphasizing any foreign elements.

These images of a community besieged by "terrorist" and "un-American" youth increased in August of 1942, when the *Los Angeles Times* and the *Los Angeles Herald* stepped up their usual invective about "un-American" groups to focus on "gang wars" and a supposed wave of terror perpetrated by Mexican-descent youth.[74] The precipitating event in this case was the discovery of the battered body of young José Diaz. Earlier, on the eve of his death, rival groups of Mexican American youth had clashed nearby, at a popular hangout known as "Sleepy Lagoon." A citywide police round-up of some three hundred young Mexican Americans followed, and culminated in seventeen being convicted—under circumstances later found unconstitutional—of complicity in Diaz's murder. Among some of the spurious evidence presented to the Grand Jury was a "Report on Mexicans" authored by Los Angeles County Sheriff Edward Duran Ayres. The "Ayres Report," as it came to be known, argued that a "biological basis" shaped Mexican criminality: the lust for violence and knives could be traced to Mexicans' bloodthirsty Aztec ancestry. This Indian background, Ayres argued, was ultimately tainted by the "Oriental characteristic" of "utter disregard for the value of life." This was part of the great "difference between the races of man."[75] Issued under the auspices of the "Foreign Relations Bureau" of the Sheriff's Department, the report implied that these genetic inferiors were foreign intruders who threatened decent society. Presuming to draw on Mexico's experience with its "Indian" element, and interpreting the Mexican Revolution far differently than the lombardistas, Ayres proposed tough punishment as the solution to "gangsterism" in the United States.[76]

Sentiments similar to those of Ayres tainted the trial of the Sleepy Lagoon seventeen, and the local chapter of the International Defense Fund initiated an appeals process. A few months after the convictions, activists from this initial nucleus of defenders worked to establish a broader coalition that tapped CIO locals, Los Angeles community groups—including minority organizations—and sympathetic U.S. and Mexican consular officials.[77] A March 1943 meeting brought together members of twenty union locals, thirty-four church, civic and youth organizations, and local branches of the Communist Party. Ignacio López represented the U.S. State Department's Office of the Coordinator of Inter-American Affairs (OCIAA) as an "interested observer." Mexican Consul General Manuel Aguilar, who quietly assisted the committee over the next year and a half, spoke at the meeting and invoked the Good Neighbor Policy, an important strategy that emerged from the meeting.

Eventually reconstituted as the Sleepy Lagoon Defense Committee, the group created a national committee with Carey McWilliams, an attorney and prolific writer on labor and minority issues, as chair. While McWilliams worked his own connections with public officials, the Defense Committee developed a wide variety of publicity, fund-raising, and letter-writing campaigns to promote the legal appeal. However, it was another set of events that brought greater attention to the case.

In June of 1943, U.S. servicemen on leave in Los Angeles provided the Defense Committee's cause with an unintended boost. Rampaging through Mexican *barrios*, they beat and stripped minority youth—many of them Mexican Americans sporting zoot suits.[78] Adding insult to injury, Los Angeles police responded by arresting many of the victims. Local papers' coverage of the so-called "Zoot Suit Riots" ("Servicemen's Riots" in some more recent scholarship) incited further anger and violence against the "un-American" minority youth. This local conflict flared into an international crisis, because Latin American media coverage of the attacks threatened to disrupt hemispheric solidarity, just as the U.S. government was seeking Mexican guest workers and other assistance for the Allied war effort. The behavior of Los Angeles' public officials in the riots confirmed the claims of defenders of the Sleepy Lagoon seventeen: these young men had been railroaded by police and justice systems that were deeply prejudiced against Mexican American youth.

The anti-Mexican discrimination in wartime Los Angeles became a crucial element in the dialogue between grassroots Good Neighbors, and their publications revealed this. A January 1943 article in the CTM organ *El Popular* painted the defendants as part of a broader population of hooligans. According to this account—written *after* the Sleepy Lagoon convictions but *before* the Servicemen's Riots—the pachucos had fallen under the influence of *sinarquistas* operating in the United States.[79] Founded in Mexico in 1937, the National Sinarquista Union was a right-wing Catholic organization opposed to cardenismo, lombardismo, and other left-wing currents. These leanings and the support that some sinarquistas gave to European fascism earned the wrath of both Mexican and U.S. leftists, who also manipulated their governments' fear of the fascist influence in the Americas.

El Popular claimed that the sinarquistas had supplied the pachucos with marijuana and asserted vaguely that "so things led" to the death of José Díaz. Thus, the lombardistas initially depicted the Sleepy Lagoon controversy as an attempt by fascist agents to provoke ill will between the Mexican and U.S. peoples, and the youths in question appeared merely to be pawns—albeit delinquent ones—in this conspiracy. This view fit with a disdain for the pachucos common to Mexican intellectuals.[80] It also illustrated the lombardista tendency to label as "fascist agents" those who posed any obstacle to Allied war operations or to the CTM. This tendency, visible in the *Mexican Labor News*, is also characteristic of Communist Party publications of the time, including the Mexican Communist Party organ, *La Voz de Mexico* (which received funds and other assistance from the CPUSA).[81]

In just a few months, however, lombardista publications transformed these youths from dope-smoking dupes of the sinarchistas to symbols of a bicultural Americanism. By June 1943, *El Popular* had rehabilitated their image: one article likened the draped pants worn by pachuco*s* to the garb of Argentine *gauchos* and gypsy flamenco artists. At the same time, it situated their flamboyant style within the popular culture of swing, declaring that it symbolized "the spirit of North American youth." The title chosen for this article, "Pachucos . . . Zoot Suits . . . Jitterbugs" made it clear that zoot suits represented not criminality but a quirky fad of the young.[82]

Then in August 1943, the lombardista magazine *Futuro* carried photos of victims of the Los Angeles violence. "Contra los 'Pachucos': Contra los Mexicanos" ("Against Pachucos, against Mexicans") declared the headline. The feature affirmed the youths' Mexican cultural identity at the same time that it decried the denial of their rights within U.S. society. By finally embracing the pachucos as *mexicanos*, the lombardistas parted company with Mexican contemporaries who disparaged these bicultural boys with an attitude. Exemplifying the negative view was the much earlier essay from 1934, "The *Pachuco* and other Extremes," in which the prominent writer Octavio Paz declared the pachuco "an orphan lacking both protectors and positive values." In contrast, the grassroots Good Neighbors—on both sides of the border—made these youth not orphans but possessors of dual parentage.[83]

The Sleepy Lagoon case became a very public part of these activists' exchanges, shaping each side's rhetoric and proving that the pachucos did indeed have "protectors." The grassroots Good Neighbors' insistence on the dual identity of the pachucos strengthens the case for using the term "Mexican American" to refer to these ethnic Mexican youth, a term insisted upon by some of their contemporaries. An interesting interplay can be seen between these U.S. developments and the lombardista attempts to redefine "American" in a continental sense that underscored parallels between progressive forces in Mexico and the United States.

By mid-June of 1943, Lombardo launched a blistering attack on Los Angeles officials and the *Mexican Labor News* published excerpts of one speech. "Race Hatred of Zoot-Suit Riots Exposed" contained Lombardo's assessment of Sheriff Ayres and like-minded bigots: they were "saboteurs of Mexican American friendship and of unity between the United States and Latin America."[84] Lombardo contrasted these saboteurs with "the labor and political leaders" whose work against discrimination proved them to be "the sincerest friends of Mexican-United States Good Neighborliness."[85]

His sincere friends in Los Angeles returned the compliments in their own publications, which also echoed the Mexicans' emphasis on fascist conspirators. A Defense Committee pamphlet affirmed that supporters of the Sleepy Lagoon appellants helped "Lombardo and other democratic leaders in Latin America" argue that "not all Americans think like Ed Duran Ayres or act like the prosecution that sent the seventeen boys to jail."[86] Thanks to Lombardo's efforts, the pamphlet argued, the "Mexican Fifth column had a limited success in capitalizing on the work of its U.S. counterpart."[87] While the Sleepy Lagoon Defense Committee's arguments incorporated rhetoric common to CP influence and organizations, the arguments also reflected a cross-border exchange of information. This exchange was shaped by Mexican leftists' interpretation of the unique relationship between Mexico and the United States, including the fact that the United States had historically sheltered many forces—*mexicano* and *gringo*—opposed to the reforms of the Mexican Revolution.

Joining in the transnational flow of alternative media, the *CIO News* took up the cause of the Sleepy Lagoon appellants. Articles with headlines such as "Race Hatred is Sabotage" and "CIO Hits Race Discrimination as Treason" turned the rhetorical tables on the media and officials who had long blasted labor and left-wing "subversives." Behind this antidiscrimination campaign were many of the same West Coast unions whose internationalist and Latino members had previously supported grassroots Good Neighbor ties with Mexican labor.

The *CIO News* also illustrated another connection to the lombardistas: in 1943 it began to cover Latin American labor, through reports by a young journalist from the Universidad Obrera, César Ortiz Tinoco. In 1942 Ortiz had toured the United States as part of a delegation of Latin American journalists, sponsored by the U.S. government in order to promote the war effort. Ortiz's trip ended on the West Coast, and he appears to have been one channel through which news of the Sleepy Lagoon case made its way to the lombardistas. After his return to Mexico, the Defense Committee stepped up its efforts to reach allies south of the border, including sending materials directly to Lombardo and Cárdenas.[88] Soon the more positive images of the *pachucos* appeared in Universidad Obrera publications such as *El Popular*, *Futuro*, and the *Mexican Labor News*.[89]

At the same time that U.S.-based civil rights activists educated the Mexican labor-left about the situation in Los Angeles, information from and about the lombardistas migrated north, as evidenced by the files of the Sleepy Lagoon Defense Committee and U.S. censors' monitoring of Latino activists. SLDC organizational files include materials discussing the CTAL and other activities of Lombardo, and the swiftness with which Universidad Obrera and SLDC publications quoted each other's representatives indicates a level of exchange. As mentioned above, censors noted pamphlets sent from the Universidad Obrera to Josefina Fierro, a member of the committee, including a publication titled "El Sinarquismo en México."[90] Like the lombardistas, the Defense Committee also inserted fears about sinarquista activities into their arguments, thus linking local struggles to international dangers. The committee's 1943 volume, *The Sleepy Lagoon Case*, combined this approach with a spin that appropriated some of the language of anticommunism, arguing that "as we take the offensive against the Axis enemies everywhere in the world, we take the offensive against their agents and stooges and dupes in California."[91]

Paralleling the rhetoric of the lombardistas, and often quoting it, Defense Committee publications framed this local civil rights struggle as part of an international battle. They too appealed to the Good Neighbor ideal, insisting that nondiscrimination and equal rights constituted *true* Americanism and that racism was a component of Nazi ideology. The grassroots Good Neighbors—on both sides of the border—also emphasized that halting discrimination was essential to preserving Latino and Latin American support for the Allied war effort. This was the argument that moved U.S. officials, at a variety of levels, to take action regarding the situation in Los Angeles. In response to the 1943 Servicemen's Riots, federal pressure curbed the anti-Mexican tone of local media, military authorities temporarily declared Los Angeles off-limits for servicemen on leave, and federal and local officials scrambled to create programs to serve Mexican American youth. Finally, in October 1944, an appeals court reversed the convictions of the Sleepy Lagoon defendants. This marked an important victory not only for the individuals freed from prison, but for the cross-ethnic, cross-border coalition that struggled for their release.

Elsewhere in the United States, cross-border connections also shaped discussions of discrimination. Soon after the Servicemen's Riots, Lombardo began to assail racism in his speeches both in Mexico and during his frequent visits to the United States. To a Fourth of July gathering of unionists in El Paso, Texas in 1943, he presented "The Falsehood of a Racial Interpretation of the History of the Americas," a speech that challenged the ideas espoused by prominent thinkers of his time, including U.S. diplomatic historian Samuel Flagg Bemis, whose book on U.S.–Latin American relations had been published that same year. Though Lombardo did not mention Bemis by name, the elements of his speech constituted a clear refutation of Bemis's claims that low "climatic energy" and the "volatility" of a racially mixed population hindered Latin Americans' progress. Lombardo instead drew on Marxist-Leninist theory to describe how imperialism had distorted economic development in Latin America. Lombardo argued that "the fundamental factor differentiating the two Americas is not race, but rather economic structure."[92]

Lombardo likened U.S. development to Latin American underdevelopment, arguing that both were "the work of a small group of big financiers, industrialists, and businessmen from North America."[93] Latin Americans' understanding of this fact, he explained, shaped their deep-seated anti-imperialist feelings. Latin Americans fought fascism, he asserted, because in accordance with the Atlantic Charter they wanted self-determination and democracy. They resisted the resurgence of "*imperialismo yanqui*" that monopoly capital could create.[94]

Though other Latin American intellectuals held and voiced some of these views, the lombardistas were unique in bringing them to popular venues in the United States.[95] In his July fourth speech, Lombardo drew on his listeners' familiarity with wartime hardships to emphasize the economic disparities in the Americas. Latin Americans, he argued, faced not temporary but "permanent privations," influenced by export monoculture's distortion of their countries' economies.[96] These arguments foreshadowed the economic plans that he and other Latin American economic nationalists would voice at the war's end.

Appropriately tapping wartime concerns, Lombardo's speech in El Paso also linked racial prejudice to fascism, thus weaving patriotism into a critique of U.S. domestic practices. "It would be absurd to combat the Nazi regime because it aims at establishing the hegemony of the German race," he argued, "if at the same time among our own people there exist discriminatory sentiments with respect to Indians, negroes, and mestizos, if people continue to be classified according to their color. No man in America can or should call himself anti-fascist or democratic if he considers negroes, Indians, or mestizos to be inferior. In this hour, all discrimination is a boost to fascism."[97]

Two days later, Lombardo continued to address social issues in the United States, as he explained to the African American congregation at El Paso's Mt. Zion Baptist Church that true Christians, like socialists, strove for justice. The two groups, he argued, needed to unite in order to preserve freedom of religious and political beliefs and to battle discrimination in all its forms.[98] No doubt appeals such as these fed reactionaries' arguments about "communists" agitating for civil rights.

Lombardo's interest in Texas manifested itself in another project that emerged in June 1944. A veritable who's who of Mexican artists, political figures, and intellectuals formed the Comité Mexicano Contra el Racismo (Mexican Committee against Racism, CMCR). Vicente Lombardo Toledano was one of several (male) vice presidents and his wife, Rosa María Otero Gama, was one of two (female) secretaries. Other prominent members included: Eduardo Villaseñor, president of the Bank of Mexico; poet and anthropologist Andrés Henestrosa; painter José Clemente Orozco; actress Dolores del Río; educator Alfonso Caso; and several senators, governors, and other officeholders.[99] Beyond the Comité's consulting council, it is likely that a number of members were simply endorsers who perhaps also provided financial support.

The Comité published *Fraternidad*, a magazine that reported on incidents of discrimination and the struggles against them. In addition to highlighting the victory of the Sleepy Lagoon Defense Committee and appointing the former SLDC secretary as a U.S. correspondent, the magazine's editors reported regularly on the work of the Texas Good Neighbor Commission and the cases that organization needed to address. Cover graphics for some of the issues were provided by Alberto Beltrán, an artist whose distinctive woodcuts and illustrations graced numerous Universidad Obrera publications.[100]

Despite *Fraternidad*'s coverage of U.S. groups and individuals working for positive changes, Ciudad Juárez Consul William Blocker resented this effort to raise the issue of discrimination. He forwarded copies of the publication to the State Department, claiming that "this magazine is not only Communistic, but radically a serious agent of racial discrimination." Though his comments do not make clear how *Fraternidad* promoted discrimination, he clearly viewed its publishers as "agents" who promoted conflict between classes and countries.[101] He complained to Ambassador Messersmith that the magazine was "becoming more and more vicious in criticizing Texas."[102] To State Department official John Carrigan he sent a particularly colorful copy, along with his complaints about its circulation across the border: "This is the rottenest magazine I have ever seen, and I am surprised that the Mexican Government is permitting it to be published, particularly with the names listed on the second page of the Consultive Commission thereon. It is as red as the red ink in which it is published, and its circulation in Texas certainly does not improve the racial discrimination situation."[103]

Blocker's complaints about *Fraternidad* echo the sentiments expressed in his aforementioned report to the State Department, in which he blasted activists who "stirred up" presumably happy "peons." Again, he saw the "reds" who raised the issue of discrimination as evidence of a spillover of Mexican labor radicalism.

Blocker continued to view this transnational activism as a threat to long-term U.S. interests in the region. "By keeping the border peaceful," he had argued in 1942, "our future with Latin America in the reorganization of the economic setup will come easier in making lasting beneficial arrangements."[104] Blocker's vision of economic cooperation paralleled that of other U.S. policyshapers—and it clashed with ideas posed by the lombardistas. Responding to the inter-American conferences of the late wartime and immediate postwar period, Lombardo and other Latin American leftists decried U.S. proposals that Latin American countries open their economies to free trade and private investors.[105]

One such important conference took place at Chapultepec Palace in Mexico City in February 1945, where representatives from the hemisphere's nations met to discuss future economic links. At this Inter-American Conference on the Problems of War and Peace, U.S. delegates called for discontinuing aid to Latin America, such as the grants and loans provided during wartime.[106] After the war, many Latin Americans expected to be rewarded for the sacrifices they had made to support the Allied effort, but by the 1947 inter-American conference in Río de Janiero, U.S. leaders had shifted away from policies to promote Latin American development, and aid was instead directed to Europe and Japan. These policymakers trumpeted private capital and free trade as the means for development in Latin America.

Many of the Latin American delegates argued that foreign public capital and state involvement in the economy were essential for their countries, and many of them supported tariff protection and curbs on foreign enterprises that threatened the "public interest" or the "just and adequate participation" of national capital. Nevertheless, in the final analysis, the Chapultepec Conference constituted a "victory" for U.S. business interests, and only a few clauses acknowledged Latin American concerns. As one historian puts it: "[The U.S. leaders'] postulates and assumptions . . . were in reality a modification of Adam Smith's division of labor thesis. The United States would produce manufactures and heavy items; Latin American countries would turn out semi-finished goods and branch off into light industry while still producing raw materials."[107]

Even during the war the lombardistas had objected to such an asymmetrical division of labor, and in the postwar period their anti-imperialist arguments resumed. In one attack on the Chapultepec plan, Lombardo described Latin America as comprised of "semicolonial countries" that served as investment zones for imperialist powers such as Great Britain and the United States. Latin America suffered "triple exploitation," in that foreign monopolies tried to gain control of important resources, set low prices for the primary materials, and set high prices for manufactured imports to the region. These trade and investment practices, he argued, distorted Latin American economies, creating regions of monoculture and thwarting development of industry, particularly heavy industry.[108]

Leaning on Marxist-Leninist theories of imperialism, Lombardo and his colleagues argued that Latin American development necessarily followed a different trajectory than in the United States and other industrialized countries of the global north. They argued that European imperialism (a system into which the United

States was eventually adopted as a junior partner) pressed colonies to specialize in the export of raw materials. Most of the wealth generated by such primary production had benefited the colonizing countries, building them into industrial powerhouses with which manufacturers in the less-developed countries could not hope to compete.[109]

Also troubling to State Department officials was the fact that the lombardistas frequently invoked Roosevelt and the Good Neighbor Policy in their critiques of postwar policies, implying that the policies marked a betrayal of FDR's progressive ideals. Like other Latin Americans who posed alternatives to U.S. postwar economic proposals, Lombardo framed his ideas as an extension of the Allied cause and the visions of its leaders. In the name of the CTAL, he even argued that the final Chapultepec agreement was "not only contrary to the interests of the peoples of Latin America, but also adversarial to the criteria expressed by the democratic sectors of the United States and of Great Britain, and in particular, the point of view expressed by the illustrious chiefs of those great powers, President Franklin Delano Roosevelt and Prime Minster Winston Churchill."[110]

The lombardistas' own proposals for protectionist and state-guided economies, including land reform and income redistribution, were, in the words of one astute State Department analyst, "in the spirit of economic nationalism and with industrialization of Latin America as the goal." This unnamed analyst argued that lombardista ideas were consistent with basic Marxist theory and strategy for the "colonial and semi-colonial world." Denying that Lombardo's de-emphasis of class struggle was a "crude switchover" decreed by Moscow, the analyst explained that this was "a far subtler shift centering about the 'anti-imperialist' (in the present historical juncture read 'anti-U.S.') facet of Marxist policy."[111] This shift helped explain why, in 1945, Lombardo sided with Mexican industrialists in opposing U.S. economic penetration in the postwar period. This act alienated him from some sectors of organized labor and confirmed the opinion, held by parties ranging from Ambassador Messersmith to left-wing contemporaries and later scholars, that Lombardo was an opportunist extraordinaire. More nuanced interpretations place some of Lombardo's political shifts within a changing Mexican political context that threatened to reverse many of the social and labor gains made under Cárdenas, though Universidad Obrera publications do reveal his *personalismo* and a degree of opportunism.[112]

Lombardo's economic nationalist alliance with Mexican industrialists also conflicted with U.S. policy shapers' goals, which framed Latin American countries not only as producers of crucial raw materials but also as investment zones for U.S. capital, a position summarized well by Messersmith in 1944: "At the end of the last war we entered into the "assembling" stage for certain products abroad; at the end of this war we shall actually have to begin manufacturing certain articles abroad. We can do this through branch American companies of the parent plant at home, using the same methods and techniques that we have at home and selling our goods under the same trademarks, but having the advantage of cheaper or more easily available raw materials, and particularly of labor cheaper than our own."[113] Despite Latin American protests, this U.S. emphasis on private capital emerged victorious, ironically, as Congress poured money and planners into the economies of Western Europe and Japan.

In addition to criticizing the economic implications of U.S. foreign policy, Lombardo continued to probe inequities in U.S. domestic affairs. In 1945 the Universidad Obrera staff mailed surveys about postwar relations to selected university professors in the United States and Canada. "What measures do you propose in order to end the racial discrimination which still exists in certain parts of the United States, against people of Latin American descent?" read one of the questions.[114] The lombardistas intended to send their findings to U.S. Congressional leaders and to the U.S. delegation to the 1945 United Nations conference in San Francisco. One State Department official reported that Lombardo himself would "be kept under scrutiny in San Francisco so it is very much hoped that he will be kept within bounds."[115]

Key State Department officials viewed Lombardo as an irritating critic of U.S. policies and practices who brought his critiques of imperialism, discrimination, and other presumed U.S. ills to a variety of forums. He was all the more dangerous to U.S. interests because, as Ambassador Messersmith put it, he was viewed "as a sort of apostle and a great leader" by many labor leaders and much of the public in Latin America.[116]

U.S. officials targeted this apostle and his allies in a variety of ways, and many of their tactics foreshadowed future forms of "containment" in the Americas. Surveillance activities, expanded during wartime, established some of the institutional and ideological bases for later intelligence-gathering on Latin American forces for social change. Much of this intelligence work crossed the line into outright intrigue, from hopes of smearing Lombardo to concerted efforts to undermine his U.S. and Latin American supporters.

From the time Lombardo rose to prominence as co-founder and Secretary General of the CTM in 1936, U.S. officials had spied and reported on his activities. A 1938 State Department directive instructed all consular officers in Mexico to prepare regular reports on labor leaders in their areas, and in 1942 officers were specifically directed to monitor Lombardo.[117] State Department records, especially from the Mexico City Embassy, include volumes of clippings about Lombardo's travels, speeches, and writings. The records also reveal FBI and embassy interception of Lombardo's telephone conversations, telegraphic and mail correspondence, and surveillance of his travels, including in the United States.[118] Lombardo usually traveled with his wife, attorney Rosa María Otero Gama, who served as "his right hand," and they often had their young daughters in tow.[119] One of them, Adriana Lombardo, remembered these trips to the United States, "always with the police right behind us," and described her father's work as "a family affair."[120] Indeed, one confidential U.S. report remarked upon this family unity, lamenting that Lombardo's "home life is simple and quiet and has never been the subject of adverse public comment."[121] If Lombardo's private life could not provide an avenue for scandal-mongering, some State Department officials hoped that his political contacts might.

Lombardo was one important target in a web of expanded wartime intelligence gathering. Beginning in 1940 and 1941, the FBI moved beyond its domestic purview by placing officers as special "attachés" in various U.S. embassies in Latin America.[122] Paralleling the bureau's targeting of U.S. unionists, the attachés in this Special Intelligence Service paid special attention to organized labor. FBI Director J. Edgar Hoover shared information with the Office of the Coordinator of Inter-American Affairs, a special wartime agency headed by Nelson Rockefeller, who established his own intelligence networks in Latin America. Hoover and Rockefeller jealously guarded their Latin American efforts from encroachments by the Office of Strategic Services (OSS), which, headed by William Donovan, was entrusted with wartime intelligence for the rest of the globe and eventually evolved into the Central Intelligence Agency (CIA).[123]

In correspondence to his superiors in the State Department, Mexico City Ambassador George Messersmith assailed these Special Intelligence operations for several reasons. For one, he argued "The FBI [was] rapidly expanding its field of activity beyond what is proper" and its "enormous staffs" at embassies created "ill-will" among Latin Americans and the potential for "serious difficulties" in future inter-American relations.[124] Messersmith's resentment of increasing numbers of FBI newcomers stationed at the embassy hinted of territoriality, yet it also demonstrated concern about intelligence activities that ran amok, often because their participants knew little about the countries and political situations in which they operated.[125] Not only, he argued, did the civil and legal attachés report on "so-called subversive activities" outside the legitimate concerns of U.S. foreign policy, their reports demonstrated "confusion and inaccuracy and lack of understanding."[126]

Despite Messersmith's protests and the questionable efficiency of the Office of the Civil Attaché in Mexico, the State Department reversed its plan to dismantle this outgrowth of the FBI at war's end. A primary factor in this decision was the reluctance to lose confidential sources who had promised evidence of "financial assistance between the Soviet Government and one of the outstanding Mexican labor leaders."[127] No Moscow gold with which to discredit Lombardo was uncovered, but the FBI operations endured beyond their wartime mandate, until the National Security Act of 1947 directed that they be taken over by the Central Intelligence Agency.[128]

The Ambassador's misgivings centered more on the clumsiness of these intelligence operations (whose staffers, he complained, received salaries far larger than those of comparable embassy personnel) than opposition to intrigue itself. No stranger to more subtle forms of intervention, Messersmith made clear to Mexican officials the U.S. government's concern with Lombardo, whom he described as "more slippery than mercury."[129] Though Lombardo's influence over Mexican labor and politics had declined dramatically once Cárdenas left office, the U.S. State Department expressed enough concern that in 1946, President Miguel Alemán promised U.S. embassy officials that he would "take care of" Lombardo Toledano and his outspoken friends, who criticized the emerging Cold War policy of the former Allies. Of particular concern were their criticisms of economic policy and their lack of hostility to the Soviet Union.[130]

A full account of the U.S. government's campaign against Lombardo and his allies cannot yet be reconstructed, because many records are still classified. As

Steven Niblo, a leading historian of Mexico in the 1940s, has noted: "From 1938 to 1954 there is no open record of the covert action that was pursued, and the United States is still withholding a considerable amount of materials relating to the man it viewed as the demon of the day, Vicente Lombardo Toledano."[131]

The present-day security risks contained in such records are unclear, though revealing the extent of State Department machinations against Lombardo and other left-wing labor leaders would certainly confirm many Latin Americans' suspicions of yanqui intervention. The available sources demonstrate that the State Department was extremely concerned with Lombardo and took action to undermine his work.

Messersmith and others in the State Department worked hard to alienate Lombardo Toledano from potential allies in U.S. government or labor unions. On several occasions the ambassador alerted Washington officials of Lombardo's pending trips to the U.S. capital; his advice for officials facing the Mexican leader's trip to Washington D.C. in 1942 was to treat Lombardo with "courtesy but discretion" and to "tell [Inter-American Affairs Coordinator Nelson] Rockefeller to watch what he says."[132] In 1943 State Department officials even headed off a visit to the president that had been requested by Mexican Minister Counselor Luis Quintanilla.[133]

Messersmith also argued repeatedly that U.S. labor leaders should be warned away from contact with Lombardo. Responding to Lombardo's 1945 visit to the United States to meet with CIO leaders, he wrote that it would be "unfortunate" if the CIO and AFL worked with the CTAL leader because "this would be adding strength to those elements in Mexico who are just waiting for an opportunity to stick us in the back."[134] In another communiqué he noted that "Lombardo is smooth and suave and he will try to make our labor people believe that he is so friendly to the United States, etc. That has been his game all along but he hates our guts, including our labor people in the United States."[135]

However, a more complex picture is revealed by the support of certain "labor people in the United States" for the lombardistas. Lombardo opposed not the United States per se, but government policies perceived to reinforce asymmetrical relations between the United States and Mexico, and discrimination against Mexican Americans. Lombardo found common ground with the U.S. left that also opposed these asymmetries, including the CPUSA, the CIO, and Vice President Henry Wallace. Many of them were New Deal supporters whom Lombardo saw as somewhat similar to the cardenistas in Mexico. Yet an important element of New Deal foreign policy that proved contentious was U.S. policymakers' desire to make Latin American markets and economies—especially Mexico's—serve the interests of U.S. capitalism. This explains some of the antipathy that Messersmith and other officials felt for the Mexican leftist.[136]

A secret State Department Policy and Information Statement draft summarizing the situation in 1946 reiterated this vision of Mexico as "an economic bulwark" for the United States, and it also spoke to the role of labor and Lombardo. The Mexican labor movement, argued the authors, needed to "become a friendly rather than a disruptive force in economic and political life . . . and a friendly and cooperative element." Closer relations with U.S. labor could promote "liberal labor policies" friendly to U.S.-based multinationals, and a "Western Hemisphere orientation among labor leaders."[137] Threatening this orientation was "possibly the most effective agent of the Soviets in the hemisphere, . . . Vicente Lombardo Toledano, whose prestige is, strangely, probably higher outside of Mexico."[138] The solution described in this policy statement was to "foster closer relations between labor in this country and labor in Mexico as well as throughout the hemisphere. Every effort, consistent with the delicacy of the problem, is being made by the Department and by the Embassy in Mexico to foster such relations."[139]

To address the "delicate" problem, a variety of U.S. machinations served to reduce Lombardo's influence among inter-American labor organizations and the CTM. One tactic was to exacerbate the rivalry between Lombardo and his successor as CTM General Secretary, Fidel Velázquez. Commenting on an invitation that the AFL had extended to Velázquez in 1944, embassy officials advised that U.S. officials should "give him all possible facilities to make his trip agreeable." In the United States, they argued, Velázquez "would not hesitate to strengthen his own position" and "have the limelight, after seeing Lombardo in it so often."[140] To avoid the appearance of direct intervention, government officials supported the AFL in its courting of Velázquez and other anti-lombardista labor leaders. Meanwhile, Lombardo's old nemesis (and AFL ally), Luis Morones of the CROM, pressured the Mexican government to take a hard line against the Mexican labor-left.[141]

The AFL became an eager ally of the State Department, undercutting its old rival, the CIO, which had played so prominent a role in grassroots Good Neighbor connections. Serving both these entities, Serafino Romualdi, a "roving ambassador" for the AFL, moved from assisting the OSS in de-radicalizing Italian trade unions at the end of the war to building U.S.-friendly unionism in Latin America. Romualdi promoted anticommunist "free" trade unionism and transported U.S. dollars to the Latin American rivals of the lombardistas. In 1946 he was in Chile, helping channel funds to the socialist rivals of Communist unionists.[142] That same year he corresponded with the head of a Catholic Union movement in Costa Rica with the news that the AFL would provide a monthly subsidy of $750 to support organizing in Nicaragua and El Salvador. In 1947 Romualdi visited Peru to encourage union groups there to form an alternate organization to the CTAL.[143] That same year the AFL offered money to Mexican unionists in exchange for their efforts to foster CTM opposition to the CTAL.[144]

By 1948 these efforts bore fruit. Anticommunist sectors of Latin American labor worked for their national organizations' withdrawal from the CTAL, often shattering unions and provoking great enmities in the process. Encouraged by the AFL, the U.S. State Department, and in some cases anticommunist political leaders at home, these same elements split the CTAL at its Inter-American Labor Conference in Lima in 1948.[145] That year, conservative elements in the CTM also expelled Lombardo (and many of his followers) from the organization he had co-founded. Ousting the main agents of grassroots Good Neighbor efforts effectively severed the ties between the main bodies of the CTM and CIO.[146] Though Lombardo remained a visible and controversial figure in the Mexican left, he never again enjoyed the prestige and influence he had held during the "Good Neighbor" years of the Roosevelt Administration.

The targeting of the lombardistas must be seen as part of a broad program of purges of leftists throughout the Americas. The changing regional and international climate shaped domestic conflicts, and the backlash against the labor-left found justification in anticommunism. Often with U.S. government or corporate prodding, Latin American regimes suppressed unions whose ideology and militancy might threaten an unencumbered influx of foreign capital.[147] In the absence of U.S. aid akin to the Marshall Plan, many Latin American elites viewed private investment as the best hope for contributing capital and technology to their countries' industrialization (and in many cases, their own enrichment). Foreign investment required the stabilization of national politics and of industrial wage levels, and thus a de-radicalization of organized labor.

Under President Miguel Alemán, the Mexican state used repression, bribery, and co-optation to effect a "taming" of the CTM. The "*charrazos*" of the late 1940s meant the replacement of militant union leaders and sectors with corrupt, often flamboyant figures who helped turn the confederation into a creature of the rightward-moving government political party.[148] Though Mexican leaders did not resort to banning Communist parties, as did some of their Latin American counterparts, they closely observed their northern neighbors' efforts to counter the progressive currents that had developed in the 1930s and earlier 1940s.[149] In the United States, the Taft-Hartley Act prohibited Communists from serving as union officers, and un-American Activities committees at a variety of levels persecuted activists, including those who had built bridges across ethnic and national lines. Many of the grassroots Good Neighbors faced such persecution and were ousted from their unions, their jobs, and even their communities. Though some had joined the Communist Party or affiliated organizations, their concerns usually lay closer to home than the aims of the Soviets. What seems to have most disturbed certain U.S. officials was the challenge such activists posed to asymmetrical relations between Latin America and the United States, and between Latinos and Anglos.

Foreign-born activists encountered additional hardships in the form of the 1952 Immigration and Naturalization Act, which expanded the grounds upon which individuals could be deported. This legislation, used against many Latinos, was foreshadowed by George Messersmith in confidential State Department correspondence in 1945. The Ambassador railed against Alonso Perales, a prominent *tejano* activist who had reported U.S. discrimination cases to Mexican papers, including the conservative *Novedades*. A middle-class founder of LULAC, the antidiscrimination organization that so vexed William Blocker, Perales was no leftist, though the publication *Fraternidad* also featured an article he had written.[150] Messersmith hoped to find out whether this Texan was in the "more precarious" state of being a naturalized citizen. (Perales was U.S.-born.) Arguing that "the time had come to throw the fear of God" into Perales, Messersmith claimed that "When an American citizen . . . begins to enter into correspondence with papers in other countries . . . or organizations in other countries and attacking his own country or members of the government of his country, I think if we do not have laws to govern this at present, we can get a law . . . I think the temper of Congress is such that we can get something done."[151]

In the Cold War period to come, "the temper of Congress" did produce legislation to thwart the type of transnational solidarity in which grassroots Good Neighbors engaged. These Mexican and U.S. activists challenged inequalities in the Americas, and their work prompted U.S. officials to respond. The lombardistas challenged the State Department's long-range economic policy, which was to promote an export-oriented Mexican economy that was "a growing market for American goods and services."[152] The cross-border coalitions in which they participated also threatened domestic structures of inequality in the United States, structures that denied many U.S. Latinos their labor, social, and political rights. The grassroots Good Neighbors left some positive legacies, especially by developing U.S. allies who sympathized with Mexicans' struggles for social and economic justice. Their efforts also helped shape the U.S. government's "containment" of movements for social change, an inter-American containment in which "foreign" and "domestic" concerns continue to be intertwined.

Notes

1. For a detailed discussion of the Universidad Obrera's activities directed toward U.S. constituencies, see Gigi Peterson, "Grassroots Good Neighbors: Connections Between Mexican and U.S. Labor and Civil Rights Activists, 1936–1945" (Ph.D. diss., University of Washington, 1998).
2. Confederación de Trabajadores de México (hereafter cited as CTM), "Informe del Comité Nacional: Acción Internacional de la C.T.M.," 25 February 1941, *C.T.M.: 50 años de lucha obrera* (Mexico: Partido Revolucionario Institucional, 1986), 779.
3. Bryce Wood's classic, *The Making of the Good Neighbor Policy* (Austin: University of Texas Press, 1985) explores this theme.
4. See Lloyd Gardner, *New Deal Foreign Policy* (Madison: University of Wisconsin, 1964) and David Green, *The Containment of Latin America: A History of the Myths and Realities of the Good Neighbor Policy* (Chicago: Quadrangle Books, 1971).
5. U.S. Department of State, "[Secret] Policy and Information Statement" Draft, 8 April 1946, p. 7. Sent by John Carrigan to Raymond Geist, Charge d'Affaires, U.S. Embassy in Mexico, 9 April 1946, Box 22, folder 1946, 710–711.5, RG 84: Mexico City Embassy General Records, 1937–1949 (hereafter cited as MCE-GR), National Archives at College Park, Maryland.
6. For Lombardo Toledano's background, see Robert Paul Millon, *Mexican Marxist: Vicente Lombardo Toledano* (Chapel Hill: University of North Carolina Press, 1966) and Enrique Krauze, *Caudillos culturales en la revolución mexicana* (México: Síglo veintiuno, 1976).
7. For Lombardo's relationships with Soviet and U.S. Communists, see Barry Carr, *Marxism and Communism in Mexico* (Lincoln: University of Nebraska Press, 1992), Harvey Levenstein, "Leninists Undone by Leninism: Communism and Unionism in the United States and Mexico, 1935–1939," *Labor History* 22 (spring 1981): 237–261, Valentín Campa, *Mi Testimonio: Memorias de un comunista mexicano*, Tercera edición, (México: Ediciónes de Cultura Popular, 1985), and José Revueltas, *Escritos politicos III: el fracaso histórico del partido comunista en México* (Mexico: Ediciónes Era, 1984).

8. Rosa María Otero Gama, *Vicente Lombardo Toledano: Datos biográficos* (México, D.F.: Universidad Obrera de México, 1988), 35–36.
9. To place Lombardo in the context of his contemporaries, see Roderic Camp, *The Making of a Government: Political Leaders in Modern Mexico* (Tucson: University of Arizona Press, 1984).
10. Millon, *Mexican Marxist*, 11.
11. See Victoria Lerner, *La educación socialista en México, vol.17: Historia de la revolución mexicana.* (Mexico: Colegio de México, 1979).
12. Héctor Aguilar Camín and Michael Meyer, *In the Shadow of the Mexican Revolution* (Austin: University of Texas Press, 1993), 128–33; Alan Knight, "Cardenismo: Juggernaut or Jalopy?" Working Paper 90-09, Mexican Center, Institute of Latin American Studies, University of Texas at Austin, n.d., 22.
13. The *Mexican Labor News* (hereafter cited as *MLN*) reveals a symbiotic though sometimes conflictive relationship between the CTM and Cárdenas. Useful English-language discussions of this relationship include Joe Ashby, *Organized Labor and the Mexican Revolution Under Lazaro Cardenas* (Chapel Hill: University of North Carolina Press, 1967); Barry Carr, *Marxism and Communism in Twentieth Century Mexico* (Lincoln: University of Nebraska Press, 1992); Alan Knight, Knight, "Cardenismo," and "Weapons and Arches in the Mexican Revolutionary Landscape," in, *Everyday Forms of State Formation: Revolution and the Negotiation of Rule in Modern Mexico*, ed. Gilbert Joseph and Daniel Nugent (Durham and London: Duke University Press, 1994), 24–66; Harvey Levenstein, *Labor Organizations in the United States and Mexico. A History of Their Relations.* (Westport: Greenwood Press, 1971); Millon, *Mexican Marxist*.
14. UOM, "Summer School [Pamphlet], First Annual Session, 1936" (Mexico: UOM, 1936), 4.
15. For analysis of *MLN* content and rhetoric, see Peterson, "Grassroots Good Neighbors," 64–88.
16. *Futuro*, 1936–45, *passim*.
17. *El Popular*, 1936–1945, *passim*.
18. Adriana Lombardo, interview by author, Mexico City, 12 September 1991.
19. Lombardo, interview; various Universidad Obrera publications.
20. A fine discussion of the changing CTM-state relations is in Ian Roxborough's, "Mexico," in *Latin America between the Second World War and the Cold War, 1944–48*, ed. Leslie Bethell and Ian Roxborough (Cambridge: Cambridge University Press, 1992), 190–216.
21. For a useful discussion see Steven Niblo, *Mexico in the 1940s: Modernity, Politics, and Corruption* (Wilmington, Del.: Scholarly Resources, 1999), 75–147.
22. This left-wing confederation enjoyed the presence of U.S. delegates at its conventions, including John L. Lewis at its founding congress; "35,000 Hear John L. Lewis Denounce Fascism," *MLN* (15 September 1938): 1.
23. Victor Alba, *Politics and the Labor Movement in Latin America* (Stanford: Stanford University Press, 1968), 325. Alba's sources include figures provided by the International Labor Organization and by U.S. Communist William Z. Foster, and like many figures for Latin American labor and left-wing organizations, these numbers should not be taken too literally.
24. Jesse H. Stiller, *George S. Messersmith, Diplomat of Democracy* (Chapel Hill: University of North Carolina Press, 1987).
25. George Messersmith to Sumner Welles, 2 December 1942, Mexico City, Box 221: 1942 850.4A-850.4L, RG 84: MCE-GR.

26. See for example: Romeyn Wormuth to Secretary of State, "Economic and Political Conditions on Nuevo Laredo District," 4 May 1938, RG 84: MCE-GR, 1937-49, Box 22, 1938, 850.4; "Los Angeles Workers Invite Lombardo," *MLN* 7:13 (28 September 1939): 2–3; "Lombardo Attends California Congresses," *MLN* 7:15 (10 October 1939): 3; "CTM Members to Visit CIO Congress," *MLN* 8:35 (20 September 1940): 2.
27. CTM, "Acción Internacional de la C.T.M.," *C.T.M.: 1936–1941* (México, D.F.: Partido Revolucionario Institucional, 1981), 41; CTAL, *Tercero Congreso de la Confederación de Trabajadores de América Latina* (Mexico: CTAL, 1948), 14.
28. "35,000 Hear John L. Lewis," *MLN* (15 September 1938): 1.
29. Samuel Flagg Bemis, *A Diplomatic History of the United States*, 5th ed. (New York: Holt, Rinehart, and Winston, 1972), 566. Bemis, a contemporary of Lombardo and a well-esteemed U.S. historian, also published a 1943 volume on U.S.-Latin American relations that espoused a critical view of cardenista labor reforms and the 1938 Mexican oil expropriation. Bemis argued that Mexico "has afforded a long trial of the sincerity . . . and self respect of the Good Neighbor of the North," and in its oil expropriation "depended on the sympathy of organized labor in the United States"; Samuel Flagg Bemis, *The Latin American Policy of the United States* (New York: W.W. Norton, 1943), 345, 347.
30. CIO, "Daily Proceedings of the Second Constitutional Convention of the Congress of Industrial Organizations," (10–13 October 1939), 58; Clete Daniel, *Chicano Workers and the Politics of Fairness* (Austin: University of Texas Press, 1991), 198n, 19.
31. CIO, "Second Constitutional Convention," (October 1939), 58; "Miss Lewis Deplores Small Labor Voice at Lima Conference," *CIO News* 2:4 (23 January 1939): 2.
32. "Confederation of Latin American Workers Holds Convention in Mexico," *MLN* 8:24 (13 June 1940): 3.
33. *MLN*, 1936–45, passim.
34. Josephus Daniels to Secretary of State, Mexico City, 18 March 18 1938, Box 14 1938 850.4, RG 84: MCE-GR.
35. "Numerous letter[s], e.g. Amameda [sic-Alameda] County, California Industrial Union to Hull, 8 May 1940, 812.6363/6807, RG 59: Records of the Department of State, National Archives; cited in Henry Weinberg Berger, "Union Diplomacy: American Labor's Foreign Policy in Latin America, 1932–1955" (Ph.D. diss., University of Wisconsin, 1966). Berger also provides insightful discussion of U.S. labor's involvement in these inter-American issues in "Crisis Diplomacy, 1930–39," in *From Colony to Empire*, ed. William Appleman Williams (New York: John Wiley and Sons, 1972), 294–336.
36. International Longshoremen's and Warehousemen's Union, *Proceedings, 1938*, 220 and "San Francisco CIO Industrial Union Council," *New York Times*, 27 March 1938, cited in Berger, "Crisis Diplomacy," 308–309.
37. See Saul Alinsky, *John L. Lewis* (Cornwall, N.Y.: Vintage Books, 1949), 201–203.
38. Within the extensive historiography on the Mexican-U.S. oil controversy, a useful English-language overview is Steven Niblo, *War, Diplomacy, and Development: The United States and Mexico, 1938–1954* (Wilmington, Del.: Scholarly Resources, 1995), 35–60.
39. Mutual assistance in CTM and CIO strikes is described in "Mexican Workers Enrolled by CIO," *New York Times*, 24 October 1938. See also D.H. Dinwoodie, "The Rise of the Mine Mill Union in Southwestern Copper," in *American Labor in the Southwest*, ed. James Foster (Tucson: University of Arizona Press, 1982), 46–56, and Mario García, *Mexican Americans* (New Haven: Yale University Press, 1989), 180–181.

40. "Mexican Labor Boycots [sic] American Ships," *MLN* 1:12 and 13 (25 November/2 December 1936): 2; "Tercer Consejo Nacional de la CTM, 1937," "Asuntos Internacionales," *CTM, 1936–1945*, 312. See also "Mexican Workers Enrolled by CIO," *New York Times*, 24 October 1938. Henry Berger defines "hot cargoes," as goods generated by an industry involved in a labor dispute; refusing to handle these goods constitutes a form of secondary boycott. Berger, "Union Diplomacy," 93.
41. Charles P. Larrowe, *Harry Bridges: The Rise and Fall of Radical Labor in the United States* (Westport, Conn.: Lawrence Hill, 1972), 7; for discussion of Latino workers under the ILWU umbrella see Mario García [and Bert Corona], *Memories of Chicano History: The Life and Narrative of Bert Corona* (Berkeley and Los Angeles: University of California Press, 1994), 87–107.
42. Useful studies of the MMSW include D. H. Dinwoodie, "The Rise of the Mine-Mill" and James Foster, "Western Federation of Miners and Mine-Mill," "Western Wobblies," and "Mexican Labor in the American Southwest," all in *American Labor in the Southwest*, ed. James Foster (Tucson: University of Arizona Press, 1982), 46–56, 13–18, 59–64, and 157–163.
43. "Metal Workers Strike in Guggenheim Smelter," *MLN* (10 September 1936); CTM Votes to Aid Striking Metal Workers," *MLN* (30 September 1936); "American Smelting/Refining Faces National Walkout," *MLN* (10 February 1937); [untitled article] *MLN* (11 January 1939).
44. "U.S. Miners Pledge Solidarity in American Smelting Conflict," *MLN* 3:21 (25 November 1937): 2–3.
45. Dinwoodie, "Rise of the Mine Mill," 48; García, *Mexican Americans*, 180–181.
46. William Blocker to Cordell Hull, Ciudad Juárez, Mexico, 11 August 1939, 812.5043/21, RG 59: Records of the Department of State; cited in Berger, "Union Diplomacy," 104.
47. William Blocker to Secretary of State, Monterrey, Mexico, 25 April 1938, Box 22 1938, 850.4, RG 84: MCE-GR. Francisco Múgica had played a crucial role in shaping some of the radical provisions of the Mexican Constitution of 1917, and in 1938 he penned the historic Cárdenas announcement of the oil expropriation. Luis Rodríguez was the president of Mexico's government party, the Partido Nacional Revolucionario (PNR).
48. William Blocker to Secretary of State, "Confidential Survey of Racial Discrimination Problem," Mexico, 8 January 1942, Ciudad Juárez Consulate, Classified General Records, 1923–1949 (hereafter cited as CJC-CGR), National Archives, College Park, Maryland.
49. William Blocker to Secretary of State, "Transmitting Results of a Confidential Survey of the Problem of Racial Discrimination Against Mexican and Latin American Citizens in Texas and New Mexico," 17–18, Ciudad Juárez, Mexico, 27 February 1942, Box 1, folder 1939–1942, RG 84: CJE-CGR.
50. Ibid., 19.
51. Here, in keeping both with the self-identification of many of these historical actors and with current scholarly usage, I use the term "ethnic Mexicans" to refer to those of Mexican descent, regardless of their country of birth or citizenship status. In both the lived history and the historiography, use of identifiers such as "Mexican" or "Mexican American" is shifting and reflects individual preferences and historical contingencies.
52. Blocker, "Confidential Survey," 4.
53. Blocker, "Confidential Survey," 6.
54. Ibid., 6, 3.

55. See, for example, Devra Weber, *Dark Sweat, White Gold: California Farm Workers, Cotton, and the New Deal* (Berkeley and Los Angeles: University of California Press, 1994); David Weber, *Walls and Mirrors: Mexican Americans, Mexican Immigrants, and the Politics of Ethnicity* (Berkeley and Los Angeles: University of California Press, 1995), and García and Corona, *Life of Bert Corona*.
56. Blocker, "Confidential Survey," 17, 23–24, 26.
57. Ibid., 25.
58. One good overview is Clete Daniel, *Chicano Workers and the Politics of Fairness: The FEPC in the Southwest, 1941–1945* (Austin: University of Texas Press, 1991).
59. Mario García, *Mexican Americans*, 182–86, 193. Archival sources illuminate Fox's campaign against labor organizers and Consul Esparza: Chris Fox to William Blocker, El Paso, Texas, 26 January 1940, Box 1, folder 1939–42, RG 84: CJC-CGR; N.D. Collaer, Inspector in Charge, U.S. Dept. of Labor/Immigration and Naturalization Service, El Paso, to William Blocker, 26 January 1940, Box 1, folder 1939–1942, RG 84: CJC-CGR.
60. Chris P. Fox to William Blocker, El Paso, 1 September 1942, 1, Box 1, folder 1939–1942, RG 84: CJE-CGR.
61. William Blocker to Secretary of State, "Apparent Variance of President's Labor Discrimination Committee at El Paso, Texas, with the Department's Views on the Racial Discrimination Problem," Ciudad Juárez, Mexico, 3 September 1942, 1, Box 1, folder 1939–1942, RG 84: CJE-CGR.
62. Clete Daniel's *Chicano Workers and the Politics of Fairness* provides an excellent discussion of the federal agencies' in-fighting over these hearings.
63. See David Gutiérrez, *Walls and Mirrors*, 110–11; García, *Mexican Americans*, 146–159.
64. CTM, "Informe que Rinde el Comité Nacional de la CTM, al X Consejo de la Misma Institución," *CTM, 1936–1941*, 793.
65. Adolfo Orive Alba to Eduardo Quevado, 22 June 1939, Box 1, folder 8, Collection M349: Papers of Eduardo Quevado, Stanford University Library Special Collections.
66. Examiner's note attached to letter from Josefina Fierro de Bright to Vicente Lombardo Toledano, Los Angeles, Calif., 1 May 1942, [Intercepted Special Delivery letter], Box 221, 1942 850.4A-850.4L, RG 84: MCE-GR.
67. Over the decades both activists and scholars have used different terms to refer to these youth of Mexican descent living in the United States, most of whom were U.S.-acculturated if not also U.S.-born. Here I prefer to use the term "Mexican American" because these youth and their defenders frequently took care to affirm both their Mexican cultural roots and their status and rights as members of U.S. society. There is, of course, some irony in using "American" to denote U.S. identity, especially because the grassroots Good Neighbors in Mexico posed a hemispheric definition of "American" that affirmed Latin Americans' right to the term.
68. An insightful firsthand account from a defender of these youth is Alice [Greenfield] McGrath. "The Education of Alice McGrath," interview by Michael Balter, 1987, UCLA Oral History Program, UCLA Special Collections.
69. McGrath, interview, 161.
70. The classic study of this targeting is Mauricio Mazón's *The Zoot-Suit Riots: The Psychology of Symbolic Annihilation* (Austin: University of Texas Press, 1984).
71. "One Killed and Ten Hurt in Boy 'Wars,'" *Los Angeles Times*, 3 August 1942.
72. One article referring to the "reign of terror" by "youthful 'pachuco' gangs" described a mass arrest of Mexican American youth as "the biggest roundup since prohibition days"; "Police Seize 300 in Boys Gang Drive," *Los Angeles Times*, 10 August 1942.

73. "Jury Delves into Boy Gang Terror Wave," *Los Angeles Times*, 5 February 1942.
74. Though the *Los Angeles Times* was not unique in identifying such youth as "Mexican," the absence of the term "American" (insisted upon by some Mexican Americans of this generation—see, for example, the memoirs of Bert Corona) is significant in light of the paper's anti-foreign rhetoric.
75. Ed Duran Ayres, "Statistics," 2. Typewritten manuscript of report given to 1942 Los Angeles County Grand Jury, 2, Box 4, folder 8, Collection 107: Sleepy Lagoon Defense Committee (hereafter cited as SLDC), UCLA Special Collections.
76. Ibid., 3.
77. Citizens' Committee for the Defense of Mexican American Youth (CCDMAY), "Minutes: Conference held March 14, 1943 in Belmont Studios, Los Angeles," Box 2, folder 11, SLDC.
78. Some photographs demonstrate that a victim did not need to wear a full-fledged zoot suit to be attacked; for example: "Contra los 'Pachucos': Contra los Mexicanos," *Futuro*, 90 (Agosto 1943): 9. Numerous sources have treated the Sleepy Lagoon trial and ensuing appeals work, including Carey McWilliams, *North from Mexico* (Westport, Conn.: Greenwood Press, 1968 reprint of 1948 edition), 230–231; and Mazón, *Zoot-Suit Riots*, 20–22.
79. See Jean Meyer's classic study, *El sinarquismo: un fascismo mexicano? 1937–1947* (Mexico: Cuadernos de Joaquín Mortiz, 1979). Sinarquismo in the United States merits further research and analysis, as evidenced by recollections such as those of historian Carlos Gil in his *Hope and Frustration: Interviews with Leaders of Mexico's Political Opposition* (Wilmington, Del: Scholarly Resources Books, 1992), 291.
80. Octavio Paz's 1934 essay, "The Pachuco and Other Extremes," is probably the best-known example of this point of view; Octavio Paz, *The Labyrinth of Solitude*, trans. Lysander Kemp, Yara Milos, and Rachel Phillips Belash (New York: Grove Press, 1985), 15.
81. Peterson, "Grassroots Good Neighbors," 98.
82. "Pachucos . . . Zoot Suits. . . y Jitterbugs," *El Popular* (25 junio 1943): 4.
83. In *Walls and Mirrors*, David Gutiérrez provides an excellent discussion of conceptions of bicultural identity that emerged in left-wing Latino circles in the late 1930s and 1940s.
84. "Race Hatred Basis of So-Called Zoot Suit Riots Exposed," *MLN* 9:4 (15 June 1943): 1–2.
85. Ibid., 2.
86. SLDC, *The Sleepy Lagoon Case* (Los Angeles, 1943), 4.
87. Idem.
88. SLDC, Office Memo, Los Angeles, California, 8 July 1944, Box 3, folder 4: Office Memo file, SLDC. This memo read: "Subject: Send autographed copy of MYSTERY [SLDC publication on the case] and a letter from Carey McWilliams to each of the Mexican government officials listed on the attached sheet."
89. See, for example, "La Verdad en la Cuestion de los 'Pachucos'," *El Popular* 1830 (18 June 1943): 5; "Pachucos . . . Zoot Suits . . . y Jitterbugs," *El Popular* (25 June 1943): 4; "La Semana en el Mundo," *El Popular* 1841 (27 June 1943); "Contra los 'Pachucos': Contra los Mexicanos," *Futuro*, 90 (Agosto 1943): 9; and "Race Hatred Basis of So-Called Zoot Suit Riots Exposed," *MLN* 9:4 (15 June 1943): 1–2.
90. Examiner's note attached to letter from Josefina Fierro de Bright to Vicente Lombardo Toledano, Los Angeles, Calif., 1 May 1942, [Intercepted Special Delivery letter], Box 221: 1942, 850.4A–850.4L, RG 84: MCE-GR.

91. SLDC, *Sleepy Lagoon Case*, 21.
92. Vicente Lombardo Toledano, "Falsedad de la Interpretación Racial de la Historia de América" (Mexico: Universidad Obrera de México, 1943), printed text of speech given on 4 July 1943 in El Paso, Texas.
93. Lombardo Toledano, "Falsedad," 11.
94. Ibid., 17–20.
95. For example, Eric Williams's *Capitalism and Slavery* was published in 1944, and in the late 1930s Brazilian scholar Gilberto Freyre had published several works arguing that the institution of slavery, rather than racial mixing in itself, had damaged Brazilian society.
96. Lombardo Toledano, "Falsedad," 12–13.
97. "Sería absurdo combatir al régimen nazi, porque pretende la hegemonía de la raza germana, como la preconiza, si dentro de nuestros pueblos existen sentimientos de discriminación respecto de los indios, de los negroes y de los mestizos, si continúan siendo clasificados los hombres en función de color. No puede ni debe llamarse antifascista ni democrática ningún hombre de América que considere inferiores a los negroes, a los indios o a los mestizos. En esta hora, toda discriminación racial es un ayuda al fascismo."; Ibid., 14.
98. Vicente Lombardo Toledano, *Cristianos y socialistas unidos contra la agresión* (Mexico: Universidad Obrera de México, 1943).
99. "El Comité Mexicano Contra el Racismo ha quedado constituido en la Capital," *El Popular* 2193 (19 June 1944): 1.
100. For example, *Vicente Lombardo Toledano: Datos biográficos* (Mexico: Universidad Obrera de México, 1987).
101. William Blocker to Secretary of State, "Subject: Forwarding Copies of the Racial Discrimination Magazine Fraternidad, Published in Mexico," Ciudad Juárez, Mexico, 25 July 1945, Box 602, 840.1, RG 84: MCE-GR.
102. William Blocker to George Messersmith, Ciudad Juárez, Mexico, 25 July 1945, Box 602, 840.1, RG 84: MCE-GR.
103. William Blocker to John Carrigan, Ciudad Juárez, Mexico, 25 July 1945, Box 602, 840.1, RG 84: MCE-GR.
104. William Blocker to George Messersmith, Ciudad Juárez, Mexico, 13 November 1942, Box 1, folder 1939–1942, RG 84: CJE-GR.
105. See for example, "Lombardo Fija la Posición del Movimiento Obrero de la América Latina sobre las Relaciónes Económicas entre las Naciones de Este Continente," *Futuro* 99 (April 1945): 43–46, and Vicente Lombardo Toledano, "Balance de la Conferencia Interamericana Sobre las Problemas de la Guerra y de la Paz," *Futuro* 99 (April 1945): 47–51.
106. For a useful overview, see David Rock, "War and Postwar Intersection: Latin America and the United States," in *Latin America in the 1940s*, ed. David Rock (Berkeley and Los Angeles: University of California Press, 1994), 15–40; and in the same volume, Ian Roxborough, "Labor Control and the Postwar Growth Model in Latin America," 248–264.
107. Gardner, *New Deal Foreign Policy*, 195.
108. "Lombardo Fija la Posición," *Futuro* 99 (April 1945): 43–46.
109. Lombardo, "Balance de la Conferencia," 47–51, and "Lombardo Fija la Posición," 44; Green, *Containment of Latin America*, 198–199.
110. "Lombardo Fija la Posición," 45.
111. Memo, "Recent Developments in CTAL Policy and Strategy, prepared by a member

Mexican Labor Left and Its U.S. Allies   275

of the Division of International, Social, and Health Affairs," sent from State Department to U.S. Embassy, Mexico City, 5 October 1945, Box 622, 850.4 Con-Lo, RG 84: MCE-GR.
112. See Steven Niblo's fine discussion in his *War, Diplomacy, and Development,* 196–200.
113. George Messersmith to Cordell Hull, Mexico City, 4 August 1944; cited in Niblo, *War, Diplomacy and Development,* 201.
114. Robert Wall, Office of the Civil Attaché, "Memo for the Ambassador," Mexico City, 11 April 1945, 1, Box 622, folder 850.4 Con-Lo. RG 84: MCE-GR.
115. John Carrigan to George Messersmith, 4 April 1945, Box 622, folder 850.4 Con-Lo, RG 84: MCE:GR.
116. George Messersmith to Spruille Braden, "Secret" letter, Mexico City, 3 January 1946, 6, 102.3–711.5, Box 22, folder 7, RG 84: Mexico City Embassy-Security: Segregated General Records (hereafter cited as MCE-SSGR), 1941–49, National Archives, College Park, Maryland.
117. Ibid., 6.
118. For example, "Record #BA12702, Letter from Rosa María Toledano [sic] to Rosa María, Adriana, Marcela Lombardo Otero," 8 October 1942, Box 221, 850.4A–850.4L, RG 84: MCE-GR.
119. Lombardo, interview; William Ailshie to Secretary of State, "Transmitting Biographical Sketch on Lis. [sic] Vicent Lombardo Toledano," ["Maximum Priority Pouch-Strictly Confidential,"] Mexico City, 28 November 1944, Box 488: 1944, 850.4E: RG 84: MCE-GR.
120. Lombardo, interview.
121. Ailshie to Secretary of State, "Biographical Sketch on Lombardo."
122. Memo, "Agreement Between MID, ONI [Office of Naval Intelligence] and FBI for Coordinating Special Intelligence Operations in the Western Hemisphere, Approved by the Department of State," 30 April 1943, Box 4, folder 1943, 102.3, RG 84: MCE-SSGR.
123. Cary Reich, *The Life of Nelson A. Rockefeller: Worlds to Conquer, 1908–1958* (New York: Doubleday, 1996), 204, 222–227.
124. George Messersmith to Adolf Berle, Assistant Secretary of State, Mexico City, 21 July, 1943 and Messersmith to Berle, 12 July 1943, Box 4, folder 1943, 102.3, RG 84: MCE-SSGR.
125. George Messersmith to John Willard Carrigan, Department of State, Mexico City, 5 December 1945, Box 20: 1945, folder 030-123, RG 84: MCE-SSGR.
126. George Messersmith to Secretary of State, Mexico City, 10 September 1944, "Confidential-First Priority, No 20.037," Box 8: 1944, folder 102.3-121 RG 84: MCE-SSGR.
127. William Ailshie to George Messersmith, 5 December 1945, 1, Box 20, 1945, folder 030-123, RG 84: MCE-SSGR.
128. John Ranelagh, *The Agency: The Rise and Decline of the CIA* (New York: Simon and Schuster, 1987), 114.
129. George Messersmith to Spruille Braden, Mexico City, 3 January 1946, Box 22: 1946, folder 102.3-711.5, RG 84: MCE-SSGR.
130. George Messersmith to Spruille Braden, Assistant Secretary of State, Mexico City, 3 January 1946, Box 22 1946 102.3–711.5, Folder 1946 690-701.1, RG 84: MCE-SGR.
131. Steven Niblo, *War, Diplomacy, and Development,* xv. My own research in archives from the Mexico City Embassy revealed many documents de-classified only in 1996, and they provided only a limited picture of activities directed at Lombardo.

132. George Messersmith to Sumner Welles, Mexico City, 2 December 1943, Box 21, folder 1942 850.4A–850.4L, RG 84: MCE-GR.
133. John Carrigan to George Messersmith, Washington, D.C., 9 February 1943, Box 6, folder 850.4, RG 84: MCE-SSGR.
134. George Messersmith to John Carrigan, Mexico City, 7 April 1945, "SECRET Air Mail Letter," Box 20, folder 701.1-790, RG 84: MCE-SSGR.
135. Messersmith to Carrigan, 7 April 1945.
136. Messersmith's correspondence also reveals a deep personal hatred of Lombardo; George Messersmith to Spruille Braden, 3 January 1946, Spruille Braden to George Messersmith, 8 January 1946, James Wright to George Messersmith, 10 January 1946, George Messersmith to James Wright, 15 January 1946, George Messersmith to Spruille Braden, 15 January 1946, Box 22, folder 7, RG 84: MCE-SSGR.
137. U.S. Department of State, "[Secret] Policy and Information Statement" Draft, 8 April 1946, 14.
138. Ibid., 23.
139. Ibid.
140. William Ailshie to Joseph McGurk, Division of Mexican Affairs, Mexico City, 21 August, 1944, Box 487, folder 1944 850.4 Gen–850.4C, RG 84: MCE-GR.
141. Niblo, *Mexico in the 1940s*, 202–203.
142. Andrew Barnard, "Chile," in *Latin America Between the Second World War and the Cold War: Crisis and Containment, 1944–1948*, ed. Leslie Bethell and Ian Roxborough (Cambridge, Mass.: Cambridge University Press, 1993), 78.
143. Rodolfo Cerdas Cruz, "Costa Rica," and Nigel Haworth, "Peru," Ibid., 287, 186.
144. W.H. Doyle to R.H. Geist, memo re: Visit of Serafin Rumualde (*sic*), 12 May 1947, Box 45, 1947 850–850.4, RG 84: MCE-SSGR.
145. Roxborough, "Labor Control," in *Latin America in the 1940s*, ed. Rock, 259.
146. Roxborough, "Mexico," in *Latin America, 1944–1948*, ed. Bethell and Roxborough, 207–208.
147. Niblo, *Mexico in the 1940s*, 216.
148. A *"charro"* is a dandified cowboy figure, and in this context the term referred to the ornate Jaliscan garb favored by some of these labor leaders. By the 1960s, Mexicans used the term *"charrismo"* to describe sell-out to the PRI. Excellent English-language discussions of the initial *charrismos* are Niblo, *Mexico in the 1940s,* and Ian Roxborough's "Mexico," in his co-edited volume on *Latin America, 1944–1948* (both cited above).
149. Useful discussions of these developments are in Bethell and Roxborough, *Latin America, 1944–1948* and Rock, *Latin America in the 1940s*.
150. Alonso Perales, "Roosevelt desea que no haya discriminación alguna," *Fraternidad* (1 September 1944): 4–5.
151. George Messersmith to John Carrigan, Division of Mexican Affairs, Department of State, 31 December 1945, Box 602, 1945 840.1, RG 84: MCE-GR. Messersmith's comment about "the fear of God" is in George Messersmith, "Memorandum to Mr. Cabot, Mr. O'Donaghue, Mr. Thomasson," Mexico City, 26 December 1945, Box 602: 1945, 840.1, RG 84: MCE-GR.
152. U.S. Department of State, "[Secret] Policy and Information Statement" Draft, 8 April 1946, 7. Sent by John Carrigan to Raymond Geist, Charge d'Affaires, U.S. Embassy in Mexico, 9 April 1946, Box 22, folder 1946, 710-711.5, RG 84: MCE-GR.

Contributors

KENNETH C. BURT, Carey McWilliams Fellow at the University of California at Berkeley, is the political director of the California Federation of Teachers. A board member for the Southwest Labor Studies Association, Burt publishes in the academic and popular press, and is writing a book on the emergence of Latinos as a political force in California.

ROBERT W. CHERNY is a professor of history at San Francisco State University. He is currently writing a biography of Harry Bridges and is engaged in other work on the history of Pacific Coast longshoremen and of communism and anticommunism in the Pacific Coast states. He has published a number of works on politics during the Gilded Age and Progressive Era.

MARVIN GETTLEMAN is emeritus professor at Brooklyn Polytechnic University and Codirector of the Project on the Comparative International History of Left Education. He served as executive director of the Abraham Lincoln Brigade Archives and is a member of the editorial board of *Science & Society*. He is coeditor of *The Middle East and Islamic World Reader* (2003).

MICHAEL K. HONEY holds the Harry Bridges Endowed Chair of Labor Studies at the University of Washington, and teaches African American and labor and ethnic studies and American history at the University of Washington, Tacoma. His books include *Southern Labor and Black Civil Rights: Organizing Memphis Workers* (1993) and *Black Workers Remember: An Oral History of Segregation, Unionism, and the Freedom Struggle* (1999).

WILLIAM ISSEL is a professor of history at San Francisco State University. He is the author of *Social Change in the United States, 1945–1983* (1985) and (with Robert W. Cherny) *San Francisco, 1865–1932* (1986). He is on the advisory board of the Northern California Labor Archives and Research Center and is writing books on Catholic Action in California and on business, labor, and politics in San Francisco.

MARGARET MILLER received her Ph.D. from the University of Washington and has taught labor studies at San Francisco State University and history at Sonoma State University. She is also the author of an historical context study of agricultural labor, written for the U.S. National Park Service. She is presently working on a book-length study of labor and welfare politics in the Pacific Northwest.

DAVID PALMER is senior lecturer in American studies at Flinders University, Adelaide, Australia. He is the author of *Organizing the Shipyards: Union Strategy in Three Northeast Shipyards* (1998) and is a member of the editorial board of *Labour History* (Australia). He is writing a book on the history of Japanese and U.S. workers' movements in war industries.

VERNON L. PEDERSEN is a professor of history and associate dean for academic affairs and student services at Montana State University–Great Falls. He is the author of *The Communist Party of Maryland, 1919–1957* (2001) and a member of the editorial board of *American Communist History*.

GIGI PETERSON is an assistant professor of history at the State University of New York College at Cortland. She is currently revising her manuscript, *Grassroots Good Neighbors: Connections between Mexican and U.S. Labor and Civil Rights Activists, 1936–1945*.

ELLEN SCHRECKER is professor of history at Yeshiva University. The author of *Many Are the Crimes: McCarthyism in America* (1998) and *No Ivory Tower: McCarthyism and the Universities* (1986), she has written extensively about the McCarthy period. Her most recent publication is an edited collection of essays, *Cold War Triumphalism: The Politics of American History After the Fall of Communism* (2003).

RANDI STORCH is an assistant professor of history at State University of New York College at Cortland. She is currently writing a book on the history of the Communist party in Chicago.

KIERAN WALSH TAYLOR is a graduate student at the University of North Carolina at Chapel Hill and serves on the boards of the Institute for Southern Studies and the Southwest Labor Studies Association. He is coeditor of *The Papers of Martin Luther King, Jr. Volume 4: Symbol of the Movement, January 1957–December 1958* (2000) and is currently working on a history of radicals in the labor movement in the 1970s.

DON WATSON is cofounder of the San Francisco Bay Area Labor History Workshop and advisory board member of the SFSU Labor Archives and Research Center. He has served as vice-president and secretary of the Southwest Labor Studies Association and has given numerous papers at conferences of this organization on the subject of farm labor.

SAMUEL W. WHITE is an assistant professor of labor education at the University of Missouri–Columbia. He teaches topics related to the history of labor, work organization, and new technology and is currently working on a manuscript dealing with labor and politics.

GERALD ZAHAVI is a professor of modern American labor and business history at the University at Albany, State University of New York. He is the cofounder and director of *Talking History*, a radio program and aural history production center at the University at Albany, and editor of the *Journal for MultiMedia History*. He is currently completing *Embers on the Land: Local and Regional Studies in Culture, Community, and Communism, 1918–1955*.

INDEX

Abner, Willougby, 79
ACLU (American Civil Liberties Union), 88
Actors Guild, 119
ACTU. *See* Association of Catholic Trade Unionists
ACWA (Amalgamated Clothing Workers of America), 123
ADC Union, 196–197, 202
AEC (Atomic Energy Commission), 12
AFL. *See* American Federation of Labor
AFL-CIO: abuse within, 3–4; ethics code of, 64; membership increase, 109n4; noncommunist clause of, 64; southern unionism and, 235, 237, 238
AFL-CIO Department of Organization, 63
AFL-CIO Industrial Union Department (IUD), 62
African Americans: attacks on soldiers, 217; Communist Party contribution in Schenectady, 47–48; discrimination in Evansville, 145; furniture union of, 234; IUMSWA organization of, 90–92; pension union and, 195, 196, 197; zoot-suiters and, 254. *See also* National Association for the Advancement of Colored People; South, labor organization in; United Packinghouse Workers of America (UPWA; CIO), in Chicago
AFSCME (American Federation of State and County Municipal Employees), 108
Agata, Joe, 104
Agricultural Workers Organizing Committee (AWOC), 63–64

Aguilar, Manuel, 255
Aid to Dependent Children (ADC), 193, 196, 197, 199, 202
Alba, Adolfo Orive, 254
ALCO (American Locomotive Company), 25
Alemán, Miguel, 264, 267
Alinsky, Saul, 59,119,124, 126
Alioto, Joseph L., 154
Allis-Chalmers Company, 13–14
Amalgamated Clothing Workers of America (ACWA; CIO), 123
Amalgamated Meat Cutters and Butcher Workmen of America (AMC; AFL), 61, 66, 67, 75
An American Dilemma, 207
American Association of Social Workers, 182
American Civil Liberties Union (ACLU), 88
American Communist Party, 29, 77
American Council of the Spanish-Speaking, 129
American Federation of Labor (AFL): antidiscrimination and, 218; attempt to resurrect Pan-American Federation of Labor, 249; Building Trades Council, 119; Central Labor Council of, 119, 120; competition with CIO, 1; Evansville membership, 141; increase in southern membership, 217, 235; labor school support by, 208; Latin American unionism and, 265, 266; loss of Masonite plant to

American Federation of Labor (AFL) (*continued*)
CIO, 222, 223; merges with CIO, 3, 19, 62; racial discrimination and, 92; San Francisco and, 158; southern unionism and, 223,; Standard Coil and, 126, 130, 132, 133; support of social welfare by, 193, 196; unemployment compensation and, 200; union expelled from, 3–4, 102. *See also* AFL-CIO; CIO; *individual union*
American Federation of State and County Municipal Employees (AFSCME), 108
American Federation of Teachers, 250
American Legion, 149
American Locomotive Company (ALCO), 25
American Smelting and Refining Company (ASARCO), 251
American Veterans Committee, 208
The Annals of Communism, 177
Antle, Bud, 63
Aptheker, Herbert, 207
Armour, 80–81
Armour Local 347, 78
Army-McCarthy hearings, 7, 184
Arsenault, Jean Jr., 56n18
ASARCO (American Smelting and Refining Company), 251
Association of Catholic Trade Unionists (ACTU), 101, 134, 147, 155, 165–166, 167, 170, 174n53–175n53
Atlantic Charter, 259
Atomic Energy Commission (AEC), 12
Avila Camacho, Manuel, 249
AWOW (Agricultural Workers Organizing Committee), 63–64
Ayres, Edward Duran, 255, 257
"Ayres Report," 255

Baltimore Sun, 183
Barry, William, 125
Bartlett, Ford, 79
Bartley, Numan, 226, 238
Beck, Dave, 3
Bell, Kathryn, 147
Bellingham Industrial Union Council, 200
Bemis, Samuel Flagg, 250, 259, 270n29
Bennett, Fay, 63, 66

Bentley, Elizabeth, 181
Berger, Sadelle, 147, 148
Berger, Sydney, 148
Bethlehem Steel, 181, 185
Beverly, Leon, 80, 81
Bezenhoffer, Joe, 80
Bittner, Van, 226–227, 231
Black Furniture Union, 234
blacklisting, in Hollywood, 119
Blocker, William, 252–254, 260–261, 262, 267
Blood, Ross, 101, 105, 106, 117n85, 181
Bloody Christmas, 121, 128
Bloor, Ella Reeve, 25
Blumberg, Albert, 179, 183
Blumberg, Dorothy Rose, 179–180, 183, 187
Boeing Company, 194
Boss, Andrew C., 166–167, 169
Boucher, Anthony, 207
Boulware, Lemuel R., 34, 37, 55n10
Boulwarism, 55n10
Bowen, Harold, 96
Bowen, Paul, 198, 200–201
Boyd, Leroy, 223, 235
Boyle Heights (LA), 123, 124, 127, 131
Boyson, Arthur, 116n74
bracero program, 59, 67, 68n5, 253
Bradley, George, 166
Brant, Carl, 133
Braverman, Maurice, 183
Brecht, Charles, 99
Breshears, Jerry, 68n5
Brewer, Roy, 58, 119
Bridges, Harry, 14, 93, 107, 164, 166, 168, 177, 208, 251
Briggs plant, 141, 147
Brophy, John, 161
Browder, Earl, 77, 191, 205, 206, 248
Brown, Archie, 166
Brown, Frank, 78
Bucyrus-Erie plant, 141, 144, 145, 146 (fig), 147, 149
Budenz, Louis, 13–14
Building Service Employees Union, 196, 200
Building Trades Council (AFL), 119
Burt, Kenneth C., 127
Butler, Hobert, 143

California Labor School, 167, 205, 206, 207, 208
California State Federation of Labor, 168
Calles, Plutarco, 247
Campbell, Charlie, 36
Cantwell, John J., 124, 125
Cárdenas, Lazaro, 246, 248, 249, 250–251, 252, 258
cardenismo, 246, 247, 248, 256
Carey, James B., 66, 87, 109n8, 122, 123, 132
Carey, James C. (Jim), 30, 34, 37, 41–43, 66, 87, 109n8, 122, 123, 132
Carlos, Grace Almanza, 122, 132
Carpenter, David, 182
Carrigan, John, 260
Carson, Jules, 207
Casey, Michael J., 160, 172n19
Caso, Alfonso, 260
A Catholic New Deal (Heineman), 170
Catholic Church, 1, 11; anticommunist stance of, 39–40, 125–126, 180, 181; criticism of red-baiting by, 130; farmworkers and, 59, 62; Jandreau and, 36–37, 52; labor institute of, 119, 120, 123, 126, 127, 131, 132, 134; labor school of, 127; red-baiting and, 154–155, 164; rights/duties of workers according to, 165; shipyard workers and, 101; sinarquistas and, 256; support of IUE at Standard Coil, 118, 119, 122, 126, 130–131, 132; support of Latinos in Los Angeles, 124–128; worker program of, 127–128. *See also* Association of Catholic Trade Unionists; San Francisco, Catholic activism in
Catholic Interracial Council of Los Angeles, 124
Catholic Labor Institute, 119, 120, 123, 126, 127, 131, 132, 134
Catholic Labor School, 127
Catholic Worker Movement, 165
Catholic Workers, 135, 154, 165
CDA. *See* Committee for Democratic Action
Central Intelligence Agency (CIA), 19, 264
Central Labor Council (AFL), 119, 120, 121
Central Labor Union, 142
Chamber of Commerce, 224
Chambers, Whittaker, 181, 182
Charles, John Patrick, 56n18
charrismo, 276n148
charro, 276n148
Chavez, Cesar, 59, 63, 135
Chicago. *See* United Packinghouse Workers of America (UPWA; CIO), in Chicago
Chicago Tribune, 80
Chicanos. *See* Mexicans/Mexican Americans
Christensen, Parley P., 119–120, 121
Christoffel, Harold, 13, 14, 16
Christopher, George, 168
Christopher, Paul, 230
Chrysler Corporation, 141
CIA. *See* Central Intelligence Agency
CIO. *See* Congress of Industrial Organizations
CIO News, 258
Citizen's Committee Against the Ober Law, 182
Citizens Public Assistance Committee (CPAC), 198
Civil Rights Congress (CRC), 78, 197
civil rights movement, 18, 62, 231, 237
Clark, Karen J., 48–50
Clark, Leroy, 228, 234, 235
closed shop, illegality of, 2, 225
Clubb, O. Edmund, 182
CMCR (Mexican Committee against Racism), 260
CNPD (National Committee in Defense of the Proletariat), 247
Coffee, John, 194
Coffield, John V., 126–128, 130–131, 132, 134, 135
Cold War: affect on labor organization in South, 223–224, 225, 230, 235, 236, 237, 238; affect on UE and Evansville community, 142
Columbia Records, 121, 131
Comité Mexicano Contra el Racismo (Mexican Committee against Racism; CMCR), 260
Commission on Equal Employment Opportunity, 168

Committee for Democratic Action (CDA), 145, 147
Committee on Education and Labor, 145
Committee on Latin American Affairs (CIO), 250
Committee to Preserve American Freedoms, 129
Communist-led union: dedication to racial equality, 9; difference from other union, 9; government attack on, 10–11. *See also* Taft-Hartley Act; *individual union*
Communist Party (CP): loses control of LA CIO Council, 119; percentage of membership in CIO unions, 8; racism and (*see* Standard Coil); support of CIO organizing efforts, 130; support of Latino for public office, 119, 120; support of UE in rivalry for Standard Coil with IUE, 118; union leadership role of, 8–9
Communist Party of Maryland: 1940 HUAC hearings, 179–180; 1944 HUAC hearings, 180; 1951 HUAC hearings, 182–184; 1954 HUAC hearings, 184; 1957 HUAC hearings, 185; influence destroyed, 185–186; intensity of hearings increased, 186–187; Local 43 of IUMSWA and, 180, 181, 186; locals associated with, 180; membership of, 180, 181; pre-HUAC investigation of, 179; Smith Act and, 181, 183–184
Communist Party of the United States of America (CPUSA), 85, 185, 249, 254, 256, 265
Communist Political Association, 77
Community Service Organization (CSO), 59, 63, 119, 120, 123, 124, 125, 128, 129, 134, 135
Confederación of Mexican Workers (CTM), 256; founding of, 245–246, 247–248; Lombardo expelled from, 266–267; relationship with CIO, 250–252, 254; relationship with Mexican state, 248–249; U.S. view toward, 252–253
Confederación Regional Obrera Mexicana (CROM; Regional Mexican Workers Confederation), 247, 266
Confederation of Latin American Workers (CTAL), 249, 250, 254, 256, 258, 262, 266

Conference of Studio Unions, 119
Congress of Industrial Organizations (CIO): competition with AFL, 1; equal rights and, 218–219; expansion of southern membership by, 217; first convention of CIO union in Jersey City, 88, 89; labor school support by, 208; Latin American unionism and, 250, 265, 266; left-led union expelled from, 1, 10, 12, 13, 26, 35, 58, 118, 130, 132, 143; loss of influence in Los Angeles, 119; merges with AFL, 19, 62; no-strike pledge and, 90, 95, 101, 104, 105, 115n67, 116n74, 205, 218; political action committee of, 181, 226; Sleepy Lagoon and, 258; social welfare support by, 193, 195, 196; Standard Coil and, 118, 126, 128, 132, 133, 135; referred to, 150, 158, 180, 181, 200, 208, 253, 254, 255, 257, 262, 265; ties with Lombardo, 249, 250; ties with Truman administration, 12. *See also* AFL; AFL-CIO; Evansville, Ind., labor movement in; South, labor organization in; *individual union*
Connelly, Matthew, 169
Connelly, Phillip "Slim," 124
Connor, Harry, 181
Copeland, W. A. "Red," 230, 232, 234
Cordiner Memo, 55n9
Corona, Bert, 121
corporate campaign, against organized labor, 16, 17 (fig)
Corridan, John M., 170
corruption/racketeering, 3
Coughlin, Charles, 170
Council for Civic Unity, 168
CPAC (Citizens Public Assistance Committee), 198
CPUSA. *See* Communist Party of the United States of America
Craig, Dale, 143
CRC. *See* Civil Rights Congress
CROM. *See* Confederación Regional Obrera Mexicana
Cronin, Bernard, 166
Cronin, John Francis, 163, 180, 187
Crouch, Paul, 183
Crowder, Earl, 230

Crump, Edward H., 220, 230
CSO. *See* Community Service Organization
CTAL. *See* Confederation of Latin American Workers
CTM. *See* Confederation of Mexican Workers
Curran, Joe, 115n72, 181

Daily Worker, 8, 13, 28, 34, 54, 184
D'Alesandro, Thomas, 179
Damato, Tom, 99
Daniel, Franz, 65
Daniels, Josephus, 250, 251
Davis, Benjamin, 91
Davis, Matthew, 220
Davis, "Red" William, 229 (fig), 231-232, 236
Davis, William, 97, 101, 114n65
Day, Dorothy, 126
Debs, Eugene, 86, 87
defense industry, left-led union and, 12–13
deindustrialization, 16
Democratic Party: after demise of labor left, 19; pension union and, 193, 194, 195; shift to right by, 149, 224, 226; shipbuilder's and, 86, 87–88; southern unionism and, 224, 226, 230, 234, 237–238; Standard Coil and, 129
Dempsey, John, 88, 90, 91, 96, 98, 99, 100, 102, 103–104
Dennis, Eugene, 77
Department of Organization (AFL-CIO), 63
deportation, 14, 148, 164
DeShetler, Irwin, 123, 124
Deslippe, Dennis, 170
Díaz, José, 255, 256
Dies, Martin, 180
Dies committee, 179–180
DiGirolamo, Carmen, 35
Divini Redemptoris, 155, 164
Dixiecrat Party, 227, 230, 235
Dobbs, Ben, 130
Donohoe, Hugh A., 160, 163–164, 165, 166–167, 173n36
Draper, Allan, 236, 237
Dubinsky, David, 86, 87, 208
DuBois, W.E.B., 195, 217

Dunlop, John T., 1
Dunne, George, 124
Dunne, Neil, 54
Durham, Earl, 81
Durkin, Martin, 97
Dutra Steel, 131

Eastern Europe, 122, 125, 128, 210
Eastland, James, 234
East Los Angeles. *See* Standard Coil
Edison, Thomas, 25
Edison Machine Works, 25. *See also* Schenectady, N.Y., history of labor unrest in
Eighth Pan American Conference, 250
Eisenhower, Dwight D., 3
Elber, Irwin, 208
El Congresso del Pueblo de Habla Española (Spanish-Speaking People's Congress), 253, 254
Elconin, William, 131, 133
Electric Boat (IUMSWA local), 106
Elliot, Al, 90–91, 98, 99
El Monte, Calif., 126–127. *See also* "Zoot Suit" riots
El Popular, 248, 256, 257, 258
Erikson, Erik, 207
Esparza, Manuel, 253
Evansville Cooperative League, 143
Evansville, Ind., labor movement in: AFL membership, 141; anticommunist faction with Local 813, 145; Bucyrus-Erie plant organization, 144, 145; Bucyrus-Erie strike, 145, 146 (fig), 147, 149; CIO attack on Communism/UE, 143; CIO membership in, 141; congressional investigation of strike, 145, 146, 147–148, 149, 152n14; elimination of UE, 150; EU pitted against other union, 144–145; IUE as prominent union, 143–144; non-Communist affidavits and, 148–149; popular anticommunism and, 142–143; UE Local 813 and, 141, 142, 144; union alignment against UE, 149–150; worker purges, 147, 149

Factories in the Field (McWilliams), 59
Fair Employment Practices Committee (FEPC), 76, 144–145, 253–254
Farmer-Labor Party, 120, 194

Faultless Caster, 141, 144, 147, 149
Federal Bureau of Investigation (FBI): CPUSA labor schools and, 206; McIntyre file of, 138n36; Mexico and, 263, 264; in Schenectady, 44, 47, 51; shipyard workers and, 101; southern unionism and, 234; Standard Coil and, 122, 126, 131, 136; surveillance of union activity by, 10. *See also* House Un-American Activities Committee
Federal Mediation and Conciliation Service, 2–3
Federal Ship. *See* Industrial Union of Marine and Shipbuilding Workers of America
Fernandez, Manuel, 52–54
Fiering, Henry, 121, 129, 133, 136
Fierro, Josefina, 254, 258
Filipelli, Ronald, 142
financial disclosure, by union, 3
Fineglass, Abe, 81
Fiorello, Frank, 34–37
Fish, Hamilton, 179
Fisher, Dave, 36
Fisher, James T., 170
Flynn, Peter, 87, 91, 95, 96, 97–98, 99, 100, 113n57–114n57
Foisie, Frank P., 162
Folsom, Jim, 222
Foner, Jack, 206
Foner, Philip, 206, 207, 232
Fones-Wolf, Elizabeth, 16
Food, Tobacco, Agricultural and Allied Workers (FTA): expelled from CIO, 58; Local 19, 233-234; Local 22, 9–10, 13, 18, 228,; southern labor organization and, 218, 222, 225, 226, 228, 230, 231, 232, 234, 236
Ford, Gerald, 1
Ford Motor Company, sued by United Auto Workers, 16
Fore River Local 5 (IUMSWA), 106–107
Foster, William Z., 80, 81, 86
Fox, Chris, 253, 254
Foy, Terry, 89, 91, 98, 99, 105, 107, 108, 114n60
Frankfeld, Philip, 181, 182, 183
Frankfeld, Regina, 181, 183
Fraternidad, 260

Friedan, Betty, 10, 130
Friedlander, Sidney, 35–36, 46, 53, 56n12
FTA. *See* Food, Tobacco, Agricultural and Allied Workers
Furniture Workers Union (CIO), 123, 232
Futuro, 248, 249, 257, 258

Galarza, Ernesto, 59, 60, 61, 62, 63, 64, 65, 66
Gallagher, Hugh, 158, 163
Gallagher, Tom, 99
Gama, Rosa Mariá Otero, 260, 263
Garcia, Victor, 92, 98
Gardner, Evelyn, 195
Gates, John, 184, 185
Gates, Ralph F., 145
General Assistance, 200
General Electric (GE) Company, 118, 121. *See also* Schenectady, N.Y., history of labor unrest in
George, Charles, 103
George Knoch & Sons, 141
Gerstle, Gary, 150
GE Worker, 46
Gillie, Ken, 59
GI Non-Partisan League, 220
Goldstein, M. H., 96–97
Goldway, David, 206, 211
Goodfriend, Bernard "Whitey," 181
Good Neighbor Policy, 245, 246, 251, 252, 254, 255, 256, 257, 258, 262, 266, 267, 268
Googe, George, 223
Gordon, Max, 55n5
Gorman, Pat, 60, 61, 65, 66, 67
Graham, Frank Porter, 63, 97, 222
Granados, Ramona Almanza, 126
Grange, 193, 194
Great Depression, 1, 130, 192, 194, 246
Green, John, 86–87, 89, 91, 95, 96, 97, 99, 101, 102, 103, 104, 105, 106, 109n8, 181
Green, William, 60, 133
Griffith, Barbara, 221, 237
Grogan, John, 101–102, 103, 106

Haggerty, Neil, 60
Hague, Frank, 87–88, 89
Halpern, Martin, 233
Hanna, Edward J., 155, 164, 171n8

Hargis, Billy James, 224
Harrison, George, 64-66
Harrison, Gregory A., 168–169
Harrison, Maurice E., 168
Hatch, Helen Almanza, 120, 122
The Haunted Wood (Weinstein), 177
Hayes, Charles, 78, 80, 81
Haynes, John, 177
Haywood, Allan S., 219
Haywood, Bill, 86
Haywood, Harry, 76, 77
Healey, Dorothy, 120
Heineman, Kenneth J., 170
Helstein, Ralph, 58, 59, 61, 64, 75
Henestrosa, Andrés, 260
Henning, John F. "Jack," 154–155, 164, 168
Henry, George, 179
Hernandez, Ignacio, 130
Hicks Camp barrio, 126
Higgins, George C., 170, 176n75
Highlander Folk School, 219, 220, 224, 230, 231, 236, 238
Hill, Herbert, 82
Hillman, Sidney, 95, 97
Hiss, Alger, 150, 177, 182
Hoffa, Jimmy, 3, 107–108
Hollcroft, Bette, 130
Holloway, George, 235
Holloway, Mrs. Ruben Ross, 179, 187n3–188n3
Hollywood Studio Strike, 124
Hollywood Ten, 7
Holton, Karl, 255
Hoosier Cardinal, 141
Hoover, J. Edgar, 12, 264
Horowitz, Daniel, 10
Horowitz, Irving, 43–46
Horton, Myles, 221, 230, 231
Horwitt, Sanford, 58
House Labor and Education Committee, 13, 14, 267
House Un-American Activities Committee (HUAC), 11, 13, 108, 119; hearings on alleged UE Communism by, 132, 133–134; hearings on alleged UPWA Communism, 64; meat packinghouse worker investigation by, 80; southern unionism and, 224, 226, 232, 235; United Auto Workers Local 248 investigation by, 13–14. *See also* Communist Party of Maryland
Hull, Cordel, 252
Hunt, Helen Almanza, 126, 132
Hutchinson, John, 184

IAF (Industrial Areas Foundation), 119
IAM. *See* International Association of Machinists
Ickes, Harold, 110n12
ILA. *See* International Longshoremen's Association
I Led Three Lives (Philbrick), 183
ILGWU. *See* International Ladies Garment Worker's Union
ILWU. *See* International Longshoremen's and Warehousemen's Union
Immigration and Naturalization Act (1952), 267
Independent Progressive Party, 120
Indiana Parents Association, 149
Indiana State Police, 146
Industrial Areas Foundation (IAF), 119
Industrial Union Council (IUC), 143, 251
Industrial Union Department (IUD; AFL-CIO), 62
Industrial Union of Marine and Shipbuilding Workers of America (IUMSWA; CIO): concurs with NWLB rulings, 104–105; delegate election, 101, 105–106; discrimination stance of, 91, 111n27, 113n51; early leader of, 86–87; early leadership of, 86–87; founding/initial success of, 85–86; Hispanic leadership of, 92; leftist leaders disperse after defeat, 106–108; leftists and, 92–94, 105–106; Local 15, anticommunist moves, 101–102; Local 22, 102; locals dismissed/dissolved, 113n53; merge with Machinist Union, 106; NWLB and Federal Shipbuilding recommendations, 112n40; preamble to constitution of, 86–87; renunciation of strikes by, 95; triumph over left in, 106; women and, 98, 113n51; worker unrest at, 100–101, 102–103, 104–105. *See also* Industrial Union of Marine and Shipbuilding Workers of America (IUMSWA; CIO), Local 16

Industrial Union of Marine and Shipbuilding Workers of America (IUMSWA; CIO), Local 16: African American worker organization by, 90–92; autonomy suspended, 103; Federal Shipbuilding contract expiration, 94–95; financial troubles/internal conflict, 96, 98–100, 114n64; maintenance-of-membership controversy, 95–98, 105; rebuilding/reforming efforts by, 100, 102; Republican right-wing leader of, 88–89; strike by, 95–96; union convention sponsorship by, 88

Industrial Workers of the World (IWW), 94, 208, 232

inflation, 2

Inter-American Conference on the Problems of War and Peace, 261, 262

Internal Revenue Service (IRS), 10, 14

International Association of Machinists (IAM), 122, 132, 134, 148, 150

International Association of Theatrical and Stage Employees, 119

International Brotherhood of Electrical Workers (IBEW; AFL). *See* Standard Coil

International Brotherhood of Teamsters: Communist issue and, 61–62; expelled from AFL, 3–4

International Harvester, 141, 147, 236

International Ladies Garment Workers Union (ILGWU), 57n21, 86, 119, 123, 208

International Longshoremen's and Warehousemen's Union (ILWU), 93, 107; Catholic Church and, 164, 166; Communist Party domination of leadership of, 9; equal rights and, 218; HUAC investigation of leadership, 14; Local 16, 121; Mexican labor left and, 251; pension union support by, 196, 200

International Longshoremen's Association (ILA), 3, 102

International Textile Workers, 180

International Union of Electrical, Radio and Machine Employees (IUE; CIO): formation of, 26; reason for chartering, 143; in Schenectady, 36–37, 40, 46. *See also* Standard Coil

International Union of Marine and Shipbuilding Workers of America (IUMSWA), 180, 181, 186

International Union of Mine, Mill and Smelter Workers, 9, 14, 107, 226, 231, 233, 236, 250, 251

International Woodworkers of America (IWA), 196, 200, 222, 229

Irish Americans, 120

Iron Curtain, 126, 130

IRS (Internal Revenue Service), 10, 14

IUC. *See* Industrial Union Council

IUD. *See* Industrial Union Department

IUMSWA. *See* Industrial Union of Marine and Shipbuilding Workers of America

IWA. *See* International Woodworkers of America

IWW. *See* Industrial Workers of the World

James, Troy, 149

Jandreau, Leo: adopted daughter of (*see* Clark, Karen J.); as Local 301 business agent, 26, 38; switches to IUE, 36–37, 40, 46; union activism of, 27, 28, 30, 33, 34, 41–42, 43, 48, 53

Jandreau, Ruth Young, 48–52

Jefferson School of Social Science, 205, 206, 207, 208, 209, 210, 211, 212

Jenkins, David, 207, 209 (fig)

Jesuit labor school, 155, 166–168, 170

Jews, 119, 121

John Birch Society, 224

Johnson, Lyndon, 201–202

Johnson, Vic, 98, 102, 103–104, 107, 114n65, 115n72

Joint Fact-Finding Committee on Un-American Activities, 198

Jones, Claudia, 77

Jones, William, 229

Justice Department: left-led union and, 14; Standard Coil and, 140n67. *See also* House Un-American Activities Committee

Kagel, Sam, 157

Kandel, Irving, 185

Kaplan, Lou, 88–89, 90, 91, 92, 93–94, 98, 99–100, 104, 105, 106, 107–108, 111n27, 113n51, 114nn60,64

Kearney, Bernard William, 44
Kearney, James Stanley, 166, 174n53–175n53
Kearney, Joseph, 131, 132
Kearny, N.J. *See* Industrial Union of Marine and Shipbuilding Workers of America
Kefauver, Carey Estes, 30, 55n7, 222
Kennedy, Stetson, 224
Kennedy, Thomas, 97
Khrushchev, Nikita, 184, 185
King, Martin Luther, Jr., 64, 108, 238
Klehr, Harvey, 177
Knight, Artie, 104
Knights of St. John, 149
Knowles, Clive, 62
Knox, Frank, 95–96, 97
Knox, H. R., 145
Korean War, 12, 14, 53, 182, 184, 233
Korean War Port Security, 7
Korndorff, Lynn, 95, 97
Korstad, Karl, 236
Korstad, Robert, 228–229, 234
Koster, Frederick J., 162
Krainock, Lou, 65
Kriss, Frank, 40, 56n13
Ku Klux Klan, 94, 147, 179, 225, 227
Kushner, Sam, 81

Labor League of Hollywood Voters (AFL), 119
Labor-Management Reporting and Disclosure Act. *See* Landrum-Griffen Act
Labor Relations Board, 27
labor school, Communist: California Labor School, 167, 205, 206, 207, 208; cooperation between, 207; curriculum at, 206, 207, 208, 209–211; employee benefits at, 208; entrance requirements, 206; extension schools, 213n2; faculty at, 206–207; forced closure of, 206, 207–208; Jefferson School of Social Science, 205, 206, 207, 208, 209, 210, 211, 212; services provided by, 208–209; student motivation at, 211–212
labor school, Jesuit, 155, 166–168, 170
Labor Youth League (successor of Young Communist league), 122
LaForge, Charlie, 30, 31–32, 33–34
Landrum-Griffen Act, 3–4, 167
Langlie, Arthur, 191, 198
LAPD. *See* Los Angeles Police Department
Lapham, Roger, 168
LaRoe, Edward, 36
Latino. *See* Mexicans/Mexican Americans
Lautner, John, 183
La Voz de Mexico, 256
Lawson, John Howard, 209 (fig)
League of Latin-American Citizens (LULAC), 253, 267
Lee, Sirkka Tuomi, 185
left-led union: congressional investigation of, 13–14; defense industry and, 12–13; effect of demise of, 12–13, 15–16, 18, 19; end of anticommunist campaign against, 14–15; leaders subpoenaed/indicted, 14; strikes by, 11, 13; Taft-Hartley affidavit effect on, 11–12. *See also individual union*
Lemlich, Clara, 57n21
Lenin, Vladimir, 120, 157
Leo XIII (pope), 155, 158, 160, 169
Levenstein, Harvey, 232–233
Levin, Nat, 88, 89, 91, 92, 96, 99, 103, 107, 108, 117n91
Lewis, John L., 109n4, 116n74, 250, 251
Lewis, Kathryn, 250
Lichtenstein, Nelson, 237
Lightfoot, Claude, 80, 81
Livingston, Jack, 63, 64, 65
Lloyd, Thomas, 66, 67
lombardistas, 246, 247, 248, 253, 256–257, 258, 259, 261, 262, 265, 267, 268
Lombardo, Adriana, 248
Lombardo Toledano, Vicente, 62; expelled from Confederación of Mexican Workers, 266–267; founds Confederation of Latin American Workers, 249; helps found Confederación of Mexican Workers, 245–246, 247–248; helps found preparatory school, 248; international activity of, 249; postwar vision of Americas criticized by, 247–248; racism in U.S. attacked by, 257, 259–260, 261–262, 263; rise of, 247; U.S. investigation of, 249–250, 262, 263–266
López, Ignacio, 255

Los Angeles: police brutality in, 121, 128, 129; Servicemen's riots in, 127, 135, 254, 256, 257, 259; Sleepy Lagoon case in, 121, 255–256, 257–258, 258, 260; wartime anti-Mexican discrimination in, 254–256
Los Angeles CIO Council, 119, 120, 124
Los Angeles Communist Party, 130
Los Angeles Herald, 255
Los Angeles Police Department (LAPD), 121, 128
Los Angeles Times, 133, 255–256
Lundgren, Lee, 122, 123, 124, 128, 132, 134

MacDonald, Ramsey, 99, 104
MacIntosh, Frank, 33–34
MacPherson, Gavin, 102, 103
Maguire, John, F., 166
Maiatico, Ben, 109n8, 116n74
maintenance-of-membership clause, 35, 95–98, 105
Male, Louis, 30
Many are the Crimes: McCarthyism in America (Schrecker), 177
March, Herbert, 64, 72–73 (fig), 74, 76, 78, 80, 81
Markward, Mary Stalcup, 182–183
Marshall, Ray, 235
Marshall Plan, 41, 122, 145, 267
Martin, Clarence, 192
Martinez, Refugio, 79
Marx, Karl, 157
Marxism, 209, 212, 245, 249, 262
Marxist-Leninism, 259
Maryland. *See* Communist Party of Maryland
Maryland Subversive Activities Unit, 185
Mason, Lucy Randolph, 217
Mastriani, Billy, 40
Matles, Esther, 50, 51
Matles, James, 50, 51, 57n22, 108
Matthews, J. B., 178–179, 180, 184, 187
Maxwell, Howard, 144
McAtee, Bernard, 148
McCarran Act, 148
McCarthy, Joseph, 26, 32, 33, 45, 50, 79, 135, 177–178, 182, 184, 209

McCarthyism, 177–178; Army-McCarthy hearings, 7, 184; definition of, 7; demise of left-wing unions under, 10; reason to target labor movement, 7–8, 135–136; in Schenectady, 33–34, 43–46; women's rights and, 10. *See also* House Un-American Activities Committee
McClellan Committee, 3
McColloch, Mark, 142
McCoy, Nora, 199 (fig)
McCrea, Ed, 228, 231–232, 236
McCullough, Thomas, 59, 62
McDonald, David, 233
McDonald, Donald, 59
McGowan, Raymond A., 125
McGrath, William, 181
McGucken, Joseph, 125, 168
McIntyre, James Francis, 124, 125, 126, 134, 135, 138n36, 168
McNulty, Al, 96, 103, 114n64
McShane, Joseph, 170
McWilliams, Carey, 59, 256
Meany, George, 3, 58, 60, 61, 63–64, 65, 66, 97, 223. *See also* American Federation of Labor
membership, union: decline in, 4, 15; post World War II, 1; pre-World War II, 1
Memphis Labor Council, 231–232
Mendelson, Mendy, 90, 101, 115n67
Mendez, James, 124
Messersmith, George, 249–250, 254, 260, 262, 263, 264, 265, 267–268
Mexican Committee against Racism (CMCR), 260
Mexican Communist, 62
Mexican Revolution, 246, 253
Mexicans/Mexican Americans: beatings of, 121; bracero worker program, 59, 67, 68n5, 253; Community Service Organization and, 59, 63, 119, 120, 123, 124, 125, 128, 129, 134, 135,; pension union and, 202; Servicemen's riots and, 127, 135, 254, 256, 257, 259; Sleepy Lagoon case and, 121, 255–256, 257–258, 258, 260; at Standard Coil, 118, 120, 123, 124, 128, 129; UPWA and, 79; wartime discrimination against, 254–256. *See also* Confederación of Mexican Workers; Lombardo Toledano, Vicente

The Mexican Labor News, 248, 249, 250, 251, 256, 258
Meyers, David, 47–48
Meyers, George, 183, 184
MIG-15 (Soviet-built jet), 130
Militant Truth, 224
Miller, Clifford, 185
Milton, David, 92–93, 115n72
Milwaukee, Wisc., 13
Minchin, Timothy, 227
Mine-Mill. *See* International Union of Mine, Mill and Smelter Workers
minimum wage, 217
Mitchell, Edward A., 145, 147, 149, 152nn14, 19
Mitchell, H. L., 59, 60, 61, 62, 63, 64, 65, 66
Mitty, John J., 155, 156, 157, 158, 160, 161, 162–163, 165, 167, 168, 169
Molotov-Ribentropp Pact, 247
The Monitor, 156, 158, 160, 162, 163, 167, 168
Monroe, Bob, 90
Mooney, Edward, 170
The Moraga Quarterly, 154
Morais, Herbert, 207
Morones, Luis, 266
Morse, Wayne, 97, 101
Moyer, Herbert, 101
Mugica, Toledano Francisco, 252
Mundy, Marie, 120
Murray, Philip, 12, 58, 133, 231
Myrdal, Gunnar, 207

NAACP. *See* National Association for the Advancement of Colored People
NAM. *See* National Association of Manufacturers
National Advisory Committee on Farm Labor (NACFL), 63
National Agricultural Workers Union (NAWU), 59–60, 64–66
National Association for the Advancement of Colored People (NAACP), 10, 29, 77, 78, 79, 201, 208, 219, 227
National Association of Manufacturers (NAM), 2, 224
National Committee in Defense of the Proletariat (CNPD), 247

National Defense Mediation Board (NDMB), 95, 112n40
National Guard, 149
National Labor Relations Act (1935), 2, 217, 221. *See also* Wagner Act
National Labor Relations Board (NLRB): denial of services to left-led union, 10, 11, 12; establishment of, 2; Standard Coil and, 121–122, 133, 134–135; UE and, 144, 148; unionism in the South and, 225, 233
National Longshoremen's Board, 157
National Maritime Union (NMU), 115n72, 180, 181, 231
National Security Act of 1947, 264
National Sinarquista Union, 256
National Union of Marine Cooks and Stewards, 182, 196, 208
National War Labor Board (NWLB), 96, 97, 101, 102–103, 104
National Welfare Rights Organization (NWRO), 196, 197
The Nation's Business, 192
NATO, 207
NAWU. *See* National Agricultural Workers Union
Nazi-Soviet Non-Aggression Pact, 121, 178, 191
NDMB. *See* National Defense Mediation Board
Negro Commission, 80
Negro Labor Council, 78
Neilson, Harold, 80
Nelson, Bruce, 236
Nemitoff, Blackie, 103, 104
Newark, N.J. *See* Industrial Union of Marine and Shipbuilding Workers of America
New Deal Democrat, 126
Newsweek, 199
New York Shipbuilding (IUMSWA local), 92, 94, 98–99, 105, 106, 107
New York Times, 1, 207
Neylan, John Francis, 157
Nickey Brothers, strike at, 229 (fig)
Nixon, Richard, 238
NLRB. *See* National Labor Relations Board
NMU. *See* National Maritime Union

non-Communist affidavit (Taft-Hartley), 11–12, 123, 148–149, 225
North Korean, 125
no-strike pledge, 90, 95, 101, 104, 105, 115n67, 116n74, 205, 218
Not Without Honor: The History of American Anticommunism (Powers), 177, 178
Nowak, Joseph, 184
Nowell, William Odell, 183
NWLB. *See* National War Labor Board
NWRO. *See* National Welfare Rights Organization

OAA. *See* Old Age Assistance
Oakland, Calif., 166
Ober, Frank B., 181
Ober Law, 181–182, 185, 186
O'Brien, David J., 164
OCCIAA. *See* Office of the Coordinator of Inter-American Affairs
O'Connell, Jerry, 194
O'Dwyer, Thomas, 124–125, 128
Office of Strategic Services (OSS), 264, 266
Office of the Coordinator of Inter-American Affairs (OCIAA), 255, 264
O'Grady, E. B., 157
O'Hanion, I. H., 179
Old Age Assistance (OAA), 191–192, 194, 195, 196, 197
O'Neil, Gordon, 163
Operation Dixie, 18, 222, 226, 227, 228, 230, 231, 234, 235, 237, 238
Orozco, José Clemente, 260
OSS. *See* Office of Strategic Services
Osslo, Max, 67

pachucos, 254, 256, 257
Pacific Northwest Labor School, 205
Pan-American Federation of Labor, 249
Parker, George, 144
Parks, Sam, 74, 78–79, 80
Parra, Leroy, 120
Patterson, Leonard, 184
Payne, James, 147, 148
Paz, Octavio, 257
Pennock, Louise, 195, 202
Pennock, William, 190, 191, 198, 199 (fig), 200, 201

Pension Builder, 202
Pension Union, 200
People's Congress/Congreso, 121
Perales, Alonso, 267
Perlin, Marshall, 55n8, 56n17
Perry, Pettis, 80
Peters, Joe, 89, 92
Petit-Chair, Al, 114n60
Pettus, Terry, 193, 195, 198, 200–201
Philbrick, Herbert, 183
Pinsky, Paul, 166
Pius XII (pope), 169
Pius XI (pope), 155, 160, 161, 163, 166, 169, 180
Plumb, Milton, 62
Plumbers Union (AFL), 120
police brutality, in Los Angeles, 121, 128, 129
Political Action Committee (CIO-PAC), 181, 226
Political Affairs, 80
Power, Richard Gid, 177–178, 186
Progressive Party, 182, 198, 216, 217, 226, 227, 231
Proposition 18 (Calif.; "Right to Work"), 168–169

Quadragesimo Anno, 155, 163, 166, 180
Quevedo, Eduardo, 121
Quintanilla, Luis, 265
Quirini, Helen, 37–41

Rabinowitz, Victor, 14
race-baiting, 18
race relations, 1; Communist-led union and, 9–10; pension union and, 196–197. *See also* African Americans; Mexicans/Mexican Americans; United Packinghouse Workers of America (UPWA; CIO), in Chicago
race riots, 92
Ramirez, R., 79
Randal, Charles, 179
Randolph, A. Philip, 63, 65, 77
Rappaport, Morris, 190–191
Rapp-Coudert investigation, 206, 208
RCA, 121, 134
Reagan, Ronald, 119, 238
red-baiting, 13, 17 (fig), 50; Catholic

Church and, 130, 154–155, 164; historical, 7–8; southern labor organization and, 18, 223, 224, 227; at Standard Coil, 130, 131
Reds and our Churches (Matthews), 184
red scare, 26, 232, 233, 234, 236, 237, 238
Reeder, Andy, 94, 105, 107, 108, 116n74
Reflections of a "Labor Priest" (Higgins), 170
Refregier, Anton, 207
Republican Party, 136, 149; shipbuilder's and, 86, 88–89; southern labor organization and, 224, 230
Republican Steel Plant, 141
Rerum Novarum, 155, 160
Reston, James, 1
Reuther, Victor, 60, 62
Reuther, Walter, 3, 58, 60–61, 64, 65, 66, 150
Revolutionary Policy Committee, 86
RGASPI. *See* Russian State Archive of Social and Political History
Rice, Charles Owen, 36, 58, 68, 176N75
Rieve, Emil, 97
Riffe, John, 59, 60, 234
"right to work," 3, 168–169, 200, 225
Ring, Daniel, 96
Rios, Tony, 121, 126, 127 (fig), 128, 129, 134, 135
Rivers, Charles, 53, 57n23
R.J. Reynolds Tobacco Company, 9, 13, 233–234
Roberts, Holland, 207, 211
Robeson, Eslanda, 195
Robeson, Paul, 80, 144, 195, 209 (fig), 231
Robinson, Arthur, 152n14
Robinson, Reid, 250
Rockefeller, Nelson, 108, 264, 265
Rodriguez, Luis, 252
Rodriquez, Manuel, 130
Rogin, Lawrence, 235
Romualdi, Serafino, 266
Roosevelt, Eleanor, 63, 216
Roosevelt, Franklin D., 230; Communist organization of CIO and, 125; formation of NWLB authorized by, 96; Good Neighbor Policy of, 246; HUAC and, 133; shipbuilding industry and, 87, 95, 97, 112n40; southern unionism and, 217

Rosellini, Albert, 200
Rosenberg, Ethel, 49, 50, 182, 185
Rosenberg, Julius, 49, 50, 177, 182, 185
Ross, Fred, 59, 119, 125, 128, 129
Rossi, Angelo, 162
Rosswurm, Steve, 170
Roth, Almon, 161
Routon, Richard, 232
Roybal, Edward R., 119, 120, 121, 124, 128, 129
runaway plant, 16
Russian State Archive of Social and Political History (RGASPI), 177
Ryan, John A., 163, 169, 180

Sabre Jet, 118, 120, 130
San Antonio De Paula Parish, 131
San Francisco, Catholic activism in: anticommunist campaign, 164; call for, 154–155; industrial problems conference, 161–162; Jesuit labor school, 166–168; labor agenda, 159 (fig); lay activism, 164–166, 169–170; papal labor encyclical use in, 155–157, 158, 160–161, 162, 163–164, 169; promotion of mainstream unionism, 164; "Right to Work" and, 168–169; Social Action School for Priests, 161, 163; during waterfront strike, 156–157; WWII business–labor campaign support by, 162–163
San Francisco Urban League, 168
San Francisco Academy of Catholic Men, 171n9
Saxton, Alexander, 207
SCEF (Southern Conference Education Fund), 231
Schachter, Leon, 61
Schatz, Ronald, 170
Schenectady, N.Y.: economic foundation of, 25. *See also* Schenectady, N.Y., history of labor unrest in
Schenectady, N.Y., history of labor unrest in: Carey account of union struggle, 41–43; child viewpoint of, 48–52; CIO expels UE and Local 301, 26; CIO organizes IUE, 26; Communist infiltration of UE, 29–30; Communist influence in, 28, 29; Communist Party contribution to

Schenectady, N.Y. (*continued*)
    black community, 47–48; Communist unionist viewpoint of GE, 52–54; company union at GE Works, 27; crisis faced by community-based Communist Party organization, 43–46; early activist account of union struggle, 27–29; Fernandez account of union struggle, 52–54; founding of GE Works, 25; GE company union broken, 27–28; Horowitz account of union struggle, 43–46; IWW strike against GE (1906), 25; lack of union support, 28–29, 35; left-wing CIO-based labor movement in, 26; management account of union struggle, 29–34; McCarthyism and, 33–34, 43–46; opposition forces to UE and Jandreau, 34–37; reason to join UE, 41–42; right-wing account of union struggle, 41–43; security issues at GE plant, 30–32, 33–34; split in UE to IUE, 40; UE barred from representing nuclear workers, 12; UE Local 301 established, 26, 27, 28, 57n23; UE workers subpoenaed, 32; UE workers sue, 32; union expulsion from GE, 52–54; union leader/plant manager relations, 33–34; union meeting control, 42–43; women activists, 37–41, 45–46; Young account of union struggle, 48–52
Schenectady Gazette, 44, 54
Schnitzler, William, 60, 63
Schrecker, Ellen, 177, 178, 186
SCHW. *See* Southern Conference for Human Welfare
Schwartz, Florence, 181
Scottsboro, Ala., 48, 76, 218
The Secret World of American Communism (Haynes & Klehr), 177
Seeger-Sunbeam, 141, 147
Seidman, Joel, 112n40
Selsam, Howard, 206, 207
Senate Internal Security Subcommittee (SISS), 232, 234
Sentner, Toni, 148
Sentner, William, 148
Serrano, Socorro, 131
Servel Inc., 141, 143, 147
Servicemen's Riots, 127, 135, 254, 256, 257, 259

Sharecropper Fund, 60, 63, 66
Shelley, John F., 163, 164, 166
shipbuilding industry: workers employed during WWII, 86; yard closings, 106. *See also* Industrial Union of Marine and Shipbuilding Workers of America
Shubsda, Thaddeus, 131
Silverman, Vincent, 174n53–175n53
Simmons, Lowell, 225
sinarquistas, 256, 258
SISS. *See* Senate Internal Security Subcommittee
Sleepy Lagoon Defense Committee, 121, 257–258, 260
Sleepy Lagoon, 255–256, 257, 258, 260
Smith, Jim, 61–62, 64–65
Smith, Laura, 166
Smith, Moranda, 228
Smith Act, 50, 148, 181, 183–184, 191, 198, 200, 207
Sobell, Morton, 56n17
SOC. *See* Southern Organizing Committee
Social Gospel, 128
Socialist Party (SP), 86, 87
Socialists, 135
Social Security Act, 192
Social Workers Council, 196
Sorrell, Herb, 125
South, labor organization in: AFL role in, 223; anticommunist stance adopted by CIO, 226–227, 230, 233–234; antiunionism and, 224–225; black/white veteran role in, 220; CIO and, 18, 217–221, 231–233; coalition for organizing labor, 218–220; Cold War affect on, 223–224, 225, 230, 235, 236, 237, 238; factors in defeat of CIO, 235–238; failure of, 18, 235–239; globalization affect on, 238–239; industrial workers post WWII, 216; Ku Klux Klan and, 225; low-wage industry and, 220–221, 222, 227–229, 237; Operation Dixie and, 18, 222–223, 226, 227, 228, 230, 231, 234–235, 237, 238; red-baiting affect on, 223, 224, 227; shift to right affect on, 224; Taft-Hartley Act affect on, 225–226, 230; union expelled from CIO, 231–233; WWII affect on unionism, 216–217

Southern Conference Education Fund (SCEF), 231
Southern Conference for Human Welfare (SCHW), 219, 220, 224, 231–232, 237–238
Southern Organizing Committee (SOC), 226, 228, 229–230, 235
Southern States Industrial Council, 224
South Korea, 130
The Soviet World of American Communism (Haynes & Klehr), 177
Soviet Union, 128, 178, 180, 187, 237
SP. *See* Socialist Party
Sparrows Point, 184, 186
Spegal, William, 182
Spellman, Francis, 125, 169
Spirit of Kilroy, 144, 149, 152n14
Squier, George, 208
St. Thomas More Society, 168
Stachel, Jack, 93
Stalin, Joseph, 128, 184
Stalinism, 150
Standard Coil: battle between IUE/UE for, 118, 119; battle for as product of time/place, 134–135; contract after second election, 134; election at, 122, 132, 133–134; firing of UE activist at, 129–130; IBEW representation at, 120, 121–122; ineligible voter at, 133; IUE strategy to take over, 122–124, 128–130; key to IUE success at, 135; Korean War and, 130–131; overview of, 120; red-baiting at, 130, 131; Roybal and, 129; support of IUE at, 118, 122, 126, 132, 140n67; support of UE at, 118; UE continued action at, 134; UE response to IUE efforts, 130–132, 133; women's issues at, 120, 130, 131–132
Stanton, Marty, 35,
State, County, and Municipal Workers of America, Local 555, 208
State's Rights Party, 227
Steinmetz, Alfred Proteus, 26
Stephens, Tony, 61, 63–64
Sterling Electric, 130
Stevens, A. C., 29–32, 33, 34
St. Mary's College, 154

Strack, Celesta, 207
Subversive Activities Control Board (SACB), 10, 191, 206
"Super Seniority," 9
Sweethearts of Servicemen, 180
Swift Local 28, 75
Swim, Pete, 230

Taft-Hartley Act (1947), 53, 143, 167, 168, 230; effect on Communist-led union, 10–11; non-Communist affidavits under, 12, 13, 14, 76, 148–149; provisions of, 2–3, 15, 75, 225, 267
Tannehill, DeWitt, 62
Taylor, George, 97
Teamsters. *See* International Brotherhood of Teamsters
Thomas, Norman, 60, 66, 87, 88
Thomas, R. J., 60
Thompson, Roy, 80
Thurmond, Strom, 227, 230
Tifton (Georgia), 225
Tinoco, César Ortiz, 258
Torre, Louis, 122, 133
Townsend Plan, 192
Transport Workers Union (TWU), 9
Tripp, Etta, 194, 195, 199 (fig)
Trotsky, Leon, 128
Trotskyists, 90, 105, 114n60, 115n67, 135
Truman, Harry, 2, 52, 53, 122, 223, 230, 231
Truman administration: shipbuilding and, 106; ties to CIO, 12
Tully, Antonio, 91, 92, 98
Tully, Henry, 90, 91, 92, 107
TWU. *See* Transport Workers Union

UAW. *See* United Auto Workers of America
UCAPAWA (United Cannery, Agricultural, Packing and Allied Workers of America), 61
UE. *See* United Electrical, Radio and Machine Workers of America
UE News, 34
Unemployed Council, 193
Union Counseling Committee, 200
union shop, 3, 225

United Auto Workers of America (UAW; CIO): accommodation to Taft-Hartley, 15; antidiscrimination and, 218; CIO purges and, 233; Communist Party influence in, 8; in Evanston, 141, 143, 145, 147; Ford Motor Company sued by Local 600, 16; Local 248, 13–14; Local 265, 143; social justice and, 82

United Cannery, Agricultural, Packing and Allied Workers of America (UCAPAWA; CIO), 61

United Electrical, Radio and Machine Workers of America (UE; CIO): barred from representing nuclear facility workers, 12; Communist domination of leadership of, 8–9; effect of anticommunist crusade on, 11, 12, 13, 14, 15; equal rights and, 218; expelled from CIO, 35; founder of, 50; Local 301, 56n15; Local 813 (*see* Evansville, Ind., labor movement in); Local 1421 (*see* Standard Coil); size in Los Angeles, 118–119; women's issues and, 10, 130, 131–132

United Furniture Workers of America (UFWA; CIO), 143, 228

United Mine Workers of America, 217, 218

United Office and Professional Workers of America, 12

United Packinghouse Workers of America (UPWA; CIO): alliance with AWOC, 66–68, 67 (fig); allies of, 59–60; charges of Communism at, 61–62, 63–64; Communists remain in, 58, 59; equal rights and, 218, 232; erosion of meatpacking base, 62–63; financial support for, 60; lettuce worker strike, 66–67 (fig); proposed merger with NAWU, 60–61; takes over CIO Local 78, 58–59. *See also* United Packinghouse Workers of America (UPWA; CIO), in Chicago

United Packinghouse Workers of America (UPWA; CIO), in Chicago: changing racial composition of workers, 72, 74, 79; civil rights affect on, 79–81; Communist support of shifting racial policy, 73–74, 76–77, 79–80; creation of Anti-Discrimination Committee, 76, 78, 79; decline of black membership in Communist Party, 77–78; demand for integration, 74–75; effect of Taft-Hartley Act on, 75; formation of, 72; interracial focus shift, 72–73; Mexican workers and, 79; number of workers, 74; race relations survey, 75–76; strike defeated (1948), 75. *See also* United Packinghouse Workers of America

United Public Workers, 14

United Service Organization (USO), 180

United States Armed Services, 133

United Steelworkers of America (USWA; CIO), 11, 14, 119, 120, 121, 122, 123, 124, 144, 218, 233

United Transport Service Workers, 233, 234

Universidad Obrera de Mexico. *See* Workers University of Mexico

UOM. *See* Workers University of Mexico

UPWA. *See* United Packinghouse Workers of America

Urban League, 77, 234

U.S. Steel Corporation, 86, 95, 97

USA. *See* United Steelworkers of America

USF Labor Management School, 155, 166–168

The USF Labor Management School Panel, 168

Vanderburgh County Council of Veterans Organizations, 144

Van Gelder, Phil, 86, 87, 91, 94, 96, 98, 99, 100, 101, 106, 107, 108, 117n85

Velázquez, Fidel, 249, 266

Velson, Irving, 117n85

Veterans of Foreign Wars, 149

Vietnam War, 19, 230, 233

Villaseñor, Eduardo, 260

Vottis, Pasquale, 27–29

Vottis, Sal, 27–28, 38

Wagner Act, 2, 4, 27, 53, 217, 221

Walker, Edwin A., 224

Wallace, George, 238

Wallace, Henry, 41, 46, 53, 54, 79, 122, 144, 182, 198, 230, 231, 265

War Labor Board, 163, 217, 220

War on Poverty, 201–202

Warren, Earl, 168

Washington Commonwealth Federation, 190, 192, 193
Washington Federation of Labor, 196
Washington Pension Union (WPU): achievement of, 199–200; alienation from mainstream politics, 198; antipathy toward alleged Communist in, 191; decline of, 200–201; formation of, 190–191, 192–193, 194; gender/race and, 196–197; grievance committee of, 194; initiatives of, 195–196; legacy of, 201–202; membership of, 193–194; opposition to, 197, 198; political career launched by, 194–195; social/cultural events of, 195; unemployment compensation and, 200
Washington State Federation of Scandinavian-American Democratic Club, 193
Weeks, Barney, 233
Weinstein, Allen, 177
Weinzapel, Matthew, 149
Welch, Robert, 224
Wells, J. Bernard, 179
Westinghouse, 118, 121
White Citizens Councils, 227
Widman, Rosalee, 61
"wildcat" strike, 2
Wilkerson, Doxey A., 207–208, 211
Wilkerson, Yolanda, 207
Winston-Salem, N.C., 9–10, 13, 18

Wobblies, 94
women's issues: early activist, 57n21; at FTA, 9, 13, 228; at IUMSWA, 98, 113n51; at pension union, 196–197; Schenectady activists, 37–41, 45–46; Southern unionism and, 228–229, 238; at Standard Coil, 120; at UE, 10, 130, 131–132
Wood, Leroy, 183
Wood, William, 185
Workers' Alliance, 193,194
Workers Education Division of the Works Progress Administration, 194
Workers University of Mexico (UOM), 245, 248, 258
Works Progress Administration (WPA), 88, 110n12
Wright, Charles E., 142, 143
Wright, George, 96, 98, 99, 100, 103, 114n64

Yates, Oleta, 207
Yorke, Peter, 164
Young, Ruth. *See* Jandreau, Ruth Young
Young Catholic Student/Young Catholic Worker program, 127–128

Zieger, Robert, 150, 196, 218, 224, 232, 234, 237
zoot suiters, 254–257
"Zoot Suit" riots, 127, 135, 254, 256, 257, 259